GCSE

MODERN WORLD HISTORY

L E SNELLGROVE

DP PUBLICATIONS LTD
Aldine Place
142/144 Uxbridge Road
Shepherds Bush Green
London W12 8AA

1989

The publishers have made every effort to trace the copyright holders but if they have, inadvertently, overlooked any, they will be pleased to make the necessary arrangements at the earliest opportunity.

A CIP catalogue record for this book is available from the British Library.

ISBN No: 1 870941 22 5

First published in Great Britain, 1989

Pageset by KAI in Times on a Macintosh IIcx computer.

Printed in Great Britain by
The Guernsey Press Company Ltd.,
Braye Road Vale,
Guernsey, Channel Islands.

Contents

Preface

AIM

The aim of this book is to provide all the support needed for a course in GCSE Modern World History since 1870. It is assumed that the book is used in *conjunction* with classroom teaching and/or as a revision aid.

NEED

GCSE History Examinations require candidates to have a *knowledge* and *understanding* of events and issues taken from one of a variety of syllabuses offered by the different Boards. **The National Criteria** for History lists the aims of a GCSE History course in some detail. The essentials can be listed under four *General Headings*.

1. **Knowledge and Understanding.** Knowledge requires a student to know a fact, understanding requires him to know the causes of that fact.

2. **Concepts.** A concept is an idea and the first idea that concerns a student of history is *cause,* as already illustrated in 1. Another concept is *change -* a potent force in history. A GCSE history student will be expected first to *identify* then understand these changes and to trace how they influence, or are influenced by, events. There is also the concept of *continuity,* the thread which often links us with quite distant times. Thus the student will be expected to see *similarities* as well as *differences* between past and present.

3. **Empathy.** This involves looking at events and issues from the perspective of people who experienced them. Naturally, such essay work requires knowledge but it also involves sympathy and understanding of the past.

4. **Skills.** This part of a GCSE course tests what you are able to do rather than what you know. It involves the study of *sources*. These can be *primary* (dating from the period studied) or *secondary* (documents written about the events in a later period, usually by an historian). Students will be expected to *evaluate* such documents - which may be books, diaries, press-cuttings, maps, paintings, cartoons or advertisements - and to distinguish where possible between fact, opinion, bias or reasoned judgment. This book contains exercises in both types of source, although the emphasis is on primary material.

The *need* was seen to reflect the above in a book written *since* the first examination took place. The opportunity has also been taken to provide something often requested by candidates - the means of knowing *how well* they are answering examination questions.

APPROACH

This book is divided up into 35 topics, or **Work Units**. These have been carefully selected after a study of the requirements of the GCSE Examining Boards.

Each topic has an extended Introduction, the purpose of which is three-fold.

1. **To stimulate interest and discussion.** The *salient* points of the topic are *summarised* in a lively and interesting way. The *essentials* are provided in order to provoke discussion and ensure all aspects of the topic are covered.

2. **To help understanding.** There is no 'final word' in history; wide varieties of interpretation and sometimes lack of material prevent it being a 'black and white' subject like mathematics. However, each Introduction provides, so to speak, the skeleton with the degree of interest stimulated and the amount of discussion ensuing providing the flesh.

3. **To help with revision.** Together with any notes made, the Introduction is a useful quick revision aid prior to the examination itself.

Following the Introduction is the Work Unit, detailing the main points of the topic. This is followed by a series of *graded exercises* and *examination questions* designed to test the *knowledge, understanding* and skills needed to be *successful* in GCSE History. A history question can be the same for GCSE, 'A' level or University; it is the *level of response* which is expected to be different. For this reason, *answers* are provided to all but the essay questions with indicators of the marks likely to be awarded to its components. In this way, the student will be able to see what *weighting* should be given to each aspect of the question.

Where subjects overlap, i.e. both Russia and the United States were involved in the Cuban Missile Crisis, adequate cross-referencing is provided in the text.

The book also contains a glossary of historical terms and terminology likely to be encountered by the student studying this subject.

There is insufficient space to thank all the individuals and schools who have helped in the preparation of this book but special mention must be made to de Stafford School, Caterham, Surrey and to Mr Andrew Thompson, Headmaster of Oakwood School, Horley, Sussex. I should also like to thank the staff of the London Library for their unfailing courtesy, helpfulness and expertise, and to my wife for assistance far beyond the call of wifely duty

L E Snellgrove, 1989

Introduction

SYLLABUSES

Each of the Examining Boards offer a wide variety of history syllabuses. These are drawn up within the guidelines set by the **National Criteria**. These stipulate that a subject must be:

(a) of sufficient historical length;
(b) able to cover key issues;
(c) historically coherent and balanced.

The Boards offer a number of different approaches to **Modern World History**. Some begin at a later date than 1870. The Midland Examining Group, for example, begin their courses in 1914. Some, like the Northern Examination Association, organise their material into *five themes:*

(a) Conflict and Conciliation.
(b) Governments in Action.
(c) International co-operation.
(d) Colonialism.
(e) Human Rights.

The London and East Anglian Board, by contrast, group topics geographically:

(a) Asia and Africa south of the Sahara.
(b) The Middle East and North Africa.
(c) Latin America and the Caribbean.
(d) North America.
(e) Western Europe including Britain.
(f) The Soviet Union and Eastern Europe.

Choice is allowed and the student does not have to answer questions on *all* these regions. Candidates should consult their teacher, or write to the particular Board whose examination they intend to take *before* commencing revision. [The addresses are on page 393]

COURSEWORK

In every GCSE syllabus at least 20% of the final assessment will consist of marks given for **coursework**, that is, work completed either in school or college, or at home, under the supervision of their teacher. *External candidates* (those not following a course at school or college) may have to take an extra examination in

1

Twenty per cent represents a minimum. Some Boards, notably London and East Anglian, Northern Examination Association and Northern Ireland Schools Examination Council, require 30% of the final assessment to be coursework. This coursework will often consist of essays of between 1000 and 1200 words set at monthly intervals but with certain topics tape recordings, photographs, models, film or computer programs may assist or augment written work.

GRADINGS

The GCSE Examination is a common method of examining at 16-plus which replaced the old GCE and CSE examinations. Certificates are awarded on a seven-point scale: A, B, C, D, E, F and G. It was proposed at first that GCSE grades at A, B and C would be linked to A, B and C at 'O' level and Grade I at CSE whilst grades D, E, F and G would be linked to grades 2, 3, 4 and 5 of the old CSE examination. Candidates who fail to reach grade G will be ungraded and receive no certificate.

1

The Franco-Prussian War
1870-1871

INTRODUCTION

In 1862 Benjamin Disraeli, a British politician, had dinner with Otto von Bismarck, the prime minister of Prussia. Later he remarked, "What an extraordinary man Bismarck is! He meets me for the first time and tells me all he is going to do. He will attack Denmark in order to get possession of Schleswig-Holstein; he will put Austria out of the German confederation; and then he will attack France - an extraordinary man!" During the next eight years Bismarck did exactly what he had promised Disraeli. First Denmark in 1864, then Austria in 1866 and France in 1870, were defeated by Prussia and other German states. Finally, victory against France inspired the Germans to achieve an age-old dream and unite in a Reich (Empire). By any standards, Bismarck's life was a success story.

Today we know that the result of Bismarck's life work was catastrophic defeats for Germany in both world wars. Why did events go so disastrously wrong? German unification was achieved, not by peaceful, democratic means as German liberals had hoped, but by ruthless trickery and violence. This led many Germans to trust in military solutions, to believe, as Bismarck said, that "policy..cannot succeed through speeches...it can only be carried out through blood and iron", a remark which gave him the nickname of the "Iron Chancellor". Militarism of this sort by other European nations besides Germany led to wars which are estimated to have cost the lives of 70,000,000 between 1914 and 1945. Even the ideal of nationalism which inspired German unity was an ideal for the winners only. Losers, like the Danes of Schleswig and the French of Alsace-Lorraine, found themselves under German rule after 1864 and 1870.

In spite of what Bismarck told Disraeli, how far did he plan his career? Was it always a certainty, never a gamble or a lucky opportunity? War is always a gamble; although Bismarck had at his disposal the best army in Europe he could not be sure of victory. Political opportunities which he could not have foreseen came his way and he seized them. But his trump card in the game was the fact that at crucial moments Austria and France wanted war. Neither country was prepared to give up its leading position in Europe without a fight. In fact, Bismarck was a cautious gambler. He was careful, for example, only to fight one opponent at a time and after 1870 he never went to war again. But the *way* he had won awakened dangerous dreams in Germany. He left a set of rules which might have saved the Reich - isolate your enemy before you go to war, never fight on two fronts, limit the damage of war by quick and merciful peace treaties. But the dreams were too powerful. They led Germany's arrogant military leaders to break the rules and lose the game.

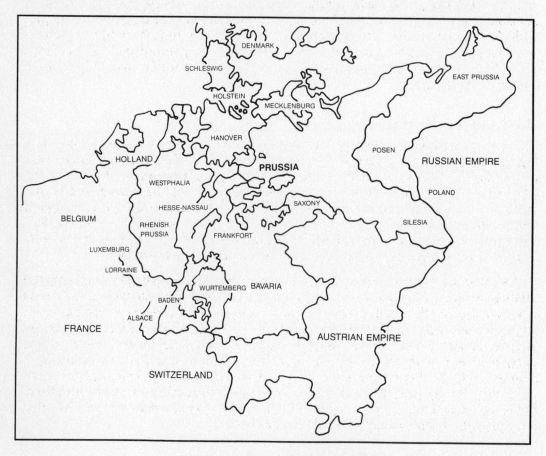

German States before Unification in 1871

THE SCHLESWIG-HOLSTEIN QUESTION

For centuries the Germans had not been united under one government but split into many states. Some were quite small, and others, like *Prussia* and *Bavaria*, large. This situation suited France, whose rulers did not want a powerful Germany on their borders (see map). *Austria* (the Austro-Hungarian empire) comprised many nationalities but it had a German ruling class and a predominant German culture. For this reason Austria regarded herself as the leading German state in Europe. *Otto von Bismarck*, who became prime minister of Prussia in 1862, aimed to make

Prussia the dominant state in Germany and Europe. He achieved this aim by three successful wars, against *Denmark* in 1864, *Austria* in 1866 and *France* in 1870-1. Such successes led the Germans to unite in a *Reich* (empire), a move which altered the balance of power in Europe. (See map on previous page).

The quarrel with Denmark concerned two border states, *Schleswig* and *Holstein*. Bismarck claimed that they should be German because many of the inhabitants spoke German. He persuaded Austria to join him, and in 1864 Prussian and Austrian troops invaded Denmark. After a quick victory, Austria took over Holstein and Prussia took over Schleswig. Bismarck knew he could pick a quarrel with Austria about the administration of Holstein any time he wished. He was confident that when he did so the Prussian army, reorganised by War Minister, *Albrecht von Roon*, and commanded by *Helmut von Moltke*, would be able to defeat the Austrians.

THE SEVEN WEEKS' WAR, 1866: CAUSES

The Prussian army had been famous for its discipline since the Napoleonic wars (1803-15). Roon had increased its efficiency, while Moltke planned to use new inventions like the railway and telegraph to speed army movements. The American Civil War (1861-5) had shown that very large armies could be moved swiftly into battle by rail, whilst their coordination could be improved by telegraphic communications. The Prussian army was equipped with the most modern weaponry and trained to move with clockwork efficiency; it was said that Moltke studied railway timetables as well as maps when planning a campaign.

As relations between Austria and Prussia grew worse, Bismarck provoked a crisis by suggesting a new *German Confederation* with Austria excluded. Austria at once called on the Confederation to join her against Prussia. Nine German states supported Austria, six joined Prussia. Italy prepared to do battle against its old enemy, Austria, over lands which it claimed should be Italian. *France* was persuaded not to intervene by Bismarck's suggestion that Prussia would help *Napoleon III*, the French emperor, to take over *Belgium*. Napoleon was not taken in by this. He realised the danger of a too powerful Prussia as a result of the war but he calculated that Austria and the German states would weaken themselves in a long struggle. Such a situation would benefit France.

THE TREATY OF PRAGUE

When the fighting began Moltke proved himself a master of strategy. A large Austrian army was encircled and defeated at *Konnigratz* (also known as *Sadowa*) on 3rd July 1866. This ended the war, although the Austrians won victories against the Italians at *Custozza* and in a sea battle off *Lissa*. Bismarck moved swiftly to sign a treaty before hostilities could spread. The *Treaty of Prague* excluded Austria from a new *North German Confederation* but did not punish her. No Austrian territory was annexed by Prussia but *Venetia* was returned to Italy. Bismarck rejected a suggestion by the Prussian generals that the army should stage a victory march through *Vienna*, the Austrian capital. Prussia annexed *Holstein* and took over *Hanover*, *Nassau*, *Hesse-Cassel* and the city of *Frankfurt* because they had fought for Austria. This gave Prussia valuable territory and four and a half million extra people.

The Seven Weeks' War, as it was called, created problems for large south German states such as *Bavaria*, *Wurrtenburg* and *Main*. Napoleon III made it clear that there would be war if they joined the new Confederation. Yet if they did not join Prussia and her allies in a future war with France they would be regarded as traitors to the German cause and would not benefit from any German victory. France knew that the war had been a severe setback to her own position; Prussia had gained a major victory which might have been stopped if the French had fought alongside the Austrians. The slogan that "France was defeated at Sadowa" served to inflame French public opinion and to make it certain that the French would go to war to settle the leadership of Europe once and for all. Such an attitude made Bismarck's next task easy.

THE HOHENZOLLERN CANDIDATE

In 1870, the Spanish were looking for another monarch, having driven their queen, *Isabella*, into exile because of her misgovernment. Bismarck suggested *Prince Leopold of Hohenzollern* as a possible candidate for the vacant throne. The Hohenzollerns were the royal family of Prussia and Leopold was a relative of *William I*, the Prussian king. The French were horrified at the thought of Hohenzollerns ruling on their Spanish as well as their German frontier and threatened war if Leopold's candidature was not withdrawn. This is what Bismarck hoped would happen but King William persuaded Leopold to stand down. This so infuriated Bismarck that he thought of resigning. The French were delighted at this diplomatic victory and decided to press home their advantage. *Count Vincent Benedetti*, their ambassador, was instructed to demand an assurance that Prussia would never put forward a Hohenzollern candidate again.

THE EMS TELEGRAM

King William was staying at *Ems* when Benedetti arrived for an interview. Before the hour of the meeting, Benedetti approached the king as he was out walking. The king refused to give any promise regarding a future candidate and when Benedetti persisted, raised his hat politely and walked on. Later, when the ambassador had his audience with the king, he again raised the matter. He was told that the king had nothing further to discuss with him. These facts were relayed by telegram to Bismarck, who was at dinner with Moltke and Roon. Bismarck saw his chance when he noticed that the king had instructed him to publish the text of this *Ems Telegram*. By shortening and altering the wording of the message, Bismarck contrived to give the impression that there had been a quarrel between king and ambassador. The effect was as he wished. The French decided that their ambassador had been snubbed; the Germans that their king had been insulted. On 19th July 1870 France declared war on Prussia and the Confederation.

GERMAN VICTORY

Moltke's careful planing ensured that the Germans moved smoothly into action, along railway lines reserved for military use only. By contrast, French mobilisation was chaotic as thousands of men were sent to distant parts along railways still being used by civilians; one unit from North Africa arrived after the war was over. The French army's best chance of success was to invade Germany because such a move might encourage Austria to attack Prussia. Two large French armies, one commanded by *Macmahon* in Lorraine and the other by *Bazaine* in Alsace, did cross the frontier and briefly capture the German town of *Saarbrucken* but did not continue the invasion after suffering several defeats. By this time it was clear that the Germans new breach-loading cannon were able to tear holes in the attacking French lines before the French could use their ultra-modern Chassepot rifle. Accurate artillery fire was to prove crucial in the weeks which followed.

Macmahon was defeated at *Froeschiller* and Bazaine at *Spicheren* (both on 6th August) as the Germans poured into France. Macmahon fell back to the river *Meuse* and was routed at *Beaumont*. His disorganised forces swarmed into the little town of *Sedan* where they were surrounded, bombarded and starved into surrender on 2nd September. This led to the collapse of the French Second Empire because Napoleon was captured with his troops. By early September the Prussians had surrounded Paris; the only means of escape was by balloon. The French capital endured a siege which lasted throughout the winter. Bazaine's army of 200,000 men retreated slowly, inflicting very heavy losses on the Germans at *Gravelotte* on 17th August. Then it, too, was surrounded in the town of *Metz* where it was starved into surrender on 29th October.

TREATY OF FRANKFURT

On 18th January 1871 Bismarck completed France's humiliation. The German princes, led by the King of Bavaria, invited King William to become emperor of the new *German Reich*; the south German states, delighted by Bismarck's success were eager to join. A new French *Assembly* (Parliament) had met at *Bordeaux* when Napoleon abdicated and Paris was surrounded. It was this government which was forced to accept the terms of the *Treaty of Frankfurt* (10th May 1871). France was ordered to pay £200 million compensation to the Germans for starting the war and German troops were to remain on French soil until this was paid. Most important for the future was the annexation by Germany of the two French border provinces of *Alsace* and *Lorraine*. Bismarck was against this but the German generals claimed they needed the provinces to make Germany easier to defend. The French were bitter. They draped the statue which represented the "lost provinces" in Paris with black cloth and dreamed of a war of revenge. But they knew that for such a war they would need allies against the new European super-state.

SELF-ASSESSMENT SECTION

1. Why was Bismarck nicknamed the "Iron Chancellor"?

2. Why did Bismarck feel confident of a German victory in war?

3. Which country took over Holstein after the German/Danish war of 1864?

4. Who was Prussia's War Minister?

5. Who commanded the German forces during the Franco-Prussian war?

6. Which new invention did most to revolutionise Bismarck's wars?

7. Which war was ended by the Treaty of Prague?

8. Why were the Spanish seeking a new monarch in 1870?

9. Why did the French oppose Leopold as a candidate for the Spanish throne?

10. Which French defeat in 1870 led to the collapse of the Second Empire?

11. The Ems Telegram:-

    a)   described King William's holiday.
    b)   mentioned an interview between the King and French ambassador.
    c)   described a meeting between the King and Prince Leopold.
    d)   described a quarrel between the King and the French ambassador.
         (TICK THE CORRECT ANSWER)

12. After the Franco-Prussian War, Moltke, the German commander-in-chief, said, "What our sword has won in half a year, our sword must guard for half a century". He was referring to:-

    a)   Paris
    b)   Alsace/Lorraine
    c)   Versailles
    d)   Bavaria
         (TICK THE CORRECT ANSWER)

13. Against the names listed below, select the correct letter in the key.

    1. SEDAN   A. German town captured by the French in 1870
    2. SPICHEREN   B. South German state
    3. SAARBRUCKEN   C. Town where Napoleon III surrendered
    4. METZ   D. Province returned to Italy in 1866
    5. KONNIGRATZ   E. Scene of Bazaine's defeat in August 1870
    6. BORDEAUX   F. Battle between Austrians and Prussians in 1866
    7. FRANKFURT   G. Sea battle between the Austrians and Italians in 1866
    8. LISSA   H. Scene of Bazaine's surrender in October, 1870
    9. BAVARIA   I. Treaty signed here ending Franco-Prussian War.
    10. VENETIA   J. Town where French Assembly met during Siege of
                            Paris

14. In 1871 an English clergyman, the Reverend W Gibson, was living in Paris. Later he wrote a book about his experiences called "Paris during the Commune", published in London in 1895. On 15th June 1871 he wrote this in a letter to a friend,

> "I regret to find that the determination to seek to take their revenge sooner or later on Prussia is again manifesting itself among the Parisians...Alas for France, and alas for the hope of peace in Europe!....Germany, when within the next few years she again encounters France in arms, will find her a very different foe from the France of 1870; and who knows but that before the end of the century there may be a similar triumph in Paris to that which is now being celebrated in Berlin? I vainly hoped that France would feel herself fairly beaten and be willing to accept her inferior position.."

 a) What was being celebrated in Berlin at that time?
 b) Why would Parisians in particular wish to take revenge on the Germans?
 c) What steps did Bismarck take to ensure that the French were not a different i.e. more dangerous foe in any future war?
 d) What particular result of the Treaty of Frankfurt made it unlikely that the French would accept their "inferior position"?

15. In what way were the French to blame for the war which broke out in 1870?

16. One of Bismarck's rules was to limit the damage caused by a war with a quick and merciful peace. Give an example of a) a merciful peace, and b) an *un*merciful treaty concluded by him.

17. Explain the difficulties faced by the south German states after the Prussian victory against Austria in 1866.

18. Imagine you are at a dinner with Roon, Moltke and Bismarck when the Ems Telegram arrives. Describe the conversation concerning what had happened at Ems, and what was the best thing to do.

19. Imagine you are a French soldier in the army surrounded at Metz. Describe your experience during the fighting leading to this surrender, and the historic events at the surrender itself.

2

Germany   1871-1914

INTRODUCTION

Germany emerged from the Franco-Prussian war a military and industrial giant. Her 41 million population compared with the 36 million of France and Austria, Britain's 31 million and Italy's 27 million. Only Russia, with 87 million, surpassed her, but Russia was far behind in industrial and economic development. One of the greatest technical achievements of the 19th century assisted the growth of German power. Her almost land-locked position in central Europe, with rivers running only into the Baltic, a short coastline and mountains to the south, was turned into an advantage by railways which made Germany the focus of the European rail network.

Building on such a foundation, Germany's Industrial Revolution was swift. Coal output rose from 30 million tons annually in 1871 to 190 million tons in 1913. A new way of processing steel, perfected in Britain, meant that ore from the Westphalian coalfields could be used in steel production. Westphalia and the industrialised parts of Alsace and Lorraine boosted iron and steel output to the point where it doubled between 1880 and 1890. Two new branches of industry, chemicals and electric generation, were virtually taken over by German scientists and technicians. At the same time, Germany enlarged her commercial activities. Her merchant ships, whose tonnage multiplied seven times in 20 years, traded with America, Africa and the Near and Far East. At home, such industrialisation led to a drift to the towns which tipped the balance in favour of urban living. Germany, mainly a nation of peasant farmers in 1800, was predominantly a nation of town dwellers by 1900.

Bismarck's political skills were strained to control such a runaway situation. On one side was the Catholic Church whose Pope had condemned "progress, liberalism and recent civilisation" in 1864. Such an attitude led Bismarck into a confrontation with Germany's Catholics which lasted until he realised that the struggle was threatening the unity won in 1871. Then he retreated, giving away as little as possible in the battle between state and Church power. On the other were the communists and socialists whose Marxist philosophy condemned the capitalist system which was making Germany rich at the expense of the poor in their opinion. Bismarck killed this threat with kindness. He realised that the bad conditions in

10

many of Germany's new factories and towns could make them a breeding ground for revolution. His answer was to give German workers Europe's first welfare system, a form of industrial insurance which was a landmark in welfare legislation.

Such "State Socialism" was accompanied by laws which banned socialist political parties and newspapers. Most German liberals, whose fathers had dreamed of uniting Germany by peaceful, democratic means, accepted a situation which brought most of them prosperity and a feeling of national pride. Consequently, the new Germany, with its Parliament, and political parties and limited franchise based on property, was not a true democracy. Freedom was one of the victims of Bismarck's victories. The new giant was presided over by a monarch who believed he ruled by divine right, supported by feudal-minded landowners who worshipped the army and its soldierly values. It was to prove a fatal combination.

THE GERMAN REICH

The *German Reich* created after victory over France in 1870 had virtually the same system of government as the old *North German Federation*, except that it was now ruled by an emperor. It was arranged that this *Kaiser* should always be chosen from the Kings of Prussia; thus the new Reich was Prussian-dominated as Bismarck had always hoped. The executive power in Germany was exercised by an Imperial Chancellor - Bismarck from 1871 until 1890. Law making was undertaken by the two houses of Assembly (Parliament), the *Bundesrat*, where each German state was represented in relation to its size and population, and the *Reichstag*, whose representatives were elected by every German man over 25.

BISMARCK AND THE KULTURKAMPF

There were three times as many Protestants as Catholics in the German empire. Bismarck was anxious to retain this imbalance. For this reason he had been against taking over any parts of the Catholic Austrian empire after the Seven Week's War in 1866. Although Bismarck was a Protestant, his quarrel with the Catholic Church was purely political. Successive popes had maintained that no state had the right to interfere in Church affairs, particularly its schools. The powerful modern states which developed during the 19th century were not prepared to let an outside authority educate, or indoctrinate, their children. This quarrel was particularly fierce in France as well as Germany.

In 1870 the Pope issued the doctrine of *Papal Infallibility*. This stated that when a pope explained Church teachings on faith or morals he could not, because of divine help, be wrong. This claim was partly the result of the Pope having lost his Italian lands to the patriots who had just united Italy. This loss of political power made the Papacy eager to assert its spiritual authority. Bismarck was drawn into the quarrel about Infallibility against his will. When thousands of German Catholics refused to accept the doctrine, he was asked to sack such *Old Catholics* from their posts as teachers and preachers. When he refused, the Germans who did support Infallibility became hostile to Bismarck's administration and formed a new *Centre* political party.

11

THE MAY LAWS

The battle which followed was called the *Kulturkampf* (Civilisation-struggle). In 1871 Bismarck abolished the Catholic department of the Prussian Ministry of Church Affairs and Education. A few months later Catholic priests were forbidden to mention politics in their sermons, and, in March 1872, the *Jesuits*, most militant of Roman Catholic religious Orders, were banned from preaching or teaching. Finally, under the *May Laws* of 1873, the government took over the training of priests. The effect of all these laws was dramatic. By 1876 every bishop in Prussia was in prison or exile and over a third of Catholic parishes were without a priest. The Kulturkampf served to increase the power and numbers of the Centre party; by 1874 its 91 seats in the Assembly made it the second largest party in Parliament.

Bismarck realised that his policies were counter-productive; they were increasing support for the Catholic cause. From the start of the Kulturkampf he had feared that the Centre party might attempt some sort of alliance with his enemies, France and Austria, whose rulers supported the Pope. Furthermore, the heir to the imperial throne, *Crown Prince Frederick* and his wife Victoria, were against him on the issue. The arrival of a more liberal pope, *Leo XIII*, in 1878 gave Bismarck the opportunity to compromise. The May laws were repealed, although Jesuits remained a banned Order.

BISMARCK AND THE SOCIALISTS

One reason Bismarck wished to heal the rift with the Church was that he feared the Socialists were a greater danger. The first German socialist party was formed by *Ferdinand Lasalle* in 1863. In 1869 this group joined south German socialists led by *August Bebel* and *Wilhelm Liebknecht* to become the *Social Democratic Labour Party*. The S.D.L.P. produced the so-called *Gotha Programme* which proposed a state takeover of industry, coalmines and banks, profit-sharing for workers and the end of many social injustices. Gotha envisaged peaceful change, not revolution, although there were extremists in the party. By 1877 there were about half a million German socialists. This caused Bismarck, a conservative-minded landowner, to worry. A powerful socialist party in the Reichstag could be a problem because he had just quarreled with his main ally, the *National Liberal Party*. The National Liberals' commitment to Free Trade had just made them opponents of the protective tariffs Bismarck had introduced to help German farmers.

STATE SOCIALISM

In 1878 two attempts were made on the Kaiser's life. After the first, Bismarck blamed the socialists although there was no evidence to link them with the crime. He introduced an anti-socialist bill into the Reichstag but it was rejected largely through National Liberal votes. After the second attempt, which nearly succeeded, Bismarck blamed the National Liberals for not protecting the Kaiser and called a General Election. The idea that the National Liberals were "disloyal" to the Kaiser caused them to lose many seats at the election. Those who were returned to the Reichstag decided to support Bismarck's proposals rather than risk another election where they might suffer further losses. Bismarck now introduced a law which banned the S.D.L.P., imprisoned its leaders and shut its offices and newspapers.

Perhaps because of these actions, socialist ideas became increasingly popular amongst the general public. Bismarck aimed to pacify Germany's workers and turn them against revolution by introducing a comprehensive scheme of *social insurance*, providing cover for illness, injury and old age. Insurance was funded by weekly contributions paid in the form of stamps, with the workers paying two-thirds and the employers one-third of the cost. There was also provision for some free medical treatment, unemployment pay for up to 23 weeks, and, in 1889, *Old Age Pensions*, funded in the same way as social insurance. Socialist leaders saw through Bismarck's *State Socialism* which they branded as mere "crumbs off the rich man's table". But such pioneer welfare schemes were copied by other European countries, notably Britain.

EDUCATION AND INDUSTRY

Imperial Germany's education system was copied from the Prussian state schools introduced in 1888. Free education was provided for children from primary schools to technical college and university. However, the rift between Church and state at the time of the Kulturkampf created two types of school, one run by the government and the other by the Church, and this had the effect of dividing people in their attitudes towards life and politics. Some grew up to be anti-clerical; others remained staunch Catholics. By 1914 German education was ahead of most European countries and mass illiteracy had been conquered. State schooling, both in Germany and elsewhere, had the effect of regimenting the population, who, after the disciplines of school, went on to the disciplines of the factory, and, in the case of most European men, the discipline of the armed forces. Mass indoctrination through newspapers and meetings, either for or against capitalism, became a possibility. The stage was set for the mass movements of the 20th century.

An efficient education system underpinned a great deal of Germany's industrial and economic progress. The chemical and electricity industries, in particular, were serviced by a stream of well trained scientists and technicians. *Werner von Siemens*, a German, had developed the *dynamo* by 1867 and *electric traction* by 1879. By 1891 Germany had a nationwide chain of power stations transmitting electricity. Chemical plants were producing *dye-stuffs* and *plastics*. The expansion of trade caused by shipping and railways was accompanied by efficient insurance and banking facilities which benefitted the economy. German industrialists, secure from foreign competition behind tariff barriers, joined together to form *cartels*, whose members fixed prices and established quotas to prevent over-production; an employer who produced more than his quota was fined by the cartel. Cartels were not just concentrations of industrial power. They could organise political power through their allies and friends in Parliament and by the end of the century no government could afford to ignore their views or interests.

KAISER WILLIAM TAKES OVER

In 1888 the old emperor William I died. He had supported Bismarck throughout his career, although he had rarely agreed with either his policies or his methods. His son, *Frederick*, reigned only a few months before dying of cancer. Frederick's son, *William II*, known to other Europeans as the *Kaiser*, dismissed Bismarck and reversed many of his policies. William wanted to found German colonies and build a powerful navy, both of which Bismarck opposed because he knew they would mean a clash with Britain. William preferred Austria as an ally rather than Russia. Bismarck had tried to remain friends with both in order to deprive France of possible allies. William also wanted to treat socialists better. He removed the ban on their political activities and by 1912 the S.D.L.P. was the largest single party in the Reichstag with 110 representatives. Its countrywide membership, based on Germany's industrial centres, stood at over a million in the same year.

SELF-ASSESSMENT SECTION

1. What exactly had the pope condemned in 1864 ?

2. Who was represented in the Bundesrat ?

3. Who were the Old Catholics ?

4. Who founded the first German socialist party ?

5. Which party represented German Catholics ?

6. Who produced the Gotha Programme ?

7. Which political party was Bismarck's ally until 1878 ?

8. Who invented the dynamo ?

9. What is a cartel ?

10. Explain the doctrine of Papal Infallibility.

11. The *Kulturkampf* was :-

    (a) a battle between Church and state.
    (b) a battle between the government and socialists.
    (c) a quarrel between Catholics and Protestants.
    (d) a quarrel between the Jesuits and the Church.
         (TICK THE CORRECT ANSWER)

12. The *Gotha Programme* was :-

    (a) a programme for armed revolution.
    (b) a plan to ban socialist parties in Germany.
    (c) a plan for an alliance between the Centre and National Liberal parties.
    (d) a proposal to nationalise major industries.
         (TICK THE CORRECT ANSWER)

13. Here is a list of dates. Put the correct event by the date by using the letters.

1. 1863.   A. the dynamo was invented.
2. 1867.   B. the year the socialist party became the single largest party in the Reichstag.
3. 1873.   C. year the first German socialist party was formed
4. 1878.   D. May Laws passed.
5. 1879.   E. two German Kaisers died in the year.
6. 1888.   F. electric traction invented.
7. 1889.   G. Bismarck dismissed by William II.
8. 1890.   H. two attempts made on the Kaiser's life.
9. 1912.   I. Old Age Pensions introduced.

14. This cartoon appeared in the British magazine "Punch" soon after the event it portrays.

DROPPING THE PILOT.

(a) Who is the pilot meant to be ?
(b) Who is looking at him from the top deck ? How does the artist indicate who he is ?
(c) What had the man descending the gangplank been "piloting" ?
(d) Why had he been "dropped" ?

15. Describe Bismarck's State Socialism. Why was it condemned by socialists ?

16. Explain the steps by which Bismarck attempted to limit Catholic influence in the German empire. How far was it successful ?

17. Imagine you are a German living in 1900. Explain your hopes and fears for the future in a letter to a friend. (Use information from both Work Units 1 and 2.)

3

The United States of America
1789-1914

INTRODUCTION

Few successful revolutionaries have had practical experience of government; the tyrannical regimes against which they rebelled generally saw to that. This was true of the leaders of the French and Russian revolutions. The American rebels against British rule in 1775 who wrote the US constitution were exceptions. Most British American colonies were limited democracies of one sort or another from their foundation in the 17th century. Consequently, George Washington, John Adams, Thomas Jefferson and their colleagues were practical men of affairs who had experienced government at provincial and state level. They brought to the making of the Constitution a unique blend of high ideals and political expertise.

The US Constitution was devised as a "piece of machinery" to operate what 18th century thinkers thought of as the "laws" of politics and government. Seventeenth century scientists, of whom the most famous is Isaac Newton, had demonstrated that immutable laws governed the earth and planets. In the same way it was believed that noble ideals and commonsense could make these political "laws" operate for the benefit of mankind. A carefully devised system of government would make impossible the twin extremes of dictatorship and anarchy. Furthermore, the American experience, if successful, would set an example to other countries as they struggled for freedom. "It has been frequently remarked that it seems to have been reserved to the people of this country, by their conduct and example, to decide ... whether societies of men are really capable of establishing good government from reflection and choice.", wrote one of the Founding Fathers, as the authors of the US Constitution are known today.

This seemingly arrogant idea came naturally to the descendants of men and women who believed that God had guided them to the New World. Unfortunately, it has made it easy for foreigners to accuse Americans of hypocrisy. They ask how a Constitution which proposed "to secure the Blessings of Liberty to ourselves and our Posterity", could have allowed black slavery until 1868. When the USA took over the Phillipine islands in 1898 they asked what had become of America's love of freedom and hatred of imperialism. Nevertheless, the American dream has influenced American men and women throughout their history, and it is essential to the understanding of a 20th century super-power.

THE USA CONSTITUTION

The original 13 colonies (See map) won independence from British rule after a war, 1775-83. At first they banded together in a loose *Confederation* but this proved unsatisfactory so in 1789 representatives of the states devised a tighter form of government under a new *Constitution*. This divided the government into three. First there was the *Executive* branch to carry out the day to day running of affairs. This was to be done by a *President* who was to be chosen by an *Electoral College*; these electors met to carry out this task every four years. Direct election by the people was considered dangerous. It was feared that it might lead a popular candidate to refuse to resign at the end of his term and try to seize power. Today this College no longer chooses a President. Each elector is known to support either the Republican or Democratic Presidential candidate. So once the balance of Republican and Democratic electors is known, the winner is proclaimed before the College votes.

Second was the *Legislative*, or law-making, branch. This job is done by *Congress* which consists of two chambers, the *Senate* and the *House of Representatives*. The Senate represents each state in the union and there are two Senators for each state, regardless of its size.The House of Representatives represents the people and each state is allocated members according to its population. Finally there is the *judiciary*, or law-enforcement branch. This consists of a *Supreme Court* and lesser courts. In later years the Supreme Court established the right to interpret and, if necessary, alter the Constitution.

THE FOUNDING FATHERS

The Founding Fathers aimed to avoid tyranny, mob rule or a sudden seizure of power by a person or group. The method they used is known as *Separation of Powers* and it means that each of the three branches of government is run by different people. The idea is to stop one group from becoming too powerful. For example, the President cannot be a member of Congress and judges take no part in Congressional business. The Founding Fathers also worked out an elaborate system of *Checks and Balances* whereby each branch of government can interfere in the working of the others. The President, for instance, appoints civil servants and judges but his appointments have to be ratified (approved) by the Senate. A judge who has tried and convicted a person can find that person pardoned by the President. Congress can refuse to take an action recommended by the President but the President can veto (cancel) a bill proposed by Congress. These arrangements slow down Federal operations but most Americans feel that such delay is a small price to pay for democracy. It should be noted that political parties were unknown when the Constitution was written. The first President, *George Washington*, was against them and they developed after his two terms of office.

The Founding Fathers included a *Bill of Rights* in the Constitution. This was modelled on the British law of the same name and its purpose was to guarantee basic freedoms of speech, assembly etc. This Bill became the first ten *Amendments* to the Constitution. Since 1789 this right of amendment has proved invaluable. It has been used sparingly but it has helped make the Constitution flexible in changing times. Notable amendments include the *Abolition of Slavery* (1868) and the *Women's Franchise* (1920).

THE PROBLEM OF SLAVERY

The USA expanded steadily during the 19th century. In 1803 *President Jefferson* negotiated the *Louisiana Purchase* with the French. In spite of its name it included far more than the modern state of Louisiana; it actually doubled the size of the existing USA. Other acquisitions by purchase or war included *Florida, New Mexico, California* and *Texas* from the Spanish and *Alaska* from the Russians. Settlers moved into these regions, forming *territories* which, when the population became sufficient, became *states*. This moving "frontier" provided a safety valve for the adventurous or discontented. It also fuelled the greatest quarrel in American history, that between the Northern and Southern states concerning negro slavery. As each territory proclaimed statehood the question arose as to whether it should be slave or free. Until about 1850 the Southern grip on the US government had been strong; they had supplied many Presidents, Senators and Representatives as well as army leaders. But as each new "free" state demanded admission to the Union, the South demanded a "slave" state to redress the balance. This would prevent it from being outnumbered by the North, whose way of life it detested.

THE AMERICAN CIVIL WAR

It was the possibility of slavery being extended *outside* the South which led to war. Whilst most Northerners disliked slavery few were prepared to demand that it should be abolished. What they would not accept was the growth of slavery in regions hitherto free, where white farmers might become unemployed as a result. Southerners felt that their distinctive way of life, based upon a cotton and tobacco economy, was being threatened by "Yankee" industrialisation. In 1860 *South Carolina* seceded (left) the Union and other states followed to form the *Confederate States of America*. The newly elected President, *Abraham Lincoln*, refused to let the South go peacefully. He declared their actions unlawful and in the war that followed (1861-5) the South was defeated after widespread fighting and devastation and the loss of 600,000 lives. (*See the map on the following page*).

The post-war occupation of the South by Northern troops is called *Reconstruction*. Its aim was to force Southerners to give equal rights to negroes. New state governments were set up, nicknamed "*Carpetbag Governments*" by the Southerners because they claimed that many of the Northerners who ran them were disreputable self-seekers who brought little more possessions than could be carried in a carpetbag. Certainly many were corrupt and Reconstruction failed, leaving a legacy of bitterness in the South which lasted well into the 20th century. The South might have been better treated had Lincoln lived, but he was murdered by a fanatic in Washington a few days after the war ended. One result of Reconstruction was the *Solid South*, a block of Southern states who voted Democrat for many years because the North had been led by the Republican party during the war and afterwards.

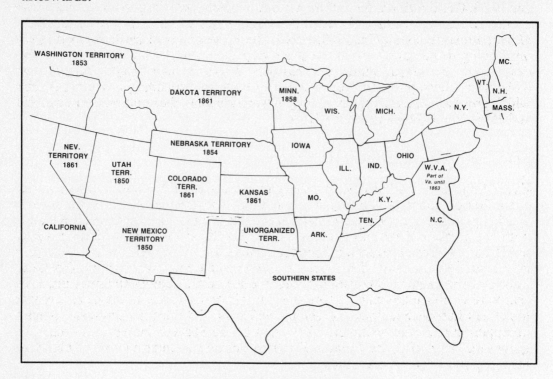

The USA at the time of the Civil War

INDUSTRIAL DEVELOPMENT

Between the end of the Civil War in 1865 and 1900 there was a vast growth in US industry with production doubling every 12 or 14 years. This development resulted from new inventions, immense natural resources, abundant capital investment and an expanding railway system. *Big Business* was headed by industrial giants, like *John D. Rockefeller's Standard Oil Trust*. This business, starting with the discovery of oil in Pennsylvania in 1859, eventually gave Rockefeller a monopoly of oil refining. Because such firms were organised by trustees, the name *Trust* is used by Americans to describe large, monopolistic corporations. Another trust was the steel empire created by *Andrew Carnegie*. Carnegie was born in Scotland in 1835 and came to the USA when he was 13. He started work in a cotton factory but shrewd investments in oil and railways made him a millionaire before he was 30. He decided to concentrate on iron and steel production because of the demand for rails, bridges, carriages and locomotives. Eventually he owned fleets of merchant ships as well as factories and iron-ore mines. Later, politicians who opposed the creation of such monopolies were dubbed "*Trustbusters*".

Railway construction in such a large country was the essential ingredient for new settlements and industrialisation and this was highlighted when the first *Transcontinental Railroad*, from Omaha to Sacramento, was completed in 1869. American cities and towns grew quickly; in 1850 *Chicago* had 30,000 inhabitants and in 1900 two million. New York grew to be the second largest city in the world by the end of the century. To feed the rising population the fertile lands of the *Middle West* became a *Cattle Kingdom* where thousands of cattle roamed freely until being driven north to the meat-packing factories of Chicago. Farmers also developed the wheat lands of *Minnesota*, *North* and *South Dakota* and *Nebraska*. These products were needed to feed the expanding urban population which grew yearly as European immigrants flooded into the country; between 1851 and 1900 16,600,000 entered the USA.

THE MONROE DOCTRINE

Expanding trade and business gradually involved the USA with foreign countries even though most of the Founding Fathers had tended to be *isolationists*. Washington, for example, had warned his countrymen against "permanent alliances with any portion of the foreign world". In 1824 President *James Monroe* issued his famous *Doctrine*, warning European states not to interfere on the American mainland, north or south. The Doctrine was a response to a series of revolutions in Latin America against Spanish rule. Monroe feared that European forces might be sent to re-establish this rule. In fact, only Britain at that time had the naval strength to prevent European nations intervening, which she did since the new states opened up opportunities of trade hitherto forbidden by the Spanish. However, as the USA grew more powerful, the Monroe Doctrine became an important principle of its foreign policy. (See Work Unit 9).

MANIFEST DESTINY

The Monroe Doctrine was resented by the newly established Latin American states, first, because it had been issued without consulting them, and second, because they felt that Latin Americans had more to fear from US interference in their affairs. Their distrust of what they termed the "*Colossus of the North*" was proved well-founded when, in 1846, the USA defeated *Mexico* and at the *Treaty of Guadaloupe Hidalgo* took *California*, *Texas* and *New Mexico* from the Mexicans. In the 1850's the USA forced *Japan* to trade with America, and in 1867 joined Britain in forcing an *Open Door* trading policy, even though the Chinese government was against such trade (See Work Unit 10). After the Civil War, some US administrations favoured a *Manifest Destiny* policy. This was the belief that the USA was "destined" to control the continent from west to east and north to south from the Arctic Ocean to the Isthmus of Panama, a move which would have taken in British Canada as well as Mexico. An outward sign of this belief was the purchase of *Alaska* from the Russians in 1867. Various disputes with Britain regarding the exact boundary between Canada and the USA were settled by the *Treaty of Washington* in 1871.

In 1895 there was a border dispute between *Venezuela* and *British Guiana*. The US attempted to intervene and, when Britain objected, invoked the Monroe Doctrine. There was talk of war between Britain and the USA but eventually Britain agreed to outside arbitration which settled the dispute in her favour. During this crisis Britain mobilised its fleet and the US government realised that it had only three modern battleships to take on the world's largest navy. Influenced by the writings of *Captain Alfred Mahan* regarding the importance of seapower in world history, Congress voted to build a *two-ocean navy*, one for the Pacific and one for the Atlantic. This laid the foundation of US naval power.

THE SPANISH-AMERICAN WAR

In 1898 the USA went to the aid of rebels objecting to Spanish rule in *Cuba*. *The Spanish-American War* was sparked off by the mysterious sinking of the US battleship *Maine* in *Havana harbour*, Cuba. The cause of the explosion has never been established but Americans, especially those influenced by *Randolph Hearst's New York Journal*, blamed the Spanish. An American army invaded Cuba, complete with volunteers including *Rough Riders* led by a future President, *Theodore Roosevelt*. US troops and the Rough Riders (mostly on foot because they had been forced to leave their horses at home) won a victory by storming *San Juan Hill* outside *Santiago*. A few days later a US fleet wiped out a Spanish squadron in the harbour. In the Pacific a US naval force commanded by *Commodore Dewey* attacked the Spanish colony of the *Phillipine Islands*. Dewey's fleet destroyed a Spanish naval force in *Manila Bay*. These victories gave the Americans an empire because, by the terms of the *Treaty of Paris*, Spain was forced to sell the Phillipines to the USA and to cede (give) *Puerto Rico, Cuba, Guam* and *Hawaii* to her also. US governments ruled Cuba directly until 1902 and intervened in her internal affairs several times later.

PANAMA

The proposed building of the *Panama Canal*, first by British engineers and then by Americans, interested the USA. During the Spanish-American war a US battleship, the *Oregon*, had been forced to sail 14,000 miles around *Cape Horn* to reach Atlantic waters. Clearly a canal at Panama would enable the two-ocean navy to move from one area to another without such costly detours. In 1901 Britain agreed to the *Hay-Pauncefote Treaty* whereby the USA might build, control and fortify a canal, so long as all ships might be charged equal tolls. A zone 6 miles wide was suggested, but the Columbian government, who owned the region, refused to ratify the sale to the USA. In November, 1903 a revolution by the Panamanians against Columbian rule was used as an excuse by *President Theodore Roosevelt*. Three days after the revolution the USA recognised Panamanian independence in return for owning the land on which the canal was to be built. Roosevelt then brought in US experts to deal with the health problems which hampered construction. The canal was completed in 1914 and is still regarded as vital to US security.

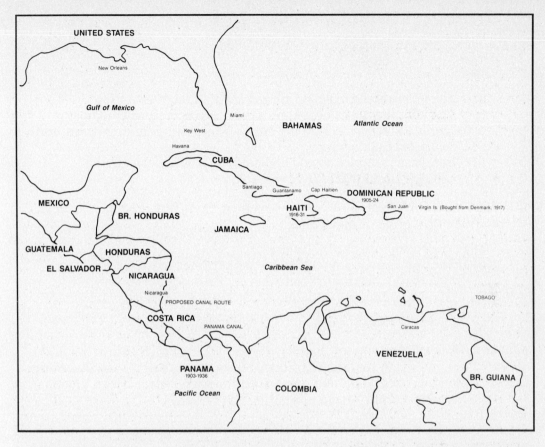

After US troops had helped put down the *Boxer Rising* in China (See Work Unit 10) the US government issued another *Open Door* policy statement which seemed to indicate that the USA was bound to protect China from other nations. This was to have far-reaching effects in the 20th century.

SELF-ASSESSMENT SECTION

1. Who was the first President of the USA?

2. What is the title given to the authors of the US Constitution?

3. Who negotiated the Louisiana Purchase?

4. Which was the first Southern state to secede from the Union?

5. Who led the North during the Civil War?

6. What was a "carpetbagger"?

7. Who founded a steel empire?

8. Where was the Cattle Kingdom?

9.   What was the Monroe Doctrine?

10. Which US President recognised Panama's independence ? Why did he do this?

11. Manifest Destiny was the belief that :-

   a)   The USA should make no alliances with foreign countries.
   b)   The US constitution would set a good example to other nations.
   c)   The USA ought to rule the North American continent from north to south and east to west.
   d)   European countries should not interfere in American affairs.
        (TICK THE CORRECT ANSWER)

12. Here are some of the causes of the American Civil War. List them in what you consider their order of importance.

   a)   The North's dislike of slavery.
   b)   The Southern desire to preserve their distinctive way of life.
   c)   The North's determination to prevent the spread of slavery.
   d)   Abraham Lincoln's declaration that secession was unlawful.

13. Two American historians, Charles and Mary Beard, wrote,

   "Among the many historic assemblies which have wrought revolutions in the affairs of mankind, it seems safe to say that there never has been one that commanded more political talent, practical experience, and sound substance than ...."

   Complete this quotation from the choices below.

   a)   The Standard Oil Trust.
   b)   The Philadelphia Convention which devised the US constitution.
   c)   The Confederate States of America.
   d)   The Congress of the United States.

14. In 1860 a senator made this election speech. Read it carefully and then answer the questions below.

   "The North is accumulating power and it means to use that power to emancipate your slaves. When that is done, no pen can describe, no tongue depict, no pencil paint the horrors that will overspread this country....Disunion is a fearful thing, but emancipation is worse. Better leave the Union in the open face of day, than be lighted from it at midnight by the incendiary's torch".

   a)   Was the speaker a Southerner or a Northerner ? Give reasons for your answer.
   b)   How was the North "accumulating power" at that time ?
   c)   What was the speaker's motive in using such language to his audience ?
   d)   Was the speaker in favour of disunion ? Give reasons for your answer.
   e)   What did the speaker think that freed slaves would do ?

15.

(Source: "History of a free people" by Bragdon and McCutchen.
The Macmillan Co. 1969.
Reproduced by Culver Pictures.)

This cartoon appeared in the 1870's. The central figure in it is General U.S. Grant, the North's most successful general, and President at that time.

a)   Explain what this cartoon is about.
b)   Who is the woman meant to be ?
c)   What is meant by the words displayed on her dress ?
d)   Explain the significance of the bag and the soldiers.
e)   What is the significance of the ruined buildings and sunken ships in the background ?
f)   Do you think the artist was for or against the subject of this cartoon ? Give reasons for your answer.

16. Read these extracts and then answer the questions below.

A. President McKinley took the decision to buy the Phillipines after the Spanish-American War. Here he describes his feelings and motives to an audience of clergymen.

"I walked the floor of the White House night after night until midnight ... And one night late it came to me this way - (1) That we could not give them (the Phillipines) back to Spain - that would be cowardly and dishonourable; (2) that we could not turn them over to ... our commercial rivals - that would be bad business and discreditable; (3) that we could not leave them to themselves - they were unfit for self-government - and ... (4) that there was nothing left for us to do but to take them all, and educate the Filipinos, and uplift and civilise and Christianise them ..."

B. Another US politician, Albert J. Beveridge, put the matter this way.

"The Phillipines are ours forever: "territory belonging to the United States", as the Constitution calls them. And just beyond the Phillipines are China's illimitable markets. We will not retreat from them either ... We will not abandon our opportunity in the Orient. We will not renounce our part in the mission of our race, trustees under God of the civilisation of the world".

a)   Which country might have taken over the Phillipines if the USA had not bought them ? (See Work Unit 21 as well).
b)   The Phillipines had been ruled by Catholic Spain. Can you think of a reason why Beveridge and McKinley could still talk of "Christianising" the Filipinos ?
c)   What were the two main reasons for the USA buying the Phillipines to judge from these extracts ? Which do you think was the *most* important ?
d)   Which parts of A. and B. remind us of Manifest Destiny ?
e)   Which extract seems less enthusiastic about taking over the Phillipines ? Give reasons for your answer.

17. Imagine you are a Southerner. Give your reasons for fighting the North.

18. Imagine you are a Northerner. Give your reasons for fighting the South.

19. List the factors which led the USA to become a world power during this period. How did these factors lead to the abandonment of the principles of the Founding Fathers ?

4

Russia   1855-1905

INTRODUCTION

For centuries Russia's backward millions had been ruled by Tsars (Caesar or Emperor). These all-powerful monarchs were supported by the Russian Orthodox Church. Despite much modernisation, Russia was still backward compared with other western European countries. This backwardness applied to social and political as well as economic life. Set against such an entrenched establishment was an almost "underground" movement, a small but influential intellectual class determined to change Tsarism in one way or another. Some of these dissidents, as they would be called today, wanted a Parliamentary democracy similar to France, Germany or Britain. Others were Marxists or Nihilists who lived an exiled, imprisoned or secret existence and plotted to overthrow the Tsar's government violently. To be successful, these groups needed mass support, either of workers or peasants. Unfortunately for them, their education cut them off from the illiterate masses, whilst their numerical weakness made them helpless against the massive forces of army and police. Consequently, they never progressed beyond talk or terror, and reform in 19th century Russia was imposed from above by well-meaning but dictatorial Tsars.

The dangers and limitations of this kind of change are shown by the career of Sergei Witte, Finance Minister to the Tsar in the 1890's. The chief weakness of the Russian economy was that it relied upon an uncertain harvest. If the harvest was good, surplus grain could be exported to earn foreign currency and buy essential imports. If the harvest was bad, Russia's financial strength abroad was weakened. This led to shortages at home and, in turn, starvation and riots. There was always an outside chance that such suffering and disturbance might give the revolutionary underground its opportunity. Witte planned to solve this problem with a crash programme of factory building, mining development and railway construction, financed by foreign loans and heavy indirect taxation.

Witte's scheme was economically successful. Between 1892 and 1901 Russia's industrial production almost doubled. But the cost in human terms was high. The poverty-stricken people saw a further reduction in their pitiful living standards because of taxation. They reacted by rioting or going on strike. Witte tried to

27

control the situation but he knew that it was a race against time. Could the benefits of industrialisation reach the people in better living standards before there was a revolution ? The gamble failed partly because of the choices Witte had to make. His largest transport project, the Trans-Siberian Railway, provided a faster link between Europe and the East than the sea-route in those days. Unfortunately, this brought Russia into conflict with Japanese expansion in the region and led to defeat in war and near-revolution at home. The Tsar saved his throne in 1905 by making temporary concessions to those who demanded Parliamentary democracy. The loans Witte raised in France led Russia to join in an alliance against Germany (See Work Unit 11). This brought Russia into the First World War, a move which led to defeat, the overthrow of the Tsar and a Communist dictatorship.

EMANCIPATION OF THE SERFS

Russia's defeat in the Crimean War (1854-6) convinced *Tsar Alexander II* that his country must be modernised. His major reform was to emancipate (free) the serfs who had been virtual slaves for centuries. Although Alexander became known as the *Liberator* because of this action, emancipation was not as beneficial a reform as it might have been. The peasants now bought their land from the *mir*, or village council, with loans repayable over 49 years. Their holdings were about half the size of the land they had worked as serfs and the problem grew worse if the plot was divided between members of a large family. Many peasants could not pay their debts and either went to work for richer farmers, known as *Kulaks*, or drifted to the towns where they worked in industry. Since the Russian population rose steadily during the last half of the 19th century and agriculture remained inefficient, there were continuous shortages and frequent famines. The landowners, on the other hand, received money for the land they sold but still retained half.

ALEXANDER II : REFORM AND DISCONTENT

The Tsars ruled without Parliament or elected Council. If Alexander wanted advice he chose a minister who was little more than a court favourite. This *autocracy* was supported by the priests of the Russian Orthodox Church who taught children and adults to regard the Tsar as "father of his people". To run such a vast country before modern communications was not easy and it was made worse by a corrupt and inefficient civil service; one Tsar remarked, "Russia is not governed by me but by my forty thousand clerks". A secret police called the *Third Section*, and, later, the *Okhrana*, censored all mail and books and arrested anybody who criticised the regime.

Critics of the system were drawn from the relatively few people who had been to university. They looked to Western Europe for inspiration and demanded democratic government with the Tsar ruling through elected Dumas (Parliaments). In 1874 thousands of students went into the countryside to try to get the peasantry to support them. They were convinced that there could be no lasting reform without such mass support; their nickname *Narodniki* comes from a Russian word meaning "to the people". This movement was not successful. Many of the peasants were too poor and ignorant to understand such protest. Those who did understand often disliked such ideas because they were western and therefore "foreign". Alexander persecuted the Narodniki but pursued his own reform policies. He allowed a certain amount of self-government through *Zemstvos* (Councils). Unlike his predecessor, Tsar Nicholas I, who had disliked railways because they made people "restless", Alexander began a large-scale railway building programme.

These reforms were too modest to satisfy the Tsar's critics who now included Anarchists, Nihilists and Marxists as well as moderates. Alexander became disillusioned by the activities of these extremists. He cut down the powers of the Zemstvos, strictly supervised university teaching and imposed press censorship. The extremists replied with a campaign of terror. In 1881, after several unsuccessful attempts, terrorists mortally wounded Alexander in a bomb attack in a St Petersburg street. His son, *Alexander III*, was a believer in strict discipline. He hit back with a policy of *Autocracy*, *Orthodoxy* and *Nationalism*, i.e. dictatorship, strict obedience to the Church and a strong belief in all things Russian being better than foreign ones.

ALEXANDER III : RUSSIFICATION AND REVOLUTION

Russia is basically a land power; in earlier centuries it had no coastline at all. For two hundred years the Tsars conducted military campaigns both north and south, first, to establish "buffer zones" between Russia and her powerful enemies and, second, to establish ports with access to the Baltic and Mediterranean Seas. Such conquests left foreign peoples under Russian rule and the problem of discontented "minorities" grew worse as the years went by. By the 1800's Russia ruled most of *Poland*, some parts of *Finland* and a southern region called the *Ukraine*. Alexander was stern in his attitude to these minorities and tried to impose Russian language, culture and religious beliefs on them. He disliked Jews and turned a blind eye to massacres of them in *pogroms* (from the Russian word for "destruction"). He also wanted the Poles and Finns to leave the Catholic Church and join the Russian Orthodox Church. His "Russification" was deeply resented by these peoples. In 1831 and 1863 there were serious revolts in Poland which were only crushed after hard fighting.

LENIN AND THE BOLSHEVIKS

Alexander's rule was opposed by extreme political parties. The Narodniki had created a "*land and liberty*" movement which aimed to give landowners' property to the peasants and establish an elected government. It had its terrorists, some of whom had murdered Alexander II. His assassination had put back the cause of moderate reform. It infuriated the millions who loved the Tsar and believed he had a God-given right to rule, and it also put a stop to beneficial reforms he had just been about to initiate. *Land and Liberty* developed into the *Social Revolutionary Party* in 1900. Another group, the *Social Democratic Party*, was an underground Marxist organisation; many of its members were imprisoned or living in exile.

At an SDP meeting in London in 1902 the SDP split into two factions, the *Bolsheviks* (Majority Men) and the *Mensheviks* (Minority Men). The Bolsheviks were led by *Vladimir Ilyich Ulyanov*, better known by his nickname, *Lenin*.

Lenin adapted the Marxist idea of a revolution led by the proletariat (urban workers) into one in which the proletariat joined with the peasantry. In articles and lectures, Lenin developed the idea of a small, well-disciplined elite becoming the "vanguard of the working class". The workers would organise strikes aimed at revolution, not for the more usual demands of better pay and conditions. The development of Russian industry by Witte in the 1890's helped Lenin's plans because the appalling conditions in the new factories and mines created a discontented and militant workforce.

TURKISH WAR AND SAN STEFANO

Throughout the 19th century Russia continued to expand into Asia, and to increase her influence amongst those *Balkan* peoples who were still ruled by the Turks. The Russians are Slavs and they used the sufferings of the Balkan Slavs as an excuse to intervene. In 1876 there was a crisis after the *Bulgars* rebelled and were crushed with great brutality. Alexander condemned these *Bulgarian Atrocities* and declared war on Turkey, proclaiming that Russian troops would drive the Turk out of Europe altogether. Russian armies swept into the Balkans, taking *Plevna* and *Adrionople*, and threatened *Constantinople*, the Turkish capital. Other Great Powers became alarmed at such an increase in Russia's power and influence in the region. Their reasons for doing so are explained more fully in Work Unit 9. Britain sent a fleet into the *Dardanelles* to warn Russia not to send warships into the Mediterranean, and *Austria*, seeing her own influence in the region at risk, demanded that the *Russo-Turkish War* end. The Russians were exhausted by their efforts and in no position to defy such pressure. By the *Treaty of San Stefano*, 1878, they forced the Turks to give *Serbia* home rule, and they set up a new state, *Bulgaria*.

CONGRESS OF BERLIN

Britain and Austria protested at the creation of this *"Big Bulgaria"* which would have enabled Russia to dominate the Balkans and the Straits. Russia agreed to an international *Congress* at *Berlin* to settle the matter. This conference, organised and dominated by Bismarck, revised the San Stefano treaty and arranged the Balkans differently. "Big Bulgaria" was divided into three, a smaller, independent *Bulgaria*, a self-governing province called *Eastern Rumelia* and a region returned to Turkey on condition that the Christian population was better treated. *Serbia* and *Montenegro* became independent and another area, *Bosnia-Herzegovina*, was administered by Austria. Britain was ceded *Cyprus* to use as a base to defend Turkey if necessary. (*See the maps on the following page*).

The *Congress of Berlin* settled the map of the Balkans until 1912 but it sowed the seeds of future trouble. Turkey was annoyed that its "friends" had benefitted at her expense; Britain with *Cyprus* and Austria with *Bosnia*. The Serbians were bitter about Austrian occupation of Bosnia because it contained a large Serb population. This resentment helped to spark off the First World War (See Work Unit 11). In later years Turkey became friendly with Germany, the one Great Power which had not gained territory from her, and this helped decide which side she fought on in the First World War.

Actual boundaries after Congress of Berlin

ANGLO-JAPANESE TREATY

During the late 19th century Russia's westward expansion into Asia was made easier by the weakness and disunity of the Chinese empire. Each year Russia took over more of *Manchuria*, a Chinese province, and built the *Chinese Eastern Railway* across it as though it was her own territory. These moves annoyed Japan which also had ambitions regarding China. As a result of the *Sino-Japanese War*, 1894-5, which she won, Japan set up *Korea* as a puppet state. Previously it had been ruled by China. Japan also took *Formosa* and *Port Arthur* on the Liaotung peninsula (See map). Russia wanted this port and, supported by Germany and France, forced the Japanese to return it to China. Japan's leaders hid their resentment, increased their war preparations, and looked around for allies. In 1902 their representatives signed the *Anglo-Japanese Treaty* with Britain. Officially this treaty was meant to safeguard China from further encroachments on her territory. In fact, it was meant to discourage France and Germany from more colonisation in the Far East and, because Japan had a strong navy, to leave Britain free to mass more warships in home waters to face the threat of German naval expansion (See Work Unit 11). The Treaty stated that each country would remain neutral if the other was at war with one power but help actively if either was attacked by two.

RUSSO-JAPANESE WAR

Japan regarded this treaty as the "red light" to settle scores with Russia. In 1904 she demanded that Russia withdraw its troops from *Manchuria* and *Korea*. When the Russians refused, the Japanese fleet made a surprise attack on *Port Arthur* which crippled the Russian Pacific fleet. In land campaigns the Japanese fought and won the three-month battle of *Mukden*. Finally, when the Russian Atlantic fleet reached Japanese waters, after sailing round the world, *Admiral Togo*, the Japanese commander, destroyed it in one hour in the Straits of *Tsushima*, May 1905. Russia, utterly defeated, was forced to sue for peace. A treaty was arranged by *President Theodore Roosevelt* at a conference held in the United States. By the *Treaty of Portsmouth (USA)* 1905, Russia lost Manchuria and Port Arthur and was forced to recognise Japan as the dominant power in Korea. This was the first defeat in modern times of a western nation by an Asiatic one. It led to near revolution inside Russia (See Work Unit 13).

SELF-ASSESSMENT SECTION

1. Why was Alexander II called the "Liberator" ?

2. What was the Okhrana ?

3. Who were the Narodniki ?

4. What is the more usual name for the "Majority Men" ?

5. What was a pogrom ?

6. Who resented "Russification" ?

7. What happened to "Big Bulgaria" ?

8. Who won the Battle of Tsushima ?

9. Who acted as peace-maker in the Russo-Japanese War ?

10. Who administered Bosnia after 1878 ?

11. Against the names listed below select the correct letter in the key.

   1. LENIN
   2. ALEXANDER II
   3. BISMARCK
   4. THEODORE ROOSEVELT
   5. ALEXANDER III

   6. NICHOLAS I
   7. COUNT WITTE

   A. was Finance Minister to the Tsar.
   B. dominated the Congress of Berlin.
   C. was assassinated in St. Petersburg.
   D. led Bolsheviks.
   E. connected with the Treaty of Portsmouth.
   F. believed in "Russification".
   G. discouraged railway development.

12. The Russo-Japanese War was fought in :-

   a) Korea.
   b) Vietnam.
   c) Mongolia.
   d) Manchuria.
   (TICK THE CORRECT ANSWER)

13. Why had Russia discontented minorities ? Give an example of the difficulties which arose because of them during this period.

14. Why was the emancipation of the serfs a "mixed blessing" ?

15. Imagine you are a Jew living in 19th century Russia. Explain what your life is like and why it is so difficult.

16. The "Punch" cartoon *on the following page* appeared in 1876.

   a) Who is the figure holding the dogs meant to represent ?
   b) Who is the figure peeping over the fence ? Why is he warning the man holding the dogs ?
   c) Who are the dogs supposed to represent ?
   d) Who is the man walking away meant to be ? Why might the dogs want to attack him ?
   e) One Great Power deeply interested in the subject of this cartoon is not shown. Which one was it ?
   f) How did this Great Power play a part in settling the subject of this cartoon ?

17. Why was the Congress of Berlin called ? How far was it successful ?

18. Explain the Turkish attitude to the decisions of the Congress. How far did this effect future events ?

19. Imagine you are Tsar Alexander III. Write a letter to a minister explaining why you will not allow democratic government in Russia.

THE DOGS OF WAR.

BULL A 1. "TAKE CARE, MY MAN! IT MIGHT BE AWK'ARD IF YOU WAS TO LET 'EM LOOSE!"

(See Question 16).

5

Africa   1885-1914

INTRODUCTION

Until 1875 most European colonies in Africa were confined to the coastal regions, although explorers and traders had penetrated the interior. These colonies were founded for trade and also, in many cases, for strategic reasons. The Dutch and, after 1815, the British, owned Cape Colony in South Africa because it commanded the Cape of Good Hope on the main sea-lane to the Far East. Britain had East African colonies partly to guard vital trade routes round Africa, through the Suez canal and into the Indian Ocean. By 1914 the scene had changed dramatically. Most of the African continent, except Abyssinia (now Ethiopia) and Liberia, had been shared out between European powers. Several questions arise from this extraordinary fact. Why did the map of Africa alter so quickly, and at this time in history ? Above all, why did the so-called "Scramble for Africa" happen at all ?

First, conditions in Europe inclined the Powers towards expansion outside the continent. Bismarck's wars and those between Russia and Turkey had produced a precarious balance of power which could only be altered at the risk of general war - as happened in 1914. France, for example, dare not attack Germany again without allies but she could expand and regain lost military prestige in Africa, where she had owned North African colonies since the 1830's. Britain, with her strong imperial tradition, world-wide trade and age-old jealousy of France, was only too happy to respond to these French moves and establish more colonies. So, whilst British imperialists tried to link Britain's possession from north to south of the continent, French imperialists tried to consolidate a broad band of French territory from west to east. Belgium was ruled by a king, Leopold, who decided to have his own profitable colony in central Africa, the vast region now known as Zaire. The new German empire felt that a Great Power should have colonies, whilst newly-united Italy dreamed of creating a new "Roman" empire in Africa. Only Russia, pre-occupied with her own expansion into Asia, and Austria, busy struggling to hold its multi-national empire together, stayed out of the "Scramble".

All this national activity was built on a solid base of trade networks and exploration which had been accelerated by traders, missionaries and explorers in the middle years of the 19th century when interest in the "Dark Continent" was intense.

The general public in Europe followed the movements of explorers, in particular, with an interest now shown for aircraft records and space travel. The quest for the source of the Nile roused international speculation, whilst famous incidents like Stanley's search for the "lost" Livingstone were followed excitedly by readers of the "Daily Telegraph" which had sponsored the mission.

The motives for individuals to go to Africa were often as mixed as those of their governments. Industrialists maintained that their fast-growing economies needed African raw materials, although this was not always true. Missionaries wanted to turn the African Christian and wipe out what they regarded as "pagan" customs. "Do-gooders" like Livingstone and Gordon wished to wipe out slavery and the slave trade in the continent. Less religious Europeans talked of taking up the "White Man's Burden". They claimed they had a mission to "civilise" the natives. Adventurers risked their lives in a mysterious, strange and dangerous environment.

Behind all this activity lay a feeling of superiority. Europeans lived in a fast-changing world of scientific discoveries and technical marvels. They believed in the idea of progress i.e. that things would steadily improve, and they felt that their technical superiority over Africans gave them the right to organise their lives. In the end they both won and lost. Africans did copy western ways. They adapted themselves to the technical marvels of another continent. But, by doing so, they disproved the theory that they were inferior to Europeans.

AFRICA : THE SLAVE TRADE

Trade was the first link between Europe and West Africa. The *Slave Trade* arose from the need for workers on American and Caribbean plantations. A *Triangle of Trade* developed. European manufactured goods were sold to the Africans in return for slaves, often prisoners from tribal wars. These slaves were taken across the Atlantic in cramped and unhygienic conditions which made the *Middle Passage* of the Triangle notorious. Once in the New World they were sold to planters for sugar, cotton and tobacco. Only when Britain banned the slave trade in 1807 and used its large fleet to capture slave ships, did this trade die out.

Normal trading in Africa was operated by private businesses, like the *Royal Niger Company* formed in 1884 to promote trade in palm oil and other commodities with territories now in *Nigeria* and the French *Compagnie Française de l'Afrique Equitoriale* which operated in the same region. A different kind of company was set up by the Belgian King *Leopold*. Called the *Association Internationale Africaine*, it was supposed to suppress the internal slave trade and open up central Africa for normal trading. In fact, Leopold ran the *Congo* (now Zaire) in a brutal manner for his own profit. His private estate was taken over by Belgium in 1908 after his death.

Companies like RNC and CFAE used private armies to protect their operations. If tribal wars interfered with trade too much their governments were usually persuaded to send in regular troops. This, in turn, often led to the region being taken over by that government. Britain gained *Nigeria* and *Ghana* in West Africa and *Uganda* and *Kenya* in East Africa in this way. The profits from such trade were immense, involving gold, diamonds, coffee, cocoa and rubber, Africa being very rich in raw materials. *West Africa*, the original base for the slave trade, was the scene of intense competition between British and French commercial interests. When Britain's oldest colony in Africa, *Gambia*, was threatened by an alliance of the Ashanti people, the British sent an army led by Sir Garnet Wolseley. Wolseley invaded Ashanti territory, defeated its warriors and temporarily occupied *Kumasi*, their capital.

GERMAN COLONIES

The *Gold Coast* (now Ghana) was colonised by the British because of French pressure on neighbouring *Porto Novo* and *Senegal*. Britain's official involvement with *Nigeria* arose from her businessmen's desire to deal directly with the palm oil producers of the *Upper Niger* region. Germany colonised *Togo*, the *Cameroon* and *South West Africa* (now Namibia). Her interest in East Africa began when *Karl Peters*, a German explorer, went there in 1884 and concluded a number of treaties with local chiefs in what is now known as *Tanzania*. When France, Britain and Germany started competing for this territory, a *Boundary Commission* was set up to settle differences. As a result, *Kenya* and *Uganda* became British, and *Tanganyika* became German.

A plantation-style economy grew up in these colonies based on cotton and coffee growing. The Arab Sultan of Zanzibar preferred British rule to German. He appointed British officers to train his army and in 1877 placed himself under British protection. *Zanzibar* became an official British Protectorate in 1890. When German business interests complained to their government about this, Britain placated Germany by agreeing that she should have the *Caprivi Strip*, a piece of territory connecting *German South-West Africa* with the Zambesi. At about the same time French control of *Madagascar* was recognised by the other Great Powers.

Italy wanted *Tunis* and, when this was occupied by the French, made moves towards *Abyssinia*, taking *Eritrea* in 1885 and *Somaliland* in 1892. In 1896 however, an Italian army was destroyed at *Adowa* by the Abyssinians and no further conquests in this region were attempted by the Italians until 1935 (See Work Unit 15). In 1911 Italy declared war on Turkey in order to take the *Tripoli* and *Cyrenaica* provinces away from the Sultan. This conquest was achieved in a year and the two provinces were later joined and called *Libya*.

The Portuguese were amongst the earliest settlers in Africa, their ships having reached the Cape of Good Hope in 1488. Later, they showed more interest in *Goa* and *Mozambique* and it was the Dutch whose own East India Company set up the Cape as a staging post on the way to the Far East. (See Work Unit 6). In 1890 Portugal recognised Britain's interest in *Mashonaland* and *Nyasaland* (now Malawi and Zimbabwe) in return for recognition of *Portuguese East Africa*.

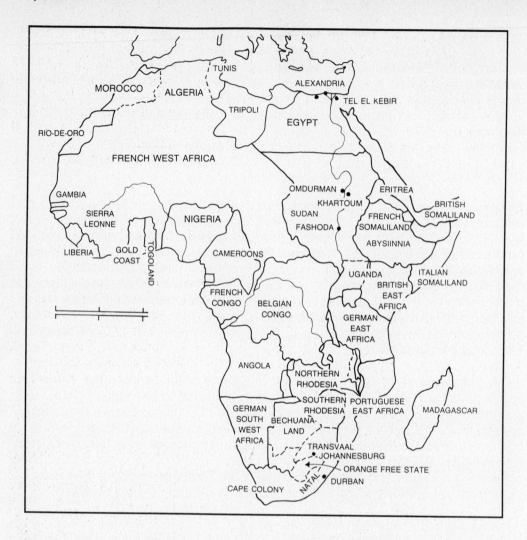

BRITAIN AND EGYPT : THE SUEZ CANAL

Egypt, although conquered by the Turks in 1517, always enjoyed a degree of self-government under the Sultan. After Napoleon's unsuccessful invasion of Egypt in 1798-9, an Albanian, *Mehemit Ali*, seized power and began a career of conquest modelled on that of Napoleon himself. He also employed French advisers and introduced French-style education and laws into Egypt. Mehemit overran *Syria* and *The Egyptian Sudan* but his success alarmed the Great Powers who feared the Ottoman Empire might collapse. Mehemit was forced to stop by pressure from Britain, Russia and Austria.

The *Suez Canal* was built in Egypt by *Ferdinand de Lesseps*, a French engineer, and financed with French money. The British at first opposed the scheme even though it shortened the route to their Eastern possessions, India, Australia and New Zealand. They thought it would be vulnerable in time of war and so preferred the old Cape of Good Hope route. The canal soon became a vital link in east-west traffic because the fast-developing steamship found it easy to use, whereas sailing captains were troubled by the variable winds in the Red Sea. In 1895 the *Khedive* (governor or ruler for the Sultan) faced bankruptcy because of unwise financial policies. He decided to sell his shares in the Suez Canal Company. *Benjamin Disraeli*, British Prime Minister at the time, saw the value of the canal to Britain. He borrowed £4,000,000 and bought fifty per cent of the shares in an unofficial deal which was afterwards ratified by the British government. This led to what is known as *Dual Control* i.e. joint administration of Egypt's financial and economic affairs by France and Britain. This lasted until 1882.

BRITISH CONQUEST : TEL-EL-KEBIR

In 1879 the Sultan deposed *Khedive Ismail*, replacing him with his son, *Tewfik*. Tewfik failed to control a nationalist movement led by *Arabi Pasha*, an Egyptian soldier. By 1882 it was clear that only British or French military intervention could save Tewfik. France was not anxious for any involvement which might leave her weak in the face of German aggression so her Assembly voted against action. Following a riot in *Alexandria* in which some Europeans were killed, a British fleet bombarded the city and troops led by *General Wolseley* landed and captured it. The canal was secured in three days and Arabi's forces defeated at *Tel-el-Kebi*r, September 1882. This battle marked the start of British rule in Egypt. *Sir Evelyn Baring* (later Lord Cromer) was sent out to administer the country. He reorganised Egypt's finances and economy in later years.

GORDON AND GLADSTONE

The Khedive had claimed sovereignty over the *Sudan* and it had been administered for some years by Egyptian officials. News of the British landing and Egyptian defeat sparked off a rising in the Sudan, led by a religious fanatic calling himself the *Mahdi*, 1883. *William Gladstone*, now Prime Minister of Britain, was not so much of an imperialist as Disraeli. He refused to allow British control to extend as far as the Sudan but agreed to send British officials to oversee the safe evacuation of Egyptian civil servants. A British soldier, *General Gordon*, who had been governor of the Sudan under the Khedive, was sent out to supervise the evacuation. Gordon, however, was anxious to smash the slave trade in the region and he lingered in Khartoum, possibly in the hope that a British army would have to be sent to his rescue and that he could use it to destroy the Mahdi's power.

Gladstone came under great pressure to save Gordon because the general was a national hero in Britain. At first he was reluctant to act. When he did send a relieving force it arrived in sight of the city two days after it had been taken by the Mahdi and Gordon killed. The Sudan was ruled by the Mahdi and his successor, the *Khalifa*, until 1896 when a British army led by *Lord Kitchener* advanced up the Nile valley and defeated the Khalifa's forces at *Omdurman*, 1898. This happened just in time from the British point of view because a small French force, led by *Captain Marchand*, had reached *Fashoda* as part of a drive across Africa to assert French sovereignty. Kitchener was under orders not to give way to

Marchand; Fashoda was at the head of the Upper Nile whose waters were vital for the Egyptian economy, especially for its cotton crop.

Marchand's tiny force would have stood no chance against Kitchener's army but the two soldiers acted more sensibly than their governments or peoples. Whilst French and British politicians made provocative speeches and public opinion in both countries was whipped into a frenzy of war-talk, Marchand and Kitchener treated each other politely. Eventually the French desire for possible allies against Germany got the better of their desire for colonies. A new French Foreign Minister negotiated a French withdrawal. Fashoda suggested that no major European power was prepared to risk a general war over a colonial matter, however bitter the dispute.

SELF-ASSESSMENT SECTION

1. Why was the Middle Passage notorious ?

2. What is the Gold Coast now called ?

3. Who defeated the Ashanti ?

4. What two previous provinces made up Libya ?

5. Who bought a half share in the Suez Canal in 1875 ?

6. Who captured Khartoum and killed Gordon ?

7. Who won the Battle of Omdurman ?

8. Why did sailing captains dislike the Suez Canal ?

9. Who led a revolt against the Khedive in 1879 ?

10. Who administered Egypt after 1882 ?

11. Gladstone was reluctant to send a relief force to the Sudan because :-

    (a) He disliked General Gordon.
    (b) He did not wish the British to take over the Sudan.
    (c) He preferred the French to take over the country.
    (d) He liked the Mahdi.
         (TICK THE CORRECT ANSWER)

12. Why was a British force sent to Egypt in 1882 ? What were the long term results of British intervention ?

13. Put the correct country (by letter) against the correct colony. Britain A, France B, Germany C, Italy D, Belgium E.

    UGANDA
    ERITREA
    MADAGASCAR
    CAMEROON
    TANGANYIKA
    EGYPT
    THE CONGO

14. Put correct details (by letter) against these names.

1. KARL PETERS.   A. He built the Suez Canal.
2. KING LEOPOLD.   B. He was deposed by the Sultan.
3. DAVID LIVINGSTONE.   C. He won the battle of Tel-el-Kebir.
4. FERDINAND DE LESSEPS   D. He made treaties with East African chiefs.
5. GENERAL GARNET   E. He ran the Congo.
   WOLSELEY
6. KHEDIVE ISMAIL.   F. He searched for Livingstone.
7. HENRY STANLEY.   G. He met Kitchener at Fashoda.
8. JEAN MARCHAND.   H. He was a famous explorer and missionary.

15. Explain the main causes of the Scramble for Africa. Which were the most important in your opinion ?

16. Discuss the role played by private companies in the European colonisation of Africa.

17. From the moment Britain purchased an interest in the Suez Canal there was disagreement in Britain about how far British influence should go in Egypt. Here are three points of view - Gladstone writing in 1877 and two MP's speaking in a debate about the matter in Parliament, July 1882.

A. "Suppose the very worst. The Canal is stopped. And what then ? ... It seems to be forgotten by many that there is a route to India round the Cape of Good Hope ... (Three weeks delay) will hardly make the difference to us between life and death in the maintenance of the Indian Empire."

(Source : Gladstone writing in the "Nineteenth Century"
Quoted Chamberlain. "The Scramble for Africa" Longman, 1974)

B. "Egypt forms our highway to India and the Far East generally ... As regards the Suez Canal, England has a double interest; it has a predominant commercial interest, because 82 per cent of the trade passing through the Canal is British trade, and it has a predominant political interest caused by the fact that the Canal is the principal highway to India, Ceylon ... British Burma ... Australia and New Zealand."

(Sir Charles Dilke M.P. speaking in the House of Commons,
25 July 1882. Quoted Chamberlain)

C. "The Suez Canal was of paramount and national importance to England; indeed, it was a common thing to say that it formed the gate and key to India. So long, therefore, as we held the Empire of India, we must, of necessity, dominate the Suez Canal."

(Mr J.C. M'Coan M.P. speaking in the same debate,
27 July 1882. Quoted Chamberlain)

(a) Which source disagrees with the other two ? In what way does it disagree ?

(b) Using Sources B and C, explain why Britain intervened in Egypt in 1882.

(c) Which source is most concerned that Britain should take firm control of Egypt?

(d) What do all three sources agree about ?

18. Imagine you are an African living in the late 19th century. Explain what you like, and dislike, about the arrival of European colonisers.

19. Imagine you are working for the Royal Niger Company. From this Work Unit, and from your own knowledge, write a letter to a friend explaining what your company is doing and why it is doing it.

6

South Africa
1815-1914

INTRODUCTION

The Boer War (1899-1902) grew out of two conflicting dreams. Paul Kruger, prime minister of the Transvaal, wanted an all-Dutch South Africa. During the 19th century his people had moved further up country to free themselves from British rule. The British had insisted in retaining some sort of control if only to protect the natives from their hard, Boer task-masters. Kruger resented the British claim to sovereignty and hoped to eliminate British power in all four South African provinces - Cape Colony, Natal, Orange Free State and Transvaal. Cecil Rhodes, the English prime minister of Cape Colony, was a fanatical imperialist. He wanted to make all South Africa, including what is now Zimbabwe, British. Enough people believed in these conflicting dreams to cause a war which lasted three years and cost 30,000 lives.

The British claimed they were fighting to get better treatment for the natives and also for the Uitlanders - European settlers digging gold in the Transvaal. Kruger refused to give voting rights to these people although his government taxed them heavily. He claimed that if he did so he would in time be handing his country over to foreigners. In his opinion, the Boers' separate identity as a white nation was threatened; the British were only interested in their gold and diamond interests. At home, the British people were deeply divided about the matter. Some felt sympathy for the hard-working, devout farmers of the Transvaal and Orange Free State. Despite this, when war came patriotic fervour led thousands of volunteers to go and fight for Queen and country in South Africa. The Boers were beaten in 1902 after a very bitter struggle during which every other European nation condemned Britain.

Eight years later the critics of the war got their way. A Liberal government formed a new dominion, the Union of South Africa, with an ex-Boer general, Louis Botha, as its President. In spite of this, Boer resentment remained. They disliked English culture and language; they thought the British were soft in their attitude towards the blacks. The key to what happened later lies in the question,

43

"Who lost the Boer War?". The British won the war. The Boers suffered only temporary defeat. The real losers were the majority populations of South Africa, the black and coloured races. The war had never been fought for them. When the British complained about the bad treatment of Uitlanders and demanded equality, they were demanding equality for whites. When Kruger talked of independence and freedom he meant independence and freedom for the Boers only. Neither British nor Boer thought of real economic or political freedom for blacks.

In the years following the formation of the Union in 1910 the Boer (now known as the Afrikaaner) gradually gained political domination over the English-descended settler as well as blacks and coloureds. The Afrikaaner was not an imperialist in the old sense of the word. He did not wish to take up the White Man's Burden or educate "inferior" races to self-rule. The Afrikaaner believed in white racial superiority and he built his own peculiar "empire" out of this prejudice. The black could work for him but he must be separated in every other way, in housing, transport, recreational facilities, even in marriage. So apartheid, "separate development" according to the South African government, vicious racial discrimination to the rest of the world, became the most lasting and tragic result of the Boer War.

THE GREAT TREK

Dutch settlers colonised the Cape region of South Africa from 1653. By the terms of the peace treaty which ended the Napoleonic Wars in 1815, *Cape Colony* became a British possession. Britain's interest in the Cape was strategic; it guarded the sea route to India. The original colonists, the *Boers* or *Afrikaaners*, were of Dutch or German descent. They remained in the majority because relatively few British settlers came to this part of Africa. The Afrikaaners resented British rule and this dislike increased when Britain freed all slaves in the British Empire in 1833. Although the Boer farmers received compensation for the loss of their slaves, they regarded the money as insufficient and the idea of freeing them wrong. One group of Afrikaaners, known as the *Voortrekkers* (pioneers), decided to get away from the British altogether by moving into the interior in covered wagons. This *Great Trek* in 1834 led to a clash between the Boers and the *Zulus*, who were eventually defeated at *Blood River* in 1838. This victory is still celebrated by white South Africans.

Sir Harry Smith, the British Governor of Cape Colony, promptly annexed the territories occupied by the Boers in the name of Britain. When the Boers rose in arms, Smith defeated them at *Boomplatz*. By this time the British government was run by the Liberal party, many of whose members were against extending the British Empire. They made an agreement with the Boers. By the terms of the *Sand River Convention*, 1852, the Boers were allowed two territories, the *Orange Free State* and the *Transvaal*, as autonomous regions.

THE ZULU WAR

In 1867 diamonds were discovered near the Orange River. The Orange Free State claimed the region but Britain maintained that *Kimberley*, the chief mining town, was in Cape Colony. It was these mines which made Cecil Rhodes, amongst others, rich. *Lord Carnarvon*, British Colonial Secretary, favoured solving South Africa's problems by creating a federation, as had been done in Canada. The Boers, unlike the Canadians, did not want to be part of a British-run federation but by the late 1870's the Transvaal was bankrupt and threatened by Zulu armies led by *King Cetewayo*. *Sir Theophilus Shepstone*, the Secretary for Native Affairs in Natal, played on the Boer fears and persuaded them to be annexed by Britain in 1878. The Boer leaders' agreement was conditional on them being allowed to pretend in public that they had been against annexation. The British Governor of Cape Colony, *Sir Bartle Frere*, had become convinced that the Zulus represented a danger to the peace of South Africa. Without consulting his government in England, Frere demanded that Cetewayo disband his army. The Zulu king refused and this brought on the *Zulu War*, 1879. A British force was slaughtered at *Isandhlwana* but, after the heroic defence of *Rorke's Drift* by a few British soldiers, a fresh army arrived to destroy the Zulu power at Ulundi, May 1879.

THE FIRST BOER WAR

Now that they were free of the Zulu threat, the Transvaal leaders again demanded their independence. In Britain the Liberal government of Gladstone debated what to do. The Boers grew impatient, rose in revolt, and at *Majuba Hill*, (1881), defeated a small British force and killed its general, *Sir George Colley*. Gladstone was advised to "avenge" Majuba but in speeches he had made it clear that he was against the annexation of the Transvaal. He refused to do so, and at two conventions, one held at *Pretoria*, the Transvaal capital, in 1881, and the other in *London* in 1884, Britain gave self-rule to the Boers on certain conditions. Britain regarded these agreements as giving her ultimate control, particularly in foreign affairs. *Kruger*, now President of the Transvaal, regarded all British rule as unacceptable. After Majuba the British army longed for revenge, whilst the Boers felt confident that their riflemen could defeat the British again if necessary.

THE JAMESON RAID

In 1885 Britain took over *Bechuanaland* to offset German activity in South West Africa. Next year gold was discovered at *Witwatersrand* in the Transvaal. Rhodes bought a stake in these mines and, as part of his plan to surround the Boer republic with British territory, concluded a treaty with *Lobengula*, chief of the Matabele. In return for money and weapons, Lobengula gave Rhodes's *British South Africa Company* the exclusive right to develop what became *Rhodesia* (now Zimbabwe). Britain reluctantly backed Rhodes in case Germans or Portuguese moved into these regions. The Boers saw their simple farming way of life threatened by the arrival of the gold miners whom they called "*Uitlanders*" (Outsiders). A sprawling, untidy mining camp grew rapidly into the city of *Johannesburg*. Its immigrants soon threatened to outnumber the Boers.

Kruger was aware of the economic power which such riches bestowed on the Transvaal but he was determined, as he said, that the Uitlanders should not take over "his" country. The Uitlanders were denied the vote, forbidden to hold government jobs but heavily taxed. Their leaders frequently protested, and some began to store ammunition and weapons for a possible rising against the Boer government. Rhodes regarded the Uitlanders' grievances as an excuse to annex the Transvaal for Britain. He stationed detachments of his Company police along the border, commanded by his friend, *Dr Starr Jameson*. The idea was that this force would cross the border the moment the Uitlander rebellion began, "to restore order". Both Rhodes and *Joseph Chamberlain*, Britain's Colonial Secretary, knew about this plan. But when the Uitlanders lost their nerve and did nothing, Jameson still crossed the border on his famous *Raid*.

Rhodes sent a telegraph message ordering Jameson to stop, but the Raiders had cut the wires. A Boer commando had shadowed their movements and at *Doornkop* they were ambushed and easily overpowered. Jameson and other raiders were handed over to the British by Kruger and they received prison sentences when they returned to England. The effects of the *Jameson Raid* were far-reaching. Rhodes was forced to resign as prime minister of the Cape Colony and return to Britain to face an enquiry. Chamberlain, although he protested his innocence, lost the confidence of most Boers and some British. The Kaiser sent a telegram to Kruger congratulating him on the failure of the Raid. This infuriated British public opinion and worried the British government who always feared an alliance between the Boers and Germany.

MILNER VERSUS KRUGER

In 1898 *Sir Alfred Milner* was sent to the Cape as High Commissioner. Milner shared Rhodes's imperialist ambitions for South Africa and was convinced that the only answer to the problem was the annexation of the Boer states, if necessary by war. It became clear that he intended to use the Uitlanders' grievances as the lever to carry out his policies when he sent his *Helot Despatch* to Chamberlain, claiming that the Uitlanders were being treated as helots (slaves). Kruger, meanwhile, bought weapons and equipment, including heavy guns, from Germany. In 1899 *Marthinus Steyn*, President of the Orange Free State, decided to call a conference at *Bloomfontein* to try to avoid a war in which the Orange Free State was bound by treaty to support the Transvaal. Kruger, starting at 15 years, eventually agreed that a Uitlander could have the vote after 7 years. Milner demanded that this period be reduced to 5 years and when this was refused abruptly broke off the conference. By this time British reinforcements were being sent to South Africa from India and Boers were being called up for military service in the Transvaal.

In early October, 1899, the Orange Free State decided to join the Transvaal in the war which was now inevitable. Kruger sent an ultimatum to the British which accused them of interfering in the Transvaal's internal affairs by taking up the Uitlander cause. It ordered them to stop all troop movements near Transvaal borders and not to land any troops on their way to South Africa by sea. When Britain rejected this ultimatum, the Boers invaded *Natal*, 12 October 1899.

SECOND BOER WAR, 1899-1902

The Boers had chosen the best time for their mounted riflemen; the spring grass was available as fodder for their horses. After their easy victory in 1881, they despised British soldiers and their methods. Boer troops were equipped with modern Mauser rifles and German Creusot and Krupp artillery. They outnumbered the British and hoped to drive them out of South Africa altogether. At first they were successful. In three engagements, at *Stormberg*, *Magersfontein* and *Colenso*, accurate Boer rifle fire, aided by swift movement and clever use of ambush, slaughtered the slow-moving British infantry. Then the Boer generals made a strategic mistake. Instead of invading Cape Colony and capturing Capetown, they wasted time besieging three towns, *Mafeking*, *Ladysmith* and *Kimberley*. This allowed time for British reinforcements to be sent from Britain, where patriotic feeling caused thousands of men to join up.

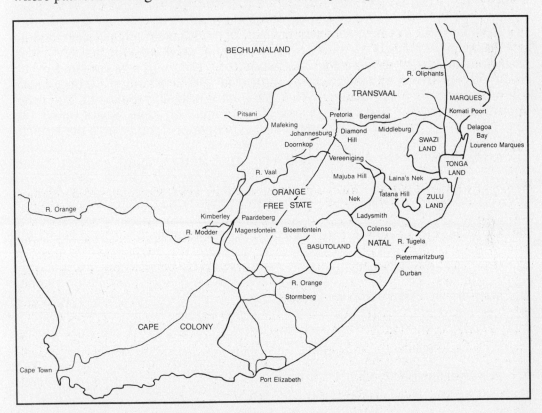

By November a well-equipped army led by *Lord Roberts* marched north, protected by masses of cavalry. The main Boer army was encircled and forced to surrender at *Paardeberg*, February 1900. In May Roberts crossed into the Orange Free State and drove on to take both *Johannesburg* and *Pretoria*, the capital of the Transvaal. Soon afterward he defeated another Boer army at *Diamond Hill*. The last regularly organised Boer army was beaten at *Bergendal* on 27 August. On 11th September Kruger fled across the border into Portuguese territory.

It seemed the war was over. But the Boers now began a guerilla campaign which continued for nearly two years. Boer commandoes would carry out hit and run attacks and then return to what appeared to be normal civilian life. Lord Kitchener, who succeeded Roberts as commander, adopted a policy of burning Boer farms used by the raiders and rounding up Boer women and children in specially-built *concentration camps*. When disease spread through these camps due to inefficiency and over-crowding, killing thousands, there was widespread condemnation of Britain throughout the world. Kitchener's methods, though unpopular, were successful and in May, 1902 the Boers admitted defeat. By the terms of the *Treaty of Vereeninging* the Transvaal and Orange Free State were annexed by Britain, although the Boers were given self-rule within the empire. A sum of £3,000,000 was paid to Boer families to rebuild and restock their farms.

UNION OF SOUTH AFRICA

In 1905 a British Liberal government granted, first the Transvaal, and then Orange Free State, autonomy. In October, 1908 delegations from all four South African states met at *Durban* to devise a constitution for a proposed new dominion. The result was the Union of South Africa, formed in 1910, with an ex-Boer general, Louis Botha, as its first President. When the First World War broke out, bitterness about the Boer War and the concentration camps led some Boers under the leadership of *Christian de Wet* to rebel at the thought of fighting *with* the British. *Jan Smuts* and *Botha* put down this rebellion, and although Botha promised his people that they would only defend South Africa in the coming conflict, South African troops did conquer *German South West Africa*, and fight in *German East Africa* as well as France.

SELF-ASSESSMENT SECTION

1. Who first settled Cape Colony ?

2. Why did the Boers go on the Great Trek ?

3. Who were the Uitlanders ?

4. Who was President of the Orange Free State ?

5. Who won the Battle of Blood River ?

6. What was the Helot Despatch ?

7. Who sent the Kruger Telegram ?

8. Where did Kruger flee after the battle of Bergendal ?

9. Who was chief of the Matabele ?

10. What was the object of the Jameson Raid ?

11. Write a sentence or two about each of these :-

    (a) The Sand River Convention.
    (b) The Bloomfontein Conference.
    (c) Treaty of Vereeninging.
    (d) The Durban Constitutional Conference.

12. Put correct details (by letter) against these names.

1. STARR JAMESON.	A.	Prime Minister of the Transvaal.
2. SIR HARRY SMITH.	B.	British general who captured Pretoria.
3. LORD ROBERTS.	C.	He led raiders into Transvaal.
4. SIR ALFRED MILNER.	D.	He won the Battle of Boomplatz.
5. JOSEPH CHAMBERLAIN.	E.	A Boer general.
6. LORD KITCHENER.	F.	First President of Union of South Africa.
7. PAUL KRUGER.	G.	Wanted Britain to annex the Boer states.
8. LOUIS BOTHA.	H.	Set up concentration camps.
9. JAN SMUTS.	I.	British Colonial Secretary.

13. Read this and then answer the questions underneath.

> "The worst moment is when you first come to the house. The people thought we had called for refreshments, and one of the women went to get milk. Then we had to tell them that we had to burn the place down. I simply didn't know which way to look ... I gave the inmates, three women and some children, ten minutes to clear their clothes and things out of the house, and my men then fetched bundles of straw and we proceeded to burn it down. The old grandmother was very angry ... Most of them, however, were too miserable to curse. The women cried and the children stood by holding on to them with large frightened eyes ... They won't forget that sight, I'll bet a sovereign, when they grow up ... "
>
> (Source : Lt. Phillips. Quoted in Thomas Pakenham's "The Boer War",
> Weidenfeld and Nicolson, 1979).

    (a) Who do you think wrote this ? Give reasons for your answer.
    (b) Whose policy was he carrying out ?
    (c) Why was the farm being burned ?
    (d) How far has the prophesy in the last sentence been fulfilled ?

14. List the reasons which made Kruger dislike the Uitlanders and refuse to give them civil rights.

15. How far were Cecil Rhodes and Alfred Milner to blame for the Boer War ?

16. Look at the following photograph and then answer the questions.

(Source : Reproduced from "To the Bitter End :
a photographic history of the Boer War, 1899-1902" by Emanoel Lee.
Penguin Books, 1985. p.178)

    (a)   Who is most likely to have set up this camp ?
    (b)   Who is most likely to have been living in it ?
    (c)   Why were these camps set up ?
    (d)   Using this photograph, and other knowledge, write a description of daily life in this camp. Explain how you feel about what is happening to you.

17. Cecil Rhodes ordered Dr. Starr Jameson to :-

    (a)   Enter the Transvaal with his troops if the Uitlanders rebelled.
    (b)   Invade the Transvaal.
    (c)   Stand guard on the Transvaal border.
    (d)   Cause a Uitlander revolt by crossing the border into the Transvaal.
        (TICK THE CORRECT ANSWER)

18. Imagine you are a Boer soldier. Write a letter home explaining :-

    (a)   how you are equipped.
    (b)   how you intend to fight the British.
    (c)   why you think the Boers will win.
    (d)   what you are fighting for.

7

France   1870-1914

INTRODUCTION

France was an ancient monarchy which became a republic after a revolution led by men who so detested the past that they rejected God, called 1792 "The Year One" and renamed the calendar months. It was a Catholic country which had been wracked by religious civil war in the 16th century and had ejected most of its Protestants in the 17th. It was for many years the world's foremost military power, a nation which under Napoleon I conquered Europe. These facts help set the scene for political events during this period.

In 1870 France lost its Napoleonic emperor who, far from reviving the military glories of his uncle, the first Napoleon, led his army to humiliating defeat. For five years afterwards the French people were split between those who wanted a return of the "ancien regime" (old monarchy) with its promise of stability and order, and those who desired another republic founded on the 1789 ideals of liberty, equality and fraternity. To some the Bourbon monarchy suggested all the economic and social abuses and bad government which had led to the revolution in the first place. To others, a republic meant rebellion, atheism, anarchy and violence. This division had a religious side. The Catholic Church supported the monarchy throughout the centuries. The revolutionaries had hated it so much that to be a priest in 1789-93 was nearly as dangerous as to be a nobleman. Yet millions of French people remained firm Catholics. By 1870 the world-wide Church was known as the enemy of "modern" ideas and progress. Many monarchists, alarmed at the rapid changes in the world, were happy to support the Pope's stand. They were, in French terms, clericals who supported, not just Church beliefs, but Church influence and political power.

Left-wing politicians, from moderate liberals to socialists and communists, were suspicious of the priest's influence in the home and school, for it led, in their opinion, to political influence. So were urban workers who were prepared to use the Church for baptisms, marriages and burials but demanded that their politics were their own business. Hence the fierce struggle, similar to that in Germany at the time, over Church control of education. "Clericalism is the enemy" proclaimed Gambetta, a famous radical politician in 1877. It was both a slogan and a rallying cry for many 19th century French people.

Finally, there was the question of the army. France's proud military tradition had bred generations of devoted soldiers and their supporters. These men and women saw the army as the guardian of the honour and glory of Catholic France. They regarded anybody who disagreed with them - left-wingers, Jews, protestants - as traitors and enemies of France. After 1870 the army was ultra-sensitive. Its disastrous showing against the Germans left deep psychological wounds which often had the effect of making the officer class more aggressive, not less. Somehow the honour of the army had to be restored, in their opinion. Perhaps one day against the Germans, but certainly in colonial affairs, they could show that Frenchmen had lost none of their military prowess. Such people often looked for a military "hero", a new Napoleon, to arise and "save" France from her anti-clerical enemies. If they could find such a man, they might attempt a military coup (takeover). Knowledge of this fact heightened the fears of those who detested what the army and the clericals stood for.

These states of mind were the underlying causes of the scandals, changes of government and policies, during this period. Yet France had an inner strength. Her recovery from the Franco-Prussian War was swift and remarkable. The foundation of a new empire in Africa and Indo-China was carried out with vigour and determination. However insecure her governments, none ever had to ban a political party, as Bismarck did in Germany. When the supreme test came in 1914 France went to war united and democratic. Although surprising in view of its political history, it was something of which every French person could be proud.

MONARCHISTS VERSUS REPUBLICANS

After the defeat of France in 1870 Napoleon III was taken prisoner by the Prussians who allowed him to end his days in exile in Britain. A new *National Assembly* (Parliament) was elected, sitting first at *Bordeaux* and then in the old royal palace at Versailles near Paris. Many Assembly members wanted a monarchy, some merely because monarchists were known to favour ending the war. Strongly republican Paris, however, was in a dangerous mood after a bitter winter of starvation and bombardment. Various factors aggravated an already tense situation. Parisians did not like an Assembly which met in the old royal palace of the Bourbons. They feared that a member of that family might be invited to fill the vacant French throne. When the Assembly decreed that all rents suspended during the war must be repaid and the Paris National Guard be disbanded, a revolt broke out.

THE COMMUNE

Beginning as a republican movement, the *Commune* rapidly grew more extreme. Some of its leaders demanded that France be split up into a loose federation. Others formed a commune-style of government, a council which claimed to be completely independent of the Assembly. *Adolphe Thiers*, head of the National Assembly, asked Bismarck's permission to increase the army to 150,000 and use it to take Paris by storm. *Marshal Macmahon*'s troops broke into the city but they had to fight every inch of the way against communards manning the street barricades.

Many buildings were destroyed and the rebels made a final stand in the Pere Lachaise cemetery. Thiers then allowed the troops to massacre many communards in what became known as "the week of blood", May 21-28 1871. A grateful Assembly made Thiers President. He had shown that a republican need not always be a revolutionary. Rich people rallied round to raise loans which paid off the German debt in three years. The Germans then left French territory.

THE THIRD REPUBLIC

Thiers' actions made a monarchy less likely. In the view of many people the fact that a republican could crush a revolution was reassuring. The monarchists wasted time arguing over which of three contenders should be king. This was because the French royal family was divided between *legitimist* and *Orleanist*, both branches of which had ruled France earlier in the century. Eventually, *Macmahon*, who had succeeded Thiers as President in 1873, suggested that the *Count of Chambord*, grandson of King Charles X, should be king. The Orleanist *Count of Paris* would succeed him. The Count insisted that France go back to her old royal flag, the *fleur-de-lys* (lilies) instead of the tricolour. Neither the army nor the middle classes would accept this. The tricolour symbolised the victories of the first Napoleon as well as the ideals of the revolution, *liberty, equality, fraternity*.

Macmahon decided to wait for Chambord's death. This waiting game proved the monarchists' undoing for each election showed a further swing towards republicanism. Seat after seat in the Assembly fell to the republicans until, in 1875, *Leon Gambetta* managed to get a republican Constitution through the Assembly by one vote. It was decided to have a *President* and two houses of parliament, the *Senate* or Upper House, elected indirectly through electoral colleges, and a *Chamber of Deputies*, or Lower House, voted for by every man over 24. Ministers were to be chosen by the President but responsible to the Senate and Chamber. This was France's *Third Republic* and it lasted until 1940.

BOULANGER

Macmahon, President from 1875 until 1879, still hoped for a monarchist revival. But the swing away from monarchy continued. In 1876, for example, an election resulted in a republican majority in the Chamber, although the monarchists still held the Senate. Next year, Macmahon called another election and this led to republican control of both Houses. Macmahon then resigned and was replaced by *Jules Grevy*, a republican. By this time the monarchy had ceased to be a serious option. The Commune had been crushed, a President with the powers of an "elected monarch" had been installed. Respectable, well-off French people no longer feared a republic. They felt sure that no matter how many changes of government - fifty between 1875 and 1914 - real power would be exercised by moderates.

The last serious threat to the stability of the republic came from *General Georges Boulanger*. He was made Minister of War in 1886. Boulanger was a military hero who made fiery speeches demanding a war of revenge to regain Alsace and Lorraine. His appeal was many-sided. He demanded a stronger army, which pleased the soldiers and those who wanted the lost provinces back. He also

53

wanted more democracy in the army which suited left-wingers and anti-clericals. He wanted a stronger Presidency, which pleased the Monarchists, and the abolition of the less democratic Senate, which pleased the republicans. This gave him support on both sides of the political spectrum. In 1888 he was so popular that six constituencies chose him as their Deputy. His supporters began to hope that he would march on the Assembly and seize power by force. The government hit back by accusing him of treason. At this critical moment Boulanger's nerve failed him and he fled to Belgium where he committed suicide three years later.

DREYFUS

In 1879, *Ferdinand de Lesseps*, the builder of the Suez Canal, began work on a canal across the *Isthmus of Panama*. After ten years' work, his company went bankrupt due to engineering mistakes and the unhealthy climate which killed off the workers. In 1892 de Lesseps was found guilty of bribing politicians to gain their support for his plans. The publicity surrounding the trial showed that many of the financiers involved in the schemes were Jewish. This led to a fresh outburst of anti-semitism which, in turn, led to a far greater scandal.

In 1894 *Alfred Dreyfus*, a captain in the French army and a Jew, was court-martialled and sentenced to life imprisonment for selling military secrets to the Germans. The case against Dreyfus hinged on an unsigned and undated piece of paper said to be in his handwriting. Dreyfus proclaimed his innocence but was ceremonially stripped of his rank and sent to the penal colony of Devil's Island. When the leakages of information continued the whole of France began to take sides, some for Dreyfus and some for the army. In 1897, *Colonel Picquart*, a protestant and head of French military intelligence, accused *C.F. Esterhazy*, another officer, of being the traitor. Picquart was promptly posted to a war zone in Tunisia, where nobody could interview him, and a fresh court-martial took three minutes to acquit Esterhazy.

ZOLA'S "J'ACCUSE"

In January, 1898, *Emile Zola*, the novelist, wrote an article in defence of Dreyfus called *"J'accuse"* (I accuse) in which he claimed that the War Ministry was engaged in a cover-up. He stated that the handwriting experts whose evidence had convicted Dreyfus were either lying or insane. Zola was prosecuted for libel and sentenced to a year in prison which he avoided by going abroad. Picquart, meanwhile, was dismissed from the army for "professional faults". By this time France was in uproar, with friends and families divided on the issue. Some thought that the army's honour was more important than any individual. Others demanded justice for Dreyfus. Those against Dreyfus included monarchists, churchmen and army officers. Those for him were usually republicans, anti-clericals and left-wingers. The quarrel was more bitter because of the anti-semitism involved. The Catholic press ran campaigns against Jews. Dreyfus's supporters claimed the whole affair was a plot by the military authorities to rid the army of Jews.

DREYFUS PARDONED

In 1898 Picquart, now a civilian, was prosecuted for his accusations against Esterhazy. The new chief of French Intelligence, *Colonel Henry*, produced evidence which turned out to be a forgery. Henry committed suicide when it became known that he had been forging documents to help prove Dreyfus guilty. Esterhazy then fled from France and later admitted that he was the traitor. A reluctant court-martial still found Dreyfus guilty "but with extenuating circumstances". It sentenced him to 10 years in prison but the President intervened to pardon Dreyfus who was finally restored to his rank in the army in 1906. The Dreyfus scandal discredited monarchists, army and Church, who had all condemned an innocent man. It revealed the deep split in French society between clericals and anti-clericals. This bitterness endured into the 20th century.

EDUCATION

There was a strong feeling in France that the country's defeat by Germany was due partly to the excellent Prussian education system which turned out skilled workers and soldiers. *Gambetta*, for example, said that the French had not been beaten by Prussian soldiers but by Prussian schoolmasters. Until the 1880's all education in France was in the hands of the Catholic Church. *Jules Ferry*, prime minister for two periods during the early 1880's, was an anti-clerical. He started a national system of education for children between 6 and 13 which was funded by the state. Ferry claimed he wanted "a generation of good citizens for our country". This involved getting rid of Church influences and stressing the great achievements of the Republic. Priests, monks and nuns were forbidden to teach in state schools and in *lycees* (state secondary schools) religious instruction was abolished. This move was followed by restrictions on Catholic religious Orders, particularly the teaching ones. "Authorised" Orders, approved by the government, could run their own *ecoles* (private schools) but without financial help from the state. The most militant Order, the *Jesuits*, were expelled from France.

ATTACK ON CATHOLIC CHURCH

The government of *Waldeck-Rousseau* (1899-1904) revised the law of association regarding groups of more than 20 members so as to strike at the Church. Such groups had to apply to continue in existence. If they failed to apply, or were not approved by the government, they were suppressed. This act led to the closure of over 1500 monasteries and convents, In 1905 an even more anti-clerical ministry made sweeping changes. The 1802 *Concordat* (agreement) with the Pope was ended. All churches and cathedrals became state property and priests were no longer paid by the government. Catholics were ordered to form "*Associations culturelles*" (Associations for Public Worship) if they wished to run cathedrals and churches. The Pope forbade French Catholics to form such associations and in 1907 the government allowed Catholics to use churches without forming an association.

POPE LEO XIII

The separation of Church and State carried out in these years had the effect of putting the French Church more directly under the control of the Papacy. It coincided with the pontificate (reign) of Pope Leo XIII, a liberal-minded pope. Leo condemned both Marxism and capitalism and pleaded for less inequality and more social justice. He told French Catholics to forget their old differences and work with the Third Republic. Unfortunately for him, his works and teaching occurred when the battle was being fought for control of French schools. The ill-feeling caused by this made reconciliation impossible. Leo also encouraged Catholics to form trade unions and socialist parties for he did not believe that either were un-Christian. Leo's successor in 1903, Pope Pius X, was more conservative. He declared "modernism", by which he meant science in particular, to be heresy. This set the Church firmly against scientific discoveries which seemed to conflict with Catholic dogma.

The attack on the Church in these years was political. The Church was viewed as the supporter of monarchy and the enemy of republicanism. It had attacked Dreyfus and supported Boulanger. In fact, successive French governments were supported by the voters, as religious belief appeared to weaken.

TRADE UNIONS AND SOCIALISM

France was still an agricultural country during this period. Its industrialisation proceeded more slowly than in other western countries. In 1884 trade unions were legalised and they set up "self-help" labour exchanges to help the unemployed. The Socialists were led by *Alexandre Millerand*. He was a moderate who believed that socialists should cooperate with other political parties; in 1893 he led 45 deputies in the Assembly. In 1895 a number of trade unions united to form the *Confederation Generale du Travail* (CGT). The CGT believed in industrial action to improve conditions, including, if necessary, strikes. When Millerand joined the government in 1899 French socialists were appalled. Many were against any cooperation with "class enemies". They were particularly shocked that Millerand was serving in the same cabinet as *General Gallifet*, who had led the troops who slaughtered the communards in 1871. By this time the French socialist party was Marxist in belief, and Millerand was expelled, to be replaced by *Jean Jaures*.

THE SECOND INTERNATIONAL

Jaures was a member of the *Second International*, a Marxist organisation formed in Paris in 1889 to celebrate the centenary of the French Revolution. The First International had been formed in 1864 with Karl Marx as one of its leaders. It had collapsed because of the disruptive tactics of anarchists led by *Michael Bakunin*. The Second International represented both socialists and trade unionists but excluded anarchists. It held congresses in various European capitals between 1891 and 1912 and was due to meet in Vienna when the First World War broke out in 1914. Socialists were against war and were supposed to oppose it actively, with strikes and sabotage. But although the international solidarity of workers was stressed, the nationalistic feelings of members kept it a theory rather than a fact.

Should Frenchmen forget about 1870 and the loss of Alsace Lorraine and join with their German comrades ? Or should they remember that they were good, loyal Frenchmen above all else ? In 1914 Jaures paid for his beliefs with his life. He was murdered because he opposed France's entry into the First World War.

Syndicalists (from "Syndicats", the French word for trade unions) believed in a single weapon, the general strike which would paralyse the government and destroy the capitalist system. Syndicalist extremists ran strikes and committed sabotage. In 1909 they organised a rail strike. *Aristide Briand*, the minister in charge of transport, called up all the strikers of military age and then sent them back to work. As soldiers their strike would then have become mutiny, a treasonable charge punishable by death. The strike collapsed.

French military conscription had been standardised in 1889 at three years. In 1905 favouritism was ruled out and all young men had to serve, regardless of their family connections or future career. Socialists often favoured the idea of a "citizen army" because it would be more democratic than the highly professional force which served the Third Republic. This scheme was rejected as leading to inefficiency and defeat. War was becoming too technical; enthusiasm and courage were no longer enough. However, the governments of these years succeeded in making army life more democratic and military service more of a training in citizenship.

Millerand was in the Waldeck-Rousseau government which fixed working hours, first at 11 a day and, later, at 10. He lived to be President of the Republic after the First World War. French socialism was divided. There were Marxists and *"possibilists"*, who rejected the all or nothing doctrines of Karl Marx. Many of these intellectuals were distrusted by the workers and the CGT would not join the socialist party. In 1905, in response to the Dreyfus troubles, the socialists combined in one parliamentary party and in 1914 there were 76 socialist deputies in the Assembly. The murder of Jaures broke this unity. In 1912, with war appearing likely, France formed a coalition government with representatives of all parties.

SELF-ASSESSMENT SECTION

1. What were the two Houses of Parliament of the Third Republic called ?

2. Which House was *indirectly* elected ?

3. Which French engineer worked on the Panama Canal ?

4. What was the "ancien regime" ?

5. What was the first meeting place of the French National Assembly in 1871 ?

6. What were "Associations culturelles" ?

7. Why was the Count of Chambord in the news in 1873 ?

8. Who led the French Socialists in 1914 ?

9. Who was Emile Zola ?

10. Who reorganised French education in the 1880's. What was his main aim ?

11. Those who claimed Dreyfus was innocent were :-

    (a) anti-clericals.
    (b) anti-semitics.
    (c) priests.
    (d) monarchists.
    (e) clericals.
         (TICK THE CORRECT ANSWER)

12. Put correct details (by letter) against these names.

    1. WALDECK-ROUSSEAU.   A. Anarchist leader.
    2. GENERAL GALLIFET.   B. Second in line to the French throne.
    3. ALEXANDRE MILLERAND.   C. Minister of Transport in 1909.
    4. MICHAEL BAKUNIN.   D. Crushed the Paris Commune.
    5. ARISTIDE BRIAND.   E. Moderate socialist leader.
    6. COUNT OF PARIS.   F. Said "Clericalism is the enemy".
    7. MARSHAL MACMAHON.   G. His government closed monasteries and
                                     convents.
    8. LEON GAMBETTA.   H. Traitor in the Dreyfus case.
    9. C.F. ESTERHAZY.   I. French monarchist President.

13. Explain the factors which led to General Boulanger's popularity. Why were French people susceptible to his appeal ?

14. Why did the Dreyfus case divide French opinion so deeply ?

15. What factors made the socialist ideals of pacifism and worker' solidarity difficult to achieve in France at this time ?

16. Write short sentences on these subjects.

    (a) The Second International.
    (b) French military conscription.
    (c) Possibilists.
    (d) Syndicalism.

17. This newspaper report appeared in England on May 27 1871. Read it carefully and then answer the questions.

    "Terrible scenes have occurred in the final conflict between the insurgents of the Red Republican faction and the troops of the regular army ... They are the effects of ... that spirit of mingled vanity and bitter fanaticism which is ever ready to sacrifice law, justice, charity and humanity, the safety and honour of the country, all prudence, decency and commonsense, to ... party ambition or party spite ... The streets of Paris were slowly but surely occupied by regular troops ... As soon as a barricade was captured, the red flag was taken down and the tricolour flag put up instead. The defenders ... sometimes yielded themselves prisoners; in other cases they refused quarter, and persisted in firing on the troops, or they rushed to a last hand-to-hand combat, with savage cries of "A la Mort !" (*To the death*). Upon these occasions not a man or woman escaped the death they sought".

(Source: Illustrated London News:
Quoted in "History As Hot News" by De Vries and Amstel.
John Murray, 1973)

(a) By what name is the "Red Republican faction" more usually known today ?

(b) What did the tricolour flag represent ? Why did the "insurgents" display a red flag ?

(c) What was unusual about some of these fighting for the "Red Republican faction" ?

(d) Which side do you think the writer supported ? Give reasons for your answers.

18. Imagine you are Alfred Dreyfus. Write a letter to a friend, describing the course of your court-martial and speculating on why you have been found guilty.

8

The Eastern Question

INTRODUCTION

During the late 19th and early 20th centuries the Eastern Question was easy to explain but almost impossible to solve. Briefly put, it was the problem of who would fill the power vacuum when the Turks were finally driven from their Balkan possessions. For centuries the Balkans had been a corridor between east and west. Vital trading routes had been used, not just by merchants and travellers, but by armies. In medieval times Crusaders had marched east along its valleys and river systems. Between the 15th and 17th centuries invading Turks had swept west in conquests which had led them across Hungary to the outskirts of Vienna. Unlike the Crusaders, the Turks had stayed, ruling a Christian Slav people with great brutality. At times they had sent in Turkish colonists or carried out forcible conversions to the Muslim faith; in the 19th century 70% of Albania's population was Muslim. By the 19th century, however, Turkey was weak and backward compared with the industrialised west. As the Turk's grip faltered on her restless subject peoples, two Great Powers, Austria and Russia, looked for ways to benefit from the Ottoman collapse.

For land-locked Russia it was a matter of gaining access to the Straits and the Mediterranean; puppet Balkan states would help her do that. For the Austrian empire the problem was more complicated. The Balkans were a "devil's brew" of conflicting racial, nationalist and religious groups. In this region Orthodox Christians, Catholics, Muslims and Jews clashed. Their nationalism was proclaimed, not just by political parties, but by secret societies who specialised in murder and terror. Of the nine rulers of Serbia during the modern period, four were murdered and four forced to abdicate; it was members of a Serbian secret society who killed the Archduke Franz Ferdinand, heir to the Austrian throne, and so sparked off the First World War.

Austria's rulers viewed this troublesome brew and worried in case its ideas infected their own Slav populations. The answer seemed to be to control them as effectively as possible; to make the Serbs of Bosnia, for example, wish to join the Serbs living in Austria. Finally, a third country, Britain, although far away geographically, was interested for a different reason. Britain was the predominant sea-power in the Mediterranean. She was determined to deny Russia's warships entry to this sea, and in 1854 had joined France in fighting the Crimean War to stop this happening. After their victory, France and Britain made sure that Russian fleets were forbidden access to the Mediterranean but by the 1870's Russia had decided to ignore this ruling.

Three major crises occurred during this period. In 1877 Russia attacked Turkey after some particularly awful massacres of Christians. In a few months her armies fought their way to the Bosphorus, where they could see Constantinople, the Turkish capital. They saw as well the masts of British warships; Britain had decided to intervene to rob Russia of the fruits of her victory. In 1908 a revolution inside Turkey seemed to promise reform and modernisation. It suggested to the Balkan states that the time was ripe to drive the Turks into the sea. The same year the Austrians annexed Bosnia, a Serb province they had administered since 1878. This caused such ill-feeling in Serbia that it led indirectly to the murder which caused the First World War. In 1912-13, the Balkan states joined in a short-lived and uneasy alliance. They drove the Turks from their European possessions, only to fall out amongst themselves afterwards. Twentieth century Balkan states were left a jigsaw of competing nationalities until, after 1945, Stalin's Soviet armies subdued every country except Albania, Yugoslavia (the old Serbia) and Greece.

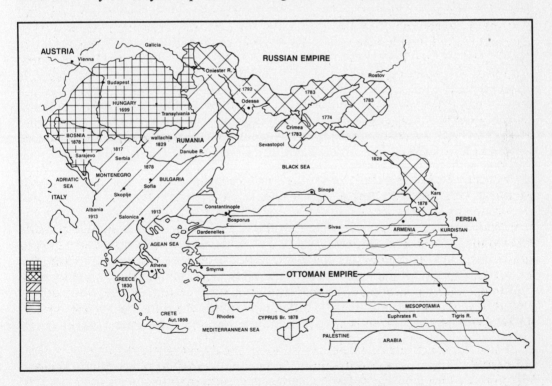

Turkish Possessions in Europe, 19th Century

THE "SICK MAN OF EUROPE"

In 1815 the *Ottoman* (Turkish) Empire comprised territories in North Africa as far as *Morocco* and Balkan regions to the rivers Danube and Pruth (See map). During the 19th century independence movements inside her frontiers led to a steady weakening of Turkish power. In 1830 the *Greeks* won independence for part of their land. *Algeria* was taken from the Turks by France. Later, the Balkan provinces of *Serbia*, *Moldavia* and *Wallachia* became autonomous (self-governing). Egypt, led by Mehemit Ali, won a similar freedom (See Work Unit 5). The problem of what to do with Turkey's European possessions when she collapsed became known as the *Eastern Question*. It was summed up by a Russian Tsar who wondered what would happen to the Ottoman lands when the "very sick man" died. For this reason Turkey was often refered to as the *sick man of Europe*. (*See map on previous page*).

THE CRIMEAN WAR

Two states who bordered these territories seemed likely to benefit if the "sick man" died, *Russia* and *Austria*. Russia's traditional policy of expansion (See Work Unit 4) had led, by the 1850's, to her conquering the *Crimea* and building the naval base at *Sebastapol*. The route from the Black Sea to the Mediterranean led through lands still ruled by the Turks - the *Straits*, the *Sea of Marmara* and the *Dardanelles* (See map). Russia's first attempt to break this Turkish hold on her lifeline led to a conflict with France and Britain. *The Crimean War*, 1854-6, resulted in the defeat of Russia, the dismantling of the Russian naval stronghold of *Sebastapol*, and the banning of Russian warships from the Mediterranean (Treaty of Paris, 1856). Russia's second attempt was made in 1877 as a reaction to the Turkish massacres after the Bulgarian rebellion. The Tsar, claiming to be the defender of Christians in the region, invaded the Balkans and beat the Turks at *Plevna*. The *Treaty of San Stefano* and the *Congress of Berlin* which followed are dealt with in Work Unit 4.

OPPOSITION TO RUSSIAN EXPANSION

Russian expansion into the Balkans in the late 19th century was opposed by Austria and Britain; France was too weakened by her defeat in the Franco-Prussian War to contemplate intervening. *Franz-Joseph*, emperor of Austria, ruled a multi-national empire (For further information read Work Unit 11). Some of these peoples were Slavs and therefore related to the Russians. Any extension of Slav power engineered by Russia near Austria's borders would make her own Slav subjects restless. Austria was also interested in gaining a port, in her case the Turkish city of *Salonika* on the Aegean Sea.

British trade routes to the Middle East, India, Australia and New Zealand converged in this region, the more so after the opening of the *Suez Canal* in 1869. Britain already regarded Russia as a threat to India through Afghanistan. Any Russian naval activity in the Mediterranean posed a further danger in the opinion of British statesmen. Consequently, although most British politicians condemned

Turkish brutality towards Christians, British governments favoured propping up the Sultan's regime to prevent a further extension of Russian power and influence. Austria and Britain, however, diverged in their policy towards independence for the Balkan states. Britain had no objection to this development. Austria preferred to control these states herself. Early in the 1880's, for example, she forced Serbia to trade almost exclusively with her.

THE FIRST WORLD WAR

The Young Turk Revolution and the *Balkan Wars* virtually ended Turkish rule in Europe (See Work Unit 11). By this time Turkey had established friendly links with Germany (See Work Unit 4). German officers reorganised the Turkish army and Germany also gave economic aid, especially with the scheme for a *Berlin to Baghdad* railway. The Kaiser was well received when he visited Turkey in 1889. The Russians, however, saw the railway project, involving driving a route through the Balkans, as a threat to their own influence in the region. When war came in 1914 Turkey's rulers decided that an Allied victory against Germany would probably lead to the partition of their own country. Turkey closed the Straits to prevent essential supplies reaching Russia. As a result the Allied Powers declared war on her, 1 November 1914. In the war which followed, the Turks suffered catastrophic defeats and the Ottoman Empire collapsed (See Work Unit 12).

GREEK AMBITIONS

As a consequence of this defeat, Turkey lost *North Africa, Syria, Iraq, Arabia* and the *Dardanelles*. Even the Turkish homeland, *Asia Minor* (also known as Anatolia) was threatened by a Paris Peace Settlement ruling which allowed Allied countries to occupy parts of Anatolia. With British warships and troops all around him at Constantinople, a new Sultan, *Mohammed VI*, feared that Turkey might cease to exist as a separate state. The *Greeks* certainly favoured this option. Until 1453 the Greeks had ruled large parts of modern Turkey in an empire known as *Byzantium*. Byzantine culture had been both Christian and Greek, and many Greeks still looked upon Turkey as "their" land. In May, 1919, they were encouraged in this attitude by *President Woodrow Wilson* of the USA and *David Lloyd George*, Britain's prime minister, especially as in the last stages of the war Greece had entered the fighting on the Allied side. However, by the time the Greeks had decided on an invasion of Turkey the advent of a pro-German Greek king and the dismissal of prime minister *Venizelos*, a favourite of the Allied leaders, had cooled such enthusiasm. Nevertheless, the Greeks embarked on their Turkish adventure in 1920.

ATATURK

In this national crisis for the Turks a military hero arrived to save them. *Kemal Ataturk* had played a vital role in defeating the Allied landings at Gallipoli in 1915 (See Work Unit 12). In January, 1920 he formed a rebel government, the *Grand National Assembly*, at *Ankara*, a town deep in Anatolia and therefore not as vulnerable to attack as Constantinople. From the Turkish point of view this action for by the *Treaty of Sevres*, August 1920, the Sultan had accepted that his country should be partitioned between *Kurdestan, Greece, Italy* and *France*. Ataturk, supported by a wave of patriotic feeling, turned on the Sultan and defeated his troops at *Inonu* in January, 1921. The Greek army, meanwhile, was advancing into the interior of Turkey. Ataturk reformed his army, fell back to the *River Sakarya* and in September, 1921, inflicted a decisive defeat on the Greeks in a three-week battle. During 1922 the Greek retreat across Anatolia became a dreadful rout, with massacres by both armies. Finally, Ataturk expelled the remnants of the Greek forces from the port of *Smyrna* (now Izmir) where the few Greek survivors were picked up by British warships. A grateful National Assembly gave Ataturk the title "Gazi" or Conqueror.

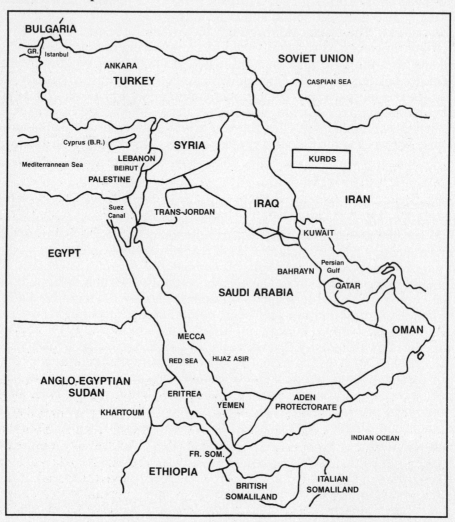

The Middle East after the collapse of the Ottoman Empire, 1919

TREATY OF LAUSANNE

By this time, Ataturk had abolished the Sultanate and been elected *President of the Turkish Republic*. When it looked as though Ataturk's troops might be drawn into hostilities with the British troops still stationed in Turkey, the British government climbed down and signed the *Mudanya Agreement* which accepted Ataturk and his republic as the lawful government of Turkey. In 1923 the *Treaty of Lausanne* recognised the Turkish Republic and declared the *River Maritsa* the frontier between Greece and Turkey. The Turks retained *Thrace*, including *Adrianople*, and the old imperial capital, Constantinople, was renamed *Istanbul*. All Greeks living in Turkey, and all Turks living in Greece, were sent home. (*See map on previous page*).

TURKISH MODERNISATION

Ataturk carried out an extensive modernisation and westernisation programme in Turkey. The Muslim faith lost its privileged position as a state religion; the position of *Caliph* (leader of the faith) which had continued after its usual holder, the *Sultan*, had abdicated, was abolished. A simplified version of Arabic was introduced in a drive against illiteracy. When religious leaders protested that the old Arabic was necessary for the reading of the scriptures they were imprisoned or executed. Women were given equal rights with men in 1926, a far-reaching reform for a Muslim country. Ataturk refused to let Turks wear the *fez*, which he said looked silly, and adopted the western-style panama hat. He toured the streets of Turkish towns with a blackboard and easel, teaching people the new alphabet. Most Turks accepted his often ruthless dictatorship, believing, probably rightly, that he had saved their national identity.

ARABS AND JEWS

During the First World War the Allies sought the help of both the Arabs in *Palestine* to fight the Turks, and of Jews worldwide. They were anxious to gain the support of the influential Jewish vote in the USA as a lever to get America to enter the war. In November, 1917, Britain promised the Jews living in Palestine that she would work for the establishment "of a national homeland for the Jewish people". (Balfour Declaration). This pleased Zionists who wanted a separate Jewish state in Palestine but dismayed Arabs who had also been promised their independence if they fought against the Turks. British agents, notably *T.E. Lawrence* (Lawrence of Arabia), assisted the Arabs in their revolt, confident in the British promise of "complete and final liberation of the peoples who have been ... oppressed by the Turk". After the war this promise proved impossible to keep. *Feisal*, son of Hussein, the chief Arab leader, went to Versailles expecting to get such lands, including Palestine. In fact, the *Mandate System* (See Work Unit 16) left many Arabs under European rule, and the Jews without a national home.

FINAL ARRANGEMENTS

Palestine was administered by Britain until 1948. During this time tension between Jew and Arab often spilled over into violence, especially as Jewish immigrants from Europe continued to enter the country. *Syria* was administered by France, and although the British allowed another of Hussein's sons, *Abdullah*, to rule *Trans-Jordan* (now Jordan), they kept ultimate control until 1956. Feisal was made king of another mandated territory, *Mesopotamia* (now Iraq). In all cases, there was a strong element of colonial rule which contrasted with promises made during the First World War. The African provinces of the old Ottoman Empire became independent much later - *Egypt* in 1952, *Tunisia* in 1955 and *Algeria* in 1959. The Balkans were divided into *Yugoslavia* (consisting of *Serbia* and *Croatia*), *Albania*, *Greece*, *Bulgaria*, *Rumania* and *Hungary* (originally part of the old Austro-Hungarian empire).

SELF-ASSESSMENT SECTION

1. Name the Russian naval base on the Black Sea.

2. Which two countries hoped to benefit from the collapse of Turkish power in Europe?

3. Who was the "sick man of Europe"?

4. Why did Russia declare war on Turkey in 1877?

5. Who conquered Algeria from the Turks?

6. Name the Emperor of Austria and the Tsars of Russia during this period.

7. Why were the Austrians interested in Salonika?

8. Who were the Young Turks?

9. Name the main religious groups living in the Balkans.

10. What was the Mudanya agreement?

11. Put the correct details (by letter) against these names.

1. SULTAN MOHAMMED VI.	A.	Greek Prime Minister.
2. DAVID LLOYD GEORGE.	B.	Led Arab revolt.
3. VENIZELOS.	C.	Last Sultan of the Ottoman Empire.
4. BALFOUR.	D.	King of Trans-Jordan.
5. ATATURK.	E.	King of Iraq.
6. ABDULLAH.	F.	Favoured Greek invasion of Asia Minor.
7. FEISAL.	G.	Founder of modern Turkey.
8. T.E. LAWRENCE.	H.	Issued famous Declaration in 1917.

12. Turkey joined Germany in the First World War because :-

    (a) The Kaiser had visited Turkey in 1889.
    (b) She had been attacked by the Balkan countries.
    (c) She had been attacked by Russia.
    (d) She feared being partitioned if the Allies beat Germany.
    (TICK THE CORRECT ANSWER)

13. Write sentences to explain ONE of these topics.

    (a) The Treaty of Paris.
    (b) The Treaty of Lausanne.
    (c) The Treaty of Sevres.

14. Look at these two maps of the Balkans in 1878. Map 1 shows the region after the Treaty of San Stefano. Map 2 shows the same region after the Congress of Berlin. Then answer the questions below. (If necessary refer to Work Unit 4).

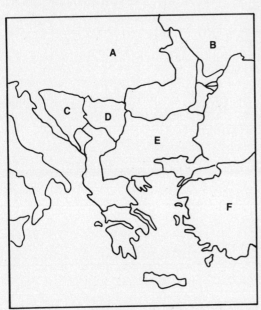 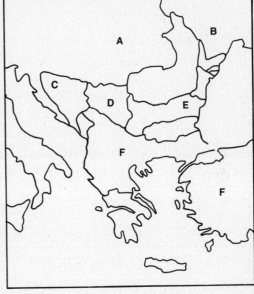

    (a) Name countries A, B and F. How did their policies disagree about this region?
    (b) Name country E.
    (c) Why is E so much smaller in Map 2?
    (d) Name province C. Which country took over this province in 1908?
    (e) Why did country A and country D have bad relations?

15. Read the following two statements. The first was issued by the British government in 1917, the second by the French and British governments in 1918.

1. "His Majesty's government view with favour the establishment in Palestine of a national home for the Jewish people, and will use their best endeavours to facilitate the achievement of this object, it being clearly understood that nothing shall be done which may prejudice the civil and religious rights of existing non-Jewish communities in Palestine ... "

2. "The goal envisaged by France and Britain ... is the complete and final liberation of the peoples who have for so long been oppressed by the Turks, and the setting up of national governments and administrations that shall derive their authority from the free exercise of the initiative and choice of the indigenous (*native*) populations."

   (a)   What is the name usually given to Document 1 ?
   (b)   How did Jews and Arabs interpret these two statements with regard to Palestine ? What has been the result of these interpretations ?
   (c)   What scheme introduced by the League of Nations after the First World War meant that neither of these promises was kept ? How far have they been realised since 1919 ? (See also Work Unit 34).
   (d)   Why were these two statement issued ?

16. Explain Austria's reasons for intervening in Balkan affairs during this period. How far was she successful in her aims ?

17. Imagine you are a Turk living in the period 1919-38. Describe the changes which have happened in your country, how you feel about them and what you think of Ataturk, President of your country.

9

Latin America

INTRODUCTION

For most Europeans Latin America is a faraway continent of which they know very little. The popular image comes from Hollywood films, in which a handful of heroic North American cowboys defeat hordes of Latin American, usually Mexican, soldiers who are betrayed by their corrupt and brutal generals. Nobody who has studied Latin American history can doubt that there is a grain of truth in this picture. But there is more to this vast continent and its peoples than such gross distortions. George Camacho, a Columbian author, has tried to correct such misconceptions. "Argentina", he wrote, "is not just a land of beef and wealthy polo players; Brazil has more to offer than burned coffee, exotic dances and star football players; and Mexico is not properly typified by a picture of the Indian seated on the ground against a wall with his knees drawn up and his sombrero tilted over his eyes".

In fact, Latin America, like the USA and Canada, is an extension of European culture into the New World. Latin Americans speak two mainstream European languages, Spanish and Portuguese. They are heirs of the culture and religion of Spain and Portugal. Their ancestors looked across the Atlantic to France and Britain for guidance; many attempts were made, for example, to copy British political institutions. Immigrants who came to work on the foreign investments in the countries served to cement these bonds. Today, these influences have a modern slant. The hydro-electric plants of Brazil, the steel factories of Chile and Columbia, the nuclear research of Argentina and other countries, show that modern technology, as well as ancient culture, have a part to play in the psychology of Latin America today.

Ignorance and prejudice about Latin America is caused partly by its geographical distance from Europe, the difficult nature of its terrain, and its history. The original conquerors came from countries ruled by dictatorial monarchs, supported by a landowning aristocracy and an all-powerful Church. This way of life was transplanted to the New World where the land, climate, and the local inhabitants, including the conquered and crushed Indians, suited such a semi-feudal system. When, after 1808, Latin Americans gained their independence, this freedom was obtained by war, not peaceful change. Consequently, the new states

69

carved out of the old Spanish and Portuguese empires, were often ruled by victorious generals. This led to a tradition of military rule in Latin America, with the army in each country acting as a sort of right-wing political party in uniform. Army leaders were willing to interfere in politics, often claiming that it was "for the good of the people". Finally, Latin America never managed to achieve the unity of a "United States" similar to that in the North. Instead, a "Balkanisation" process occurred and South America, in particular, became a patchwork of quarrelling states, competing for the available land and minerals.

The continent is very rich but this has proved a mixed blessing. On the one hand, gold, silver, coffee, fruit, cotton, sisal, wheat, hides, wool and fertilisers have attracted European and American investment. On the other, such mineral and agricultural riches have led to wars between South American states over their ownership, and economic instability caused by fluctuations in world demand. Booms and slumps have led, in turn, to political instability, fuelled by the chronic poverty of the peasantry in many countries. The industrialisation which has occurred has created a discontented urban population which in some cases, notably in Argentina, has become a powerful political force. The Latin American worker often has to support a large, unproductive population, caused by unemployment and the rising birthrate; growth in the economy is often cancelled out by a rise in births. Today the problem of world over-population is shown most vividly in Latin America.

Looming over the whole continent is the so-called "Colossus of the North", the USA. In some ways Latin America's mighty neighbour has been a help, in other ways a hindrance. Dislike and distrust of "Yankee imperialism" is widespread throughout Latin America. US politicians, for their part, worry in case the struggle for economic and social justice leads Latin American countries towards communism, as it did in Cuba. An interesting new development in recent years is the alliance between protest and revolutionary movements and the priesthood. The Catholic Church, so often the supporter of reactionary forces in the past, is now often seen as a friend of the poor and oppressed. US Presidents have frequently been torn between their genuine desire to improve the conditions in Latin America and their equally genuine fear of communism. Nineteenth century liberal idealists engineered political revolutions. Their victories were exploited by men who were determined there should not be a social and economic revolution. In most cases, Latin Americans are still waiting for this second revolution.

RACIAL MIX

The American continent from Mexico downwards was originally colonised by the Spanish and Portuguese. Because the Spanish and Portuguese languages grew out of Latin, the entire area is known as *Latin America*. Although Latin America is divided politically into 22 separate states, most of its peoples share a common language, culture and religion (Catholic). The population is a racial mix, consisting of descendants of the Spanish and Portuguese settlers, people of mixed race (part Spanish, part Indian), the Indians, and the descendants of slaves brought over from Africa. Over the centuries inter-breeding has taken place freely because there is relatively little race prejudice in Latin America.

When Latin America was first colonised, both Spain and Portugal were ruled by ancient monarchies, and had social systems based on a land-owning aristocracy and a powerful Church. This was reproduced in Latin America and in large parts of the continent it has persisted to the present time. A typical scenario involves a poor, dependent peasantry working for landowners who take a share of the crops. Such economic dependence leads to political dependence. In most cases a landowning class runs the country, supported by an army whose officers are drawn from the ranks of the wealthy.

END OF COLONIAL RULE

Until 1808 the Spanish and Portuguese empires were ruled by their respective monarchs through provincial governors and their *juntas* (Councils). In that year Napoleon's armies invaded Portugal and Spain. *Ferdinand VII*, the Spanish king, was deposed in favour of Napoleon's brother *Joseph Bonaparte. Dom Joao*, king of Portugal, was also deposed and he fled to Brazil, the Portuguese colony in the New World. Most provincial governors and the ruling classes in Spanish America rejected Joseph, and, although Ferdinand was reinstated by the victorious Allies in 1814, there began a series of risings which, over the next 25 years, led to the formation of many independent Latin American countries. The new rulers were frequently military dictators, although the most famous soldier, *Simon Bolivar* (known as the "Liberator" because of the number of liberation movements he led), hoped that some of these states would become liberal democracies of the British type. In fact, because such risings had been led by, and developed from, the discontent of the ruling classes, rather than the peasantry, the new political systems resembled the ones they had replaced. And because such independence had been gained by war, a tradition of army interference in politics was established. Even the monarchy survived in a different form because many of the *Presidents* who ruled the new countries were monarchs in all but name. (*See map on the following page*).

INDUSTRY

From 1850 onwards the capital and technical skill needed to create Latin American industries and build the necessary infrastructure of roads, railways and ports, was supplied from Europe, particularly Britain and France. In return, European countries acquired access to raw materials and cheap food for their urban populations. *Argentina*'s railways - 5848 miles by 1890 - were built by British engineers and workers with private British capital. *Chile*'s valuable nitrate industry, in demand for explosives and fertilisers, was financed by British businessmen, notably *Thomas North*, nicknamed the *"Nitrate King"*. *Chile* fought a long and costly war with *Bolivia* and *Peru* over disputed nitrate fields which resulted in a victory for Chile (1879-83). *Mexico*'s *oil industry* benefitted from infusions of British and US capital during the long dictatorship of *Porfirio Diaz* (1877-1911). Production rose from 10,000 barrels a year in 1901 to 13,000,000 in 1911.

AGRICULTURE

Another long-serving President, *Juan Gomez* of Venezuela (1908-33), struck deals with British, Dutch and US investors which helped to make Venezuela's oil industry the world's second largest exporter by 1928. Brazil developed with British help *sugar*, *cotton* and *rubber* industries. Rubber became a prosperous industry because of the growing need for tyres and electrical insulation. Until 1876 Brazil had a monopoly of rubber production. In that year an Englishman smuggled seeds out of Brazil and founded the rubber plantations of the Far East. Argentinian cattlemen imported pedigree British stock on which their flourishing meat industry is based. This would not have been possible without refrigerated ships, pioneered by the French with their *"Frigorifique"* (1876). By 1910 278 refrigerated ships were carrying Argentine meat to Britain. This industry was built largely by immigrants who founded a new middle-class in expanding cities like *Buenos Aires*, the main port for meat shipments to Britain.

US INVOLVEMENT

The USA at first took relatively little interest in such Latin American development because its available capital was being used to finance its own continental expansion. By the 1890's, however, the entire territory of the USA from *Maine* to *California* had been explored and occupied. With its own "frontier" closed, the USA mounted a campaign for foreign markets targeted at British investment in Latin America. US investors also took a keen interest in *Cuba*, both economically, because of its sugar industry, and strategically, because of its nearness to the US mainland and the proposed *Panama Canal*. When the Cubans rebelled against Spanish rule, US troops invaded Cuba and in the war that followed, defeated the Spanish, depriving them of both *Cuba* and the *Phillipines* in the Pacific (See Work Unit 3).

THE USA AND CUBA

In the years which followed the *Spanish-American War*, 1898, US administrations often intervened militarily and politically in Cuban affairs and this encouraged US investment in sugar-fields, sugar-mills, corporations, land and property on the island. During the long dictatorship of *Fulgencio Batista* (1933-58), Cuba became little more than an economic satellite of the United States; in 1956 US officials admitted that US companies in Cuba owned 90% of the telephone and electric services, 50% of the railways and 40% of the sugar industry.

This situation, plus the brutality of the Batista regime, led to a successful rising by *Fidel Castro* (1956-9). When the USA showed itself hostile to this development, Castro began to seek help from the communist world. In February, 1960, a Russian official visited Cuba and arranged for Russia to buy most of the Cuban sugar crop during the next five years. In 1962 the USA made sure that Cuba was expelled from the Organisation of American States. *The Cuban Missile Crisis* of that year made the hostility between Cuba and the USA a permanent feature of late 20th century Latin American politics. (See Work Unit 35). *Cuba* has remained a Soviet satellite, and its troops have been used in Russian-backed ventures like the war in *Angola*, Africa.

MEXICAN REVOLUTION

Some Latin American countries have developed peacefully and democratically. *Uruguay*, under the leadership of *Jose Batlle y Ordonez* (1903-7 and 1911-5) set up a two-party political system and an infant welfare state. Batlle's influence continued even after his death in 1929. The Uruguayan Constitution of 1952 did away with the Presidency, although it was restored in 1966. Part of Uruguay's success is due to the fact that the gap between rich and poor, and the ethnic differences between classes, is not so pronounced as elsewhere in Latin America.

Mexico's history has been stormy. In the 1860's it became the only Latin American country to experience active European military interference. *Napoleon III*, Emperor of France, suggested that *Maximilian*, brother of the Austrian emperor Franz Joseph, should become ruler of Mexico. In June 1863 Maximilian, supported by Mexican conservatives and French troops, entered Mexico City. The USA was engaged in its own civil war and so could not intervene. But revolutionary forces led by *Benito Juarez* and *Porfirio Diaz* fought a long campaign which eventually caused the French to withdraw, June 1867. Maximilian was captured by the revolutionaries and shot.

In 1911 Diaz himself was overthrown by discontented middle-class groups headed by *Francisco Madero*. He was joined by armies commanded by semi-bandits like *Pancho Villa* and *Emiliano Zapata*. Both men died violently, but whereas Villa is little more than a colourful folk-memory, Zapata's ideas have influenced Mexican life. In 1917 he published his *Avala Plan*. This proposed to give sugar-growing land to the peasants, and to allocate a third of every *hacienda* (large plantation) to the local people. After a long and savage civil war, Mexicans established a reforming government which nationalised and redistributed the land throughout the Twenties and Thirties. Nationalisation of land, minerals and water prevented foreign exploitation. The Church, always identified in those days with the original Spanish conquerors, was deprived of much of its power, including its control of education. In recent years Mexico has benefitted from bordering the USA because a flourishing tourist industry, as well as cheap transport costs for freight, have helped the economy.

MONROE DOCTRINE

In 1823 President *James Monroe* of the USA issued his famous *Doctrine* regarding Latin America. It laid down four main principles. First, that it was not US policy to interfere in European affairs. Second, that any attempt to extend European monarchical rule to the New World would be regarded by the USA as a danger to peace. Third, the USA would not interfere with existing European possessions in the hemisphere. Finally, that any attempt to regain the lost colonies by a European power would be regarded as an unfriendly act by the USA. At the time it had little effect; the only power who stood any chance of stopping European interference was Britain with its powerful navy. Later, nearly every principle was broken or ignored by the USA. Europeans did interfere in Latin America, at the time of Napoleon III's Mexican adventure. The USA interfered frequently in Latin American affairs, as with the Mexican War and with Cuba. Above all, the USA's involvement in two world wars has been welcomed by many Europeans, although it breaks the terms of the Monroe Doctrine.

PANAMA

The case of the Panama Canal also contradicted the Monroe Doctrine. When *Columbia* refused to lease land across the *Isthmus of Panama* to build a canal considered vital for the US navy, *President Theodore Roosevelt* took advantage of a revolution in *Panama City*, then a part of Columbia. When the rebels declared their independence from Columbian rule, the USA recognised them as the lawful government within three days. Columbian troops needed to crush the revolt were refused transport on the US-owned railway and those who had reached the area were confronted by US marines who "by a curious coincidence", to quote an American historian, happened to be on the Atlantic side of the Isthmus. Twelve days after recognition, the new Republic of Panama signed an agreement with the USA leasing a strip ten miles wide across the Isthmus for the construction of a canal.

THE "BIG STICK" POLICY

Theodore Roosevelt always maintained that these incidents were a coincidence and that the US had no part in engineering the Panamanian revolt. However, heavy-handed moves of this type against Latin America were summarised by Roosevelt himself in the motto, "Speak softly and carry a big stick". Newspapers dubbed Roosevelt's actions as the *Big Stick Policy* and it was this policy which led him later to announce his *Corollary* (follow-up) to the Monroe Doctrine which stated that the US might have to act as a "policeman" if Latin American countries were guilty of "wrongdoing" or "impotence". As an example of this, in 1905 Roosevelt appointed a receiver to take over all Dominican customs houses when that country got into debt. In 1915-16 the Corollary was again used to justify US troops landing in *Haiti* and the *Dominican Republic* to put down disorders.

At the time of the Venezuelan debt dispute (see Work Unit 3) *Luis Drago*, Foreign Minister of Argentina, declared that just as imprisonment for debt for individuals had been abolished, so nations had no right to collect debts from other nations by force (*Drago Doctrine* 1902). Later US administrations have taken a more reasonable and friendly line with Latin American countries. In 1914 the US government apologised for its actions in the Panama case and paid 25 million dollars compensation to Columbia. In the 1930's *President Franklin Roosevelt* tried a *Good Neighbour* policy towards Latin America which involved supplying money for technical assistance and welfare schemes.

PERONISMO

In recent years a new development in Latin America has been that Presidents like *Getulio Vargas* in Brazil and *Juan Peron* in Argentina have been supported by urban industrial workers. Vargas introduced better conditions for factory workers and encouraged the expansion of Brazil's important steel industry. He exploited Brazil's mineral resources, drained swamp lands, encouraged oil exploration and built roads, railways and factories. In spite of having a reputation as a fascist, Vargas entered the Second World War on the side of the Allies and his troops fought well in the Italian campaign. *Peron*, aided by the public relations work of his beautiful wife, *Eva*, created a style of government called *Peronismo*. Peron, a general, started to improve the conditions of the workers. This annoyed the middle classes and some sections of the army but the policy was helped by a substantial foreign currency reserve and the need for high-priced exports to Europe after the Second World War.

Peron nationalised many key industries and bought out foreign investors. In 1947 he declared that Argentina had gained its economic independence but a collapse in world prices caused economic crisis and inflation. He was forced to seek large loans from the USA. His attempt to create fascism "without Mussolini's errors", as he said, did not help his post-war image and he was overthrown by the army in 1955. Nevertheless, *peronista* ideas are still potent in Argentina. Many workers still worship the myth of Peron and Eva, although Peron never attempted to break up the big estates - the real cause of social unrest in the country.

INFLATION AND OVER-POPULATION

Two serious Latin American problems often have political results. *Inflation* was one cause of a serious crisis in *Chile* in 1973. With inflation running at an annual 168%, *President Allende*, a Marxist, was overthrown and killed by a military group led by *General Augusto Pinochet. Overpopulation* is often the background to much unrest. The Catholic Church's condemnation of artificial birth control is very effective in a continent where most people are Catholic. Latin American men often feel that they must prove their virility by fathering large families; women regard motherhood as their primary purpose in life. The poor, unable to rely on any welfare benefits when they grow old, look on a large family as an insurance.

Population growth in Latin America has been startling. In Brazil the population rose from 52 million in 1950 to 116 million in 1978. Such growth cancels out any benefits which result from increased trade or industry. It also leads to large shanty towns around major cities. Half the inhabitants of *Bogota*, the capital of *Columbia*, live in wooden and cardboard huts. Such conditions lead to dangerous social unrest and this protest has been supported in recent years by the rank and file Roman Catholic clergy. The Church helped rural education in both Columbia and Brazil. Its priests condemned police brutality in Brazil and in Columbia supported agricultural reform.

SELF-ASSESSMENT SECTION

1. Which Spanish king was deposed by Napoleon ?

2. Which Latin American country was colonised by the Portuguese ?

3. Why was Simon Bolivar called the "Liberator" ?

4. Which country had a flourishing nitrate industry in the 19th century ?

5. Who ruled Cuba from 1933 until 1958 ?

6. Which Habsburg prince was shot by the Mexicans in 1867 ?

7. Who published the Ayala Plan ?

8. What was the Drago Doctrine ?

9. What was the Roosevelt Corollary to the Monroe Doctrine ?

10. What is the "Colossus of the North" ?

11. Explain the main principles of the Monroe Doctrine. How far has US policy followed them since 1823 ?

12. This document was written by Hiram Bingham in a book called "Across South America", published in 1911. Read it carefully and then answer the questions.

> "In Buenos Aires (*in 1908*) one looks in vain for an American bank or an agency of any well-known Wall Street house. American financial institutions are like American merchant steamers, conspicuous by their absence. The Anglo-Saxons that you see briskly walking along the sidewalks are not Americans, but clean-shaven, red-cheeked, vigorous Britishers ... Thousands of energetic young Englishmen, backed by this enormous British capital, have aided the extraordinary progress that Argentina has made."

    a)   Do you think the author of this extract was British or American ? Give reasons for your answer.
    b)   Why were there so many British people in Buenos Aires in 1908 ?
    c)   What Argentinian industry had been helped by British capital ?
    d)   What inventions helped this industry ?
    e)   In what ways did the situation change in the 30 years after this was written, and why ?

13. Put the correct details (by letter) against these names.

1. PRESIDENT ALLENDE.	A.	Tried "Good Neighbour" policy.
2. JUAN PERON.	B.	Shot by Mexican revolutionaries.
3. THEODORE ROOSEVELT.	C.	President of Mexico for many years.
4. FRANKLIN ROOSEVELT.	D.	Issued famous Doctrine.
5. MAXIMILIAN.	E.	Led revolt against Diaz.
6. PORFIRIO DIAZ.	F.	Led "Rough Riders" into Cuba.
7. JAMES MONROE.	G.	Argentinian President.
8. FRANCESCO MADERO.	H.	Marxist President of Chile.

14. Peronismo is :-

    a)   Military government.
    b)   A left-wing working class movement.
    c)   A fascist-style government which helps the workers.
    d)   A land reform movement.
    e)   A peasant political party.
    (TICK THE CORRECT ANSWER)

15.

Reproduced from "History of a free people" by Bragdon and McCutchen.
The Macmillan Co. 1969

a) Explain the significance of the warship, shovel and guns in this cartoon.
b) Why is the "Roosevelt Doctrine" being used as a gangplank ?
c) Explain the word "Panama" written in the water.
d) Do you think the artist was for or against the events he has drawn ?
    Give reasons for your answer.

16. Imagine you are Latin American. Write a letter to a friend explaining why you
     resent "Yankee imperialism".

10

China   1840-1949

INTRODUCTION

In 1793 the Emperor of China told a trade embassy from Britain, "The Celestial Empire possesses all things ... and lacks no product within its borders. There is therefore no need to import manufactures of outside barbarians". Forty years later, as the pressure on China to trade increased, a Chinese official told Queen Victoria in a letter, "Articles coming from outside China can only be used as toys". Unfortunately for the Chinese, the "barbarians" who sold "toys" also had iron-clad warships and modern weapons. Profits from the China trade, especially in opium, made the British determined to open up more markets on the Chinese mainland. When the Chinese burnt a consignment of opium, the British beat them in two "Opium Wars"; Chinese soldiers often had only bows and arrows with which to face cannons and rifles. The despised foreign "barbarian" took over five Chinese ports where they enjoyed extra-territorial rights, that is, they did not have to obey Chinese law. Other European nations, plus the Americans and Japanese, joined in this international smash and grab. China's arrogant attitude to outsiders, expressed so clearly by the old emperor, was turned within a hundred years into one of helpless humiliation. China became little more than a colony with five or six imperial masters.

Reformers realised that China's only hope was to modernise, as Japan had done in the 1860's. The Manchu dynasty, headed by a cruel, reactionary empress, stood in the way of such a development; several officials who suggested reforms were cut in half on her orders. Japan had copied the west and still kept its emperor and ancient culture. This was not possible in China and in 1911, three years after the empress's death, a revolution established a republic with Sun Yat Sen as its President. This political revolution was not accompanied by a technological one and China still could not resist foreign interference. When the First World War started, Japan, taking advantage of her position as an ally of Britain, France and Russia, seized the opportunity of a free hand in the Far East to force more concessions out of China. The Twenty One Demands of 1915 turned the country into little more than a Japanese satellite, and the republic, now run by warlords, did nothing to remedy the situation. After the war Japan had to be more careful of her wartime allies who were also interested in China. But the attitude of the rest of the world to

China's rights was shown by the peace-makers of Versailles who gave the German possessions in China, not to their rightful owners, but to the Japanese. A Koumintang (Nationalist) army led by Chiang Kai Shek tried to restore order in the 1920's but it spent much of its energies in fighting the new Chinese Communist army led by Mao Tse Tung.

By 1931 Japan was ruled by an aggressive military regime. Manchuria, a Chinese province, was invaded by a Japanese army, and six years later, China itself was attacked. After Mao's communist victory in 1949, he used to tell Japanese officials not to apologise too much for these invasions. Without them, he argued, the communists might not have won power in China. Until 1937 the Koumintang forces were on top and had driven the communists out of the main cities and into the inaccessible Shensi province. The Japanese invasion forced Chiang to do a deal with Mao, and this gave the communists a much-needed breathing space. Chiang was driven from most of the city-centres and lines of communication by the Japanese, whilst the communists still controlled the countryside. Mao, whose philosophy inclined him to rely on the peasantry, subjected vast areas of the countryside and tens of millions of people to a rigid but honest regime. From this grass-roots power base he was able to present himself as the patriotic defender of the homeland. Chiang's regime, meanwhile, was crippled by corruption and defeat.

When Japan surrendered in 1945 no amount of US supplies, weapons and equipment could save the Koumintang. By 1949 Mao's progress in the renewed civil war began to resemble a triumphal march rather than a fighting advance; town after town fell to the communists without a struggle. The Chinese rejected a regime which had failed economically and militarily and turned to Mao, who seemed to offer a new order to China.

OPIUM WARS

From 1644 until 1911 China was ruled by the *Manchus*, conquerors from Manchuria, who supplied a ruling class as well as a succession of emperors. Although foreigners, the Manchus tried to preserve Chinese civilisation. For example, they kept rigidly to the teachings of the Chinese philosopher, *Confucius*. Early attempts by Dutch, British and Portuguese traders to open up Chinese markets were not successful. The Chinese felt themselves to be self-sufficient and looked upon all non-Chinese people as barbarians. In the late 18th century the *British East India Company*'s ships began to bring opium from India to China. The Chinese authorities, worried by the effect of the drug habit on their people, made the import and smoking of opium illegal. The British traders ignored this ban, and when the Chinese authorities burned a large stock of opium at *Canton* in 1839, Britain declared war on China. Two Opium Wars (1839-42) resulted in the defeat of the Chinese who were technologically backward compared with the West.

TREATY PORTS

By the *Treaty of Nanking* (1842) China was forced to open five ports - *Canton*, *Amoy*, *Foochow*, *Ningpo* and *Shanghai* - for foreign trade, and *Hongkong* island was ceded to Britain. The British were granted *extra-territorial rights* in China which meant that their nationals did not have to obey Chinese law. The Chinese were forbidden to charge more than 5% duty on manufactured imports, a rule which greatly helped foreign industry but handicapped the development of Chinese industry. The Chinese also had to pay a large *indemnity* as compensation to the British traders for the destroyed opium. In 1844 the United States and France secured similar privileges in China. The effect of all this inside China was catastrophic. For centuries China had exported textiles. Now she became an importer and thousands of weavers were ruined. Her inland waterways were neglected because trade travelled through the so-called *Treaty Ports*; This threw thousands of canal men and their families out of work. As taxes rose to pay the indemnity, China was afflicted with an increase in population which led to famine.

TAIPING REBELLION

The result of this discontent and misery was a series of peasant risings which turned into the *Taiping Rebellion*, the greatest man-made disaster in China's history. The Taipings were led by a Christian, *Hung Haiu Chuan*, whose aim was to overthrow the Manchus and give the land to the peasants, reform the nation's morals, abolish slavery and give equal rights to women. By 1853 the Taiping army numbered a million. It captured two important cities, *Wuhan* and *Nanking*, and from the latter the Taipings ruled large parts of China for the next eleven years. But when they pushed north to take *Peking* and break the power of the Manchus once and for all, the Taipings were driven back by the re-organised *Ching* (government) forces. In the meantime there had been another *Opium War* (1856-8) between the French and British on one side and the Chinese on the other. This followed the arrest of a British ship, the "*Arrow*" on suspicion of smuggling. The treaty ending this war involved further humiliating concessions on the part of the Chinese who had to agree to their people being taken to foreign countries to work as labourers. In later years Chinese *coolies* were transported to *Malaya* and the *USA*, where they worked on the first Trans-continental railway.

The European powers now offered to help the Manchus in their war against the Taipings, mainly because the rebels were more efficient in stopping the opium trade. Modern weapons and equipment, plus the use of a mercenary army, called the "Ever-Victorious Army" and led by *General Gordon*, began to have an effect and in 1864 *Nanking* fell to government forces. The Taipings were crushed but the death-toll has been estimated at between 20 and 30 million.

SINO-JAPANESE WAR, 1894-5.

From 1861 until her death in 1908 China was ruled by the *Empress Tze Hsi*, originally the mother of a child-emperor but effective co-regent and ruler of the country from the age of 25. Known to the Chinese as "*The Old Buddha*", she was a cruel tyrant who resisted all attempts to reform the country. Her long reign coincided with even more foreign pressure, this time on lands over which the Chinese had claimed over-lordship for centuries. In the 1880's *Burma* was taken over by Britain and *Vietnam* by France. Newly westernised *Japan* also began to expand onto the Asian mainland. In 1890 a revolt broke out against the ruler of

Korea and he appealed to the Manchu government for help. The Empress regarded Korea as part of her domains so she sent troops into Korea to help the ruler against the rebels. Japan then intervened, attacking the Chinese fleet, invading China itself and occupying *Port Arthur* and *Weihaiwei* (*Sino-Japanese War*). By the *Treaty of Shimonoseki*, 1895, China lost her claims to be overlord of Korea and gave the islands of *Formosa* (now Taiwan) and the *Pescadores* to Japan. Japan also took *Port Arthur* and *Dairen* but was forced to give them back to China by Russia, France and Germany who were opposed to Japanese interference in China's affairs. Japan's resentment over this matter led to the *Russo-Japanese War* 1904-5. (See Work Unit 4).

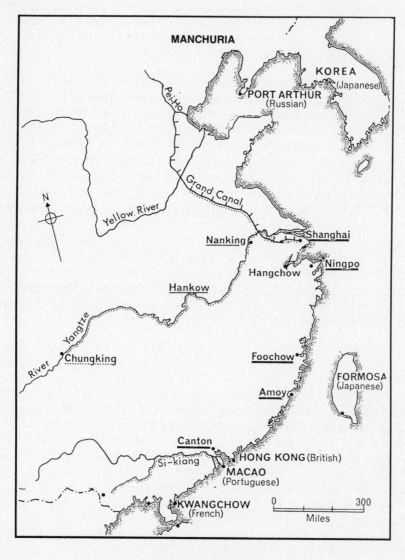

Far East, 1900

THE HUNDRED DAYS AND THE "BOXERS"

China's humiliation was now complete. Any concessions she was forced to make to one foreign country were deemed to apply to all the others, under what was known as the *"Most Favoured Nation" Clause.*In 1898 Chinese resentment at this state of affairs led to an attempt to reform China from the top. A new young emperor, *Kwang Hsu*, gathered a group of advisors around him and set out plans for economic and social reforms. He issued a number of decrees during a period known as *"The Hundred Days"*. These proposed a modern education system to replace the old one which was still based on learning the sayings and writings of Confucius, abolition of all privileges enjoyed by Manchus inside China, and a start on industrialisation with mining and railway development. These plans were betrayed to the Empress who imprisoned the Emperor for the rest of his short life and executed those officials who had not escaped.

Another attempt at reform, this time from the people not the court, started about a year later. A secret peasant society, the *Yi Ho Tuan* - the *Society of Righteous and Harmonious Fists* - began a rising aimed at driving all foreigners out of China. The *Boxers*, as they were nicknamed by westerners because of their physical training, attacked Christian missionaries in various parts of the country. When they attempted to attack foreign legations and missions, the Empress, taken aback and frightened by the extent of the disorder, agreed to lend her troops to help them take Peking. By the time the Boxer army reached the city, *Tze Hsi* had changed her mind. The Boxers occupied the city and laid siege to the foreign legation part of the city for 45 days. Most of the foreign powers involved in China organised a joint force of US, German, Japanese, French and British troops which beat the Boxers, took over Peking and wrecked the Imperial Summer Palace. By the 1901 *Protocol (Agreement)* China was forced to pay another large indemnity and to execute large numbers of the rebels. Ten nations sent troops to Peking and guarded the railway from the city to the coast. A final humiliation came in 1904-5 when the Japanese and Russians fought a major land campaign on Chinese soil to decide who should rule *Manchuria*, a Chinese province.

SUN YAT SEN

In spite of these setbacks, by the time the Empress died in 1908 China was taking her first steps towards becoming a modern, industrialised state. Western-style education was introduced to replace Confucianism and English became China's second language. Coal mines, iron mills and cotton factories were developed. Behind the scenes various revolutionary groups had united in a *Revolutionary League* led by *Sun Yat Sen*, a Christian who had been educated in Hawaii where he had adopted many western ideas. He became a doctor but in 1895 had to flee abroad because of his anti-government activities. He lived for a time in London, where he was kidnapped by Chinese agents but released by the British Foreign Office.

THE THREE PEOPLE'S PRINCIPLES

The Revolutionaries believed in what were called the *Three People's Principles*. These were *Nationalism* (ridding China of foreigners), *Democracy* (the overthrow of the Manchu dynasty and its replacement by a democratic state) and *Livelihood* (taking the land from the landowners and giving it to the peasants). In 1911 the Manchu government began to mortgage private railways to foreign companies. This sparked off risings during which the soldiers at *Wuchang* joined in. When naval units were sent to disarm the mutinous troops they, too, disobeyed the government. This rising, which overthrew the Manchu dynasty and established the first Chinese Republic is known as the *Double Tenth* because it started on the 10th October 1911 - the tenth day of the tenth month.

THE TWENTY-ONE DEMANDS

The child-emperor, *Pu Yi*, was deposed and *Sun Yat Sen* became President of the Republic. Within a year a warlord, *Tuan Shih Kai*, seized power with foreign support. Although he became leader of the Republic he did little to further the aims of the Revolutionary League. Many Manchu princes retained their privileges and no land was given to the peasants. Foreign interference continued and Tuan became a military dictator who, in 1914, made himself President for life. When the First World War broke out China at first remained neutral. Japan used her position as an ally of France, Russia and Britain to force Tuan into agreeing to her *Twenty One Demands*. By these the Japanese were to control all Chinese ports, factories and mines. Japanese "advisers" were to run the political, military and financial branches of the country. These demands, which represented a Japanese takeover of the country, were not resisted by Tuan because he saw them as a way of staying in power with Japanese support. National risings against these terms led China into anarchy, with only local warlords benefitting from the chaos.

CHIANG AND MAO

This disastrous outcome of the Double Tenth revolution led China's reformers in two directions. First, there were those who still believed in Sun's ideals. They formed themselves into the *National People's Party*, the *Koumintang*. Another group founded the *Chinese Communist Party* in Shanghai in 1922. In their early days both these movements received support and inspiration from the Russian communist government. Later, the communists, led by *Mao Tse Tung*, began to turn to the peasants for support, rather than follow the traditional Marxist line of using urban workers as the vanguard of the revolution. Both the Koumintang and the Communists at first worked together to defeat the warlords and bring order back to China. A military school set up at *Whampoa* trained an army which defeated the warlords' troops. *Chiang Kai Shek*, who had been the Republic's military adviser, ran this academy and later he became ruler of the Koumintang. After the Koumintang won this battle and set up a Nationalist Government at *Nanking* in 1927, Chiang turned against the communists. He drove them out of the main cities and proclaimed himself Generalissimo (Supreme Commander). He was supported by foreign loans and did little to lessen foreign interference in China's affairs.

THE LONG MARCH

At first Chiang drove all before him. He marched across the country, imposing order, and in 1931 overran the Communist *Chinese Soviet Republic* which had been set up at *Huan*. The communist answer in this crisis was to retreat still further into the interior, to the remote *Shansi province*. This was not easy because the *Long March* (1934-5), as it became known, involved marching 6,000 miles whilst under constant attack from Chiang's troops and aircraft. About 300,000 soldiers, with their wives and children, managed to cross mountain regions and large rivers, notably the *Yangtse* and *Tatu*. They also crossed swamp lands and wild areas where the tribesmen attacked any Chinese troops, whether Koumintang or Communist. Eventually, they set up a base at *Yenan*, in a deep gorge where many people lived in caves in the cliffs. By this time the Japanese were in Manchuria and the Communists appealed to Chiang to unite with them in fighting the foreign invader. He refused, and this was probably a mistake which lost him the support of many patriotic Chinese.

JAPANESE INVASION

The Japanese invasion of China in 1937 came, not only via *Manchuria*, but from the sea, where the Chinese had no navy to match Japan's. Chiang's troops were beaten and forced to retreat to *Chungking*. The Japanese set up the last emperor, *Pu Yi*, as head of a puppet state called *Manchukuo* (Manchuria). Consequently, by the time the USA and Japan went to war in 1941, China had three governments, the Koumintang, the Communists and the Japanese. The long years of war saw a gradual weakening of Chiang's hold on the people. The Koumintang came to be regarded as just another Chinese government in the pay of foreigners. By contrast, Mao's Communist administration lived with the people in the countryside. They stood for land reform and no foreign interference. It was a policy which every Chinese could understand and it was aided by the ruthless efficiency and honesty of the Communist Red Army. A clear sign of how feelings were running inside China came in 1944 when the Japanese defeated a Koumintang army. The survivors were attacked by the peasants who treated them as their enemies.

THE PEOPLE'S REPUBLIC

In August 1945, after the defeat of Japan, the Koumintang and the Communists reached a temporary agreement in a last attempt to prevent civil war. But the differences between the two sides were fundamental. The Communists were determined to carry out a social revolution with re-distribution of land to the peasants. The Koumintang and its wealthy supporters, many of them landowners, could never agree to this. In fact, the tide of popular feeling was running strongly for the Communists and when the war was renewed in 1947-8 the Koumintang gained only a temporary success with the capture of *Yenan*. By the time Mao launched his final offensive in 1948 Chiang's men were hated for their brutality and corruption and the Generalissimo himself had lost all credibility because of the fortunes he and his family had made during the war. The Koumintang forces were driven from north-east China and *Peking* was captured without a battle. In the spring of 1949 *Nanking*, the Koumintang capital, fell to the Communists and Chiang fled south to the island of *Taiwan* where he set up a government-in-exile, *Nationalist China*. On 1st October 1949 Mao Tse Tung proclaimed the founding of the *People's Republic of China*. (See also Work Unit 31).

SELF-ASSESSMENT SECTION

1. What was the "Celestial Empire" ?

2. Whom did the Chinese call barbarians ?

3. Why did the British wish to trade with China in the 1840's ?

4. Who were the Manchus ?

5. What is the significance of the ship "Arrow" in Chinese history ?

6. What were "coolies" ?

7. Who was the "Old Buddha" ?

8. What was the Most Favoured Nation Clause ?

9. What happened during China's "Hundred Days" ?

10. How did the Boxers get their name ?

11. The Boxers wished to :-

    a) Overthrow the Manchu dynasty.
    b) Kill all Christian missionaries.
    c) Drive all foreigners out of China.
    d) Capture Peking.
        (TICK THE CORRECT ANSWER)

12. Trace the course of Japanese involvement in Chinese history, from the Sino-Japanese War to the end of World War Two. What factors contributed to Japanese success and failure ?

13. Describe the events which led to the victory of the Chinese Communists in 1949. What, in your opinion, were the most significant factors in that victory ?

14. Read these two documents and then answer the questions.

    A. "(*He*) knows about the rotten conditions, but he can't do anything ... Sixtieth (*Chinese*) Army can't be moved - they would refuse to obey the order. Opium traffic in Yunnan still enormous ... Big stocks of hoarded gas, cloth and other commodities ... The Chinese Red Cross is a racket. Stealing and sale of medicine is rampant. The army gets nothing. Malnutrition and sickness is ruining the army; the high-ups steal the soldier's food. A pretty picture."
        [Source : US General Stillwell, quoted in "A Short History of China" by Hilda Hookham. Longmans, 1969]

B. "This party almost from the time it came to power had tolerated among its officials of all grades graft and greed, idleness and inefficiency, nepotism and factional rivalries - all the evils in short of the corrupt bureaucracy it had overthrown. These evils had become more pronounced after V.J. Day (*1945*) in the attempts to crush communism by a combination of military strength and secret police .."

[Source : US missionary, quoted Hookham, above]

a) Which army is being described in A ?
b) Who is the "he" the writer in A is describing ?
c) What happened to "this army" in 1949 ?
d) In B, what corrupt bureaucracy had been overthrown by "this party" ?
e) What theme connects A and B ? How did it contribute to a change of government in China in 1949 ?
f) Why were the army and regime described in A and B more likely to concentrate on fighting the communists *after* V.J. Day ?

15. Put the correct details (by letter) against these subjects.

1. YI HO TUAN.	A.	Young reforming emperor of China.
2. KOUMINTANG.	B.	Nickname for Boxers.
3. SUN YAT SEN.	C.	Chinese warlord.
4. PU YI.	D.	Empress of China.
5. TUAN SHIH KAI.	E.	President of first Chinese Republic.
6. CHIANG KAI SHEK.	F.	Leader of Chinese Communists.
7. MAO TSE TUNG.	G.	Last Emperor of China.
8. TZE HSI.	H.	Chinese Nationalist Government.
9. KWANG HSU.	I.	Leader of Koumintang.

16.

(Source: 'Awakening of China' by Roger Pelissier.
Reprinted by permission of Martin Secker & Warburg Ltd.)

The photograph (*on the previous page*) is of Yenan in Shensi province. Look at it carefully and then answer the following questions.

    a)   What is the name given to the Chinese who settled here in 1935 ?
    b)   What is the significance of the caves seen in the photograph ?
    c)   Why was Yenan chosen by the settlers ?
    d)   Explain the importance of Yenan in the history of modern China.

17. Imagine you are a Taiping. Explain to a friend what you hope to do for China and how you hope to do it.

11

Causes of the
First World War

INTRODUCTION

In August, 1914, age-old European feuds burst once more into war. Because Germany emerged from the Franco-Prussian War as the most powerful nation-state in Europe, and because her leaders were reactionary and militaristic, it is easy to blame her for causing the First World War. Yet no nation was blameless. Britain was prepared to fight rather than lose her supremacy at sea, and world-wide empire. France would have liked to regain the pre-eminence she had exercised over Europe for centuries. Austria-Hungary, in particular, pursued a reckless policy against Serbia, although it must have been obvious that this might lead to war with Russia. Russia, for her part, still dreamed of expansion into the Balkans and towards Turkey.

Smaller countries behaved no better. On the spot in Sarajevo where Gavrilo Princip murdered the Archduke Franz Ferdinand, heir to the Austrian throne, is a memorial which contains these words, "Here, in this historic spot, Gavrilo Princip was the initiator of Liberty on the day of St. Vitus, the 28th of June, 1914". If a modern state like Yugoslavia, successor to Serbia, can honour a teenager who senseless murder sparked off one of the worst wars in history simply because it led to Yugoslav independence, it shows what irrational feelings drove men to fight in 1914. Nationalism by both independent and subject peoples played a major part in causing the catastrophe which engulfed Europe.

By 1914 two hostile alliances faced each other across Europe, the Triple Alliance of Germany, Austria-Hungary and Italy, and the Triple Entente of France, Russia and Britain. All these countries, except Britain, were pledged to go to war to help the others, and everyone, except Italy, did so. Britain had only an "entente cordiale" with France. This "understanding" was supposedly about colonies. It gave France a free hand in Morocco in return for leaving Britain in charge of Egypt. But it also led to military talks which had nothing to do with Africa and everything to do with armies in Europe. Few doubted that in any future war Britain's fear of Germany's new fleet would cause her to join the side of Germany's enemies.

Within these secret agreements - their texts were not published until after the war - was the recognition of one stark, military fact. Each nation, whatever the reason for war, would have to attack its most dangerous enemy first. Germany would need to attack France and Russia must attack Germany. And once the mobilisation of millions of men had begun, it would be almost impossible to stop the troop trains rolling. Consequently, a war between Austria and Serbia actually involved heavy fighting in Germany and France before the Austrian army invaded Serbia ! There was no chance of localising a dispute in these circumstances. In the feverish atmosphere of the early 1900's any incident, however small or faraway, could lead to general war. It might have been a quarrel about the size of battleships. In the end a shot in Sarajevo did it.

HOSTILE ALLIANCES

The defeat of France by Prussia and her allies in 1870-1 (See Work Unit 1) left Germany the most powerful state in Europe. The various German states (See map) joined Prussia to form a German empire in January, 1871. This military and political success resulted from the policies of Prussia's chief minister, *Otto von Bismarck*. France was forced to pay compensation to Germany, and deprived of two frontier provinces, *Alsace* and *Lorraine*. From 1871, therefore, Bismarck's aim was to isolate France and so deter her from a war of revenge against Germany.

The most satisfactory alliance from Bismarck's point of view was Germany, Austria and Russia. This would leave France without a major ally and remove the possibility of a two-front war (See map), In 1873 Bismarck negotiated a *League of Three Emperors* (the Dreikaiserbund) - Germany, Russia and Austria - but it remained more sentimental than practical. This was because of the continuing feud between Austria and Russia over their respective influence in the Balkans (See Work Unit 8). When Bismarck realised that he could not have effective alliances with both countries, he chose Austria, whose language, cultural and geographical ties with Germany were strong. In 1879 he negotiated a *Dual Alliance* between Austria and Germany. Italy joined in 1882 after a colonial quarrel with France and it became the *Triple Alliance*. Bismarck tried to limit the possible danger of this arrangement by concluding a *Reinsurance Treaty* with Russia, whereby each country agreed to remain neutral if the other went to war with a third party, except if Russia attacked Austria or Germany attacked France.

IMPERIALISM

One threat to Bismarck's policies came from within Germany where imperialists demanded that Germany copy France and found colonies. Bismarck was against this scheme because it might lead to a confrontation with Britain which, in turn, might give France an ally. He was over-ruled, however, by powerful vested interests and in 1884-5 Germany founded colonies in *South-West Africa*, the *Cameroons* and *Togoland* (See map). At the *Congress of Berlin* the Great Powers agreed that "effective occupation" of a colonial territory by a European power gave that country the legal right to rule it. This accelerated the so-called *Scramble for Africa* (See Work Unit 5).

THE KAISER

In 1888 William II, usually known as the *Kaiser* from the German word for emperor, succeeded to the German throne. William had grandiose ideas about Germany's greatness and opposed Bismarck's cautious policies. One of William's first actions after sacking Bismarck was to let the Reinsurance Treaty lapse so that Germany could be free to compete with Russia for power and influence in the Balkans. This drove Russia into a *Dual Entente* with France in which the two countries promised to help each other if attacked by Germany (1892). This was a crucial factor leading to general war in 1914 because it gave France an ally and posed a two-front war threat to Germany. Although all these pre-war treaties were supposed to be secret, there were enough rumours and leaks concerning them to increase suspicion and tension between countries.

GERMANY'S NAVY

The Kaiser, influenced by his navy chief, *Admiral Tirpitz*, began to build a modern navy. This was seen as a direct threat by the British whose empire was guarded by the world's largest navy. In fact, from 1889 Britain applied a rule of thumb in naval matters, the so-called *Two-Power Standard*. By this, Britain's navy had to be larger than the combined fleets of the next two largest navies. Vested interests within Germany favoured a German fleet to support and protect her expanding colonies and trade. Tirpitz replied to criticism of such a plan by claiming that the German fleet would deter Britain from confronting Germany. In reality it had the opposite effect, as Bismarck had feared. Britain started a naval building race with Germany; in 1909, when the British government wondered whether to build four or six battleships, the British Navy League invented the slogan "We want eight and we won't wait" and eight were built. In 1906 Britain's naval designers produced *HMS Dreadnought*, a ship more powerful than any other warship afloat. This ship's name became the description of a type, and soon Germany was building dreadnoughts. At the same time Britain gave up what had been termed her *"Splendid Isolation"* - she had not engaged in land campaigns in Europe since Waterloo in 1815 - and began to look for allies. A factor in this move was the isolation of Britain at the time of the Boer War (See Work Unit 6) which had been far from splendid.

TRIPLE ENTENTE

In 1902 Britain signed a naval treaty with Japan. By the *Anglo-Japanese Treaty*, the two agreed to remain neutral if either was engaged in a war in the Far East. One aim of this treaty was to deter Russia and France from further colonial expansion in that part of the world. It also left the British free to concentrate their warships in the North Sea to contain any German threat. Its immediate effect was to leave Japan free to fight, and defeat, Russia in the *Russo-Japanese War* (See Work Unit 4).

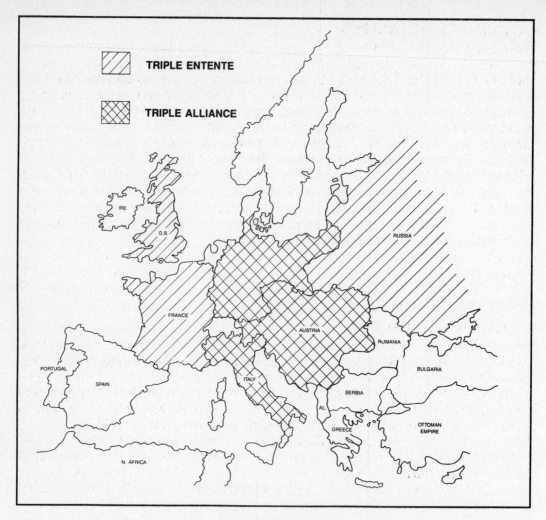

Pre-1914 Alliances

Meanwhile, Britain and France, traditional enemies for centuries, moved closer towards an alliance. In 1904 came the *Entente Cordiale* (Friendly Agreement), pioneered by the British *King Edward VII* during a visit to France. Edward loved all things French and disliked his nephew, the Kaiser. Two years later British and French officers began talks about possible military co-operation in the event of war in Europe. The French also tried to make Britain and Russia allies. This was not easy. The two countries had frequently quarrelled about India and the regions bordering it, whilst the British public and many of its politicians disliked the Tsar's tyrannical regime. However, Russia, anxious to please France, promised to stop further expansion into territories on the Indian border - *Afghanistan* and *Tibet* - and *Persia* (now Iran) was divided into "spheres of influence" between Russia and Britain. Consequently, in 1907 Britain joined what then became the *Triple Entente*, although she was not committed to go to war.

COLONIAL CLASHES

German attempts to curb French expansion in Morocco led to several serious crises which nearly caused a war. In 1905 a German minister visited *Tangier* and made a speech stressing the right of the Sultan of Morocco to rule his country free from outside influences. To prevent this quarrel leading to war, an international conference was held at *Algeciras*, Spain, in 1906. Every country except Austria backed France and the delegates reaffirmed the right of France to rule Morocco. Germany gave way, but in 1911, when there was a Moroccan revolt against French rule, the Germans sent first a gunboat, the *"Panther"*, and then a cruiser, the *"Berlin"* to the Moroccan port of Agadir to "protect German interests". This broke the Algeciras Agreement, where only France and Spain were to "police" Morocco.

The *Agadir Crisis* showed just how sensitive the British were to naval threats. The use of German warships set alarm bells ringing in the minds of many British politicians, and a cabinet minister, *David Lloyd George*, made a speech at the Mansion House in London in which he practically threatened war if British interests were ignored. His chief worry was that the Germans might set up an Atlantic naval base in Morocco. Germany again gave way, leaving the French firmly in control after crushing the rebellion.

BALKAN PROBLEMS

For centuries the Balkan countries had been ruled by the *Ottoman Empire* (See Work Units 4 and 8). After the Treaty of San Stefano in 1878, Austria tightened her grip on Serbia by imposing an economic stranglehold on her trade. A commercial treaty compelled Serbia to send most of her manufactured goods to Austria where they received preferential terms. Serbia's main export, pigs, had to be sent to Austria for slaughter because she possessed no processing plants. A "Swine Fever" clause in this agreement enabled the Austrians to close their border to Serbian pigs if there was any fear of infection to their own animals. The Austrians did this nine times between 1881 and 1906 and between 1906 and 1909 she closed the frontier altogether. This so-called "Pig War" caused bitter resentment in Serbia, although it forced her to establish a Serbian meat processing industry.

In 1908 a group of army officers, nicknamed the "Young Turks" overthrew the Sultan and tried to establish a more democratic regime. Such internal disorder encouraged Turkey's many enemies to act against her. First, Austria annexed *Bosnia-Herzegovina*, a move which infuriated Serbia because it meant Austria now ruled an extra million Serbs. Second, in 1912 *Greece*, *Serbia* and *Bulgaria* formed a *Balkan League* which aimed to drive the Turks out of Europe altogether. The swift military success of their combined armies alarmed the Great Powers who called a conference in London in 1913 to try to stabilise the situation. Before the decisions of this conference could be acted upon, a *Second Balkan War* broke out when Bulgaria, angry at losing the port of Salonika to the Greeks, attacked her former allies. Unfortunately for the Bulgars, Rumania joined in the war and they were defeated. Later, Bulgaria was the only Balkan country to fight on Germany's side in the First World War.

By the Treaty of *Bucharest*, 1913, Greece received southern Macedonia, and Serbia the north. Rumania got a strip of the Black Sea coast. Serbia failed to get an outlet to the sea because Austria blocked her claims.

THE AUSTRO-HUNGARIAN EMPIRE

Austria-Hungary was a multi-national empire, formed over the centuries by the marriages, treaties and wars of one dynasty, the *Habsburgs*. The Habsburgs ruled 11 nationalities - Germans, Hungarians, Czechs, Poles, Ruthenians, Rumanians, Croats, Serbs, Slovaks, Slovenes and Italians. Of these, two, the Germans and Hungarians, were dominant; the ruling culture and language of the empire was German. By the 20th century such dynastic imperialism was out of date. Nationalist feelings were rife amongst the subject peoples, especially where some, like Serbia and Italy, had an independent state as well. Russia, being a Slav nation, had done her best to stir up trouble by supporting the cause of Pan-Slavism. However, even without Russia, there was always trouble with these turbulent peoples who quarrelled with each other over boundaries, coastlines and minorities.

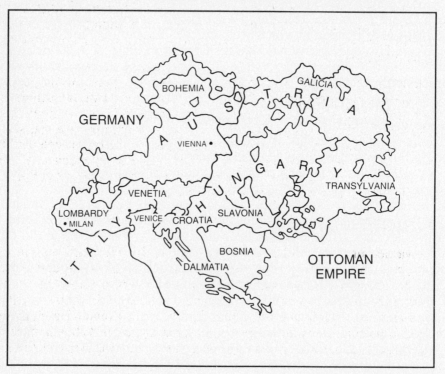

Geographical Distribution of Nationalities in Austro-Hungarian Empire, 1848.

The Habsburgs and their ministers saw the stability, even the existence, of their ramshackle empire threatened by such ideas and movements. In 1859 Pan-Italianist feeling had resulted in the Austrians being driven out of Northern Italy, partly as a result of French help for the Italians. In 1866 Pan-Germanism had led to their defeat in the war of 1866 (See Work Unit 1), and the loss of their position as the pre-dominant German state in Europe. Now Pan-Slavism seemed to pose an even more dangerous threat. Military men, led by the Austrian Chief of Staff, *Conrad von Hortzendorf*, wanted a swift, preventative war to crush Serbia once and for all. They argued that as long as Germany supported them, they could do this without a general war. On several occasions before 1914, Germany assured the Habsburg government of such support. This was the Kaiser's so-called *"Blank Cheque"* for the Austrians which led to disaster.

MURDER AT SARAJEVO

From 1908 Serbia demanded freedom for the 6 million Serbs living inside the Habsburg empire. The Serbs living in Bosnia, taken over against their will in 1908, were particularly troublesome. On 28th June 1914 the heir to the Austrian throne, *Archduke Franz Ferdinand*, and his wife, were assassinated by conspirators who crossed the border from Serbia. The actual assassin was *Gavrilo Princip*, a student. Their murders were not ordered by the Serbian government but seem to have been the work of a Serbian secret society, the *Union of Death* or *Black Hand Society*, whose leader, a *Colonel Apis*, was head of Serbian intelligence. Serbia was exhausted after the Balkan Wars and was in no condition to fight another war. Her prime minister actually warned the Austrian government that the murder gang had crossed into Bosnia.

This murder was seen as an opportunity by the war-party inside Austria. On 23rd July, having been assured of German support, the Austrian authorities sent impossible terms to Serbia. They demanded that the Serbian government suppress all anti-Austrian activity, dismiss all officials not favoured by Austria, and allow Austrian police to enter Serbia to investigate the murder. Serbia accepted all but the last demand, which she felt would mean the end of her independence. The Kaiser advised Austria to accept but the war-party had gained the upper hand in Vienna. On 28th July 1914, Austria declared war on Serbia.

FINAL MOVES TOWARDS WAR

Germany warned France and Russia not to interfere. Russia could not allow a Slav country to be wiped off the map, a disaster which would have ended her own influence in the region. Russia mobilised her army on 30th July with most of her divisions massed on the German border where the greatest threat lay; an attack on Germany was also the only way she could help her ally, France. Germany ordered Russia to stop mobilising and told France to remain neutral. When neither heeded these warnings, Germany declared war on Russia (1st August) and France (3rd August).

Britain might have remained neutral, at least for a time, if the German army had not invaded Belgium as part of its plan to encircle Paris and end the war at a blow. By the *Treaty of London*, 1839, Britain was pledged to defend Belgium. Prussia had also signed this treaty but the German government did not feel bound by this undertaking, especially as the German army had asked the Belgians if they could march through their country. When Britain's protests were ignored, she declared war on Germany on the 4th of August. The German Chancellor spoke of Britain as going to war over a *"scrap of paper"*. In fact, Britain was not prepared to have a strong naval power so near her shores. This is why she had guaranteed Belgium neutrality in the first place.

Pre-War Europe

SELF-ASSESSMENT SECTION

1. What was the Dreikaiserbund ?
2. What was the "two-power standard" ?
3. Which country in North Africa was France colonising during this period ?
4. Who pioneered the "entente cordiale" ?
5. Why did Lloyd George make his Mansion House speech in 1911 ?
6. What was the objective of the "Young Turk" revolution ?
7. Why was there a "pig war" between Austria and Serbia ?

8. Why did Serbia not want war with Austria in 1914 ?

9. Why was the "Panther" sent to Morocco ?

10. What was a dreadnought ? What was its significance at the time ?

11. Bismarck chose Austria-Hungary as an ally because :-

   a) Russia had quarrelled with Germany.
   b) Russia and Austria had quarrelled.
   c) Turkey and Germany had quarrelled.
   d) He did not want Russia as an ally.
   (TICK THE CORRECT ANSWER)

12. On 14 May 1914 Count Czernin, Austrian minister in Bucharest, wrote this. The letter is kept in the State Archives in Vienna.

   "Before our eyes the encirclement of the Monarchy proceeds in the full light of day, openly and explicitly ... step by step; under Russian patronage a new Balkan League is being welded together - against the Monarchy! And we stand by with folded arms watching with interest the progress of the deployment."

   a) To what Monarchy was Czernin referring ?
   b) What did he mean by "under Russian patronage" ?
   c) From this evidence do you think Czernin supported the war-party inside Austria ? Give reasons for your answer.
   d) Was it correct to say that Austria was "standing by with folded arms" and doing nothing about the situation ?

13.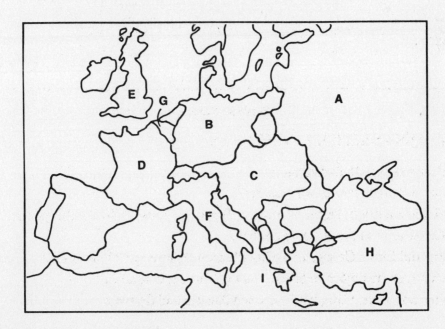

    a)   Which two countries went to war on 28th July 1914 ?
    b)   Name the countries in the Triple Alliance.
    c)   Name the countries in the Triple Entente.
    d)   Which country was invaded by Germany in 1914 ?
    e)   Which member country of the Triple Alliance did NOT join them in the war ?
    f)   Which country had a revolution in 1908 ?

14.

This cartoon by F.H. Townsend appeared in the British magazine "Punch" on 12 August 1914.

    a)   Which figure is meant to be Belgium and which Germany ? Why is one figure shown as an adult and the other as a child ?
    b)   What is the significance of the sign "No Thoroughfare" ?
    c)   Make a list of the things in this drawing which indicate that the artist was *against* Germany.
    d)   The artist illustrates only one reason why Britain went to war over Belgium. What was the other reason ?
    e)   What effect do you think the artist hoped this cartoon would have on the magazine's readers?

15. In what ways did the Kaiser's policies differ from Bismarck's ? Which were the more successful ?

16. Why did Britain oppose German naval expansion ? Why did the Germans embark on such a policy ?

17. Imagine you are a British politician anxious to persuade men to join the army in 1914. Make a speech to encourage them to join up.

18. Imagine you are an Austrian diplomat in Sarajevo on the day of the murder of Franz Ferdinand. Write a letter to your colleagues in Vienna to persuade them not to go to war.

12

The First World War
1914-1918

INTRODUCTION

The First World War cost the lives of at least 11 million men. Such huge losses were the result of large armies, and these, in turn, resulted from increased populations and expanding industrial development; only factory complexes could produce the quantities of weapons, ammunition and equipment necessary for modern warfare. Their size might have made them slow and difficult to move, for motor transport was in its infancy. But in 1914 sophisticated rail networks carried men swiftly into battle. In this way the Industrial Revolution helped magnify and multiply war.

The appalling losses arose partly because weapons of defence had obtained a supremacy over weapons of offence. Prolonged artillery bombardments tore up the ground, slowing down the infantry. Fields of barbed wire often brought the attack to a halt. Machine guns then mowed the men down, whilst poison gas clouds destroyed their lungs and lives. Cavalry, which had created wars of movement in the past, were useless in these conditions. Tanks, the modern army's "cavalry" arrived too late and in too few numbers to prevent the slaughter. Aircraft were too primitive to transform a land battle as air-power often did in the Second World War.

This dreadful stalemate in the west forced men to look for other ways to win the war. Britain's naval blockade of Europe caused suffering and starvation but it could not win a war quickly. Another scheme was to attack what a so-called "Eastern school" of strategists called the "soft underbelly" of the enemy. This involved an invasion through the Balkans and the Dardanelles which would knock Germany's two weak partners, Austria and Turkey, out of the war as well as link up with the Russians. An amphibious landing in the Dardanelles against the Turks was mishandled and proved a costly failure. Another expedition, which landed in neutral Greece, was turned into a farce when the Russians blocked Greece's entry into the war because of distrust of her claims on the Turkish empire. It was 1918, when Russia had left the war through revolution, before Greece entered the war and provided the springboard for an offensive which did, in fact, conquer the Balkans within a few weeks.

Consequently, the war was fought to a finish in the west, where certain strategists, notably General Douglas Haig, the British commander, had always maintained it would have to be, since military victory would only come when the mighty German was beaten. Haig's victory was achieved but at an awful cost. The peculiar intensity of fighting on the Western Front arose because large armies were crushed together in a comparatively small space, and were supplied by industries which could stand the strain of keeping the fighting going with weapons and ammunition; for one assault on Vimy Ridge in 1917 the Allies used nearly 3,000 guns and over 40,000 tons of ammunition. A battle of this sort, waged in the same place for months and years, has a horror of its own. On a quiet day at the front, one survivor remembered, "The sun was high and the warm day brought out the veritable thousands of big, black-green, bloated flies, searching for pieces of decayed human flesh unearthed by the bursting of shells".

Had only a few men experienced such a war it might have been forgotten. But this was a war which left more survivors than dead. Men returned to tell their stories in talk, plays, novels, poetry and memoirs. Even film footage gave future generations a flickering monochrome glimpse of the slaughter, devastation and misery. This is why the First World War is a vivid folk memory as well as an historical event.

THE SCHLIEFFEN PLAN

The war on the *Western Front* began with a massive German thrust through *Belgium, Luxembourg* and *France*. This was part of the so-called *Schlieffen Plan. Count Alfred von Schlieffen* had been Chief of Staff of the German Army until 1906. The Triple Entente between Russia, Britain and France meant a two-front war for Germany. Schlieffen planned a knock out blow through Belgium and northern France (See map), rather than a slow advance across the hilly and well-defended Franco-German border further south. The "hammer" of this blow, an army of 1,500,000 men, would descend on Paris from the north across the flat countryside of Belgium. France would be out of the war before the slow-moving Russians were fully mobilised. The French knew of the Schlieffen Plan but kept to their own *Plan 17*, an offensive which would bring four French armies into Germany as far as the Rhine. But the French attackers, including cavalry in brightly coloured uniforms, were slaughtered by machine gun fire and fell back in disorder.

The German commander-in-chief in 1914, *von Moltke*, a nephew of the victor of Sedan and Metz (See Work Unit 1), had modified the Schlieffen Plan even before the war began by making the "handle" of the "hammer" stronger at the expense of the head. The actual attack was slowed by unexpectedly tough Belgian resistance, and the numbers of German troops cut down when two Army Corps had to be sent back to deal with a Russian invasion of East Prussia. Even so, the German advance at first proved unstoppable. A small *British Expeditionary Force* (BEF) joined the French and fought delaying actions at *Mons* and *Le Cateau* before retreating. On 28th August the Germans swung east of Paris rather than try to encircle the city. The French government retired to *Bordeaux* in case Paris fell.

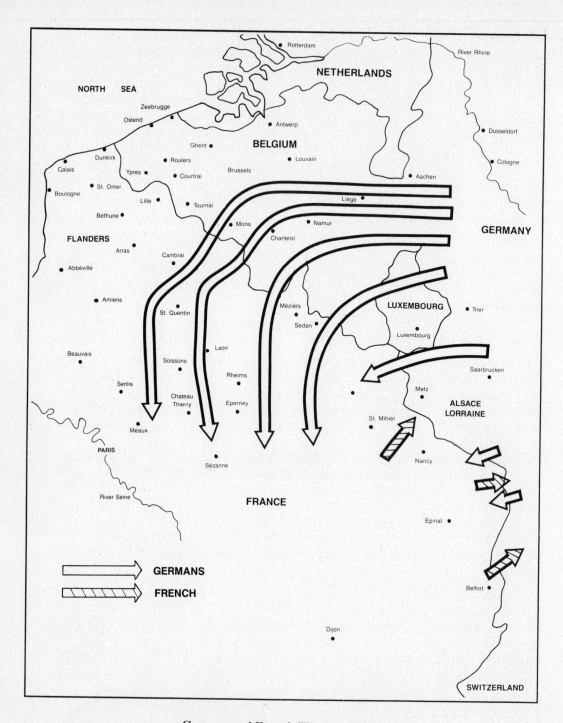

German and French Thrusts, 1914.

THE MARNE AND YPRES

By this time the Germans were tired and their line was becoming extended, leaving gaps. Their position to the east of the French capital also made them vulnerable to attacks from the city. In early September, *Joffre*, the French commander, counter-attacked, ordering British and French troops into these gaps. Another French army came out of Paris in *taxis* and joined in the fighting which raged for nearly a week over a hundred miles of countryside. During the *Battle of the Marne*, Moltke, far away in Luxembourg, lost control of operations. He ordered a retreat which was opposed by some of his commanders on the spot. The Germans fell back, first to the river *Marne* itself, and then to the river *Aisne* where they settled into a hastily constructed trench system. The Schlieffen Plan had failed, and the war was "frozen" into a pattern which continued until 1918.

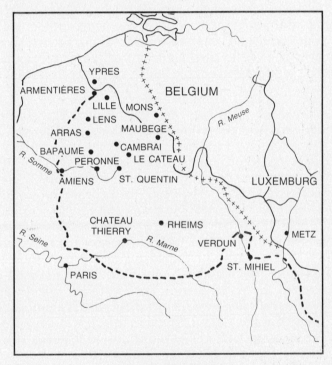

The Western Front

Both sides now "raced for the sea", hoping to outflank the other and seize the French and Belgian *Channel Ports*. The British managed to save the ports for the Allies by fighting a desperate two-month battle at *Ypres* in Belgium (October-November, 1914). The front-line now ran from near Ostend on the Belgian coast to the Swiss frontier; there was no hope of peace talks whilst the Germans occupied large parts of northern France. During 1915 the French made unsuccessful attacks in the *Champagne region* and at *Vimy Ridge*, a high-point in an otherwise flat landscape near the Belgian border. The British supported these offensives with attacks which captured *Loos* but failed to break through because the reserves were too far behind the line. This failure led to the sacking of the British commander, *Lord French*, and his replacement by *General Haig*. Until 1916 the British were the only belligerent not using military conscription so recruiting campaigns were used to get volunteers; the most famous poster was the "Kitchener Wants You" which featured the famous general.

VERDUN AND THE SOMME

During 1916 some of the most memorable battles of the war took place at *Verdun* and near the river *Somme* (See map). *Verdun* was a French fortress-town commanding a salient (corner) in the line. The German generals planned to draw the French army into a pointless battle in which it would be destroyed. The French fell into the trap, sending hundreds of thousands of men up the *"Sacred Way"*, the road leading to the town, and inspiring them with *General Petain's* slogan *"They shall not pass"*. The plan rebounded on the Germans when they found themselves engaged in a battle from which they could not disengage either, whilst the German public became as determined to capture Verdun as the French were to defend it. *Verdun*, fought over one of the smallest fronts of the war, became the so-called *"Mill on the Meuse"*, a mincing machine which swallowed up 700,000 men in five months.

In July, 1916 *General Haig* launched the planned British offensive on the *Somme* one month early to help relieve pressure on the French. The troops, all volunteers, had been promised a walkover after the greatest artillery bombardment of the war so far. But the deep German trench system had not been destroyed and the British troops were mowed down by accurate machine gun fire; on the first day the British army suffered 47,000 casualties. The battle continued until November. Some ground was captured from the Germans and *tanks* were used for the first time. At the end, both sides had suffered a total of 250,000 casualties but the German line remained intact. In 1917 the British, now using conscription, fought the *Battle of Arras* and an army of Canadians and British took *Vimy Ridge* in April, 1917. Meanwhile, the French *General Nivelle* promised another "war-winning" offensive on the river *Aisne*. The Germans found out about it and retreated to the so-called *Hindenberg Line*, a move which shortened their own line by 5 miles and wiped out the salient Nivelle's attack was supposed to take. The French attack was a disaster, with 187,000 men lost in ten days, and it brought the French army to mutiny. Some men left the line altogether. Others stayed to defend their positions but refused to attack. Order was restored and some men were shot. The Germans do not seem to have been aware of what was happening.

PASSCHENDALE AND THE FINAL OFFENSIVES

On 7 July 1917 the British blew up the German positions with a huge landmine near *Messines*. Soon afterwards, Haig launched an all out attack at *Ypres*. At first things went well for the British. Then the weather turned bad with days of heavy rain. The old 1914 battlefields near the village of Passchendale where the drainage system had been destroyed by shellfire, became a quagmire; thousands of men were drowned in the mud. In November, 1917 the British used nearly 400 tanks in an offensive near *Cambrai*. They broke through the German lines. taking 8,000 prisoners; more ground was captured in six hours than had been captured in four months at *Third Ypres*. But by evening many of the primitive tanks had broken down or become stuck in ditches and shell-holes. The Germans brought up reinforcements by train and counter-attacked, recovering most of the lost ground.

By 1918 Germany faced eventual defeat because of the entry of the USA into the war on the Allied side (See later). Their generals decided to gamble on a knock-out blow before this massive "blood transfusion" of Americans arrived to tip the scales against them once and for all. Russia had now left the war (See later) so there were more troops available for these offensives. Between March and May, 1918, the Germans attacked, first between the *Somme* and *Cambrai*, second at *Hazebrouk* and, finally, on the *Aisne*. It was a mighty effort which nearly succeeded. In many places they broke through and threatened Paris for the first time since 1914. But the effort had been too much for the men. Exhaustion, and extended supply lines, slowed them down. There were also signs of indiscipline and low morale among some of the troops. The new Allied supreme commander, the French *General Foch*, launched a series of powerful counter-attacks based on *Amiens*. The German lines were shattered; 8 August is known as the "Black Day" in the history of the German army. Their main defence, the *Hindenberg Line*, was breached and the Germans began a fighting retreat which ended when an armistice was signed on 11 November 1918. By this time revolution had broken out in Germany and the Kaiser had abdicated and fled to Holland.

EASTERN FRONT

Russia mobilised her armies quicker than expected and invaded *East Prussia*, a German province. This forced the German High Command to send troops from the attack on Paris. Armies commanded by *Hindenberg* surrounded and virtually destroyed two Russian armies at *Tannenberg* and the *Masurian Lakes*, killing or capturing 250,000 men. The Russians were driven out of Germany. In the south, however, the Russians defeated an Austrian army in *Galicia* (Russian Poland). The Serbs managed to hold their own and defeat the Austrians. In November Turkey declared war on the Allies.

Italy had not gone to war with the Triple Alliance, claiming that the agreement did not commit her to fight Britain. She was also interested in obtaining what Italians regarded as "their" lands inside Austrian territory. In 1915 the Italians signed a secret treaty in *London* which promised Italy the *Trentino* (South Tyrol) and the port of *Trieste* if she joined the Allies. Italy declared war on Austria in May and Germany in August. This created another battle-front in the Alps (See map). In June, 1916 a Russian army commanded by *General Brusilov* scored a great success against the Austrians, breaking through their lines and advancing 50 miles before running out of supplies. This success encouraged *Rumania* to enter the war on the Allied side when offered *Transylvania* and other territories. When the Brusilov offensive slowed down, Rumania was overrun by the Germans and the valuable Rumanian oil-fields fell into their hands, although British agents inflicted some damage before these troops arrived. In November, 1916 *Bulgaria* joined the

Italians launched a major offensive to capture *Trieste*. They were routed so badly at *Caparetto* that British troops had to be sent to Italy to stabilise the situation.

The Italian Front

In March, 1917 Russia experienced her first *revolution*. *Tsar Nicholas* abdicated and a *Provisional Government* led by *Alexander Kerensky* decided to carry on with the war. This led to further defeats at the hands of the Germans, and in October another revolution, led by the communist *Lenin*, caused Russia to leave the war by the *Treaty of Brest Litovsk*, March, 1918. (See Work Unit 13). Fighting continued between the Allies and Austria until October, 1918. By this time the multi-national empire was falling apart, with Czechs, Poles, Slovaks and Croats declaring their independence of the Habsburgs. The Austrians were finally defeated at the battle of *Vittorio Veneto* and on 11th November 1918 the last emperor *Charles* (Karl) abdicated.

THE WAR AGAINST TURKEY

A possible solution to the deadlock on the Western Front was to attack Austria-Hungary via Turkey and the Balkans, thus linking up with the Russians. An Anglo-French army was sent to *Salonika* in 1915 in the hope that Greece would enter the war but this did not happen because of Russian pressure. An amphibious assault was planned through the *Dardanelles* to capture *Constantinople*, the Turkish capital. An attempt by the fleet to break through was abandoned when two battleships hit mines and sank. Although this had warned the Turks of a possible attack, British and *Anzac* (Australian and New Zealand Army Corps) troops landed on the *Gallipoli* peninsula in April, 1915. The Turks, ably commanded by *Kemal Ataturk*, and the German general, *von Sanders*, managed to hold the high ground. This pinned the attackers on the beaches. From this cramped situation, the Allied troops launched a series of unsuccessful attacks throughout the summer. Heat and disease took their toll, and after another unsuccessful landing at *Suvla Bay* in August, the entire expedition was evacuated in November.

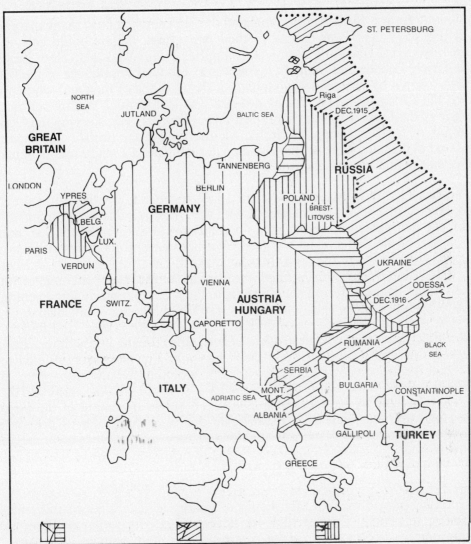

NORTH SEA

JUTLAND

BALTIC SEA

ST. PETERSBURG

Riga

DEC.1915

GREAT BRITAIN

LONDON

YPRES

TANNENBERG

RUSSIA

BELG.

GERMANY

BERLIN

POLAND

BREST-LITOVSK

LUX.

PARIS

VERDUN

UKRAINE

ODESSA

VIENNA

DEC.1916

FRANCE

SWITZ.

AUSTRIA HUNGARY

CAPORETTO

RUMANIA

BLACK SEA

SERBIA

ITALY

ADRIATIC SEA

MONT.

BULGARIA

CONSTANTINOPLE

ALBANIA

GALLIPOLI

TURKEY

GREECE

1914-18 War Zones

Campaigns were fought against the Turks by Indian, Australian and British troops to save *Egypt* and protect Persian oil supplies by holding *Palestine*. An Arab revolt against Turkish rule was assisted by Colonel *T.E. Lawrence* (Lawrence of Arabia), a scholar turned soldier. The Turks beat the regular British forces at *Kut-el-Amara* in 1916 but the following year British reinforcements led by *General Allenby* won a series of victories. In December, 1917 Allenby captured *Jerusalem* and next year, in a final offensive, his troops, many of them cavalry, defeated the Turks at *Megiddo*, took *Damascus* and brought about the Turkish surrender on 30 October 1918.

THE WAR AT SEA

Throughout the war the Allies commanded the sea supply routes, thanks largely to the British navy. This was crucial to their war effort. Britain could call on her empire resources, bringing troops and supplies from Australia, New Zealand, South Africa, Canada and India. In home waters the vital importance of the British fleet was shown by what did *not* happen; of the millions of men and women who crossed the Channel and North Sea not one was lost through enemy action. The blockade of the Central Powers continued throughout the war, starving the German war-effort of food and supplies. In the Mediterranean the French fleet operated freely, and in the later stages of the war the US fleet played a major role in defeating the German submarine campaign.

The fine German surface fleet created before the war was not big enough to ensure victory in a general engagement with the British *Grand Fleet. Admiral von Scheer*, the German commander, made regular sorties into the North Sea. hoping to catch part of the British fleet and destroy it before reinforcements could arrive. This policy led to the only major fleet action of the war off *Jutland*, 31 May - 1 June, 1916. Both Scheer and *Jellicoe*, the British commander, sent smaller forces forward in the hopes of luring enemy ships to their destruction. In late evening, as dusk was falling, *Scheer* nearly fell into a trap involving the entire British Grand Fleet. He escaped under cover of darkness and a smoke screen, and during the night, whilst the cruisers and destroyers of both sides fought a desperate action, he managed to get his *High Seas Fleet* back into port. The Germans inflicted more losses than they received; 14 British warships, including 3 battleships, were sunk and 6,000 sailors killed against the Germans' loss of 11 smaller ships and 2,500 men. This was due to the superior gunnery and better armament of the German ships. However, the High Seas Fleet never again ventured out of port in any strength so in this sense Jutland was an Allied victory.

THE "U" BOAT CAMPAIGN

The Germans pinned most of their hopes of victory at sea on their submarines or *'U' Boats*. In reply to the British blockade, 'U' Boats sank merchant ships bringing supplies to Britain or France. Since much of these supplies were carried in neutral ships, the German policy led to a confrontation with some neutral countries, notably the USA. After the sinking of the British liner *"Lusitania"* in May, 1915, in which over 100 Americans were lost, the Germans tried to avoid antagonising the USA. In 1917, however, squeezed by the Allied blockade and anxious to win the war quickly, they declared *"Unrestricted 'U' Boat warfare"* on all merchant shipping bringing goods to their enemies. This was very effective; in early 1917 Britain had only 6 weeks' food supplies left. But it caused *President Woodrow Wilson* of the USA to declare war on Germany in April, 1917. The US fleet joined the British in fighting the 'U' Boats in the Atlantic and this, plus the *convoy system* (in which warships escorted merchant ships in large groups or convoys), helped save Britain's seaborne supplies.

THE USA AND JAPAN

Most US people had mixed feelings about the war. This was not surprising considering America's many nationalities, including German-Americans. A majority probably wanted the Allies to win but most favoured *Isolationism* i.e. that the USA should have nothing to do with a European quarrel. Apart from the 'U' Boats campaign, other factors which drove the USA to war with Germany were that large amounts of money loaned to the Allies by American financiers would be lost if they were defeated, the desire of some American Jews to see a Jewish state established in Palestine once the Turks were driven out, and the affair of the *Zimmerman Telegram. Zimmerman*, the German foreign minister, foolishly sent a telegram to the Mexican government offering to help them regain territories lost to the USA in 1848 (See Work Unit 3). The British intercepted the telegram, decoded it, and made sure it was published in the USA, where it outraged public opinion and helped create a climate in favour of war with Germany.

In August, 1914 *Japan* declared war on Germany in accordance with the terms of the *Anglo-Japanese Treaty*, 1902. A British-Japanese force captured *Tsingtau*, a German-owned base on the China coast. The powerful Japanese navy then patrolled Pacific waters, whilst the Japanese government used the opportunity to impose terms on the Chinese government (See Work Unit 10).

SELF-ASSESSMENT SECTION

1.   What was the "soft underbelly" of the Central Powers ?

2.   Who commanded the British army in France from 1915 to 1918 ?

3.   How did the Schlieffen Plan get its name ?

4.   What was Plan 17 ?

5.   What did BEF stand for ?

6.   Who said "They shall not pass" ?

7.   Which side did Rumania fight on in the war ?

8.   Who commanded the British troops fighting the Turks ?

9.   What was the convoy system ?

10. What was the significance of the Zimmerman Telegram ?

11. Put the correct details (by letter) against these names.

1. SCHEER.	A.	German Chief of Staff in 1914.
2. FRENCH.	B.	Led successful Russian offensive in 1916.
3. MOLTKE.	C.	Commander of German High Seas Fleet.
4. JELLICOE.	D.	Won Battle of Tannanberg in 1914.
5. FOCH.	E.	Leader of Russian Provincial government in 1917.
6. HINDENBERG.	F.	Commander of British Grand Fleet.
7. KERENSKY.	G.	German general assisting the Turks.
8. BRUSILOV.	H.	US President who declared war on Germany.
9. SANDERS.	I.	Supreme Allied commander in 1918.
10. WILSON.	J.	British commander at Mons and Le Cateau.

12. Italy entered the First World War because :-

    (a)   She did not wish to fight Britain.
    (b)   She had been promised Trentino and Trieste.
    (c)   She had quarrelled with Austria-Hungary.
    (d)   She wished to honour her obligations to the Triple Alliance.
    (e)   She wished to help Serbia.
    (TICK THE CORRECT ANSWER)

13. The Treaty of Brest-Litovsk :-

    (a)   Took Russia out of the war.
    (b)   Took Bulgaria out of the war.
    (c)   Ended the First World War.
    (d)   Brought Greece into the war.
    (e)   Took Rumania out of the war.
    (TICK THE CORRECT ANSWER)

14. On 7 May 1915 the liner "Lusitania", carrying 1,959 passengers, was torpedoed off Ireland by a German 'U' boat. Only 761 people survived. Here, two who did survive describe their feelings.

  A. "There was no acute feeling of fear whilst one was floating in the water. I can remember feeling thankful that I had not been drowned underneath, but had reached the surface safely ... The life-belt held one up in a comfortable sitting position, with one's head lying rather back, as if one were in a hammock ... At moments I wondered whether the whole thing was perhaps a nightmare from which I would awake ... "

(Viscountess Rhondda)

  B. "As the liner tilted sharply downwards, the fantail soared a hundred feet into the air, exposing four nearly motionless propellers, as well as the immense sixty-five ton rudder. And, to complete the nightmare, she stopped there, frozen still, her forward motion suddenly and strangely arrested. A long, lingering moan arose and lasted many moments, as though the waters were wailing in horror."

(A.A. and Mary Hoelling)
[Source : both quoted in "Voices from the Great War"
edited by Peter Vansittart. Jonathan Cape, 1981.]

    (a)   Which source, A or B, suggests that the "Lusitania" was very large ?
    (b)   What *one word* describes how both sources regarded the tragedy ?
    (c)   Do you think the passengers were expecting the liner to sink ? Give reasons for your answer.
    (d)   What had caused the "Lusitania" to sink ?
    (e)   Which country was most affected by the sinking, and how did it react ?
    (f)   In what way did this sinking affect events later in the war ?

15. From the following guide, write an account of the part played by the British army in the First World War.

    FIRST YPRES ... LOOS ... SOMME ... THIRD YPRES ... ITALIAN FRONT ...CAMBRAI ... LAST BATTLES.

16. It was said that Admiral Jellicoe was the only man who could have lost the war in an afternoon. Explain exactly what was meant by this, referring particularly to the Allied Blockade and Jutland.

17. Imagine you are an airman who has flown over the Somme battle-field on 1 July 1916. Write a letter to a friend explaining what you had expected to see, and what you saw.

18. From information in this Unit, and from your previous knowledge of the subject, describe a typical day in the trenches of the Western Front during the First World War.

13

The Russian Revolution

INTRODUCTION

There was more than one Russian Revolution. In March, 1917 riots in the streets of Petrograd (now Leningrad) and an army mutiny forced Tsar Nicholas to abdicate. A Provisional government, led by Alexander Kerensky, established a more democratic republic. In October a Bolshevik (Marxist) group led by Lenin and Trotsky seized power. There were also rebellions of subject peoples, like the Poles and Ukrainians, and, running like wildfire through all this disorder, disorganised peasant risings, springing from centuries of misery and misrule.

Why did all this upheaval happen at this particular time? Three years of unsuccessful war with huge loss of life had shown up the industrial and economic weaknesses of Russia in relation to her enemies. Russia's peasant soldiers did not lack courage but they lacked almost everything else - guns, rifles, equipment, transport. The call-ups and casualties had denuded the countryside of labourers, whilst the demands of war production had produced an over-worked, discontented and sometimes revolutionary workforce. Rising prices and food shortages had plagued Russia throughout the war; the first riot about price rises took place as early as December, 1914, and the riots increased as prices rose. It was no coincidence that a 'bread riot' in Petrograd lit the fire which engulfed Russia for 4 years. As Lenin remarked, war was 'a mighty accelerator' of the process of revolution.

The question as to why one revolution, rather than another, succeeded is more difficult to answer. Really it was a question of which group or leader could master an existing situation because the revolution had begun on its own. "The collapse of the Romanov autocracy in March, 1917 was one of the most leaderless, spontaneous, anonymous revolutions of all time", wrote William Chamberlain, an American who spent many years in Bolshevik Russia. Kerensky claimed that he failed because of a betrayal by violent conspirators, (the Marxists), and lack of support by moderates of other parties. The decision of the Provisional government to continue the war was probably a fatal mistake; to fight on when war had led to revolution in the first place was unwise, even though the new regime hoped for victory and Allied help. For the communists the answer is simple. "The Bolshevik Party could not have won in October, 1917 if its foremost men had not mastered the theory of Marxism, if they had not learned to regard this theory as a guide to action", states the official Communist Party History of the Soviet Union. Non-Communists may wonder about this, although the dedicated ruthlessness of the Bolsheviks proved a decisive factor.

Two Bolshevik decisions, to give land to the peasants and to stop the war, probably brought them early control and eventual victory. Even in this matter, however, only the ending of the war was entirely their decision. In 1917 peasants started taking over the estates of landowners anyway; the figure, only 17 in March, rose to over 1,000 by July. So the Bolsheviks were merely acknowledging an accomplished fact when they proclaimed "land for the peasants'. One can see what Chamberlain meant when he wrote of a "leaderless' revolution.

THE 1905 UPRISING

Russian defeats in the Russo-Japanese War caused near civil war in Russia. Protests against Tsar Nicholas's autocratic rule reached a crisis in January, 1905, when a crowd of strikers and their families led by a priest, *Father Gapon*, marched on the *Winter Palace* in *St. Petersburg* (later Petrograd and now Leningrad). They hoped to present a petition to the Tsar asking for various reforms, including an 8 hour day for workers, a free press and a democratically-elected *Duma* (Parliament). Owing to a misunderstanding - the Tsar was not in the Palace - there was a confrontation between the authorities and the marchers which ended when the police opened fire. The official death toll for *"Bloody Sunday'* was 92, including women and children, but it was probably much higher.

This tragedy provoked further unrest - peasant riots, and more strikes. In June, 1905 there was a mutiny by sailors on the battleship *"Potemkin"*, a violent strike at *Odessa* on the Black Sea, and the setting up of revolutionary Workers' *Soviets* (Councils) in St. Petersburg by Marxists led by *Lenin* and *Trotsky*. The Tsar promised reforms, including a wider franchise, some law-making powers for the Duma and freedom of meeting and association. These half-hearted promises were made under the influence of *Witte*, his chief minister (See Work Unit 4).

At the same time the Tsarist government pursued a policy of repression and it is estimated that 15,000 workers and rioters were killed during this period, although there was also violence by its opponents. The St. Petersburg Soviet was crushed and Lenin and Trotsky fled to Finland. By the time the *Duma* met in April, 1906, the Tsar had changed his mind about reform. Witte was dismissed and all demands for genuine improvement refused. The Bolsheviks had boycotted the Duma, and their Soviets continued in an illegal, underground form. Witte's successor, *Peter Stolypin*, crushed anti-government activity with executions and mass deportations to *Siberia* (a remote region in Russia used as a prison).

However, he allowed the peasants far greater freedom to sell, divide or leave their land, or even become independent owners. The Tsar soon went back to ruling as an autocrat. Only three Dumas met between 1906 and 1914 and they had little power. Russia's economy was backed up by an enormous French loan of 2.25 billion francs.

FIRST (MARCH) REVOLUTION (1917)

Russia had suffered more than most countries engaged in the first world war. Her losses of men had been immense. Her industries provided less munitions than either her allies or enemies. The Tsarist government was very unpopular, especially as the Tsarina wielded great influence and was, in turn, influenced by a fake holy man called *Rasputin*. In March, 1917, more defeats at the front caused strikes and food riots in St. Petersburg. The situation became revolutionary when the troops refused to fire on the demonstrators; even members of the Duma would not disperse when ordered to do so. Nicholas was advised to abdicate by his generals. This he did on 15 March ,1917 in favour of his brother, *Grand-Duke Michael*. Michael declined to take over and a *Provisional Government*, headed by *Prince Lvov*, took charge.

These developments were welcomed by Britain and France whose government and electorate had never been happy about fighting for "freedom" in alliance with a tyranny like Tsarist Russia. The new regime, led from May by *Alexander Kerensky*, introduced many reforms but continued the war. Kerensky represented the liberal, reforming tradition in Russian politics and because of this he was opposed by the revolutionary tradition, represented by the Bolsheviks. To Lenin and Trotsky, both in exile when the March revolution started, the war had to be stopped. As far as they were concerned it was part of a capitalist "conspiracy' and of no benefit to the workers. The Germans realised the value of such men to them so they arranged for Lenin to have safe passage from Switzerland to the Russian frontier. He arrived in St. Petersburg in April and began to campaign for power with the slogan, *'Peace, bread, land'*. In July the Bolsheviks staged a rising against the Kerensky government but it was put down. Lenin and Trotsky fled again to Finland and waited for another opportunity.

SECOND (OCTOBER) REVOLUTION

In August, 1917 the Russians launched another offensive in *Galicia*. They were badly beaten and the army began to disintegrate. Peasant soldiers, hearing of the government's plan to give them land, left the army in their thousands and went home, shooting any officers who tried to stop them. Kerensky struggled to keep control of affairs and managed to put down a rising of officers led by *General Kornilov*.

The time seemed ripe for the Bolsheviks. Lenin returned from Finland to a hero's welcome in Petrograd. Together with his brilliant assistant, *Trotsky*, he seized power on the night of 7-8 November (October by the old Julian calender still in use in Russia). The coup was supported by soldiers, sailors and party members. By the morning Russia was officially ruled by a *Congress of Soviets*. Lenin's aim was the establishment of a 'dictatorship of the proletariat'\ which would destroy capitalism and lead eventually to a classless society. Such a radical programme was not possible whilst Russia was at war so Trotsky was sent to negotiate and sign a peace treaty with the Germans.

Germany was in a strong position. After the Russian defeats in August her troops had driven deep into Russia. The Treaty concluded at *Brest-Litovsk* in April, 1918 took from Russia nearly all the territory she had gained since the 17th century. The *Ukraine* and *Finland* became independent. *Poland, Latvia, Lithuania* and *Estonia* came under German administration. Other territories were given to *Turkey. Brest-Litovsk* was a humiliation for Russia and it gave the world an idea of what might happen if Germany won the war. But it gave Lenin the time he needed to consolidate his slender hold on power, a hold already under attack from his enemies.

THE CIVIL WAR

Russia was now ruled by a *Council of Commissars* with Lenin in overall charge and Trotsky responsible for defence and foreign affairs. Its military branch, the *Red Guards*, was expanded until it became the *Red Army*. Its secret police, the *Cheka*, silenced all opposition as ruthlessly as the old Tsarist police had done. The communist excuse for this repression was that Russia was in chaos and this was certainly true. Opponents of the Bolsheviks, organised into "White' (as opposed to Red) armies, controlled many parts of the country. They were helped by France and Britain whose leaders hoped that Russia would re-enter the war if the Bolsheviks were overthrown. Allied troops were landed at *'Archangel, Murmansk, Sebastapol,* and *Vladivostock*, officially to guard large dumps of Allied war-supplies. Japanese troops helped the 'White' *Admiral Kolchak* and his army in Siberia, the French helped the White *General Denikin* in the Caucusus, and the British helped another White, *General Yudenitch*, in the Gulf of Finland region.

Victory went to the Red Army, organised and sometimes led by Trotsky. His widely dispersed and disorganised enemies were defeated in separate campaigns.

The First World War itself had ended before this civil war finished, and the Allies grew tired of trying to help, especially as they feared that their troops might become infected with communist and revolutionary ideas. By 1920, all the Bolshevik's enemies had been defeated except the Poles. The Poles were aided by the French whose leaders wished to keep communism out of central Europe. Red Army forces almost captured *Warsaw* but the fighting was ended by the *Treaty of Riga* in 1920. This gave Poland some Russian territory, a fact which was to cause trouble in later years. The last White commander, *General Wrangel*, was rescued from the *Crimea* with nearly 30,000 men and many Tsarist officials and noblemen by warships.

During the early part of the fighting Tsar Nicholas and his family were murdered at *Ekaterinburg* when there seemed a chance of them being rescued by a White Army approaching the town. This White force consisted of a legion of *Czechs* who had fought in the old Tsarist army against Austria. They had been given permission to go to Vladivostock when the revolution began with the idea of eventually sailing west and joining the fighting in France and Belgium. The Bolsheviks tried to disarm this legion and a peaceful railway journey turned into a fighting advance. It was the Czech Legion, plus other White troops, who were moving on the town at the time.

LENIN'S RUSSIA

The Bolsheviks inherited a ruined economy. Many parts of the country has been devastated by war. Some rich regions like Poland, the Donetz Basin and the Urals, were no longer under Russian control. The supply of cotton from central Asia had been cut off. Consequently, there were shortages of everything from food to raw materials like iron and coal; locomotives were run on wood fires. With transport and industry dislocated, inflation got out of hand; 1922 railway fares were a million times what they had been in 1917. Peasants who sold their crops could no longer hope to live on the money until the next harvest. They began to hoard supplies of grain and this led to a vicious circle in which factories were not producing enough goods to sell to the peasants, who, in reply, would not produce food for the factory workers.

Lenin's answer was a system called *War Communism* - a total mobilisation of the country's resources by force if necessary. To supply the Red armies fighting the civil war, Lenin ordered all hoarded grain to be confiscated.Soldiers ransacked villages, looking for hidden grain. Informers were given half of what was discovered. Peasants found guilty of hoarding were imprisoned or shot. The peasantry hit back with savage killings of *commissars* (Communist Party officials) when they could, and a widespread refusal to grow sufficient grain. This helped cause a fearful famine which killed 5 million people in 1921-2.

NEW ECONOMIC POLICY

War Communism dealt a blow to the Bolshevik ideal of a partnership between workers and peasants; now there was deep hostility between the two. It made communism as a system unpopular and led to many revolts, the most significant being the mutiny of sailors at *Kronstadt* in March, 1921. The rebel sailors demanded *'Soviets without communism'*, and democratic reforms like freedom of the press. They wanted a revival of small scale private industry - the Bolsheviks had nationalised even one-worker firms - a fairer rationing system and a better deal for the peasants. The mutiny was crushed after bloody fighting with Red Army troops and the ringleaders were executed. Other peasants risings were put down in a similar way.

Such unrest caused Lenin to change his policy. He decided to stop forcing the peasants to hand over their grain and to soften the nationalisation policy by allowing small business to be run privately. This 'U' turn was called the *New Economic Policy* (NEP). Traders, called *Nepmen*, were allowed to set up in business. Their job as middlemen was to get the economy working again, to get food to shops, goods to villages and supplies to factories. Peasants were to pay a fixed tax in kind and then allowed to sell the remainder of their produce at a profit. All enterprises with less than 20 workers were to be de-nationalised but the *'commanding heights'* of the economy, as Lenin called them (main industries like coal, steel, railways, banks) were still to be state owned.

Any benefits from NEP were hampered by a famine. This was so bad that outside aid was accepted. Religious groups such as the *Quakers*, and international relief organisations like that run by *Herbert Hoover* (later US President) and *Fridtjof Nansen*, the explorer, poured in nearly a million tons of goods, including food and medicines. It was 1926 before Russian industry reached its pre-First World War level and by that time Lenin's successors had decided to reverse a policy which might have taken Russia permanently away from communism.

NATIONAL MINORITIES

The Bolsheviks had maintained that the foreign minorities included in the old Russian empire should be free to rule themselves. In fact, they hoped that such states would want to join Bolshevik Russia once they had workers' governments. The reality of the situation was far different. *Finland* was granted independence in 1918. When a 'Trojan Horse' of Bolsheviks inside the country tried to seize power they were defeated by German and Finnish troops led by *General Mannerheim*. The *Ukraine* proclaimed its independence in 1918 also but was forced into a 'Soviet Republic' after the communist victory in the civil war. *Byelorussia* (White Russia) tried to be free of Russian control but a successful communist revolt ended with the country's absorption into Russia. *Georgia* and *Azerbaijan* enjoyed a similar autonomy until invaded by the Red army troops in 1921. However, the defeat of the Red Army by the Poles meant that *Latvia, Lithuania* and *Estonia* remained free until the Second World War. In 1924 Bolshevik Russia became the *Union of Soviet Socialist Republics* (USSR), a title which indicated that Russia was made up of more than one nationality.

CHRISTIANS AND MOSLEMS

Communism is an atheistic movement so its leaders tried to break the power of the Church amongst the people. Church property was taken over by the state and converted into hospitals, schools, prisons and barracks. Sunday was abolished from 1929 until 1940 and a six-day week was introduced. The only legal weddings were civil ones, and New Year and May Day replaced Christmas and Easter as public holidays. However, Lenin in particular trod carefully where Christianity was concerned because he realised the strong hold it had on the peasantry who comprised the majority of the population. The *Moslem* inhabitants of Russia had to be subdued by force; in 1929 a moslem was torn to pieces by a mob when he erected a statue of Lenin in a holy shrine. Some Christians and Moslems decided to work with the authorities; one sect of Moslems even maintained that the *Aga Khan*, their spiritual leader, was Lenin's father. The Russian Orthodox Church was split during this period and its leaders did not take a firm line. *Patriarch Tikhon* at first opposed Communism but in 1922, just before he was due to be put on trial on a charge of counter-revolutionary activity, he changed his mind and decided to support the government.

In 1918 *Dora Kaplan* fired three shots at Lenin which severely wounded the Bolshevik leader. He never really recovered and died prematurely in 1924. His power passed to three men, *Joseph Stalin, Leon Trotsky* and *Gregori Zinoviev*.

Note: In 1917 Russia was still using the Julian Calender which had been abandoned by other western countries during the 16-18th centuries. (Britain changed in 1752). This calender was behind the Gregorian one and so the "March' revolution in Russia was dated February and the 'October' revolution was actually in November.

SELF-ASSESSMENT SECTION

1. Who was Father Gapon?

2. What happened on the battleship "Potemkin'?

3. What was Siberia used for?

4. What were the 'commanding heights' of the Russian economy according to Lenin?

5. How did Herbert Hoover help Russia after the First World War?

6. What was a Nepman?

7. Why did the Bolsheviks abolish Sunday?

8. Who tried to kill Lenin?

9. Why was a Czech Legion involved in the Russian Civil War?

10. Why did the Bolsheviks gain control of Russia in 1917, according to the Russian Communist Party.

11. Put the correct details (by letter) against these names.

    1. FATHER GAPON   A. Leader of the Russian Church
    2. GENERAL MANNERHEIM B. Led 'White' armies in the Crimea.
    3. PETER STOLYPIN   C. Murdered by Bolsheviks at Ekaterinberg.
    4. GENERAL WRANGEL   D. Lenin's right-hand man.
    5. TSAR NICHOLAS   E. Led march on winter Palace in 1905.
    6. LEON TROTSKY   F. Crushed anti-government activity,
                                           1906-12.
    7. FRIDTJOF NANSEN   G. Leader of Finns in war against Russia.
    8. PATRIARCH TIKHON   H. One of Lenin's successors.
    9. GRIGORI ZINOVIEV   I. Headed famine relief organisation for
                                           Russia.

12. This decree was issued by the All-Russian Soviet Executive Committee on 23 March 1921. Read it carefully and then answer the questions.

    "In order to assure an efficient and untroubled economic life on the basis of a freer use by the farmer of the products of his labour and of his economic resources... requisitioning, as a means of state collection of food supplies, raw material and fodder, is to be replaced by a tax in kind... This tax must be less than what the peasant has given up to this time through requisitions. The sum of the tax must be reckoned so as to cover the most essential needs of the army, the city workers, the non-agricultural population.."

    a) What is the name usually given to this decree?

    b) Why was it issued?

    c) Why did the army have 'essential needs' at this time?

    d) In what way did this decree represent a "U" turn by the government?

    e) What other title is sometimes given to the "requisitioning' mentioned in the decree?

13. This is the text of a telegram sent to the German ambassador in Sweden on 7 April 1917. Read it carefully and then answer the questions.

    "A number of Russian revolutionaries in Switzerland (exact number not yet decided) is to be given permission to travel through Germany in order to return to Russia via Sweden. They will be accompanied by the Secretary of the Swiss Social Democratic party, Platten. Provisionally, they will probably arrive at Sassnitz on Wednesday, 11 April.

    Please make the necessary arrangement with the Swedish government, in confidence.

    Report their attitude by telegram.

    Zimmerman".

a) Who was Zimmerman? (See Work Unit 12 if you do not know the answer)

b) Why were Russian revolutionaries living in Switzerland?

c) Why did Zimmerman want the Swedish government to be contacted "in confidence'?

d) Why did the Germans allow this journey?

e) What were the long-term consequences of the arrangement made in this telegram?

14. Read these two sources and then answer the questions.

A. ".have we not... a right to turn this liberal philosophy of the February (March) revolution exactly upside down? Yes, we have the right to say: At the same time that the official society, all that many-storied superstructure of ruling classes.... lived from day to day by inertia and automatism, nourishing themselves with the relics of worn out ideas, deaf to the.. demands of evolution, flattering themselves with phantoms and foreseeing nothing - at the same time, in the working masses there was taking place an independent....process of growth, not only of hatred for the rulers, but of critical understanding of their impotence, an accumulation of experience and creative consciousness which the revolutionary insurrection and its victory only completed".

B. "They knew that all the organised and quite free public opinion of Russia was against any kind of dictatorship, against changes of the system of government till the summons of the Constituent Assembly. Only by way of conspiracy, only by way of a treacherous armed struggle was it possible to break up the Provisional Government and stop the establishment of a democratic system in Russia after the Revolution."

(Sources: Kerensky - "Policy of the Provisional Govt" and
Trotsky - "History of Russian Revolution".
Quoted "Russian Revolution and Bolshevik Victory" Ed. Adams.
D.C. Heath, 1960)

a) One of these sources was written by *Alexander Kerensky*, the other by *Leon Trotsky*. Explain which source was written by which man, and give reasons for your choice.

b) Which source claims that only the workers who understood Marxism could lead a genuine revolution?

c) Who were the conspirators who carried out a "treacherous armed struggle"?

d) In what way do these two source disagree about what the Russian people wanted in 1917?

e) Can you think of a reason why *both* these sources might be regarded as unreliable and biased?

15. Put the correct details (by letter) against these places.

1. KRONSTADT	A.	This state remained free until 1940.
2. WINTER PALACE	B.	Scene of violent strike in 1905.
3. BREST-LITOVSK	C.	Scene of naval mutiny in 1920.
4. PETROGRAD	D.	Treaty between Russia and Germany signed here, 1918.
5. EKATERINBURG.	E.	Scene of protest march, 1905.
6. GEORGIA	F.	Treaty between Russia and Poland signed here.
7. LATVIA	G.	This state failed to keep its independence.
8. ODESSA	H.	City where the Bolsheviks first seized power.
9. RIGA	I.	Scene of murder of the Tsar and his family.

16. *War Communism* was:-

   a)   the forcible expropriation of goods for war purposes
   b)   the nationalising of most industries.
   c)   a battle between communists.
   d)   a system of supplying food to the peasants.
   e)   propaganda in favour of communism.
        (TICK THE CORRECT ANSWER)

17. Fill in the blank spaces from the words below.

   "Lenin and the ...., called communists after March 1918, were bewildered by the difficulties produced by the ...., the .... shortages and the failure of the .... to produce as much as they had in ...... Most of the factories were .... and inspectors were appointed to watch over the ...."

   (1) Bolsheviks   (2) Civil War   (3) 1914   (4) factories   (5) food
   (6) nationalised   (7) Factory managers.

   (Source from 'Lenin and the Russian Revolution' by Donald W. Mack, Longman, 1970)

18. Write short essays on *two* of the following topics.

   New Economic Policy.   The March Revolution.
   The Russian civil war.   Russian minorities.

19. Explain the background to the treaty of Brest-Litovsk. How did it:

   a)   affect Russia and
   b)   affect Germany?

14

The Versailles Settlement

INTRODUCTION

President Woodrow Wilson of the United States, on his way to the Paris Peace Conference in 1919, told his advisers, "The world is faced by a task of terrible proportions and only the adoption of a cleansing process can regenerate the world". He wanted a fair share for both winners and losers and the establishment of an international organisation to prevent war. He found a devastated Europe, mourning its dead, whose victors were demanding both security and revenge on Germany, two aims which proved to be contradictory. Italy wanted those Austrian territories promised to her in the secret Treaty of London. Poland, restored to nationhood, was fighting to get back some of the lands taken from her in the 18th century. Czechs and Yugoslavs were set to quarrel over frontier lines.

France, in particular, demanded a punishing peace which would make another 1870 or 1914-style invasion of her soil impossible. Clemenceau, the fierce old French prime minister, had led France through some of the worst days of the war. To him there was no doubt what needed to be done and it had little to do with cleaning or regeneration. German expansion must be stopped in the Rhineland, Czechoslovakia and Austria. Years after the conference he pointed to a map of Europe, put his finger on Bohemia (a province of Czechoslovakia) and his thumb on France's Rhineland frontier and remarked, "These are the critical points....That is security. But if Germany is allowed to fortify the Rhineland, then she would move against Bohemia, will be free to raise the issue of the Sudeteneland[1], settle the question of Anschluss[2] and take off in any direction she may decide". By 1939 Hitler had made all Clemenceau's fears a reality.

What went wrong? Why did Woodrow Wilson's 'cleansing process' not happen, and why did the 'security' of which Clemenceau spoke fail to materialize? The clue, perhaps, can be found in some remarks of Harold Nicholson who attended the Peace conference as a member of the British delegation. Nicholson left some vivid pen portraits of the three principle leaders, the 'tired and contemptuous eyelids' of Clemenceau, the black-button boots of Woodrow Wilson, the 'jovial

[1] A German-speaking region of Czechoslovakia

[2] Union between Germany and Austria

gestures of Lloyd George's hands'. However, he added, "We arrived determined that a Peace of Justice and wisdom should be negotiated; we left it, conscious that the treaties imposed upon our enemies were neither just nor wise".

Two key words in this extract are 'enemies' and 'imposed'. There was no real hope of lasting peace if the German people as a whole were punished for a war started by their leaders. Yet the victorious nations of Europe, not just their governments or representatives, were determined that Germany must pay for all the human misery and material devastation caused by the war. Consequently, no ex-enemy country was consulted or considered about the settlements. How could such agreements arrived at in such a way defuse age-old grievances? Furthermore, Bolshevik Russia was not represented in Paris, whilst the US Congress bound by its constitution to ratify all treaties, refused to accept either the Versailles Treaty or the League of Nations. A peace settlement which ignored the two largest European nations, Germany and Russia, and was boycotted by the USA, was unlikely to be permanent. In such circumstances, as Clemenceau predicted, Germany would soon be free 'to take off in any direction she may decide'. With wise German leaders this might not have happened. But in 1933 Adolf Hitler became Chancellor of Germany.

WILSON, CLEMENCEAU AND LLOYD GEORGE

The delegates of 32 states assembled in and around *Paris* in January, 1919. Turkish, German and Austrian representatives could only read draft treaties, make comments and suggestions, and sign any document presented to them. The *Treaty of Versailles* was signed in the *Hall of Mirrors* where the German empire had been proclaimed in 1871, on 28th June 1919, the fifth anniversary of the murder of the Archduke Ferdinand. This treaty was concerned with Germany. Other treaties were named after the Paris suburbs where they were concluded - *Neuilly* with *Bulgaria, St. Germain* with *Austria, Trianon* with *Hungary* (now an independent country) and *Sevres* with *Turkey*. (For further details of the Sevres treaty see Work Unit 8).

Most important decisions at the conference were made by *Woodrow Wilson* (USA), *Georges Clemenceau* (France) and *David Lloyd George* (Britain). The aims of these three men did not always co-incide. Clemenceau, nicknamed the 'Tiger' because of his courage and determination, wanted to punish Germany in such a way that she would never again be a threat to France. Lloyd George had just won the so-called *Khaki Election* in which anti-German feelings had run high with slogans like *'Hang the Kaiser'* and *Make the Germans pay'* commonplace. Woodrow Wilson, whose country had suffered least in the war, was an idealist who wanted to "save" the world. Clemenceau despised this attitude but Wilson had to be listened to; by 1918 the USA was the most powerful nation in the world and her relief agencies were pouring food and other aid into the devastated parts of Europe.

Wilson's ideas about peace were already known. In January, 1918 they had been published as *Wilson's Fourteen Points* (Clemenceau remarked that God only needed ten!) At that time Germany was undefeated and about to launch the last great "war-winning" offensives on the Western Front. The Germans ignored these *Points*, and in April, 1918, showed at *Brest-Litovsk* that their idea of a peace settlement was wholescale confiscation of enemy property and territory. When defeat and disaster threatened them in November, 1918, however, they agreed to Wilson's plan which was obviously better for Germany than anything France or Britain might suggest.

THE FOURTEEN POINTS

Wilson's Fourteen Points can be summarised under three headings. First, there were those concerned with the causes of war and how to abolish them. General disarmament was suggested and an end to *secret diplomacy* and *colonial quarrels* of the kind which had helped cause the First World War. The right for the shipping of all nations to have *freedom of the seas* was suggested also. Second, there were those clauses which embodied Wilson's ideas on *self-determination*. These maintained that people had a right to live under a government of their own nationality *and* choosing; the exact opposite of the principles on which the Turkish, Austrian and Russian empires had been founded.

To the question,"What constitutes a nation?" Wilson decided to use the rough guide of the language spoken by the people. This was probably the only possible rule but it was not a good one. Many peoples speak the language of their conquerors like the Indians and Pakistanis who speak English. Another problem in this connection was that in eastern Europe many nationalities were so mixed up that only large-scale movements of population could have produced a nationally 'pure' people. Finally, and most important from Wilson's point of view, was the proposal to set up an international organisation of states to prevent war and settle disputes. From this Point arose the *League of Nations.*

Some of Wilson's Points were accepted. Others were either rejected or ignored, both during the conference and in the final settlement. The rule against secret diplomacy was broken when the Big Three leaders began to meet in secret without consulting other delegates. Britain thought the freedom of the seas clause might mean that she could not stop and search merchant vessels in time of war. She refused to give up her traditional weapon of blockade. The *mandate system* (See later) actually increased the extent of colonial territories for France and Britain in particular, and may be said to have caused, rather than stopped, the number of colonial quarrels. The Italian prime minister, *Vittorio Orlando,* was furious when the Austrian territories promised Italy in secret Treaty of London were refused because it had been a *secret* agreement. Wilson tried to appeal over his head to the Italian people and found that they agreed with their prime minister. Finally, although the frontier-lines of the new Europe represented a triumph for *nationalism*, with far more people governing themselves than ever before in Europe's history, there were anomalies. *Czechoslovakia* and *Poland*, for example, ended up with large German minorities inside their borders.

TREATY OF VERSAILLES

By the terms of this treaty Germany gave back *Alsace-Lorraine* to France and a frontier area, *Eupen* and *Malmedy*, to Belgium. A great deal of Germany's eastern territories, including *Silesia*, went to the newly-established state of Poland; they had been taken in the 18th century, when Poland had been dismembered by neighbouring states. Land-locked Poland was allowed a *'corridor'* through Germany to the port of *Danzig* (now Gdansk) which was taken from Germany and made a 'free' port. The rich coalmining region of the *Saarland* in Germany was taken over by France for 15 years so as to compensate for the damage done to French coalmines during the war. Germany lost all her colonies, including *German East Africa*, the *Cameroons* and *German South West Africa* (See later).

Germany was forced to disarm. Her army was reduced to 100,000 volunteers and she was deprived of tanks, artillery and military aircraft. Her navy was fixed at 6 battleships of no more than 10,000 tons, 6 light cruisers, 12 destroyers and 12 torpedo boats. The old imperial *High Seas Fleet* was ordered to the British naval base at *Scapa Flow* but its crews scuttled their ships so that they would not fall in Allied hands. It was arranged for an Anglo-French army of occupation to remain in the Rhineland for 15 years.

The German representatives objected most strongly to the *'War Guilt'* Clause 231 in the treaty which blamed Germany for starting the war. When it seemed that they would refuse to agree the Allied Powers threatened to renew the war within 5 days unless it was signed; it is worth noting that the Allied blockade of Germany had only finished in March, 1919. It was decided that the Germans should pay *Reparations* (compensation) to the countries in which the war had been fought. This was difficult to calculate and at first it consisted of payments in kind, of coal, timber, livestock and ships. It was not easy for Germany to pay because by the terms of the treaty she had lost some of her richest industrial areas, *Silesia, Lorraine* and the *Saar*. Eventually a figure of £6,600 million was agreed. Some experts, notably *J.McKeynes* in his book, *'The Economic Consequences of the Peace'* maintained that Germany could not afford to pay this sum. If it was paid in kind it might have meant that workers in Allied countries would have been unemployed. Germany paid the bills at first by borrowing. Later, when she felt strong enough, she refused to pay. It has since been pointed out that Germany spent far more in re-arming under Hitler and fighting the Second World War than she would have had to pay in reparations.

HABSBURG COLLAPSE

Wilson's principle of self-determination - that there should be no subject races in Europe - was not needed in Austria. The Habsburg empire had begun to collapse before the war ended. *Hungary* and *Austria* broke into separate states. *Czechoslovakia* was made up of the Czechs and Slovaks. An enlarged *Serbia*, now including Montenegro, Bosnia and the Croats and Slovenes of the old empire, became *Yugoslavia, Hungary* lost subject races to *Rumania*, whilst *Austria* gave *Trieste, Istria* and *Tyrol* to Italy. *Poland* was able to get back much of its former territory now that the Treaty of Brest-Litovsk was cancelled. *Turkey* lost her former Arab provinces of *Iraq, Syria* and *Palestine* (See Work Unit 8). The treaty forbade Germany and Austria to be united.

These divisions created more frontiers and trade barriers than had existed under the old empires. Austria itself was now quarter of the original area of the empire, and contained a fifth of the population. Her army was reduced to 30,000 men and her navy to three police boats. She gave *Rumania* more territory than her existing frontiers and also agreed to pay reparations to ex-enemies. *Hungary* became land-locked; she also lost many of her old subject nationalities. *Bulgaria* suffered from having fought for Germany. She was restricted to the territories she had ruled in 1914, although she had to give eastern *Thrace* to Greece. The beneficiaries of the war in this region were Rumania which doubled in size and *Greece* which gained land from the collapse of Turkey. *Poland* was looked upon as a possible ally by France in a future war with Germany; in 1921 the two countries signed an alliance. Four other states of the old Russian empire, *Finland, Latvia, Lithuania* and *Estonia* gained their independence.

MANDATED TERRITORIES

The colonial territories taken from Germany and Turkey were not owned outright by the Allied countries. If they had, it would have been against many of the ideals of freedom and self-government which they had claimed to be fighting for. Each country or region was *mandated* to a Great Power which promised to administer it until such time as the inhabitants were judged fit to rule themselves. Such territories were legally the property of the *League of Nations* who required the occupying powers to answer to it with regular reports. This scheme was not successful. Most of these countries had been promised their freedom if they helped in the fight against the Turk. In fact, they found themselves ruled by a less brutal, but nevertheless, foreign power. The French were hated in *Syria*. The British had trouble in *Palestine* where the Arabs felt betrayed by the British commitment to the founding of a Jewish home in Palestine (Balfour Declaration). The British had also promised that nothing should be done 'which may prejudice the civil and religious rights of existing non-Jewish communities in Palestine'. Since the Jews and Arabs came to no agreement a smouldering civil war continued until the end of the Second World War.

The mandate system had been suggested by the South African *General Smuts*. It pleased South Africa and Australia who had both felt threatened by German colonies near their frontiers. It caused little trouble in Africa where German colonies were taken over and eventually given their independence by Britain, France and South Africa. Most Germans were far more concerned about losses in Europe than they were about their colonial losses.

THE LEAGUE OF NATIONS

Wilson insisted that his 14th point should be set out in the first part of the treaty - the formation of a *League of Nations* with headquarters at *Geneva* in Switzerland, a traditionally neutral country. The obligations of each member state were embodied in a *Covenant* in which they promised to decrease armaments to the 'lowest point consistent with national safety', to honour the integrity and independence of member states, to submit all disputes to a peaceful settlement and to take action against an aggressor. This last point was called the *'Sanctions Clause'* because the most effective means of deterring an aggressor without war was thought to be by economic sanctions. The League members also promised to keep their armament programmes public, to work for humane and better conditions for their workers and to try and control such international problems as disease, drugs and the slave trade.

An *Assembly*, with representatives from each member state, was to be the League's Parliament. An executive *Council* with representatives of each Great Power, plus delegates from each smaller state holding office in rotation, was to deal with the day to day running of the League. The purpose of the League was to prevent general war and solve disputes between smaller states. Other organisations included an *International Court*, based at the *Hague* in Holland (another neutral state) which was to settle legal quarrels between nations and an *International Labour Organisation* to deal with workers', health and social problems.

USA REJECTS LEAGUE AND TREATY

No ex-enemy nation was invited to join any of these organisations. It was assumed they would join later. *Soviet Russia* was also excluded. The most surprising omission came when the US Congress refused to ratify either the Treaty or the League, both set up by their President. Partly this rejection was the result of *Wilson*, a Democrat , having lost control of Congress to the rival Republican party. More importantly, it was the result of the Amercian feeling of *isolationism*, that is the desire to avoid involvement in European wars and disputes. Many Americans had not wished to join in the war which had been forced on them by the German 'U' Boat campaign. Their anti-European feelings were strengthened afterwards when many US loans to European countries, especially France, were repudiated. The US's racial mix, with large numbers of German, Russian and Irish immigrants, also made many reluctant to take sides in a European quarrel.

Without *Germany, Russia* or the *USA* in the League there was little chance of its work being successful. The situation in Europe after 1919 was in important ways more dangerous than in 1914. The French had given way on some of their demands for border security on the understanding that the arrangement would be backed by the USA. This guarantee no longer applied after the US Congress failed to ratify the Treaty of Versailles or the League. Germany was relatively stronger than in 1914 because, instead of two large empires on her borders, she was now surrounded by a string of weaker states. German bitterness over the 'War Guilt' clause and territorial losses could be dampened down by sensible leaders. On the other hand, it could be inflamed by unscrupulous ones like Hitler. Wilson told the US electorate that if they did not join the League there would be general war again within a 'a generation'. He was right almost to the day.

SELF-ASSESSMENT SECTION

1. Where is the Sudetenland?
2. Who led France at the Paris Peace Conference?

3. Which treaty was concerned with Austria?

4. What test was used to determine a nation?

5. What was the 'War Guilt' clause in the Versailles Treaty?

6. Why was Poland given a 'corridor' through to Danzig?

7. Who wrote 'The Economic Consequences of the Peace'?

8. Which country opposed 'freedom of the seas'?

9. Name one *new* country formed after the First World War.

10. What was a mandated territory?

11. Here is a speech made by Woodrow Wilson to the Peace conference on 25 January 1919. Read it carefully and then answer the questions.

> "We are here to see ..... that the very foundations of this war are swept away. (A) Those foundations were the private choice of small coteries *(groups)* of civil rulers and military staffs. (B) Those foundations were the aggression of great powers upon small. (C) Those foundations were the folding together of empires of unwilling subjects by the force of arms...."

    a) Name a country which was an example of A.
    b) Give an example of what Wilson had in mind when he said B.
    c) Give an example of a country which fits description C.
    d) In what particular way did Wilson hope to sweep away the 'foundations of war'?

12. Which of these countries were winners (put A) and which were losers (put B) in the First World War?

    HUNGARY   ITALY   BULGARIA   RUMANIA   TURKEY
    GERMANY   POLAND   AUSTRIA   GREECE   YUGOSLAVIA

13. Self-determination is:-

    a) a democratic system of government.
    b) government by your own people.
    c) a way of adjusting frontier lines.
    d) a way of finding out about nationalities.
        (TICK THE CORRECT ANSWER)

14. The cartoon (see p129) appeared in an American newspaper in 1920 under the heading 'Wilson goes to the the boss'.

    a) What does the artist mean by calling the US people 'the boss'?
    b) Why is Wilson leaving this office?
    c) What happened when Wilson met 'the boss'?
    d) How did it affect events in other parts of the world?

(Source: Bragden and McCutchen)

15. "When I encouraged Keynes to write his book *(The Economic Consequences of the Peace)* I knew his views about the statesmen at Paris ..... I did not expect him to turn Wilson into a figure of fun. These few pages about Wilson in Keynes's book made an aunt Sally of the noblest figure - perhaps the only noble figure - in the history of the war"

General Jan Smuts

(Source: 'The Carthaginian Peace or the Economic Consequences of Mr. Keynes' by Etienne Mantoux, New York, 1952)

Explain the reasons why Smuts thought Wilson was a noble figure.

16. Explain the ways in which Germany was 'punished' by the terms of the Treaty of Versailles. How far were such terms successful?

17. Explain these terms.

   a) Sanctions Clause.
   b) Covenant of League of Nations
   c) Isolationism.
   d) Secret diplomacy.
   e) Khaki Election.

15

The League of Nations

INTRODUCTION

The League of Nations was born out of the slaughter and devastation of the First World War. Its job was to prevent war, and, as such, it represented a noble ideal. But it was formed by the nations who won the war. Its foundation was one of the Allies' war aims, proclaimed before the conflict ended. For this reason it was regarded with suspicion by neutral countries who wanted no part of the war-aims of either side, and with dislike by the losers. This latter feeling was particularly strong in Germany where the League was often seen as part of a treaty they regarded as wrong and unfair. The 'Diktat', the dictated peace of Versailles, was in many ways the 'wicked witch' who spoiled the christening and doomed the future 'child'.

Woodrow Wilson, 'father' of this unhappy child, attended the christening with some optimism. He felt sure that a major cause of the war, nationalism, would be less dangerous now that the rights of minority peoples had been secured by the so-called 'successor-states' to the old empires. In fact, nationalism, in the form of Fascism and Nazism, grew more aggressive in the years which followed, often feeding on the grievances of those minorities who had not received self-determination; the Sudeten Germans of Czechoslovakia and the Hungarians of Rumania and Yugoslavia, for example, Wilson also believed that now the old autocracies had gone, most countries would be more democratic and therefore peaceable. Whether democracies are more peace-loving than totalitarian states is debatable. What is certain is that qualification for League membership was that a state should be 'self-governing', not necessarily democratic. Consequently the League soon included a number of dictatorships.

Each state joining the League was, in effect, signing a multi-lateral treaty binding it to seek peaceful solutions to its own international problems, and to help member-states if they became the victim of armed aggression. This system was called collective security, and, ultimately, it involved going to war when not party to a quarrel. This was something which a democratic government, dependant upon public opinion, might find more difficult to do than a dictatorship. Collective security in fact could only work if nations rejected war as an instrument of policy. During the Twenties and Thirties extremists in Italy, Germany and Japan not only rejected such a notion. They glorified war and militarism and, in the case of Italy and Germany, maintained that grievances, left over from the Peace Settlement, justified any violent aggression.

The First World War saw the growth of pacifism, the belief that wars would only cease if individuals refused to take part in them, and that to kill for one's country was a sin. It was ironic that this movement, although a minority one, was strong in Britain, where it helped influence foreign policy and suggested to the dictators that they had nothing to fear from the British. Both Hitler and Mussolini were gamblers. They bluffed their way through the Thirties relying on the weak nerves of their opponents to get their way. Of the two, Mussolini was never more than a bluffer. Hitler, when his bluff was called, plunged the world into war. During the final crisis which led to the Second World War the League was not even consulted, and no debates about the serious situation took place. It had by 1939 failed so often that it had ceased to be relevant.

BACKGROUND TO THE LEAGUE

Wilson's idea of a League of Nations to prevent war was not new; it had been suggested at various times since the Middle Ages. Even before the First World War ended 'League of Nations Societies' had been formed in France, Britain and the USA. The Pope favoured such an organisation, and *General Jan Smuts*, the South African soldier and politician, had written a pamphlet giving practical suggestions as to how it could be set up. Wars often give an impetus to such ideas as the generation which has experienced them says 'never again'. A *'Concert of Europe'* was instituted in 1815 at the end of the *Napoleonic Wars*, at which European kings and emperors met to try to preserve the balance of power. It died out in the 1820's after a French invasion of Spain. The League of Nations, however, was far more than a meeting of a few monarchs. It was seen as a literally life-saving operation, and was launched with a sense of urgency and mission. The Western world had seemed to be progressing steadily during the 19th century, only to plunge into a new 'dark age' in 1914. Many people were determined to prevent such a catastrophe happening again. It was out of such convictions that the League of Nations was born.

SETTING THE LEAGUE UP

Soon after the Paris Peace conference began in 1919, a special committee was formed to draft a *Covenant*, that is, an agreement binding on all member states. Amongst the Covenant's 26 Articles were ones stipulating that all disputes be taken to the League, and any league decision should be observed for at least 3 months. The French suggestion of an armed force to back up the League's decisions was rejected. Although the first meeting of the League was held in *Paris*, it was decided that its permanent headquarters should be on neutral soil, at *Geneva* in Switzerland. A special building, the *Palace of Nations*, was built on a hillside beside Lake Geneva between 1929 and 1936. This building is still used by the United Nations, mainly for Disarmament Talks.

The League was headed by a *Director-General*; the first was British, *Sir Eric Drummond*. The League's main component was the *Assembly*. This was the debating chamber of the League and was made up of three delegates for each member-state who exercised one vote on behalf of their country. Small nations had the same voting rights as large ones and all votes had to be unanimous. This proved a weakness. States who disagreed with a proposal usually abstained from voting, but any state, however small and uninvolved in the problem, could veto resolutions. This delayed possible action and was time-wasting in times of crisis.

ORGANISATIONS AND COMMISSIONS

An executive *Council* had permanent seats for *Britain, France, Italy* and *Japan*; the USA would have had a seat but the US Congress refused to ratify the Versailles Treaty or the League (See Work Unit 14). Other states held seats on the council on a rotating basis for a period of 3 years. In addition, a *Secretariat* acted as a civil service to administer the League's activities and an *International Labour Organisation* dealt with workers' conditions throughout the world. The ILO campaigned for an 8 hour working day and a 48 hour working week, the right of workers to form trade unions, annual paid holidays and no person to go to work until they were 15, thus ensuring an adequate period of schooling. An *International Court of Justice*, formed originally in 1900 to settle legal disputes between nations, became part of the League in 1922; its headquarters was at the *Hague* in Holland. The ICJ consisted of 15 judges chosen from member-states. Some of the League's most useful work was done through special commissions. There were permanent commissions for the *Mandated Territories* (See Work Unit 14), for *ethnic minorities, world health, disease, drugs,* the *Saar* region of Germany and the free port of *Danzig* (now Gdansk). There were also League *research institutes* for *intellectual cooperation, refugees*, and *leprosy*.

THE LEAGUE AND THE GREAT POWERS

One of the chief weaknesses of the League was the fact that some Great Powers never joined it, others resigned and one, *Russia*, was expelled. The refusal of the USA to join is dealt with in Work Unit 14. German applications to join were blacked at first by the French, whose prime minister, *Raymond Poincare*, was anti-German. Not every German wished to join anyway for many looked on it as part of the hated *Versailles Treaty* which had blamed Germany for starting the First World War. The beneficial effects of the *Locarno Pact* (See Work Unit 19), and the appointment of a more moderate French prime minister, *Edouard Herriot*, led to Germany joining the League in 1926. In 1930 the Germans asked for a larger army and navy than that allowed by the Versailles Treaty (see Work Unit 14). Discussions were still going on about this when *Adolf Hitler* came to power in Germany in 1933. Hitler withdrew Germany from the *Disarmament Conference* which was considering the matter, and also from membership of the League. Later, he defied the League and the terms of the Versailles Treaty by starting a German re-armament programme. *Japan* also left the League in 1933 when her invasion of *Manchuria* was condemned by it (See Work Unit 21).

Soviet Russia was excluded for many years owing to the dislike and distrust of communism felt by many authorities in the capitalist west. The activities of *Trotskyite* communists, whose aim was world revolution through an organisation called the *Communist International*, helped keep this distrust alive. Bolshevik leaders like *Trotsky* looked upon the League as little more than a 'rich man's club' of capitalist nations. Western nations, for their part, could not forgive the Bolsheviks for cancelling all foreign debts at the time of the revolution. These were very large, being mainly payments for the Tsarist war-effort. Certain developments gradually softened attitudes on both sides. The overthrow of Trotsky in 1929 and the emergence of *Joseph Stalin* as dictator of Russia, led to a change of policy (See Work Unit 23) with Stalin working for what he called *'Socialism in one country'* - Russia - and not for world revolution. A sign of this thaw was the Russo-German friendship treaty of 1926. Russia was admitted a member of the League in 1934 but expelled in 1939 after her attack on *Finland*.

SUCCESS AND FAILURE

If a nation was prepared to submit its dispute to the *Assembly* and abide by its decisions, the League's peace-making machinery worked. The province of *Silesia*, a bone of contention between Germans and Poles, was divided between the two countries after a *Plebiscite* (referendum) in 1921. When *Finland* and *Sweden* quarreled about the ownership of the *Aaland Islands* the dispute was resolved in favour of Finland and a Greek invasion of *Bulgaria* in 1925 was halted by the League which forced Greece to pay compensation to the Bulgars, However, on the debit side, the town of *Vilna* in *Lithuania* was taken by the Poles in 1923 and despite the League's condemnation, they refused to hand it back. Soon afterwards *Lithuania* replied by seizing *Memel* and ignoring a similar decision of the League.

The League was not successful when dealing with the Great Powers. In 1923 an Italian general working for the conference of ambassadors in Paris was murdered at *Janina* in northern Greece. *Mussolini*, at that time Italian prime minister but soon to become dictator, demanded financial compensation and sent troops to occupy the Greek island of *Corfu* before the Greeks had time to pay. The League suggested that Greece pay the money into a neutral Swiss bank until the matter was settled, but the ambassadors' conference, strongly influenced by Mussolini, overruled them. Greece was forced to pay and the Italian forces then evacuated Corfu.

MANCHURIA AND ABYSSINIA

In 1931 Japanese military leaders in *Manchuria*, faking an incident between their troops and the Chinese at *Mukden*, invaded *Manchuria* and set up a puppet state called *Manchukuo*. The Council of the League ordered Japan to withdraw from Manchuria but the Japanese government in *Tokyo* supported this action and refused to do so. A *League Commission*, led by *Lord Lytton*, was sent to Manchuria to investigate. The *Lytton Report* condemned Japanese aggressions and requested the withdrawal of all their troops from Manchuria. This was passed by the League Council, although the Japanese delegates voted against. As a result of this resolution *Japan* left the League in 1933. This was the first important test of the League's ability to prevent aggression and it failed.

In October, 1935 Mussolini ordered the invasion of *Abyssinia* (now Ethiopia) as part of his scheme to form a new 'Roman empire' in North Africa. (See Work Unit 16). The League branded Italy an aggressor and a special committee was appointed to work out ways of putting pressure on her to withdraw her troops. The commission recommended only *trade sanctions*, not military action. Member-states were forbidden to receive Italian imports or supply money or war material to help the Italian war effort. These sanctions were never operated properly. *Britain* and *France* were very half-hearted about the matter because they hoped Italy might prove an ally against German expansion into Austria. Although they condemned the unofficial *Hoare-Laval Pact* by which their two countries would have accepted the Italian conquest of Abyssinia (See Work Unit 16), they made sure that Italy's economy was unaffected by the sanctions. The war, which saw some easy victories by modern, well equipped troops against brave but primitive tribesmen, was popular with the Italian people. Mussolini resented the imposition of sanctions and was angry with Britain and France. He moved towards an alliance with Hitler's Germany and in 1937 took Italy out of the League. The Abyssinian fiasco marked the end of the League's credibility as a world peace-keeping force.

FINAL FAILURES

The crises which marked Hitler's successive aggressions (See Work Unit 20) took place without any real action from the League; the 1938 crisis in which Hitler met British, French and Italian leaders in Germany, was not even discussed at *Geneva*. By that time Britain and France had decided to compete in the arms race with Germany, whilst pacts like that between Hitler and the western leaders, and between Hitler and Stalin, were reminiscent of the hostile alliances which helped lead to the First World War. They were signed without reference to the League and showed dramatically how far the League had failed in its principal aim. After the Second World War, on 8 April 1946, the Assembly of the League of Nations held its last meeting at Geneva. Its affairs were wound up and its records and other documents handed over to the newly-formed *United Nations*. This organisation was now entrusted with keeping world peace (See Work Unit 24).

SELF-ASSESSMENT SECTION

1. Who pioneered the idea of a League of Nations?

2. What were the 'successor-states'?

3. What was the job of the League Secretariat?

4. When was the 'Concert of Europe' founded?

5. Who was the first Director-General of the League?

6. Where is the 'Palace of Nations?

7. Which two countries quarrelled over Vilna?

8. Where was a plebiscite held in 1921?

9. What was the aim of the Communist International?

10. Who occupied Memel?

11. Put the correct details (by letter) against these places.

    1. MANCHUKUO   A. Permanent home of the League
    2. MUKDEN   B. Awarded to Finland by the League.
    3. GENEVA   C. Headquarters of the International Court of Justice.
    4. HAGUE   D. Scene of skirmish between Chinese and Japanese.
    5. PARIS   E. Polish free port.
    6. DANZIG   F. First meeting place of the League.
    7. SILESIA   G. Puppet state set up by the Japanese.
    8. AALAND   H. Country divided between Germany and Poland.
       ISLANDS

12. At the inaugural meeting of the United Nations in 1946 a British delegate, Philip Noel Baker, said,

    "A. We know the World War began in Manchuria fifteen years ago. B. We know we could easily have stopped it *if* we had taken sanctions against Mussolini, if we had closed the Suez Canal and stopped his oil".

    a) Explain what is meant by sentence A.
    b) Why were sanctions taken against Italy?
    c) Why would the stoppage of oil supplies have been critical for Italy?
    d) Bearing in mind that the League did impose sanctions, what does the 'if' in B refer to?

13. Germany left the League in 1933 because:-

    a) Disarmament talks had dragged on too long.
    b) Germany had never wanted to be a member.
    c) Germany was expelled by the League Council.
    d) Hitler came to power in Germany.

14. Japan invaded Manchuria in 1931 because:-

    a) There was an incident at Mukden.
    b) The Manchurians wanted to be ruled by Japan.
    c) Japanese generals decided to invade.
    d) The Japanese government order the invasion.
    (TICK THE CORRECT ANSWER)

15. Give examples of how the League's peace-keeping role was hindered by its fluctuating membership between 1919-39.

16. David Low, the British Cartoonist, drew the cartoon on the next page for the 'Evening Standard' He called it 'The Doormat'

a) Why is Japan shown in military uniform?
b) In what way had Japan used the League as a 'doormat'?
c) Which nation in particular had its 'honour' trampled on by Japan?
d) Why might a 'pact saving outfit' help revive the League?

(Source: Trustees of 'Evening Standard'. reproduced in 'League and UNO' by Gibbon and Morican, Longman, 1970, page 52)

17. Read this and then answer the questions.

"I..... am here today to claim that justice is due to my people, and the assistance promised to it eight months ago when fifty nations asserted that aggression had been committed...I assert that the problem submitted to the Assembly today is a much wider one than the removal of sanctions... It is the very existence of the League of Nations .... it is the value of promises made to small states that their integrity and independence be respected...."

(Source: Quoted in Gibbon and Morican (as above) p64)

This speech was delivered in:-

a) Geneva.   b) The Hague, Holland.
c) Paris.   d) Versailles.
e) London.

It was spoken by:-

a) China's General Chiang Kai Shek.
b) Woodrow Wilson.
c) Benito Mussolini.
d) Emperor Haile Salassie of Abyssinia.
e) Sir Eric Drummond.
(TICK THE CORRECT ANSWERS)

18. Explain how the League was organised to carry out its various functions.

136

16

Italy   1870-1940

INTRODUCTION

The Italian dictator, Benito Mussolini, was essentially a journalist with a gift for words. His exciting speeches, delivered in a rousing manner, could inspire an audience; one lady said that his voice was the most beautiful she had ever heard. For twenty years he ruled Italy, treated at times like a god. 'Mussolini is always right' was his slogan, printed on posters throughout the country, and most Italians believed it.

The truth was different. Mussolini gained power when his Fascist followers staged a well-publicised 'March on Rome'. This show of force led Victor Emanuel, the Italian King, to appoint Mussolini prime minister. Yet the marchers got no nearer than 40 miles to the capital. Mussolini remained in Milan and only came to Rome by train when the king sent for him. The whole march could have been dispersed with ease had the authorities acted against it. The incident was typical of the man and his career.

Mussolini told the Italian people he would revive the glories of ancient Rome. Italian armies invaded Albania and Abyssinia and won cheap victories against outclassed foes. Yet when the Second World War came, Mussolini's 'African empire' fell to a small British force within months. His attack on Greece led to near defeat, from which he had to be saved by Hitler's armies. Mussolini made pacts with Hitler and talked of their undying friendship. Yet in 1939 he did not go to war with his ally and only entered the war when he thought it was over.

His entry into the Second World War was fatal for himself and his country. The Italian army was neglected and ill-equipped. His soldiers either could not, or would not, fight on the side of the Germans, and surrendered in their thousands. Finally, when the Allies landed in Sicily in 1943 Mussolini was overthrown and Italy left the war. From 1943-45 the Italian people paid a terrible price for Mussolini's dreams of glory. The countryside was devastated as Allied and German troops fought bitter battles on its soil. In the end Mussolini was captured and shot by Italian communist partisans. A woman spat on his body 'for her dead sons'.

The man who loved to show off in front of crowds ended as a grim public spectacle, hanging upside down from a garage roof in Milan. The man who dreamed of being a modern Caesar was dubbed by his enemies the "Sawdust Caesar". His achievements had turned out to be no more solid than sawdust.

ITALIAN COLONIALISM

When Italy became a united state in 1870, both governments and people favoured founding colonies as part of a bid to be regarded as a Great Power. In 1885 Italy took over *Eritrea* and in 1892 part of *Somaliland*. But when her troops attacked *Abyssinia* in May 1896 they were wiped out at *Adowa* by the warriors of the *Emperor Menelik*. In the early 20th century the Italians turned their attention to *Tripoli*, the last remaining province of the Ottoman empire in North Africa. In 1911, when other nations were distracted by the *Agadir Crisis* (See Work Unit 11), Italy declared war on Turkey and managed to conquer *Tripoli* and neighbouring *Cyrenaica*; the two were later united as *Libya*. This attack on Turkey, with which Germany was friendly, weakened Italy's position in the *Triple Alliance* (See Work Unit 11). When the First World War broke out Italy refused to join Germany and Austria, maintaining that she was under no obligation to fight Britain. In May, 1915 she declared war on the *Central Powers*, after being promised the *Trentino* in south Tyrol and *Trieste* on the Adriatic, if the Allies won.

POST WAR PROBLEMS

The First World War, with its defeats and heavy loss of life, weakened the economy and social fabric of Italy. At the Peace conference she received *Trieste, Istria* and the *Tyrol* up to the Brenner Pass. This did not satisfy Italian nationalists and in 1919 an Italian adventurer and poet, *Gabrielle d'Annunzio*, seized *Fiume*, a port allocated to the newly formed *Yugoslavia*, although it had a large Italian population. He managed to hold it for 15 months, an action which served as an inspiration to nationalists and fascists. Italy, meanwhile, was in a state of chaos with communists, nationalists and army deserters causing trouble wherever they could. The country was desperately poor as a result of the war and Parliament was the scene of struggles between a number of parties, none of which could obtain an overall majority at elections. Strikes, sit-ins, bombing and murder were common-place. Nationalists, in particular, were able to benefit from the general feeling that Italy had been unfairly treated at the Peace Conference.

BENITO MUSSOLINI

Benito Mussolini was born in 1883 and qualified as a teacher before going into journalism. Until 1914 he was a socialist but the war seemed to him an opportunity to enlarge Italian boundaries so he became a nationalist. He wrote speeches and articles urging war with Austria, the traditional enemy of Italy, and when war came, joined up, but was injured in an accidental grenade explosion. His dramatic return to civilian life saw him pose as a wounded war hero, or, as he put it, 'a survivor'. In 1919 he formed the *Fascio de Combattimento* (Fighting Group) in *Milan*. He claimed these were a group of 'superior men', an elite bound together as firmly as the rods and axes of the *Fascinae*, the symbol of Roman power. For this reason his men were known as *'Fascists'* and their beliefs, *Fascism*. Although there were some socialists among them, the fascists stood for extreme nationalism and imperialism. Italy became a battleground between these men in their black shirts, and the red-shirted communists.

THE MARCH ON ROME

Fascism made a strong appeal to middle class people who saw it as the only defence against "godless" communism. Mussolini played on these feelings, and stressed that his men, formed in gangs called "Squadristi", were only restoring law and order when they had street fights with communists. As a result, Mussolini's party began to win seats at elections - 35 in 1921 - and when the communists staged a general strike in August, 1922, the Fascists broke it up with extreme violence. Then, in October, 1922 Mussolini ordered the Blackshirt *March on Rome*, with four columns converging on the capital from different parts of the country. The King, *Victor Emanuel*, favoured the fascists because of their anti-communism and their claim to stand for law and order. He made sure the authorities took no police action to stop the marchers and, long before they reached Rome, summoned Mussolini to Rome and appointed him prime minister. A show of force had given Mussolini power, although in later years he was sustained by strong support from the people.

FASCIST DICTATORSHIP

Initially, Mussolini included representatives of other parties in his government, His rule was popular, and in 1923, he won an overall electoral victory and began to move towards a one-party state. The turning point of this drift away from democracy came in 1924 with the murder of *Giacomo Matteotti*, a socialist critic of Fascism. Mussolini may not have known about the murder; there are some who think Matteotti's death was an accident. But his death caused uproar amongst Mussolini's political opponents and pushed him further towards totalitarianism. His reaction to criticism was to dismiss all non-fascists from his cabinet , disband other political parties and impose censorship and rule by secret police. He became, as President of the *Fascist Grand Council*, not just prime minister, but *'Il Duce'* - the leader.

Between 1925-9 Mussolini's regime got the credit for improving economic conditions which were mainly the result of a world boom. It engaged in prestigious public buildings programmes. Swamps were reclaimed and bridges, canals, roads, hospitals and schools started, although not always finished. To the outside world he seemed the man who had made the trains run on time and the Italians work hard, At home, however, repression increased. During these years a *Corporate State* was established, in which *corporations* of employers and workers replaced free trade unions, and these corporations nominated candidates to be members of Parliament

A firm achievement of these years was the concluding of the *Lateran Treaties* with the Pope which ended the age-long quarrel between the Catholic Church and various Italian political authorities. The Pope at last recognised Italy as a sovereign state, ruled by a monarch of the house (family) of *Savoy*. In return, the Holy Father was granted the right to rule an independent political state, *Vatican City*, consisting of about a square mile inside Rome. The Catholic religion was made Italy's state religion and religious teaching became compulsory in all schools. This was a clever move on Mussolini's part because it pleased a devoutly religious population who were worried about some of the anti-religious propaganda of Fascism.

COLONIAL ADVENTURES

Apart from occupying *Corfu* for a short time in 1923 (See Work Unit 15) Mussolini refrained from aggressive military adventures during the Twenties, and joined in peace-keeping efforts like *Locarno* (See Work Unit 19). In the 1930's he planned to recreate the 'Roman' empire in North Africa. In particular, he wished to avenge the defeat at Adowa. After an incident between Italian and Abyssinian troops at *Wal Wal*, well inside Abyssinia, Mussolini demanded compensation from the Abyssinians. The Abyssinian emperor, *Haile Selassie*, appealed to the League of Nations (See Work Unit 15) but Mussolini's reply was to stage a full-scale *invasion of Abyssinia*, September, 1935. He did not expect any opposition from Britain or France; they had just joined in talks with Italy, the so-called *Stresa Front*, to see if the three countries could prevent Hitler from forcing *Anschluss* on Austria.

Because of their commitment to the League of Nations, both Britain and France officially took a strong line. They voted for *sanctions* against Italy which included denying her money or war materials, and refusing to buy her own goods. The Italian people were furious and rallied behind Mussolini. They thought it hypocritical of two countries with large empires to object to Italy having colonies, and they looked upon Abyssinia as a barbarous country, whose slavery had just been condemned by many League members, including Britain. Behind the scenes, negotiations between the foreign ministers of Britain and France, *Sir Samuel Hoare* and *Pierre Laval*, agreed to let Italy have two-thirds of Abyssinia and the Abyssinians to have an outlet to the sea through *British Somaliland*. There was little point in this agreement because by May, 1936, Mussolini's forces had achieved complete victory after a brutal campaign which included the use of mustard gas and bombs against the tribesmen.

THE AXIS

The *Hoare-Laval Pact* was repudiated by both the French and British governments; in Britain, Hoare was forced to resign. His successor, *Anthony Eden* applied sanctions yet again, although not on oil. Mussolini threatened war, and in 1936 took *Italy* out of the *League of Nations*. He never forgave Britain or France for imposing sanctions, and began to move towards friendship with Germany. When *Hitler* suggested an alliance, Mussolini responded by talking about friendship which would create 'a Rome-Berlin axis round which all European states that desire peace may revolve'. The word *'Axis'* stuck as a description of the alliance between Germany and Italy. In November, 1937 the two signed the *Anti-Comintern Pact* to oppose communism. At home, these moves made the Italian dictator unpopular. The Italian people had no particular liking for Germany, and were horrified when Mussolini did not even protest at Germany's occupation of (largely catholic) *Austria*, thus achieving *Anschluss*, in 1938. (See Work Unit 20). Mussolini, who at first despised Hitler as a person, had by this time fallen under his spell and tried to copy him in many ways.

THE PACT OF STEEL

In April, 1939, Mussolini was encouraged by Hitler's takeover of *Czechoslovakia* (See Work Unit 20) to occupy *Albania* without much fighting. This may have been because the Albanians disliked their government and their king, *Zog*. In May, the Germans and Italians concluded the *Pact of Steel*. Each country promised to help the other in time of war. Privately, Mussolini begged Hitler not to risk general war, and admitted that Italy would not be ready to fight until 1942. In August, came the *Nazi-Soviet Pact* (See Work Unit 20). This came as a blow to the Italians and to their leader. Both Hitler and Mussolini had built their careers and reputations around being the enemies of communism. Now Hitler had concluded a pact with his arch-enemy, *Joseph Stalin*.

When it became clear that Hitler intended to attack *Poland*, Mussolini said he could only join in the fighting if given huge amounts of supplies by Germany. Hitler knew these demands were impossible, and merely asked for Italy's political support in any future conflict. Italians watched in horror as two "atheist" powers, Russia and Germany, divided Catholic Poland between them. Feelings ran so high that when Russia attacked *Finland*, many Italians volunteered to go and fight with the Finns. German successes, leading to the *Fall of France* in June, 1940 (See Work Unit 22) caused Hitler to suggest Italy declare war on France and Britain. Mussolini agreed. He was anxious to join in so that Italy would have a say at the peace conference. Although almost totally unprepared militarily, Italy declared war on France and Britain in June, 1940; this was referred to by *Winston Churchill* as 'a stab in the back'. On 28 October, 1940 Mussolini sent his troops across the Albanian frontier into *Greece*, thus copying Hitler, whose soldiers had just overrun *Rumania*.

SELF-ASSESSMENT SECTION

1. What was Mussolini before he became a journalist?

2. Who were the 'Squadristi'?

3. Why did Italy refuse to go to war as part of the Triple Alliance in 1914?

4. Name a region promised to Italy in the Treaty of London?

5. What was the 'Fascinae'?

6. What was the Corfu incident?

7. How did the Hoare-Laval Pact get its name?

8.   What is the origin of the term 'Axis' to describe the German-Italian alliance?

9.   Who killed Mussolini?

10. Why did Italy leave the war in 1943?

11. The *Stresa Front* was:-
     a)   A pact between Italy, France and Britain
     b)   A plan to achieve Anschluss
     c)   A plan to stop Austrian expansion
     d)   Disarmament talks
     e)   A suggested alliance against Germany to oppose Anschluss.

12. A Fascist Corporation was:-
     a)   A trade union organisation.
     b)   An employers' organisation
     c)   A large private company.
     d)   An organisation of employer and workers.
     e)   A Parliamentary constituency.
          (TICK THE CORRECT ANSWER)

13. Read these sources and then answer the questions.

     A. "Very urgent. Top priority. Mussolini. Milan. H.M. the King asks you
         to proceed immediately to Rome as he wishes to offer you the
         responsibility of forming a ministry. With respect. Cittadeni, General.
         28 October 1922.

     B. "He *(Mussolini)* was still in Milan. His offices were surrounded by
         Units of the Army and Police, and he kept looking out of the window
         and telephoning constantly for news. He was making a strenuous
         effort to appear calm and controlled, but his excitement was close to
         hysteria. When a squadron of tanks rolled through the streets.... he
         ran out of the building with a rifle in his hands shouting incoherently
         and was nearly shot by a supporter even more excited than he was. In
         fact there was practically no opposition to the march of fascism. Both
         the Army and the police were prepared to stand aside and let it take its
         course".

              (From "Benito Mussolini' by Christopher Hibbert, Longmans, 1962)

     C. "I could have transformed this grey hall into an armed camp of
         Blackshirts, a bivouac of corpses. I could have nailed up the doors of
         Parliament".

     Mussolini, in his first speech to the Italian parliament as prime minister, 1922.

     a)   To what historical event do these sources refer?
     b)   Which source constitutes *secondary evidence?* Explain why this is so.
     c)   Explain the background to Source A. What was the immediate result?
     d)   Sources B. and C. paint a very different picture of the event. Which
          source seems to you to be the more reliable? Give reasons for your
          answer.

14. Put the correct details (by letter) against these names.

1. GIACOMO MATTEOTTI.	A. Disliked by Albanians.
2. EMPEROR MENELIK.	B. King of Italy.
3. GABRIELLE d'ANNUNZIO	C. Italian Socialist.
4. PIERRE LAVAL	D. British Foreign Minister.
5. KING ZOG	E. Condemned Italy's attack on France.
6. VICTOR EMANUEL	F. Victor of Adowa.
7. ANTHONY EDEN	G. Colleague of Sir Samuel Hoare.
8. WINSTON CHURCHILL	H. Seized Fiume for Italy.

15. This cartoon was drawn by David Low in June, 1940.

ORDER OF THE DAY

DON'T STAB UNTIL THE VICTIM'S BACK IS TURNED

a) Why is Mussolini draped in a Roman toga?
b) Who is holding the revolver (*right*) which is forcing the soldiers on?
c) Which country are these soldiers marching to attack?
d) Why were the soldiers going to war at this time, and what is the significance of the 'Order of the Day'?

16. Trace the course of events which changed Mussolini's policy towards Germany from hostility to friendship. What was the long term result of this change in a) Italy and b) the outside world?

17. Imagine living in Italy after the First World War. Describe what life is like and why you feel Mussolini and his Fascists may be the answer to Italy's problems.

18. Explain the significance of the Lateran Treaties. Why did they make Mussolini popular with the Italian people?

17

Spain 1900-1939

INTRODUCTION

The Spanish civil war (1936-9) boiled up from old and bitter grievances. A poor, technologically backward nation, distracted by gross unfairness and inequality, was deeply divided. By the 1930's the usual struggle between conservatives and liberals, churchmen and progressives, common in many European countries, had been overtaken in Spain by far more dangerous divisions. Separatists, who wanted independence for their region, communists who wanted a workers' state, socialists who wanted a democratic, state-run democracy, found themselves in uneasy alliance with anarchists, who wanted to destroy all government. Landowners, industrialists, the property-owing middle class, Catholics and Falangists (Fascists), feared these extremists and reacted by supporting authoritarian regimes. It was a recipe for disaster, and disaster duly came with a war which devastated Spain and cost 600,000 lives.

The powerful anarchist movement was unique to Spain. It thrived in two environments. First, in the industrial area where workers were exploited and downtrodden. Second, in country districts afflicted with latifundia. This is the name given to agricultural regions consisting of large estates owned by a few rich families. Such inequality reduces peasants to the status of *braceros* - landless labourers employed fitfully by the week or even the day. The poverty and misery of these two groups gave Spanish anarchism a peculiar violence. Elsewhere anarchists sometimes adopted passive resistance and civil disobedience to authority. In Spain they went on strike, burnt churches, derailed trains, wrecked houses and murdered monks, priests and nuns, in their attempt to do away with the church, monarchy, army and government.

Such terrorism affected both friends and enemies. Communists and socialists were compelled to be more extreme in order to avoid losing recruits to the CNT, the anarchist trade union. Old-style progressives were so terrified of such revolutionary working class movements that they entered into an unofficial but very effective alliance with their political opponents. Two political parties, the Liberals and Conservatives, faked elections every two years so that one or the other was in power. In this desperate manner they hoped to stave off a communist or anarchist revolution.

When a moderate left-wing government was elected in 1936, its enemies saw the floodgates of revolution opening. Their reply was the traditional Spanish one, an attempted military takeover led this time by General Francisco Franco. Two factors turned what might have been a swift coup d'etat into a 3 year war. The hatred of the dispossessed masses was too deep and well organised to be overcome by a few divisions of the regular army. And the outside world, obsessed with the conflicting 'isms' of the Thirties, chose to see this Spanish quarrel in international terms, as just another Fascist or Nazi campaign against freedom. This it was not, but such an attitude led to foreign aid pouring into the country for both sides. Thus outside interference prolonged the conflict and made it in many ways a dress rehearsal for the Second World War.

This taking of sides by the outside world did not meet with Franco's approval, although he accepted the aid given by Fascist Italy and Nazi Germany. Anti-communists might rejoice that a 'Fascist' general was leading a rebellion against a lawful, but 'red' government. Franco, although he hated communism as the arch enemy of church and state, did not see the war in this light. He saw separatism as just as great a danger as any other 'ism' and was determined that no Catalan or Basque was going to destroy the unity of the Spanish state. He believed, probably rightly, that the Republic was the enemy of the Catholic church and its privileges, and these things he claimed to defend with all the enthusiasm of an old-time Crusader. But he used fascists only to win, and refused any effective help either to Hitler or Mussolini during the Second World War.

In the end massive German and Italian aid, plus the fighting ability of his own troops and the quarrels in the ranks of his enemies, gave Franco victory. But the problems of Spain had been crushed, not solved. Only after his death in 1975 did the Spanish start moving towards democracy and social justice.

SPANISH POVERTY

During the 19th century Spain was too poor to have an industrial revolution similar to that of Britain, France, Germany or the USA. Only two regions were developed, the iron foundries of *Bilbao* and the textile factories of *Barcelona*. Poverty was rife in the countryside, and in areas of *Latifundia* there were about 2,500,000 braceros. The bitter feelings aroused by these inequalities fanned the flames of *separatism*, particularly in *Catalonia* and the *Basque country*. Traditionalists who supported the Church, monarchy and army often combined with liberals who wanted a more democratic regime when faced by the revolutionary tactics - risings, violent strikes and murder - employed by their opponents, the communists, anarchists and socialists.

RIVERA'S DICTATORSHIP

Spain enjoyed a period of prosperity during the First World War when there was increased demand for her mineral products, particularly iron ore, by the belligerents (nations at war). She suffered afterwards, from the world economic depression. Spain at this time was ruled mainly by military-style governments, headed by a militarist king, *Alfonso XIII*. The occasional civilian government elected found it difficult to survive for long; between 1918 and 1923 Spain had 12 governments. In 1923 *General Miguel Primo de Rivera* became dictator, supported by the king, the army and the rich factory owners. He gave Spain firm government but no freedom, and fled abroad in 1930 after losing army and monarchial backing. In the general election which followed large votes were cast against the old regime. The king decided that if he stayed there might be civil war between his supporters and opponents. In 1931 he abdicated and left the country. A republic was proclaimed and a liberal and socialist ministry took over led by *Anzana, Quiroga* and *Barrio*. Against this government was arrayed an opposition consisting of monarchists, landowners and the *Falange*, a fascist party founded by Rivera's son.

Between 1931 and 1936 the Spanish experienced continual disorder because neither left nor right was prepared to let the other rule in peace. In 1933 a right-wing government was formed after an electoral victory. This result led to a *rising* by the communist miners of *Asturias*. This was put down by the *Spanish Foreign Legion*, ordered over from *Morocco* and led by its commander, *General Franco*. The miners were experts in dynamiting and they used this explosive against the shells and bullets of the troops. During the fierce fighting the town of *Oviedo* was devastated and thousands of people killed. The troops then engaged in an orgy of murder and looting as revenge for the brutality shown by the miners.

POPULAR FRONT

In the Thirties left-wing people often advocated what was called a *Popular Front* to fight Fascism. This took the form of a coalition of communist, socialist and liberal parties. A *Popular Front* government was elected in France in 1936 with *Leon Blum* as prime minister. The 1934 rising in Asturias and the brutality with which it was put down led to widespread revulsion against the right, and as a result a similar government was elected in Spain led by *Manual Anzana* as President and *Casares Quiroga* as prime minister. This government was attacked by both sides. The right-wing believed that Popular Front policies would threaten traditional Spanish values. Certainly most left-wingers wanted to ban church schools and limit the powers of both the army and the Church. At the same time, the Popular Front was not extreme enough for the anarchists and even some communists. The anarchists wanted an end to all government and their hatred of religion led them to burn down churches and kill monks, priests and nuns. The right-wing also engaged in murder and street violence and each blamed the other, claiming that they alone stood for law and order.

In July, 1936 *Calvo Sotelo*, a right-wing leader who had been a finance minister in Rivera's government, was murdered. This was used as an excuse for a *military rising* headed by *General Jose Sanjurjo* which began in *Morocco* and Spain on 18th July. Sanjurjo was killed in a plane crash soon afterwards and his place as taken by *Generals Emilio Mola* and *Franco;* Mola also died in a plane crash during the war. Franco was in semi-exile at the time on the *Canary Islands* as a result of anti-government activity. He managed to slip away in a British plane to the mainland, whilst his troops were ferried across the Mediterranean in German planes.

INTERNATIONAL BRIGADES

In the past such military takeovers had been swift and effective. This time, however, there was a fierce reaction from the workers of *Madrid* and *Barcelona*. The government armed them, and they destroyed the army rebels in fierce clashes. An international outcry at what seemed like another Fascist coup caused many volunteers to come to Spain to fight for the Republic against the *Nationalists* (Franco's men). These were organised as *International Brigades* and such brigades contained veterans of the First World War.

The Nationalist advance across Spain (See map) was stopped in the suburbs of *Madrid* by armed workers and the arrival of the first International Brigade units in November. The capital remained divided between the two sides until the end of the war. Franco was aided by Italian troops and German air squadrons, as well as massive material supplies from the axis powers. The Republic was promised aid by Russia and as a result sent its available *gold reserves* to Stalin. However, although the Russian leader posed as the defender of communism, his real attitude was far less straightforward. He did not want Franco to win, but he suspected that western capitalist countries would never tolerate a communist Spain. He also liked the thought of a long war which would tie down the forces of Germany and Italy and so prevent the Nazi attack on Russia which he always feared. Hitler looked on the war as a useful proving ground for new weapons and tactics and, whilst he helped Franco, he never stopped German firms from supplying the Republic if they wished. Mussolini was hoping that Italian troops would cover themselves with glory. None of the countries were there to help the Spanish in their struggle, a fact which Franco never forgot.

NON-INTERVENTION

Germany and Italy recognised the *Nationalists* as the government of Spain almost at once. *Britain* and *France* suggested a *non-intervention* policy for foreign nations, and set up a committee for this purpose. Germany and Italy joined this committee, but made its proceedings a farce by openly helping the Franco forces. France would have taken a more active line in helping the Republic; it had, after all, a Popular Front government similar to its own. Britain opposed French intervention, and this, plus fear of what Germany might do if France became too involved in Spain, held back the French government until late in the war.

When it became clear that supplies were pouring into Spain for Franco, Britain and France convened a *conference* at *Nyon* in France. This move was ignored by Italy and Germany. At Nyon it was proposed to set up naval patrols to stop foreign aid reaching either side. This was because 'unknown' submarines (actually Italian) were sinking merchant ships carrying supplies to the Republicans. *President Franklin Roosevelt* of the USA kept to the usual American policy of neutrality during foreign wars, a policy which meant no aid for either side and a ban on US citizens taking part in the fighting. This was broken by some Americans who fought in the *Abraham Lincoln* and *George Washington* International Brigades.

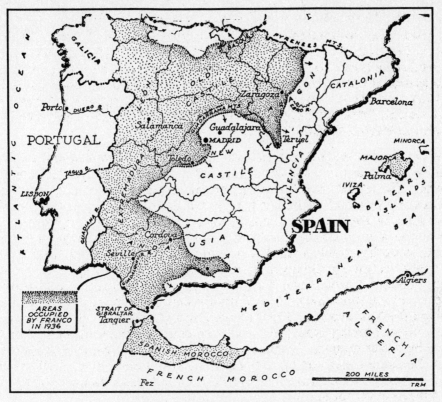

Spanish Civil War situation in 1936.

By the end of 1936 spain was divided roughly in half (See map). The *Nationalist* regime was based at *Burgos*; the increasingly left-wing *Republican* government had retired to *Valencia* where it was led by *Largo Caballero*, a socialist. First World War-style battle-lines extended across Spain and through *Madrid* and the war proceeded by stops and starts as one or the other side received fresh injections of men and materials. Both sides committed atrocities behind the lines and Franco's Spain became steadily more fascist and the Republic more communist. In Barcelona and elsewhere the communists set up prison and torture chambers reminiscent of Stalin's regime in Russia.

TERUEL, EBRO AND GUERNICA

The key moments for the Republic were, first, when the International Brigades arrived to help and, second, when in early 1938 France opened her frontiers to allow aid to reach its armies. Franco's war effort was started by the German and Italian troop planes which ferried his elite troops from Morocco. It received a massive increase of supplies to prevent a Nationalist collapse after the setback at Madrid in late 1936 and, finally, it was given the necessary equipment and supplies to finish the war after Franco had reluctantly granted 40% mineral rights to Germany. Some of the biggest battles of the war were fought at *Teruel* and on the river *Ebro*, where initial Republican successes were turned into defeats. The Basques were crushed ruthlessly and their town of *Guernica* heavily damaged by German bombers practising blitzkrieg tactics. During the final Nationalist offensives, *Barcelona*, stronghold of anarchism, was taken in January, 1939 and *Madrid* fell in March. Thousands of Republican soldiers fled across the border into France and safety at the end of the war. Many who did not escape were executed by the Nationalists in retaliation for the killings in the first weeks of the war. Reprisals went on throughout the Forties and Fifties and few trade unionist, communist, socialist or anarchist officials stood a chance of surviving if caught.

AFTERMATH

Spain was too weakened by the civil war to help Germany or Italy in the Second World War. The *Caudillo* (leader) met *Hitler* at *Hendaye* in 1940 after the fall of France. He refused to let German troops across Spain to attack *Gibraltar* and the Allied armies in North Africa. Hitler wisely refrained from invading Spain, whose mountainous terrain and barren plains had helped lead to Napoleon's downfall 150 years before. Franco did allow a *Blue Division* of Spanish 'volunteers' to fight with the Germans on the Russian front, a move which showed how he felt about communism in general and Russian aid to the Republic in particular. As the war turned against the Axis powers, Franco softened his approach to the Allies and his refusal to enter the war saved his regime. After the Second World War he was left to rule Spain, a fact which surprised and disappointed many of his old left-wing opponents in France and Britain.

After the Second World War, Franco presided over a slow economic recovery, helped by allowing US bases in Spain and by a growing tourist industry. He became increasingly authoritarian but curtailed the powers of the Falange, possibly because there were now no fascist countries in the outside world. Throughout his rule Spain was officially a monarchy but without a king; he arranged for *Juan Carlos* to be educated to take over as king after his death. When he died in 1975 Juan Carlos established a moderate democratic government which has survived sporadic military coups and separatist bomb attacks by Basques and Catalans.

ATTITUDES TO THE WAR

The Spanish civil war provided a focal point in the intellectual and political development of a whole western generation, rather as CND and the Green movement have done in more recent times. Most sided with the Republic and a few went and fought in the war, either with the International Brigades or as individuals. Most writers, intellectuals and poets favoured the Republic, although there were exceptions to this. There was almost universal condemnation of the actions of Britain and France, particularly as regards 'non-intervention' which was seen as a farce and also a key factor in the defeat of the Republic. The war provided the first opportunity to fight fascism militarily and the *Battle of Guadalajara*, where an Italian force was badly beaten, was the first fascist defeat. In Barcelona and elsewhere, as the communists tightened their grip, a Stalinist-style terror was established, something which the writer *George Orwell* saw and immortalised in *'Animal Farm'* and *'1984'*. This terror was later repeated on a large scale in eastern Europe after Stalin's victory in the Second World War.

Franco remained aloof from all this intellectual ferment. He had fought the war to preserve the Church and traditional values and to prevent separatists from breaking up Spain. His rule stifled freedom and intellectual development but it gave Spain what he regarded as far more important, firm law and order.

SELF-ASSESSMENT SECTION

1. Who wrote 'Animal Farm'?

2. What was the Falange?

3. Who was Calvo Sotelo?

4. What was the purpose of the Nyon conference?

5. Name one Nationalist general killed in an air crash.

6. Name the capital of Republican Spain during the civil war.

7. Who bombed Guernica?

8. What was the Blue Division?

9. Who won the Battle of Tereul?

10. Who commanded the Spanish Foreign Legion?

11. International Brigades went to Spain to fight:-

   a) for the Nationalists.
   b) for the Communists.
   c) for the Republic.
   d) for the Falange.
   e) to establish a workers' state.
   (TICK THE CORRECT ANSWER)

12. Non-intervention was meant:-

   a) to aid Franco
   b) to aid neither side.
   c) to prevent Germany and Italy helping France.
   d) to stop the war.
   e) to prevent a world war.
   (TICK THE CORRECT ANSWER)

13. Fill in the blanks in this passage from the selection of words below.

   "There could be no doubt which side Franco was on in divided Spain. His love of .... and unity made him hate the ...... with their dream of no government at all, and the .... who wished to divide Spain. The working class societies of the Socialists and Communists were equally disliked by Franco. In 1923 he was appointed commander of the .... In July, 1936 he led a rebellion against

151

the .... Spanish government and later became leader of ....
Spain. Helped by the .... and the Germans, he won the civil war
and ruled Spain until .... as ...."

1. Separatists	2. Caudillo	3. Nationalist
4. Spanish Foreign Legion		5. Republican
6. Italians	7. Anarchists	8. military disciplines
9. 1975.		

14. Read this source and then answer the questions.

"A. The plan was for all the workers in one factory to delegate
members to a 'syndicate', which would negotiate with other
syndicates the question of lodging, food and entertainment. B. The
second, rural group, notably in Andalusia... idealised their own town,
the *pueblo*, all of whose inhabitants would cooperate to form their
own self-sufficient government"

(Slightly adapted from 'The Spanish Civil War' copyright © 1961, 1965, 1977
by Hugh Thomas, reproduced by permission of Curtis Brown Ltd.)

a) What system is this source describing?
b) Name the city where the workers might have behaved in the manner
described in A.
c) What is the name given to the agricultural system in Andalusia? Why did
it cause bitterness and discontent?
d) In what ways would Franco have disagreed with these arrangements?

15. Read these Sources and then answer the questions.

A. "A country can live under a monarchy, or a republic, with a
parliamentary or presidential system, under communism or fascism.
But it cannot live under anarchy .... we are today present at the funeral
service of a democracy".

Gill Robles. Leader of the CEDA (Catholic political party).

B. "That ill-assorted, loose group of tribes known as the UGT[1], the
CNT[2], the FAI[3], the POUM[4], the PUSC[5]... The very aim of
these tribes was not, as might have been thought, to win the war
against the Rebels. For most of the time it was to achieve a proletarian
(workers) revolution, though not the same, for each tribe had a
revolution of its own to achieve".

Salvador de Madariaga, Spanish liberal writer.

---

[1] Socialist trade unions

[2] Anarchist trade unions

[3] Anarchist secret society

[4] Communist group against Russia

[5] Catalan Socialist-Communist party

C. "Why have the Republicans failed to stop the Nationalists? Is it because they have lacked enthusiasm? A thousand times no. ls it because they have lacked courage? I say ten thousand times no. There are three things they have lacked, three things which we *must* have - political unity, military leaders and discipline".

> Andre Marty, in charge of training the International Brigades.

a) Who are the 'Rebels' in B?
b) Which system was A. likely to have been against?
c) Why does the writer of B. use the word 'tribe'? Which side was he against?
d) In what year is A. likely to have been written?

1931   1934   1936   1939?

e) On what matter do all three Sources agree? How did this contribute to the defeat of the Republic?
f) In B., what was the main difference between the revolution desired by the CNT and the revolution desired by the other unions?
g) The writer of Source C. lists three essentials for a Republican victory. Which two can be said to have been achieved by the International Brigades, and which aim was *not* achieved?

16. In 1936 George Orwell , the British author, went to Spain to fight for the Republic. In his book about his experiences, 'Homage to Catalonia' (Martin, Secker and Warburg) he describes what he saw in Barcelona at the beginning of the civil war.

> "It was the first time that I had been in a town where the working class were in the saddle. Practically every building of any size had been seized by the workers and was draped with red flags or with the red and black flags of the Anarchists; every wall was scrawled with the hammer and sickle and with the initials of the revolutionary parties; almost every church had been gutted and its images burnt....... Every shop and cafe had an inscription saying it had been collectivised; even the boot blacks had their boxes painted red and black. Waiters and shopwalkers looked you in the face and treated you as an equal ...... Tipping was forbidden by law".
>
>   (Ack: The Estate of the late Sonia Brownell Orwell).

a) Whose badge is the hammer and sickle?
b) What is another word for 'collectivised'?
c) Which group was most likely to have destroyed the churches?
d) Indicate the parts of this Source which suggest that there might be trouble in the future.
e) Using this Source, and your previous knowledge of the subject describe life in Barcelona from 1936 until 1939.

18

The United States 1918-1939

INTRODUCTION

In certain ways Roosevelt's New Deal policies were a failure. He became President in 1933 at a time of national crisis. The USA stood on the brink of financial and economic ruin. Millions were unemployed, thousands evicted from their homes through inability to pay rent, and the land of opportunity had become the home of despair. Roosevelt's attempts to restore national confidence and get the country back to work did not proceed smoothly. Some New Deal measures were declared unconstitutional by the Supreme Court and had to be dropped. Others were rendered ineffective in parts of the USA by natural disaster, floods, droughts and dust storms. The rich and powerful condemned New Deal Plans as 'communist' and worked hard, not always unsuccessfully, to spoil them. Only another world war put the US people back to work and wiped away the effects of the Great Depression.

Why, in view of these facts, was the New Deal an historic turning point in American history? Basically because the US federal government took a grip on the lives of the average American as never before. The USA is a collection of highly individual states, originally independent of each other, who came together in a loose federation. An American looks to his state administration for the basic needs of civilised life, education, health, welfare, work, law and order. The federal government exists to deal with foreign governments, to make treaties, and, if necessary, fight wars. The New Deal introduced a huge amount of what its opponents condemned as 'government interference' into political and social life. An American historian, writing of the New Deal, had this to say, "The federal government was invading the daily lives and activities of business, farmers and labourers through collective bargaining guarantees, deduction of social security taxes for payrolls ... relief payments, home loans, bank deposit guarantees, the fixing of minimum wages and maximum hours..." It was not surprising that old-style Americans, brought up to believe that the 'land of the free' had been built by rugged individuals with spade, axe and rifle, talked of New Deal 'communism' and branded Roosevelt a 'dictator'. Certainly the New Deal made future presidents more powerful and the USA a more centralised country than it had been before.

Herbert Hoover, the President before Roosevelt, and FDR (Franklin Delano Roosevelt), as he was known, were not so different in their policies as some pro-New Dealers claim. A glance at the list of remedies suggested for the 1929-32 crisis by Hoover, and those actually put into practice by Roosevelt are not all that different in essence. Both proposed public building programmes for the unemployed, fixed farm prices, shorter working hours and guaranteed minimum wages. The real difference between the two men lay in their personalities. Hoover was an able administrator with little political experience. Roosevelt was a clever politician who 'sold' himself to the American people by every means of publicity at his disposal, including, particularly, the new medium of radio,. Because of his personal charm, Roosevelt restored the peoples' confidence. Hoover, whose presidency had co-incided with the Stock Market Crash of 1929 and the Great Depression which followed, could not restore confidence to a people who blamed him for what had happened. The evicted farmers who paraded through the street with banners declaring 'In Hoover we trusted, now we are busted', said it all. In modern terms, Hoover's image never recovered from the high hopes and prosperity at the start of his presidency and the catastrophies which followed.

American historians disagree as to whether Roosevelt was a revolutionary and his New Deal a revolution. It was certainly not a revolution in any sense understood by Europeans. At best, it seems to have been an acceleration of processes which would have come anyway. The basis of US capitalism, Big Business, far from being overthrown, was actually strengthened by federal contracts and legal support. Trade unions grew in numbers and power during the period 1933-9 but US trade unions still take no direct part in politics, as they do in many European countries. What the New Deal did was to shift the balance between federal and state power firmly in the direction of the former. To do this in a country the size of the USA, and with the individualistic attitudes of its people, was a mighty achievement which has affected US life to the present. The revolution, if there was one, was in the minds of the American people.

POST-WAR CONSTITUTIONAL AMENDMENTS

After the First World War the USA retreated into what Woodrow Wilson called 'sullen and selfish isolation'. She refused to sign the Versailles Treaty or join the League of Nations (See Work Unit 14). Consequently, it was 1921 before the USA formally ended hostilities with Germany. Two important constitutional amendments were passed during this post-war period, *Amendment 19* which gave *women the vote*, and *Amendment 18* which banned the manufacture, sale or consumption of alcohol *(Prohibition)* .(Prohibition was repealed by the 21st Amendment in 1933 after leading to a vast increase in organised crime because criminals ran an "underground" drinks industry.)

WASHINGTON NAVAL CONFERENCE

In 1921 a conference took place at *Washington* to deal with the situation caused by Japan's expansion in the Pacific area as a result of the First World War. The Versailles Treaty had given her all Germany's Pacific islands north of the equator, plus the German possession of *Kiaochow*.Her strong position in relation to China has already been dealt with in Work Unit 10. The USA was suspicious of all these Japanese moves which seemed to threaten her own Pacific interests. Various treaties were signed as a result of this conference. One regulated the commercial rights of the USA and most interested European states in *China*. Another, signed between the *USA, France, Britain, Italy* and *Japan*, 'froze' the naval strengths at 5-5-3 between Britain, the USA and Japan, and a 1.75 ratio for Italy and France. The Pacific 'frontier' between Japan and the USA was pushed back to *Pearl Harbour* in *Hawaii*, a move which left the US possessions of the *Phillipines* and the island of *Guam* defenceless. At the same time it was agreed that there could be unlimited production of ships under 10,000 tons, which included light cruisers, destroyers and submarines. The land forces of the countries involved were not affected by these arrangements. The *Anglo-Japanese* Treaty of 1902 was cancelled. The British were anxious to get rid of a commitment which might lead to friction with the USA, and which was disliked by *Australia, New Zealand* and *Canada*. In any case, Britain no longer needed it now the German naval threat had been removed. (See Work Unit 11).

JOHNSON ACT

Immigration into the USA, running at 1,000,000 a year before 1914, was restricted by *Warren Harding*, Wilson's successor as President. The *Emergency quota*, or *Johnson Act* reversed the USA's traditional policy regarding immigrants, cutting the number of people admitted from any one country in a year to 3% of that nationality living in the USA in 1910. Three years later this restriction was made permanent. The quota was reduced still further, to 2% of the nationality resident in the USA in 1890, whilst immigrants from Asia or Africa were either assigned very small quotas, or, as in the case of the Japanese, barred entirely. The racism behind these laws, and the insult to the Japanese after the goodwill fostered by the Washington Conference, meant that 85% of all immigrants were now from northern or western Europe. *Japan* reacted by calling a national day of mourning, and more extreme, anti-American politicians began to take control.

HARDING AND COOLIDGE

Harding's administration was corrupt, and there were sensational disclosures, notably the *Teapot Dome Scandal*, in which two of his ministers were found to have bought oil-fields reserved for the use of the US navy on Teapot Dome hill in *Wyoming*, and fake contracts negotiated by the head of the *Veterans* (ex-servicemen) Bureau, which cost the US taxpayer about 200 million dollars. Harding appears to have been innocent in these affairs. In 1923 he died suddenly and was succeeded by his vice-president, *Calvin Coolidge*, who won the Presidential election the following year.

Coolidge was intensely conservative. He believed in letting Big Business run its affairs with as little government interference as possible. In fact, he turned doing as little as possible into a principle and once said, "Four-fifths of all our troubles in this life would disappear if we would only sit down and keep still". His presidency was a period of prosperity but there were signs of future trouble. As a result of war loans to the Allies during the First World War, the USA had changed from a *creditor nation*, in which foreign investments in the USA exceeded American investments abroad, to a *debtor nation*, owed money by her ex-allies. This had the effect of reducing US trade, as her trading partners of pre-war days attempted to sell as much and buy as little as possible. The *US credit balance*, made up by US exports, particularly of *wheat* and *cotton*, dwindled, causing the price of these commodities to slump. This development served to further cripple *US agriculture*, which was already hit by *Prohibition*, which cut down the demand for wheat, changing eating habits which cut down the consumption of *meat* and *bread,* and the invention of *artificial fibres* for clothing manufacture which reduced cotton sales. This *agriculture slump* was the key to the disaster which followed. It reduced the purchasing power of a large part of the population\ which, in turn, cut down factory production, and the declining value of farms made credit difficult and threatened banks which had invested in farm mortgages.

THE WALL STREET CRASH

Coolidge decided not to stand for re-election, and was succeeded by *Herbert Hoover,* another Republican, in 1928. In his electioneering, Hoover promised further good times, with slogans like 'Two cars in every garage' and 'Two chickens in every pot'. Hoover believed in what Americans term, *rugged individualism*, the pioneering spirit which tamed the frontier and 'made America great'. To this way of thinking any but the most essential government regulation of private life or business is 'undemocratic' and even 'communist'. Hoover agreed that the federal government might need to control natural resources, flood barriers, which might involve rivers running through more than one state, and scientific research. But when American farmers asked him to use government money to buy their surplus food and sell it abroad, he replied that this was no part of the federal administration's job. His only concession to the farmers' plight was to approve the *Agricultural Market Act* 1929 which set up a *Federal Farm Board*, funded by the government, whose job was to loan farming cooperatives money to keep prices stable by buying and selling in the open market. This measure was both too little and too late.

The Twenties saw a fantastic rise in speculation on the US Stock Exchange *(Wall Street,* New York) in which both the rich and the not so rich bought and sold shares to cash in on US prosperity. Small investors often borrowed money to buy shares, promising to repay on demand but confident that they would never have to do so. Under the pressure of this buying spree, the face value of securities (shares) tripled between 1925 and 1929. The bubble burst when some investors realised that no profits could ever equal the prices being paid and began to sell. This soon became an avalanche of selling which caused the *Market Crash*. On 24th October

1929, called *'Black Thursday'*, millions of shares were sold; in three days 12 million shares changed hands and by mid-November investors had lost an amount equal to the cost of the US's participation in the First World War - 30 billion dollars. Thousands of small investors lost their savings, as people stopped buying products, thus leading to unemployment, which, in turn, led to less purchasing power.

THE GREAT DEPRESSION

The administration, true to its free market principles, had done nothing to restrict speculation on the Stock Exchange or regulate its dealings. When the crisis broke, however, Hoover realised the seriousness of the situation. He called an emergency meeting of leaders of industry, finance and labour at the *White House* (the Presidential residence in Washington) and called on trade unionists to abandon wage demands, industrialists to keep up employment and banks to continue lending. He realised that the real problem was a loss of confidence and so he began to issue a series of optimistic statements, one of which, 'prosperity is just around the corner' became a national joke as the Depression worsened. Unfortunately, Hoover, a Republican, had lost control of the House of Representatives to the Democrats in the 1930 mid-term elections. A hostile Congress forced him to sign the *Hawley-Smoot* bill which placed higher tariffs on almost all foreign imports. This backfired when 25 foreign nations replied by placing tariffs on US exports. Consequently, an act designed to promote business activity in the USA caused US trade to drop and created employment abroad.

HOOVER'S REMEDIES

Between 1929 and 1933 American farmers' incomes were halved. The *Farm Board* tried to maintain the price of wheat and cotton by buying surpluses off the market. Eventually, the immense quantities of these products held by the federal government caused prices to drop even further because buyers were afraid the government would sell as soon as there was a rise. In 1931 the board gave up and stopped buying surpluses. Apart from a loss of 200 million dollars, this action caused a further steep drop in prices; in 1932 farmers were receiving only 38 cents for wheat which had sold for over a dollar in 1929 and cotton suffered a similar drop. *Hoover* decided to pour federal money into road building, land reclamation and dam construction. He also founded the *Reconstruction Finance Corporation* (RFC) which lent banks and businesses money for new projects. However, because these projects were expected to make profits and eventually pay their way, the RFC favoured toll-bridges and dams producing electric power rather than non-profit making projects such as schools, playgrounds and townhalls.

When Congress passed a bill to pay relief to the unemployed, Hoover vetoed it on the grounds that such aid would 'undermine self-respect'. He preferred that private charities should provide such relief. By this time there were bread queues and soup kitchens in most major cities, and the cardboard and wooden shacks in which the homeless lived were nicknamed 'hoovervilles'. A young singer called *Bing Crosby* made a hit with a ballad which became the theme tune of the

Depression, 'Buddy, can you spare a dime?'. In May, 1932 columns of ex-servicemen marched on Washington to demand immediate payment of army bonuses not due until 1944. The nation was horrified when these ex-soldiers were dispersed by armed troops with tear gas. In that year the USA had 12 million people out of work.

NEW DEAL

In the 1932 Presidential election *Franklin D. Roosevelt* stood against Hoover. Roosevelt, a Democrat, ran a whirlwind campaign and in one of his many speeches promised *'a new deal for the American people'*. When he won the election his policies to combat the Depression became known as the *New Deal*, In those days a US President was elected in November but did not take office until the following March (it is now January). During this three-month period of 'non-government' the situation worsened. The US economy came to a standstill and the banking system nearly collapsed under the strain of unpaid debts. On *Roosevelt's Inauguration Day* in 1933, he warned the people of the gravity of the crisis but told them 'all they had to fear was fear itself'. Millions heard this speech on the radio, a medium Roosevelt used to great effect with his periodical *Fireside Chats*.

F.D. ROOSEVELT

Roosevelt had been born into a wealthy family and was distantly related to a previous president, *Theodore Roosevelt* (See Work Unit 3). He had served Woodrow Wilson as Assistant Secretary of the Navy during the First World War and, despite being partially crippled by infantile paralysis in 1921, survived to win the Governorship of New York in 1928. This was the key post from which to launch a successful bid for the Presidency. Roosevelt was a good communicator - he virtually invented the press conference - and an astute politician who knew how to manipulate the powerful groups who ran the Democratic party at that time. Unlike Hoover, he was not tied down by rigid principles. He was prepared to use the full resources of the federal government in a way which Hoover was not. For this reason Roosevelt's policies were sometimes attacked as a threat to individual freedom and as 'creeping socialism'.

Roosevelt began with a *Hundred Days (4 March-16 June 1933)* of emergency action during which Congress gave him free hand to pass any laws he wished. On 4th March Roosevelt declared a public holiday which shut the banks. Five days later the *Emergency Banking Act* was passed which forced weak banks out of business but gave federal help to strong ones. Then, in one of his Fireside Chats, Roosevelt explained that no bank could stay solvent if everybody withdrew their money at the same time. This restored the public's confidence and US banks were able to open again for normal trading. The other acts passed by Roosevelt's administration over the years until 1939 are usually known by their initials; they were, as one wit remarked, *'Roosevelt's Alphabet Soup'*.

NATIONAL RECOVERY ACT

The *National Recovery Act* (NRA) was the keystone of Roosevelt's New Deal. It proposed that businessmen, trade unionists and government join together to tackle the emergency. The NRA required representatives of both management and workers to draw up *codes of fair competition* which would help avoid over-production and share profits out more fairly. Employers were encouraged to limit working hours and so spread employment amongst more workers. They were also asked to set a minimum wage and offer fair prices. Industrialists and shopkeepers who signed such *code agreements* displayed a *blue eagle* badge with the motto. *'We do our part'*. Over 600 such codes were soon signed and operating, and nationwide production rose temporarily by 93%. But prices increased more rapidly than wages and some employers, notably *Henry Ford*, the car magnate, refused to operate the scheme at all because, amongst other things, it gave the workers bargaining rights with their employers. Trade unions soon clashed with employers on this issue and there were several strikes in which men were killed. In 1935 the NRA was declared unconstitutional by the Supreme Court on the grounds that Congress could not delegate its law-making powers to the President and the various code authorities.

AGRICULTURAL ADJUSTMENT ACT

The *Agricultural Adjustment Act* (AAA) aimed to give farmers the purchasing power they had enjoyed in the prosperous years, 1909-14. Farmers were paid cash bonuses to reduce their production of basic crops. During 1933, for example, cotton farmers ploughed under a quarter of their acreage, whilst pig producers killed 6 million pigs instead of fattening them up for market. This helped reduce *over-production*, a major cause of the Depression in the first place. During the next two years farm surpluses fell by half, although some experts think that the widespread *drought* was partly responsible for the drop. The drought struck the *Great Plains region* where unsuitable land had been used for crop growing during the boom years of the First World War. This had broken up the tough topsoil, which was carried away by *dust storms*. This created arid deserts, and between 1934 and 1939 350,000 farmers and their families were forced to leave these *Dust Bowls*. The government's reply was to pay the farmers to plant millions of trees to stop the erosion and to return the area to its original use, cattle-grazing.

C.C.C. AND P.W.A.

A *Civilian Conservation Corps* (CCC) was formed under New Deal legislation. It enlisted the 18 to 25 year-olds in outdoor work such as cleaning beaches, building reservoirs and planting trees. The *Public Works Administration* (PWA) gave similar employment to the unemployed who were put to work on dam building, sewer system renovation, waterworks and ship-building. The PWA worked through private contractors, rather than hiring men directly. A crucial factor in the misery caused by the Depression was the eviction of families who could not keep up their mortgage payments. One remedy was a *Home Owners' Loan Corporation* which was set up to re-finance small mortgages at lower rates of interest. A *Federal Housing Agency* gave a boost to the building industry by providing bank loans to pay for new house - building and house repairs.

TENNESSEE VALLEY AUTHORITY

The most permanent of the New Deal schemes was the *Tennessee Valley Authority* (TVA). The TVA aimed to revitalise the huge area drained by the *Tennessee* and *Cumberland* rivers. Employing as many as 40,000 men at a time, it built or improved 25 large dams, reforested millions of acres, established power plants, fertilizer factories and new towns. The Tennessee river was transformed into an inland waterway, 600 miles long, carrying heavy freight on barges. New man-made lakes provided recreational areas, whilst an immense amount of cheap electricity was generated. This attracted heavy industry as well as providing housewives with washing machines and electric stoves. The TVA was heavily criticised as a 'communist' measure which benefitted one part of the country at the expense of the remainder, and cut across the traditional rights of the states through which its authority ran. The opposition was so well organised and powerful that no other similar scheme was ever attempted. However, one other power plant, the *Grand Coulee Dam* on the *Columbia river* was built and remains the largest man-made construction apart from the Great Wall of China.

RESULTS

The New Deal caused organised and mounting criticism. Prominent businessmen formed an *American Liberty League* to 'defend the Constitution' and restore respect for private property. *Hoover* joined this League, and wrote a book, *'The Challenge to Liberty'* attacking the expansion of federal power over individual lives. Roosevelt was accused of being both a fascist and a communist. He replied by direct appeals to the people which led him to win more elections than any other US President (four - 1932, 1936, 1940 and 1944).

The New Deal did not end the Depression which continued until defence contracts resulting from the Second World War revived the economy. Its effects were patchy and some groups unable to exert effective political pressure, particularly the poor white farmers of the South and the negroes, did not benefit. In 1935 Roosevelt tried a *Social Security Act* to help the unemployed, the sick and the old. It was based on European examples, and worked through a payroll tax paid by employers. At first it was meagre, insufficient and in some ways unworkable, but it was improved as the years went by. Later New Deal measures also extended the government's control of banking, and increased taxes on the wealthy. The *Wagner Act* of 1935 set up a *Labour Relations Board* which had the power to hold secret elections in a factory to find out whether the workers wished to join a union or not, and to stop employers engaging in anti-union activity, This act stimulated trade union development and the *American Federation of Labour*, headed by the powerful *John L. Lewis*, managed to do deals with leaders of the steel industry and to defeat, after a long battle, the bosses of the motor industry.

SUPREME COURT DEFEAT

The New Deal increased the power of the President and the federal government but private enterprise remained dominant and even more secure as a result of some of its enactments. When the NRA and the AAA were declared unconstitutional by the Supreme court, Roosevelt tried to increase the number of judges from 9 to 15 in order to bring in lawyers who agreed with his policies. This attempt to 'pack' the highest court in the land was condemned by both Republicans and Democrats in Congress and it failed. Just before the Second World War broke out in Europe (1939) another recession wiped away some of the ground gained in the years since 1933.

SELF-ASSESSMENT SECTION

1. To which previous US president was Franklin Roosevelt related?

2. What cabinet post did Roosevelt hold during the First World War?

3. What disease partially paralysed Roosevelt?

4. Who sang, 'Buddy, can you spare a dime?'

5. Who took over Germany's Pacific possessions after the First World War?

6. What became available cheaply as a result of the TVA?

7. What was Prohibition?

8. What was the American Liberty League?

9. Who promised 'Two cars in every garage?

10. How many Presidential elections did Franklin Roosevelt win?

11. Herbert Hoover was against dole payments to the unemployed because:-

    a)   It discouraged people from working.
    b)   It was not necessary.
    c)   It undermined personal self-respect.
    d)   It was proposed by Congress.
    e)   It was suggested by Roosevelt.
         (TICK THE CORRECT ANSWER)

12. Write short paragraphs on *four* of the following:-

    a)   Teapot Dome Scandal
    b)   Johnson Act
    c)   Hawley-Smoot Act
    d)   Hoovervilles
    e)   Alphabet Soup
    f)   Fireside Chats
    g)   Blue Eagle badge

13. Explain these terms.

   a)   rugged individualism
   b)   Constitutional amendment
   c)   debtor nation
   d)   Black Thursday
   e)   pioneer spirit

14. Put the correct description (by letter) to these initials.

   1. A.A.A.   A. harnessed water power from two rivers
   2. N.R.A.   B. gave outdoor work to young unemployed
   3. T.V.A.   C. paid farmers to limit production
   4. R.F.C.   D. organised public work programmes
   5. C.C.C.   E. a code of practice for employers and workers
   6. P.W.A.   F. lent banks and businesses money for new projects.

15.

(Source: cartoon in 'Washington Post'.)

   a)   What is the subject of this cartoon?
   b)   Who is the figure in the left foreground?
   c)   What do we call these men? What position do they hold in the USA?
   d)   Why do all men at the back look the same as the left foreground figure?
   e)   What do you think the cartoonist's opinion was about this matter?
   f)   What was the end result of the subject of this cartoon?

16. The chart on the following page shows prices US farmers received for their products and the price they had to pay for goods during this period. Listed underneath are the causes of the fluctuations, designated by letter. Put each letter in its correct place on the chart.

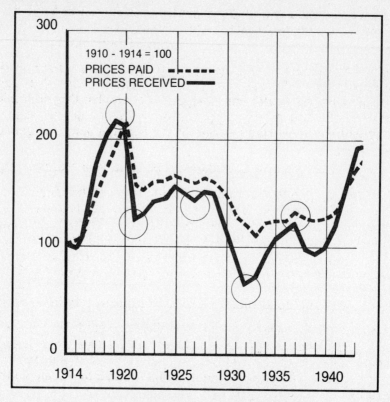

1910 - 1914 = 100
PRICES PAID ------
PRICES RECEIVED ━━━

(Source : adapted from 'History of a Free People'
by Bragdon and McCutchen, the Macmillan Company, 1954, p.626.)

A. FIRST WORLD WAR PROSPERITY
B. CRASH
C. POSTWAR DEPRESSION
D. FAILURE TO SHARE IN BUSINESS PROSPERITY
E. RECESSION
F. IMPROVEMENT DUE TO A.A.A. MEASURES

17. Read these documents and then answer the questions.

A. "National Regimentation *(under the New Deal)* ... is a vast shift from the American concept of human rights which even the government may not infringe, to those social philosophies where men are wholly subjective to the state. It is a vast casualty to Liberty if it shall continue."

Herbert Hoover. 'The Challenge to Liberty' Scribner, 1934.

B. "Democracy has disappeared in several other great nations, not because the people of these nations disliked democracy, but because they had grown tired of unemployment and insecurity, of seeing their children hungry while they sat helpless in the face of government confusion and government weakness through lack of leadership

....Finally, in desperation, they chose to sacrifice liberty in the hope of getting something to eat".

Franklin Roosevelt, Fireside chat, 1938

C. "*(The New Deal)* ... was the acceptance of the principle of the responsibility of the state for the welfare and security of its people - for employment, health and general welfare. That this principle was aggressively and bitterly opposed now seems hard to believe; its establishment must stand as one of the cardinal achievements of the New Deal.

Henry Steele Commager. 'The American Mercury' April, 1945.

D. "Hoover, an engineer born in Iowa, represented the moral traditions of native Protestant politics. An amateur in politics who had never run for office before he was elected President in 1928, he had no patience with the politician's willingness to accommodate *(compromise)*, and he hung on, as inflexibly as the situation would permit, to the private and voluntary methods which had always worked well in his administrative career".

Richard Hofstadter. 'The Age of Reform' Alfred. A. Knopf., 1955

E. "Franklin D. Roosevelt and the New Deal restored the confidence of the typical American in himself and in his country's destiny. This was achievement, even if many of the programmes failed or fell short of their purpose and even if the end-results seemed to threaten unknown perils".

Louis B. Hacker. 'The Shaping of the American Tradition'. Columbia University Press, 1947.

a) Which of these Sources is against the New Deal?
b) Which other Source mentions the characteristics shown in A.?
c) Which Source describes the great danger if the Depression continued?
d) What US historical document enshrines the 'concept of human rights' mentioned in A?
e) What 'social philosophy' had the writer of A. in mind? Why was he against it?
f) Name one great nation which had succumbed to the danger mentioned in B. at that time?
g) In what ways did Roosevelt's and Hoover's ideas of Liberty differ?
h) How would the writer of A. have defined the 'unknown perils' mentioned in E.
i) From these Sources, write two paragraphs assessing the New Deal's strengths and weaknesses.

18. Imagine you are a farmer living in an area affected by the TVA. Describe its effects on yourself and your family.

19

The Rise of Hitler
1918-1933

INTRODUCTION

Few questions loom so large in modern history as, "Why did the Nazis gain control of Germany?'. How was it possible for a bunch of gangsters to seize power in one of the most civilised European countries? Many answers have been given to this question, all of them containing elements of the truth. Some historians maintain that it was defeat in the First World War and the Versailles Diktat which turned the Germans towards dictatorship. Hitler, after all, denied that there had been a genuine military defeat and promised to defy the terms of the Treaty if he came to power.

Other experts think that it was Hitler's appeal to force to settle political arguments which gained him the support of a warrior nation. One German writer of the time exclaimed, 'The German people have always tended to worship force; they are always impressed by the cavalryman's boot and fist banged upon the table'. Whether this was true or not, dislike of rule by consent was common amongst Germans, particularly the Junker class (noblemen) who ran the army. In 1932 over half of the Germany electorate voted either for the communists or the nazis, both of whom were undemocratic. Furthermore, it was representatives of the Germany army - half of whose generals in 1925 were Junkers - who invited Hitler to be Chancellor in 1933.

It is often said that Hitler appealed to the worst in human nature and this refers, above all, to his hatred of Jews. Hitler did not invent anti-semitism; it had been a widespread European evil for centuries. But he used his own genuine hatred of Jews to gain him mass support, claiming not only that there was a world-wide Jewish conspiracy against non-Jews but, more specifically, that it was Jewish leaders who had 'stabbed the Germany army' in the back in 1918. Thus the Jews provided the scapegoat essential to explain away Germany's troubles.

Hitler 's other useful 'hate' was communism. Fear of a workers' revolution, with wholesale seizure of private property, was strong in Germany, which had experienced an attempted communist takeover in Berlin in 1919. By 1932 the

166

German communists were the largest single party outside Russia. Hitler stood four-square against communism; his first paid job after the war had been as an agitator, employed to turn soldiers against pacifist, democratic and socialist ideas. The National Socialists (nazis) were socialist only in name. As far as Hitler was concerned, the word was put in to catch a few left-wing votes.

The Great Depression is a factor in the nazi success story. Poverty and unemployment, plus the effects of runaway inflation, gave the nazis large electoral votes at key moments in their rise to power, particularly in 1932 when they emerged as the largest single party in the Reichstag. Young, unemployed men were eager recruits to the ranks of the nazi stormtroopers where they were given a square meal, a uniform and the chance of a street fight. More law-abiding people were impressed by the nazi promise to get Germany back to work. One typical nazi propaganda poster showed a sturdy German labourer rolling up his sleeves against a background of smoking factory chimneys, above the slogan, 'To Work. The Future is Ours'. This was a promise Hitler kept with his re-armament programme.

Psychologists provide another answer to our question. Nazism was an evil creed but it was a creed nonetheless. It seemed to offer hope to the hopeless. It told a defeated people that they were, in fact, the master race. Many nazi supporters experienced a feeling of 'togetherness' at Party rallies with their songs, speeches, slogans, uniforms, badges and flags. They were given also, as with many creeds, a messiah or saviour, in this case, Adolf Hitler. Thus it may not have been the distinctive Germany character, but deep feelings of insecurity common to all humans, which gave Hitler power. All that was needed were certain economic, social and historical circumstances, and these were supplied by the Germany of 1918-33.

Finally, the personality and political skill of Hitler should not be underestimated. The Fuhrer (leader) played an evil game but he played it superbly, controlling first his party and then Germany with ruthless skill. Hitler portrayed himself as an honest, ordinary man, horrified at his country's defeat and angry at its betrayal. He revelled in his extremism, claiming that only extreme measures could solve such a serious crisis. Indeed, his ideas were so extreme that few of the ruling elites took him seriously. This was true in particular, of the German general staff, who only realised the full extent of his plans of conquest when it was too late. His opponents often dismissed him as a mad clown, talking nonsense in incomprehensible speeches. After the worst war in history and the holocaust, the world realised that the nazi leader had meant what he said.

KAPP AND THE SPARTAKISTS

The new *German Republic* which succeeded the Kaiser's Reich, was based at *Weimar* because of unrest and rioting in Berlin. It is usually known as the *Weimar Republic*. It won an election in January, 1919 but was threatened by violent extremists of both left and right. Two weeks before election day there was a rising of *Spartakists*, revolutionary socialists who took their name from Spartacus, leader of a slave revolt against Rome. The Spartakists, led by *Karl Liebknecht* and *Rosa Luxembourg*, denounced the alliance between *Frederick Ebert*, socialist head of

Karl Liebknecht
Rosa Luxembourg

SOCIALIST

Not much support in Reichstag

the Weimar Government, and reactionary right-wingers like Field-Marshal *Erich von Ludendorf*, commander of the German army during the war. They demanded the nationalisation of heavy industry. After a week of street fighting, the Spartakists were crushed by soldiers of the old imperial army, enrolled as irregulars called *Freecorps*. Both Liebknecht and Luxembourg were captured and shot. Those Spartakists who survived went on to form the German communist party.

Three months later a similar rising in *Munich* was led by a group of poets and intellectuals who formed a *Soviet* on the Bolshevik model. This rebellion was put down by Freecorps units, aided by peasant rifle clubs. The threat from the right camp came in 1920 when Freecorps units occupied Berlin and set up a regime dedicated to the suppression of democracy in general and free trade unions in particular. They also favoured resistance to the Versailles Treaty. The rebels were led by *Dr. Wolfgang Kapp*. The Republican government called a general strike against this *putsch* (armed seizure of power) but its fate was sealed when it failed to get the support of the army. The rebellion collapsed and Kapp fled to Sweden.

THE WEIMAR CONSTITUTION

Reaction to the Versailles terms (See Work Unit 14) inside Germany was violent, particularly to the *'War Guilt'* clause. The settlement was denounced by Germans of all shades of political opinion and there was even wild talk of starting the war again. Few Germans stopped to think of the sort of treaty they had imposed upon Russia at *Brest-Litovsk* a year before (See Work Unit 13). Dislike of the Treaty remained a vital factor in Germany politics throughout this period, and led to electoral support for any party which condemned it.

In 1919 a new Constitution was formulated for Germany, the first truly democratic one in her history. Under its terms, the central government dealt with foreign affairs, defence, finance and economic planning. The provincial governments organised by Bismarck at the time of unification remained intact. Each separate province *(Lander)* was in charge of its own education, health and justice, and these provinces corresponded with the old historic divisions of Germany. A head of state, the *President*, was elected directly by the voters. The President was given emergency powers to rule by decree if necessary. The *Reichstag* (German Parliament) was in charge of law-making but it was more democratically elected than in pre-war days. All citizens over 20 had the vote, and seats were allocated under a system of proportional representation. This method makes it difficult for any single party to secure a working majority and lends itself to *coalition* government, in which one or two parties of the larger parties form an alliance.

The Weimar Constitution was never popular with the German people. Some felt that it was an arrangement virtually forced upon them by the Allies who were determined there should be a more democratic system in Germany. Moderate parties, like the *Social Democrats, Catholic Centre, Democrats* and *People's Party*, found themselves sandwiched between an extreme right consisting of the *Nazi* and *Nationalist* parties and an extreme left consisting of communist and socialist groups. A sizeable proportion of the electorate did not agree with democracy in any form and this proved a handicap to the republic during its short existence.

REPARATIONS AND INFLATION

The Weimar Republic inherited an inflationary situation caused by Germany's war effort having been financed by loans rather than taxation. This colossal debt stood at 156 milliard marks in March, 1919. It was also faced with the problems of *Reparations* (See Work Unit 14) which were finally fixed at £6,600,000,000 in 1921. Germany maintained she could not afford these penalties. The French, in particular, were determined to get some compensation for the damage caused by German armies during the war. When the Germans fell behind with deliveries of coal and timber French troops marched into the *Ruhr* industrial area of Germany in 1923. This led to chaos and economic stagnation, as German workers went on strike and used other form of passive resistance against the invader. Key German industries came to a standstill and the result was runaway *inflation*; the mark dropped from 500 to the £ in 1922 to 25 million to the £ in August, 1923. The Reichsbank was forced to work 300 paper mills and 2,000 printing works on 24 hour shifts to keep Germany supplied with such worthless paper.

[handwritten: PASSIVE RESISTANCE]

THE MUNICH PUTSCH *[handwritten: - Nov 1923]*

By this time violence and disorder was escalating and political murders became common. Two leading politicians, *Matthias Erzberger*, and Foreign Minister, *Emile Rathenau*, were assassinated; Erzberger had signed the Versailles treaty and Rathenau had stated publicly that Germany should pay reparations. Altogether, a total of 376 murders were committed between 1918-1922, 22 by the left and 354 by the right. In November, 1923, Adolf Hitler, assisted by Bavarians who wanted their royal dynasty back, as well as nazis, staged a *putsch* in *Munich*. Hitler's aim was to start what he called 'a national revolution', overthrow the Weimar Republic and execute the *November criminals* i.e. those politicians who had set up the new government at the end of the war in November, 1918. He hoped to persuade the Bavarian authorities to assist him in a *March on Berlin* similar to Mussolini's March on Rome the previous year (See Work Unit 16).

After formally proclaiming the revolution on a table in a *beer-hall*, Hitler and his men set out to march through Munich the following day. *Gustav Stresemann* was now Chancellor. He invoked emergency powers under the constitution and ordered the local army chief to crush the revolt. This the general promised to do, thus dooming the putsch. The nazis, including *Herman Goering*, an ex-fighter ace, and *Field Marshal Ludendorf*, were fired at by armed police when they refused to stop. Sixteen nazis were killed. Goering was badly wounded but managed to escape from the country. Ludendorf and Hitler were put on trial on charges of high treason.

The judges were anti-Weimar. They proved sympathetic to the conspirators' aims if not their methods, and allowed Hitler in particular, to make long political speeches. This helped make him become a national, as opposed to a local, leader. Hitler was sentenced to 5 years in jail but he served only 9 months. He spent the

[handwritten: Good advertisement for Hitler]

time quite comfortably with his friend, *Rudolf Hess*, writing a book which later became the nazi 'Bible' - *Mein Kampf* (My Struggle). This autobiography by Hitler was strongly propagandist and explained Hitler's future plan for conquering *'lebensraum'* (living space) in eastern Europe at the expense of Russia.

DAWES PLAN

Stresemann tackled inflation by stabilising the currency with a new *Rentenmark*; each mark was worth one trillion of the old. This currency was guaranteed by the value of the country's land and so people with property were safe. Thousands of middle and upper class Germans had seen their savings disappear, and the trauma of this experience helped to de-stabilise Germany politically. Stresemann also negotiated a compromise agreement with the Allies over reparation. Under the *Dawes Plan*, named after the chairman of one of the committees, they were to be paid on a graduated scale beginning at £5 million the first year and rising to 127 million in the fifth. The Dawes Plan, like everything else to do with the reparations, was unpopular in Germany, although it helped lead to an economic boom which she enjoyed through the Twenties. Protest votes against it benefitted the nazis who won 32 seats in the Reichstag.

LOCARNO PACT ~ 1925

Stresemann worked hard to give Germany military security and to end the state of semi-warfare between Germany and France following the march into the Ruhr. This was urgent, in his opinion, because, whilst Germany was disarmed, *France* was forging military links with countries around Germany in what became known as the *Little Entente*. In negotiations with *Aristotle Briand* of France and *Austin Chamberlain* of Britain, Stresemann hammered out a far-reaching agreement, the *Locarno Pact*, 1925. Under its terms Britain guaranteed Germany's frontiers with France and Belgium on condition that Germany did not try to change her eastern boundaries by force. In effect, Germany was promised that there would not be another Ruhr-type takeover of her territory by the French, providing she did not try to alter the position of *Danzig* and the *Polish corridor* militarily. All the signatories to Locarno pledged themselves to seek only peaceful solutions to their problems. Both Britain and Italy promised to assist either Germany or France if they were attacked by the other.

As a result of this agreement Allied troops began to withdraw from German territory, in which they had been stationed since 1918. It seemed the dawn of a new era in European history but behind the scenes the small German army allowed by Versailles was being trained as an elite force. Secret German army research into weapons systems was carried out in Sweden, Holland and Switzerland. Another sign that things were not as peaceful as they seemed was the election of *Field Marshal Paul Hindenburg*, victor of Tannanburg in the First World War, as President. Although the old soldier behaved strictly within the Weimar Constitution, his election was hardly a sign that the Germans had forgotten their military past.

Young Plan - '29

When Stresemann died in 1929 his achievements seemed considerable. He had saved the country from inflation and established her as an equal partner with other European countries and a member of the League of Nations. But a great deal of Germany's prosperity was based on loans raised in the USA. In the month he died the Great Depression began.

1926
L of N

ADOLF HITLER

Adolf Hitler was born in April, 1889 at *Braunau*, a small village in what was then the Austro-Hungarian empire. He led a poverty-stricken life before the First World War, mostly in Vienna where he was an unsuccessful artist. He served in the German, not Austrian army during the war, fighting on the Western Front where he won the *Iron Cross*, first class - a rare honour for a corporal. After the war he became a paid agitator in Munich, hired to turn soldiers against pacifist, democratic and socialist ideas. His speech-making excited both admiration and mockery. People were either spellbound by it or regarded it as the ravings of a madman. In 1920 he became leader of the *National Socialist Workers' Party* (nazi), which had the swastika as its badge. The nazis stood for *ultra-nationalism*. This meant the uniting of all German peoples, wherever they might live, in a *Greater Germany*, and the expulsion of all 'alien' elements from the country. The nazis attracted support from the classes who had been ruined by inflation or hated the Versailles Diktat.

After the failure of the *Beerhall Putsch*, Hitler never again tried to seize power illegally. He realised that in Germany the support of the old ruling classes, the army, industry and landowners, was essential for political success. During the boom years of the Twenties progress was slow. The country was contented and the nazi share of votes at elections increased only slowly. Hitler spent the time organising his party. He defeated the attempts of one of his lieutenants, *Gregor Strasser*, to make the party truly socialist and he enlisted the services of a clever, unscrupulous journalist, *Josef Goebbels*, as publicity chief. A *Hitler Youth* Movement was established, run by *Baldur von Shirach*, and a rival to free trade unions, the so-called *German Labour Front*, was set up, headed by *Robert Ley*. These, and the various Stormtrooper groups, were controlled from Hitler's headquarters, *Brown House* in Munich.

In the 1928 Reichstag elections 12 nazi deputies, including *Goering* and *Goebbels*, were returned with a total vote of 800,000. This compared unfavourably with the 9 million vote cast for the moderate *Social Democrats* and the 4 million for the right-wing *Nationalists*. Soon afterwards, Hitler formed an alliance with the Nationalists who were led by newspaper-owner, *Alfred Hugenberg*. Both Hitler and Hugenberg were objecting to the *Young Plan* which aimed to spread reparation payments over 59 years. Hitler found that this connection gave him the support of some of the most powerful industrialists in the country, including steel magnate, *Fritz von Thyssen*, who saw the advantages to him of Hitler's plan for rearmament, The nazis now had the organisation and the finance to become a national party.

THE GREAT DEPRESSION

The *US Stock Market Crash* (See Work Unit 18) hit Germany hard; unemployment rose from 1,300,000 in 1929 to 6,000,000 in 1933. This was because the German economy was dependant upon US loans which were not renewed. In 1930 the German government decided to cut expenditure on social services to save money. Arguments about this produced a split inside the leading party, the *Social Democrats*. When the Reichstag refused to pass the so-called *'economy law'* the new Chancellor, *Heinrich Bruening*, persuaded Hindenberg to use the emergency powers allowed him under the constitution. Unemployment pay and pensions were then cut by the signature of one man. This was a blow from which Weimar democracy did not recover.

As unemployment rose, violence increased on the streets. The nazis had a 'Gymnastic and Sports Division' i.e. Stormtroopers, who were trained and willing for such fighting. The nationalists had the *Stah-helm* (steel-helmet) groups and against them were the *Red Fighters* of the communists. These battles developed from fists and boots to rifles and machine guns. During one street battle, *Horst Wessel*, a nazi composer who had written their official anthem, was killed. He was turned into a martyr in later years by clever propaganda, and the *Horst Wessel* song was a feature of party rallies and other Hitler occasions.

During 1930 the nazi share of seats in the Reichstag increased to 107. Provincial elections showed a similar trend, and in one in *Brunswick*, the nazis formed the government. This was important because this administration granted Hitler German citizenship, thus enabling him to stand for elections for the first time. In 1932 Hitler challenged Hindenburg for the Presidency, polling 13 million votes against the Field-Marshal's 19 million. The deadlock in the Reichstag caused Hindenburg to dismiss Bruening, replacing him by *Franz von Papen*. Papen favoured excluding the Social Democrats and admitting the Nationalists, in other words, a swing to the right. His Minister of Defence, *General von Schleicher*, disagreed. He wanted Hitler as a minister in the cabinet so that he could be 'tamed'. Schleicher began behind-the-scenes negotiations with *Ernest Roehm*, leader of the Brownshirts, but Hitler refused to enter the government except on his own terms.

HITLER BECOMES CHANCELLOR

In July, 1932 *Papan* dissolved the Reichstag and called a general election. The Hitler election campaign, master-minded by Goebbels, consisted of huge rallies all over the country, addressed by Hitler who travelled from one to the other by aeroplane. This *Hitler over Germany* campaign involved the dramatic night arrival of Hitler's plane over the waiting crowds, caught in the glare of the searchlight. His speeches were frenzied and were designed to work his audiences into a rage. He hammered home the familiar themes, the 'stab in the back' of 1918, the Versailles 'diktat', the inflation and unemployment caused, so he claimed, by weak government. It represented a tremendous effort and gave the nazis 230 seats in the Reichstag. This made them the largest single political party represented in parliament.

Papen offered Hitler the Vice-Chancellorship but he refused. Papen then asked Hindenburg to declare a state of emergency so that the President could rule by decree. Finally, even as fresh elections revealed a 2 million drop on Nazi votes, Schleicher, Hitler and Papen did a deal. Hitler, together with his Nationalist allies, was admitted to the government. On 30 January 1933, a reluctant Hindenburg formally swore in Hitler as Chancellor. At first, out of a cabinet of 12, only 3 were nazis.

THE REICHSTAG FIRE, 1933

Just before the election of 1933 the Reichstag building in *Berlin* was set on fire by a Dutch communist, *Marinus van der Lubbe*. Arguments have continued ever since as to who was responsible for this act. The nazis claimed it was part of a communist plot to overthrow the government. The communists said it was a nazi move to discredit them. Modern evidence seems to suggest that it was the work of van der Lubbe, acting alone. The day after the fire Hitler persuaded Hindenberg to suspend all democratic rights and arrest the communist deputies. When the election took place, the nazis received 43% of the vote. This, when added to the 8% polled by their allies, the Nationalists, gave them the half share they needed to govern Germany.

THE ENABLING LAW

When the new Reichstag met, lines of stormtroopers guarded the corridors - a visible sign of the new power about to take over Germany. With the 81 communist deputies absent, Hitler promised the Catholic Centre Party that he would negotiate a treaty with the Pope similar to the Lateran treaty concluded by Mussolini. (See Work Unit 16) if they supported him in passing an *Enabling Law*. This swung them to the Nazi-Nationalist side and the vote for the bill was 441 and 94 against. In this way Hitler abolished democracy by legal means. The Enabling Law banned all political parties except the Nazis, abolished all personal freedom and disbanded free trade unions, absorbing them in the Nazi-run *Labour Front*. Goebbels took over as Minister of Propaganda. He imposed a complete censorship on newspapers, radio and cinema. Opponents of the regime were executed or placed in *concentration camps*, where the discipline and brutality usually killed them. A *Gestapo* (Secret State Police), commanded by *Heinrich Himmler*, crushed all opposition. His *Shutz Staffel* (Protective Squad), the *S.S.*, took over from Roehm's brownshirt stormtroopers. Hitler never kept his promise to the Catholic Centre.

'THE NIGHT OF THE LONG KNIVES'

The changeover from S.A. (Stormtroopers) to S.S. took place in June, 1934. For some months there had been serious differences between Hitler and Roehm. Roehm wanted to nationalise industrial firms and re-allocate wealth on socialist principles. He also wanted his 2 million brownshirts to be turned into a peoples' army. Hitler knew this would offend his right-wing supporters in industry and the army. Encouraged by Goering and Himmler, he decided to strike. A conference was arranged at *Weissee* in Bavaria. Once the leading Brownshirts were assembled in the town they were arrested and shot. *Roehm* and one of the chief lieutenants were dragged from their bed in the early morning, taken to Munich and executed. Similar murders took place all over Germany, particularly in Berlin. Some old scores were settled, and most of the men who had assisted in crushing Hitler's 1923 putsch died. This purge, nicknamed the *Night of the Long Knives,* cost 62 lives according to Hitler. There were probably many more dead. Next day Hitler announced that he had foiled a plot by Roehm and others to overthrow the state. This satisfied Hindenburg and most Germans, especially as the brutal Roehm had few friends.

SELF-ASSESSMENT SECTION

1. Who were the Brownshirts?

2. How did the Weimar Republic get its name?

3. What were the Freecorps?

4. Who was leader of the German Nationalist Party?

5. What was the Reichstag?

6. What was the Little Entente?

7. What was the significance of the rentenmark?

8. Who led the German Labour Front?

9. What was the name of Hitler's headquarters in Munich?

10. What did S.S. stand for?

11. Write short notes on *four* of the following:-

    a)   Concentration camps
    b)   The Gestapo
    c)   The Kapp Putsch
    d)   Ernst Roehm
    e)   Paul Hindenburg
    f)   Mein Kampf
    g)   Lebensraum

12. The Enabling Law:-

    a)   Restricted immigration into Germany.
    b)   Expelled 'alien' elements from Germany.
    c)   Abolished the Reichstag.
    d)   Abolished all civil liberties.
    e)   Legalised the Nazi Party.
        (TICK THE CORRECT ANSWER)

13. Gustav Stresemann:-

    a) Signed the Versailles Treaty
    b) Signed the Locarno Pact.
    c) Negotiated the Little Entente.
    d) Opposed the Dawes Plan.
    e) Sent German troops into the Ruhr.
    (TICK THE CORRECT ANSWER)

14. Put the correct details (by letter) against these names.

1.	KARL LIEBKNECHT	A.	Ex-fighter pilot and Nazi leader
2.	JOSEF GOEBBELS	B.	Murdered for signing the Versailles Treaty
3.	ERICH VON LUDENDORF	C.	French Foreign Minister
4.	MATTHIAS ERZBERGER	D.	Nazi Propaganda Chief
5.	HERMAN GOERING	E.	Leader of Hitler Youth
6.	ARISTIDE BRIAND	F.	Spartakist leader
7.	GREGOR STRASSER	G.	German Field Marshal
8.	BALDUR VON SCHIRACH	H.	Socialist Nazi

15. Examine these two sources and then answer the questions.

    A. On the following page is a nazi cartoon of 1934. The words on the flag read, 'Loyalty, Honour and Order'.

    B. "Since the masses have only a poor acquaintance with abstract ideas, their reactions lie more in the domain of feelings, where the roots of their positive as well as their negative attitudes are implanted .... It is always more difficult to fight against faith than against knowledge ... Whoever wishes to win over the masses must know the key that will open the door to their hearts .... The receptive powers of the masses are very restricted, and their understanding is feeble. On the other hand, they quickly forget. Such being the case, all effective propaganda must be confined to a few bare necessities and then expressed in a few stereotyped formulas'.

    Hitler Mein Kampf. Quoted Bullock 'Hitler'
    Odhams and Penguin, 1952 and 1962.

    a) Who is the woman meant to represent in A ?
    b) In A., what is the significance of showing her leaning on Hitler?
    c) In A., what is Hitler's grip on the flagpole meant to tell the German people?
    d) In what way does A. deal with the 'few bare necessities' and 'stereotyped formulas' mentioned in B.?
    e) What does B. tell us regarding Hitler's attitude towards 'the masses'?
    f) Name one fact Hitler wanted the people to forget, and one he wanted them to remember.

16. Explain the steps by which Stresemann restored economic and political stability to Germany after the First World War.

17. Imagine you are a German worker in 1923. Explain what happened to you when you drew your wages and went shopping.

20

Causes of the
Second World War

INTRODUCTION

The pressures of nationalism, industrialisation and empire-building led to the breakdown of the balance of power in Europe in 1914. The Versailles Settlement, to which Germany in particular objected, was left to Britain and France to enforce after the USA withdrew from European affairs. During the 21 years between the wars a power struggle inside Russia and isolationist feeling in the USA meant that neither country played a significant role in events leading to the Second World War. Three Great Powers, Japan, Italy and Germany, fell under the sway of strongly nationalist regimes and started to defy both the terms of the Versailles Treaty and the principles of the League of Nations.

Japan invaded Manchuria and, later, China; Italy conquered Abyssinia. When Hitler came to power he planned first to make Germany supreme in eastern Europe by creating a 'Mitteleuropa' (Middle Europe) of client states. This involved German occupation of Austria, Czechoslovakia and Poland. Hitler expected to achieve these goals without a major war. The second stage of his plan, the conquest of lebensraum (living space) in Russia, would lead to war which he expected to start in 1942. Germany's victory in this titanic struggle would amount to world conquest, placing her within striking distance of India as well as vital French and British interests in the Middle East.

France and Britain were hesitant and cautious in the face of these threats, dependant, as they were, on fluctuating public opinion. Consequently they were later condemned for doing too little in the face of Italian and Japanese aggression. Neville Chamberlain, the British prime minister from 1937, has been criticised for his so-called 'appeasement' policy towards the dictators, in particular Hitler . Basically, this policy gave the German leader a free hand to redraw the map of Europe in those regions where the Versailles Treaty was thought to have been unfair to Germany. For this reason Hitler was allowed to re-occupy the Rhineland (1936) and take over Austria (1938) without hindrance. At a meeting at Munich later in 1938 he was given the Sudeten (German-speaking) provinces of Czechoslovakia, 'a faraway country of whose people we know nothing', as Chamberlain tactlessly called it.

The end of appeasement came six months later when German troops occupied the remainder of Czechoslovakia. This was a non-German country unconnected with any grievance left over from Versailles. The Allies decided that it was time to halt Hitler's onward march. They hastily guaranteed the security of several smaller nations, in particular Poland, against which Hitler was making threatening moves. Unfortunately, appeasement had led Hitler to underestimate the British and French leadership. In spite of the quickening pace of British and French re-armament, he was convinced that neither country would fight over Poland. 'Our enemies are small fry. I saw them at Munich', he remarked contemptuously. It proved a fatal mistake on his part.

Why did Britain and France go to war at this particular time? It was true they could not save Poland, a country even further away than Czechoslovakia. 'Nothing more completely fatuous or lunatic could be possibly imagined,' wrote a clergyman to the 'Manchester Guardian' about the British pledge to the Poles. However, the British and French had decided, probably rightly, that their continuance as great powers was at stake, not the territorial integrity of Poland. What could be saved by going to war in 1939, were their empires. Most British politicians in 1938-9 had grown up in the 'high-noon' of empire. They were proud of the world's largest empire and determined to defend Britain's supremacy, if necessary by war. The French adopted a similar attitude towards their colonies, stressing the glories of French culture and its benefits to their subject peoples.

Furthermore, both countries believed they could defeat Germany by attrition and blockade without Russian or American help and both thought 1939 a suitable time for war if it had to come. Hitler did not seem to be aware of this 'U' turn from appeasement. He thought that his masterstroke, the Nazi-Soviet Pact with Stalin, dividing Poland between Russian and Germany, would convince the British and French that Poland was indeed a lost country. In fact, they needed no such persuading and chose to go to war for other reasons. It is strange that a dedicated nationalist and imperialist like Hitler should have failed to see the nationalist and imperialist reasons for their decision.

DISARMAMENT AND ANSCHLUSS

Hitler faced a Europe less hostile to Germany than had been the case in the Twenties. Reparations had been abandoned finally in 1931. Britain was prepared to accept a revision of the Versailles treaty. France was not keen to do this but needed to keep on friendly terms with Britain, her only powerful ally. Hitler showed his own attitude almost at once by taking Germany out of the *Disarmament Talks* and the League of Nations; Germans voted 90% in favour of this decision in a *plebiscite* (referendum).

In July, 1934 the nazis tried their first coup. The strong Austrian nazi party staged a rebellion to obtain *Anschluss* - union between Germany and Austria - which was forbidden by the terms of Versailles. There was a short period of confusion and violence during which *Englebert Dolfuss*, a Christian Socialist opponent of nazism, staged his own counter rising. The nazis murdered Dolfuss but his successor, *Kurt Schusnigg* - so small he was nicknamed 'the pocket Chancellor' - regained control and executed the rebels. *Mussolini* was opposed to having Germany on his border and sent troops to the frontier. Hitler then denied all knowledge of the risings and guaranteed Austrian sovereignty (independence) because he did not want a confrontation with Italy at this stage. France, worried by German re-armament, signed a pact of mutual assistance with Russia in 1935.

THE RHINELAND

Hitler made his first serious move in March, 1936, when the Allies were involved in the Abyssinian crisis (See Work Unit 16), He complained that the new Franco-Russian treaty violated the terms of Locarno and used this as an excuse to *re-occupy the Rhineland*, a German border region demilitarised by the Versailles treaty. This time Italy did nothing because Mussolini was furious with Britain and France over sanctions. The French army could have driven the Germans out but public opinion in France was divided about risking war on such an issue. The British reacted calmly, some ministers talking about Germany having walked into its own backyard. Secretly, Hitler had told his commanders to retreat at the first sign of resistance and was delighted when his dangerous gamble paid off. The first act of aggression by Germany since 1918 overturned part of the Peace Settlement by force and broke the concept of collective security embodied in the League of Nation's covenant. For this reason it is usually regarded as a crucial point in the drift to war.

Hitler had violated the Locarno Pact himself and upset the limits placed on the Franco-German frontier. Strategically, the re-occupation gave the Germans a more easily defended frontier. They started to build a system of fortifications, called the *Westwall* or *Siegfried Line*, to counter a similar French defence, the *Maginot Line*. France was now isolated from her *Little Entente* allies - *Poland, Czechoslovakia, Rumania* and *Yugoslavia*.

CHAMBERLAIN AND APPEASEMENT

In 1937 *Neville Chamberlain* became British prime minister. He believed as did many others, that sections of the Versailles treaty relating to Germany were unfair and should be altered. He hoped that Hitler's policies were meant to remedy these injustices only, and he wanted to negotiate a final settlement of the issue. This policy became known as *appeasement*. Two important factors lay behind it. The ruling classes of Britain saw communism as a greater danger than nazism, and Hitler as a possible ally against Russia. The British people a a whole did not want another war, particularly as the effects of *bombing*, although, of course, unknown then, were thought to be too fearful to contemplate. 'The bomber will always get through', although untrue, was a powerful slogan in any pacifist campaign. The government shared this fear of the bomber but reacted in a positive way to the threat by increasing the *Royal Air Force* to give it parity with the *Luftewaffe* (German airforce). The French had also begun to re-arm but were obsessed with the concept of a defensive war, fought behind a deep belt of impregnable fortification, the Maginot Line. The appalling losses they had suffered in First World War attacks had produced a 'defensive' mentality and this line stood as its visible symbol.

179

Post-1918 Europe

Appeasement represented a total break with the policies of the Great Powers since 1918. It ignored collective security and proposed jettisoning important clauses of the Peace Settlement. Chamberlain also hoped to detach Italy from the *Rome-*

Berlin Axis (See Work Unit 16). He negotiated an agreement, signed in April, 1938, by which Britain and Italy promised to co-operate in the Mediterranean, and to try to get all foreign volunteers, including the Italian army, out of Spain (See Work Unit 17). But in spite of this agreement Mussolini continued to move towards alliance with Hitler. He was still angry with Britain over sanctions and deeply involved with Hitler in helping Franco's Nationalist troops in Spain.

ANSCHLUSS

Anschluss was the dream of many Germans and some Austrians. The two countries shared a common language and culture, although Austria had never been under German rule. In February, 1938 Hitler invited *Schusnigg* to discuss a possible union. *Schusnigg* had been trying to cement an alliance with Italy to stop this happening but the situation had changed since 1934. Italy was too deeply involved in the Spanish Civil war to do anything militarily to help Austria. Hitler told Schusnigg that he resented the Austrian Chancellor's attempt to get closer links with Italy and the Little Entente countries, and bullied him into accepting *Arthur Seyss-Inquart*, a nazi, as Austrian Minister of Security. Schusnigg returned home and tried to arrange a plebiscite to find out if the Austrian people wanted a union with Germany. The nazi 'Trojan horse' inside the country promptly stirred up riots and disorder. At this, Schusnigg resigned and *Seyss-Inquart* was made Chancellor in his place. Inquart at once invited the Germans to cross the border and 'restore order'. On 12 March 1938 German army units occupied *Vienna*, the Austrian capital, and other key towns. They also moved up the *Brenner Pass* to confront any possible Italian troop concentrations.

In about 24 hours Hitler had added 7 million people to his 'Greater Germany'. Austria became a province of the Reich with Seyss-Inquart as its governor. This was a severe economic blow to Italy which had traded extensively with Austria. Strategically, Germany now controlled all road, rail and river communications in the middle *Danube Valley.* She shared borders with Italy, Hungary and Yugoslavia and enclosed Czechoslovakia on three sides. The Austrian army was incorporated into the *Reichwehr* (German Army) and most opponents of the Nazis were sent to concentration camps. This included Schusnigg who was very badly treated.

CZECHOSLOVAKIA

Czechoslovakia was a key member of the Little Entente with effective armed forces supplied by the huge *Skoda* armaments works. Hitler had a particular hatred of this country which he regarded as a mere hotch-potch of 'inferior' races bound together in a haphazard way after the First World War. He made his first move by complaining about the treatment of 3 million German-speaking people living in a region called the *Sudetenland.* A well organised and fanatical nazi party inside Czechoslovakia. led by *Konrad Henlein*, soon began to stir up trouble against the government of President *Eduard Benes* and Prime Minister, *Milan Hodza.* They reacted by passing an *Enabling Law*, banning all extremist parties. This was aimed specifically at the nazis but it affected other nationalist groups of *Magyars, Slovaks* and *Ruthenians.* Heinlein protested at this restriction of freedom for the German minority and Hitler made speeches complaining about the law.

Czechoslovakia had military alliances with France and Russia. The Russians were pledged to help the Czechs only after the French had given them assistance. In March, 1938 both France and Russia renewed their promise of aid in the event of attack. Chamberlain, however, stated that Britain would not necessarily support France in any conflict over Czechoslovakia. This gave Hitler an opportunity. He realised that France would be unlikely to act without Britain, and, under the terms of the alliance, Russia would not act before France. In April *Henlein* demanded semi-independence for the Sudetenland. Benes and Hodza rejected these demands and, during elections, the nazis staged their usual violence and intimidation. The Czech government, remembering what had happened to Austria in similar circumstances, mobilised their army. Chamberlain changed direction and warned Germany that Britain might become involved in any war between France, Czechoslovakia and Germany. This stayed Hitler's hand only temporarily. Secretly he was furious with the Czechs and ordered his general staff to prepare plans for a military attack on Czechoslovakia, *Code Green*, to be ready for 1 October at the latest.

MEETING AT BERCHTESGARDEN

There was no doubt that according to the principles of self-determination the Sudeten people had the right to be under German rule. The problems also fitted Chamberlain's appeasement policy for here was another case of the Versailles settlement being unfair to a German minority. Both France and Britain sent diplomats to *Prague*, the Czech capital, to persuade Benes's government to grant Henlein's demands for autonomy. Henlein, of course, was aiming at a complete German takeover. He rejected these offers, whilst Hitler made speeches condemning the Czech leadership. Chamberlain decided to make a direct appeal to Hitler and on 15 September 1938 flew to the Fuhrer's mountain retreat, *Berchtesgarden* in *Bavaria*. At this meeting Hitler told Chamberlain that nothing but complete independence would satisfy the Sudeten Germans and that he was prepared for war if this demand was not met. Chamberlain's response was to meet *Eduoard Daladier*, the French prime minister, and persuade him that they should both force the Czechs to cede this region to Germany.

This was a complete betrayal of the Czechs who were told that they must give up all territory where more than half the population were German. This meant that 800,000 Czechs would become German subjects, the powerful Czech defences in the Bohemian mountains abandoned and all French treaty obligations to Czechoslovakia broken. Benes and Hodza had no alternative but to agree and when Chamberlain flew for a second meeting with Hitler he carried with him the Czech document of surrender. The meeting was held at *Godesberg* and it seems to have dispelled any illusions Chamberlain still had about Hitler's character and future plans. The German went into one of his notorious rages and demanded that his troops be allowed to march immediately into the disputed areas, instead of gradually as Britain suggested. Chamberlain reproached Hitler for not responding more positively to the Allied peace efforts. Hitler said he would delay entry until 1 October (the date he had already planned with his generals) and promised the British prime minister that he had no more territorial ambitions in Europe. The meeting ended with no firm decisions being reached.

Europe 1936-39

BETRAYAL AT MUNICH

Both the Czechs and French now carried out partial mobilisations of their forces whilst the British put their fleet on alert. *Chamberlain* proposed a four-power meeting between Italy, France, Britain and Germany to be held at *Munich*. The Czechs were not allowed to participate at this conference. The result was an agreement similar to the Godesberg proposals; Hitler had got the Sudetenland. Chamberlain returned to Britain and announced, 'This is peace in our time'. Although he was later condemned for this Munich 'sell-out' of the Czechs, many people at the time applauded what he had done. King George VI issued a proclamation of thanksgiving and Roosevelt cabled him, 'Good man'. However, Chamberlain now began the largest re-armament programme in British history and introduced peacetime military conscription for the first time. Defenders of his actions at Munich point to this as proof that he was playing for time in order to get Britain better prepared for war.

THE TAKEOVER OF CZECHOSLOVAKIA

The loss of the resources of Czechoslovakia was a severe blow to the Allies. Hitler's economic and military power had been enlarged enormously and he had gained powerful defences, vital communications and key factories and industries. Six months later, in March 1939, Hitler wiped the country off the map. After Nazi - inspired disorders inside Czechoslovakia, the Czech President, *Hacha*, was summoned to Berlin and told that Prague would be bombed if he did not let the Germans in. The President gave way, although he had no legal right to do so. German troops occupied the rest of the country, taking over the Skoda factories, large stocks of munitions and planes, and rich resources of timber and agriculture.

The breaking of the Munich agreement within six months killed *appeasement* once and for all. Such a takeover had nothing to do with righting the wrongs of Versailles; Czechoslovakia had never been part of Germany and was a non-German nation. However, Hitler had taken Munich as the 'green-light' for German control of eastern Europe, especially as his Foreign Minister, *Joachim von Ribbentrop*, assured him that Britain and France were decadent and would not fight. In fact, Britain and France were now preparing to hold a line of countries in eastern Europe, including *Poland, Rumania* and *Yugoslavia*. They also guaranteed Greek independence against attack by Italy, and concluded a pact of mutual assistance with *Turkey*. Negotiations between the Allies and Russia failed because Stalin demanded that he must be allowed to send troops into Poland, Finland and the Baltic States. This was not agreeable to Britain and France and was opposed by the Poles.

POLAND

Hitler now began a propaganda campaign against *Poland*, stressing the unfairness to Germany of the Polish 'corridor' which led to the free city of *Danzig* but cut off East Prussia from the rest of Germany. (See Work Unit 14). He knew that Russia would never let him take over Poland without a fight so in August, 1939, he concluded a *Nazi-Soviet Pact* with Stalin. This amazing 'U' turn by the 'enemy of communism' could only be concluded by promising Stalin eastern *Poland, Bessarabia, Finland* and the Baltic states except *Lithuania*. This saved Hitler from the danger of a two-front war, whilst his supposed ally, Stalin, hoped that a long war between the Allies and German would benefit Russia. Hitler, or course, intended to attack Russia at a later date.

On 31 August Hitler presented a *Sixteen-Point Plan* to Britain. Poland was not informed of this plan which involved the return of *Danzig* to Germany and the holding of plebiscites to decide the future of the *corridor*. Before there was any response, Hitler announced that his patience was exhausted and, after a fake incident on the Polish border, his troops invaded Poland. Within days Britain and France declared war on Germany (3 September 1939) and Russian troops began moving into Poland.

SELF-ASSESSMENT SECTION.

1.   When did reparations end?

2.   Which Chancellor of Austria was murdered by Nazis?

3. Name a country in the Little Entente?

4. What was the German airforce called?

5. What was the Rome-Berlin Axis?

6. What was the Westwall?

7. What was 'lebensraum'?

8. In which country were the Skoda armament works?

9. Who lived at Berchtesgarden?

10. What was Code Green?

11. Put in correct details (by letter) against these names.

1.	EDUARD BENES	A.	Leader of Austrian Nazis.
2.	KONRAD HEINLEIN	B.	French Prime Minister.
3.	ARTHUR SEYSS-INQUART	C.	President of Czechoslovakia.
4.	JOACHIM VON RIBBENTROP	D.	Led counter-revolt against Austrian nazis.
5.	EDUARD DALADIER	E.	Leader of Sudeten nazis.
6.	ENGLEBERT DOLFUSS	F.	Chancellor of Austria.
7.	KURT SCHUSNIGG	G.	German Foreign Minister.

12. The Nazi-Soviet Pact

    a) Made war between Poland and Germany certain.
    b) Made war between Britain and France and Germany certain.
    c) Made war between Russia and Germany likely.
    d) Made a two-front war for Germany unlikely.
    (TICK THE CORRECT ANSWER)

13. Appeasement was a policy aimed at:-

    a) Detaching Italy from alliance with Germany.
    b) Abolishing the Versailles Treaty.
    c) Allowing Germany to take over non-German minorities.
    d) Maintaining collective security.
    e) Allowing Germany to take over German minorities.
    (TICK THE CORRECT ANSWER)

14. Look at the map on the following page and then answer these questions.

    a) Name the area occupied by Hitler in 1936.
    b) Name the two countries who signed a pact in August, 1939.
    c) Which frontier area was taken by Germany as a result of the Munich agreement, September, 1938?
    d) Which country was united with Germany in March, 1938?
    e) Which country was occupied entirely by Germany in March, 1939?

f)   Which country did Germany go to war with on 1 September 1939?

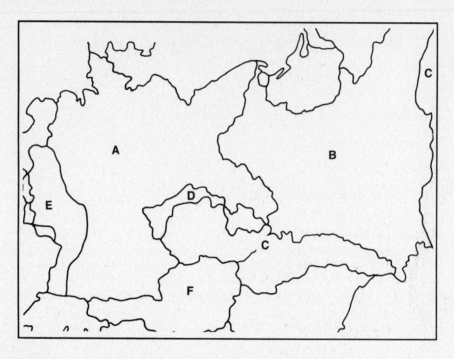

15.   Read these sources and then answer the questions.

A.   "Further steps towards the full Nazification of Austria were announced
     today.... the National Socialist culture office is appointing commissars
     for all institutions such as the Burgtheater *(Austrian National
     Theatre)*, the film studios and associations of architects, painters and
     sculptors ... Regarding the regulations for the April 10th plebiscite on
     the annexation of Austria, Jews - who have been forbidden to take
     part - are defined as:- "Persons at least three of whose grandparents
     were pure Jews by race; persons of mixed Jewish race with two pure
     Jewish grandparents; and all who, on September 16 1935, were
     members of the Jewish religious community". Anyone who married a
     Jew or Jewess on or after that date, will also be regarded as a Jew".
                              Daily Telegraph report, 17 March 1938.

B.   "We have a clear conscience, we have done all that any country could
     do to establish peace, but a situation in which no word given by
     Germany's ruler could be trusted, and no people or country could feel
     themselves safe, had become intolerable... For it is evil things we
     shall be fighting against, brute force, bad faith, injustice, oppression
     and persecution. But against them I am certain that the right will
     prevail".
               Neville Chamberlain, announcing the declaration of war on the radio,
                              Sunday, 3 September 1939.

C. "I have conquered chaos in Germany, re-established order, enormously increased production ... I have succeeded in finding useful work once more for the whole of seven million unemployed .... I have brought back to the Reich provinces stolen from us in 1919, I have led back to their native country millions of Germans who were torn away from us and in misery.."

Adolf Hitler, speech to Reichstag, 28 April 1939.

(in reply to letter from President Roosevelt, asking him if he was ready to promise not to attack a list of 30 countries)

Quoted Bullock, 'Hitler', Odhams and Penguin, p503.

a) In Source A., was there any point in having a plebiscite about Anschluss on 10th April 1938? Explain your answer.
b) Why were there laws against Jews in Germany?
c) In Source A., what was the point of the date relating to the Jewish faith?
d) Using Source B. and C. as guides, give examples of
   i) Hitler's persecution.
   ii) Hitler's bad faith.
   iii) Nazi brute force.
e) What parts of Source C. are untrue?
f) In what way had Chamberlain done everything he could to establish peace? (Source B.)

16.
   A.

B. "This choice *(the Nazi-Soviet Pact)* was a wise and far-sighted act of Soviet foreign policy under the conditions which then obtained. This step by the Soviet government to an enormous extent predetermined the favourable outcome of the Second World War for the Soviet Union and for all freedom-loving peoples'.

Published by Soviet Information Bureau , 1948.
Quoted in 'The Outbreak of the Second World War'
ed. by John L. Snell. D.C. Heath and Co., 1965.

a) In source A. name the man on the left and the man on the right.

b) In Source A. what is the significance of the remarks they are making to each other? For clarity, the remarks are reproduced hereunder.

Man on the left: ....."*The scum of the earth I believe?*"
Man on the right: ..."*The bloody assassin of the workers I presume?*"

c) Who is the figure lying between them meant to be?

d) Explain what each side hoped to gain from the Pact.

e) Explain why the viewpoints expressed in A. and B. are so different.

f) Why were people so surprised by the Nazi-Soviet Pact?

g) Do you agree with B? Give reasons for your answer.

17. Why is Hitler's re-occupation of the Rhineland regarded as the turning point in the events leading to the Second World War?

18. Imagine you are an Austrian living at the time of the Anschluss. Describe what happened to you in the weeks which followed the German occupation.

21

Japan 1853-1941

INTRODUCTION

Japan's contacts with the modern world are quite recent. Hardly anybody was allowed into Japan , and no Japanese were allowed out, for 200 years. Then the Russians (1804), the British (1842) and the Americans (1853) gave this 'sleeping beauty' a rude awakening. They forced the Japanese, literally at gunpoint, to open up trading links with the west. The Japanese response to this economic 'rape' was unusual. Instead of sinking into a semi-colonial state, as happened in similar circumstances to China, Japan began an extensive modernisation programme. A new regime, set up in the 1860's, re-organised the social, educational and economic life of the Japanese, crushing conservative resistance to such changes on the way. The Japanese genius for imitation at first surprised, then worried, and finally, frightened, the world.

Japan let western engineers, architects, educationalists, soldiers and sailors into the country as employees, not colonialists. Once their particular expertise had been assimilated, they were sent away. This arrangement worked so well that by 1894 an independent but modern Japan was able to defeat China, her old rival, and in 1904-5 become the first Asiatic power to defeat a western one. The effect of these victories on the Japanese was similar to military success on the Germans after 1870. Bushido, the fierce fighting code of the samurai warriors, was taught to the men of a modern army, navy and, later airforce. Military leaders were admired more than politicians, and by the Thirties and Forties such men had gained control of the government, which lost the trappings of democracy it had been given in the 19th century. Aggressive imperialism became the usual policy, as the Japanese treated first Korea, and then Manchuria and China, as satellite states.

Japan had two major handicaps in any contest for world domination. She had no raw materials worth speaking of, and her islands were vastly overcrowded by an expanding population. Yet it was these weaknesses which drove her leaders to conquest in the search for empty land and minerals. From 1895 onwards Japan encroached on Manchuria and China, and looked enviously at the rich Dutch, French, and British possessions in the Far East. Nevertheless, her advance faced two large obstacles, Russia, who opposed her expansion into Manchuria, and the

189

USA, who was likely to resent her advance into both China and the Pacific. Clashes with Russia over Manchuria occurred in 1904-5, when Japan won, and in 1939 when an undeclared war with the Soviet Union led to her defeat. Japanese expansion into South East Asia and the Pacific became possible after the German conquest of France and Holland in June, 1940. The French and Dutch could hardly administer, let alone defend, their possessions. Britain, meanwhile, was engaged in a life and death struggle with Germany which left Malaya, Singapore and possibly Burma and Australia, soft targets.

Faced with these opportunities, Japan was nevertheless still up against the two obstacles. Any more Chinese conquests might lead to a confrontation with Russia. Any encroachments on Dutch, French or British Far East possessions might lead to war with the USA. In late 1940 Japan began tentative moves against some of these colonies. The Americans answered with an economic blockade of Japan . As far as the Japanese military were concerned, this merely confirmed the need to fight. But it left them wondering in which direction to strike, north against Manchuria or south against the colonial empires. Their dilemma was solved when Germany invaded Russia in June, 1941. Now there could be no fear of a Russian 'stab in the back' if Japanese amphibious forces attacked the Phillipines, Malaya and Singapore, the Dutch East Indies and French Indo-China. This left only one obstacle - but a mighty one. President Roosevelt of the USA made it clear that he would continue his economic blockade of Japan unless she retreated from China and ceased aggression in the Pacific. This stranglehold was so strong, that Japan, starved of raw materials, experienced a financial crisis in late 1941.

The Japanese military leadership had two choices, either give up in its Chinese 'adventure' or be ruined by the US embargo. Given Japan's military tradition, there was no doubt which alternative she would choose. In any case, the rich pickings of the old Far Eastern empires were too great a prize *not* to risk a war in her opinion. There were also those in Japan who wondered whether the USA would fight. Would the deeply isolationist Americans go to war to save colonial empires they detested and with an ally, Soviet Russia, whom many regarded as the Great Satan? Others thought, like Hitler, that in December, 1941, Russia was close to defeat and that Germany would soon be able to join Japan in the war against the USA. Both calculations proved wrong. Rather like the Allies over Poland, the Americans did not go to war to save decaying empires, but to preserve their country's status as a Great Power. And Russia went on to destroy German military power.

It was on these incorrect assumptions that the Japanese committed a form of national suicide by going to war with a far stronger power on 7 December 1941.

THE PERRY EXPEDITIONS

Japan chose to remain cut off from the outside world from 1640 until the 19th century when she was 'opened up' as the result of western pressure. In 1853 two US warships, commanded by *Commodore Matthew Perry* arrived off *Tokyo*. Perry brought letters from the US government addressed to the *Mikado*, or emperor, of Japan. In fact, real power in Japan was exercised by the *Shogun*, originally the military commander but for many years Japan's ruler. Western countries were interested in Japan both for trade and as a refuelling stop for steamships and whalers, The Japanese viewed the arrival of the *'Black Ships'* with horror and contempt, but their refusal to trade led Perry to prepare his ships for action. He warned the Shogun that he would return the following year and arrived in 1854 with 9 warships. The Japanese were forced to sign a treaty which gave American ships the right to use two Japanese ports, and insisted that they provide protection for ship-wrecked sailors. The latter provision was because the Japanese usually executed any foreigners who came ashore. They were also forced to agree that foreigners in Japan would not have to obey Japanese laws; these were the *extra-territorial rights* which were being extracted from the Chinese at the same time. (See Work Unit 10)

THE MEIJI REVOLUTION

Until that time Japan had been a feudal nation. Her society was divided into *samurai*, or noblemen (who owned the land), peasants, *farmers, town workers* and *merchants*. The initial reaction of the ruling classes was *'Expel the Barbarian'*, and anybody who suggested an alternative was either ignored or murdered. The struggle between these traditionalists, and those who wished to modernise Japan, developed into a civil war. The modernisers won this war at the *Battle of Fushima* in 1868. They promptly restored the emperor *Meiji* to his former powers, broke the stranglehold of the Shogun on government, and initiated a programme of radical reform. The Emperor took his motto, 'Knowledge must be sought from all over the world' but from the start the ideal behind all modernisation was to beat the 'barbarians' at their own game.

In 1871 the samurai's feudal control of the land was abolished and replaced by a system under which the emperor owned all the land. The samurai, reduced to receiving a salary, joined the new national army in large numbers. Two years later, new taxes, based on the supposed value of land if sold, gave the government a steady income, even if it was sometimes unfair to peasants who had to find 3% regardless of a bad harvest. Central banking, telegraph and postal services, and a new coinage based on the *yen*, helped *Count Matsukata* reorganise the finances of the country and reduce the national debt.

NINETEENTH CENTURY MODERNISATION

Industrialisation was introduced by way of a partnership between government and private enterprise. Rich merchant families, like those who founded the *Mitsubishi* conglomerate, were helped initially by government loans. Mitsubishi diversified into shipping, ship-yards, mines and factories. At the same time the need to create home, as well as foreign, markets, led the government to improve the peasant economy. Instead of relying on rice farming, farmers were encouraged to move into two new industries, *fishing* and *silk farming*. Both proved very profitable, and so gave Japanese industry the market it needed to sell its goods. Farming itself was improved by large-scale irrigation and fertilisation schemes which made barren lands fruitful.

Compulsory education was established in Japan in 1872. A Ministry of Education exercised close control over teachers, who were really civil servants, and ensured that as people learned to read and write they were also indoctrinated with the 'right' ideas. These were summed up in the slogan, ' *A Rich Country and a Strong Army'*. Altogether 54,000 new schools were built in the last years of the 19th century. In 1889 Japan received a democratic *Constitution* with a *Diet* (Parliament) elected by property owners. However, power lay with the few ministers, chosen from the samurai, who exercised control on behalf of the emperor.

NEW ARMY AND NAVY

Both the army and the government tried to live up to the samurai ideals of *bushido* - the way of the warrior. These included chivalry, courage, honour and loyalty, and also an indifference to death. A samurai who was dishonoured or defeated would commit *hara-kiri* which means 'ripping the belly'. This is what the victim did literally in a traditional ceremony. After conscription was introduced in 1872, requiring all men of 20 to serve in the forces for 3 years, these ideals were taught to the entire Japanese nation. It made the Japanese armed forces a formidable fighting force. The army was re-organised by German officers because the Japanese were impressed by Bismarck's victories. The navy was reformed and built by British naval officers and architects because the British navy was then the largest and most powerful in the world. These experts were sent home as soon as they had served their purpose. The Japanese did not intend to end up as puppets of the west as was happening in China.

WAR WITH CHINA

Japan's remarkable economic progress created its own problems. By the 1890's she needed new markets for her thriving silk industry; a *Japanese Spinners' Association* worked hard to sell in the Chinese region. It was then that the martial spirit of the Japanese took over control of national policy. A patriotic society called *Genyosha* aimed to spread Japanese influence by armed force if necessary. In 1894 the Japanese government managed to persuade Britain and the USA to give up their claims to extra-territorial rights. In the same year they copied the westerners in 1853 and forced *Korea*, a Chinese protectorate, to open two ports to Japanese traders. This led to the *Sino-Japanese War* (See Work Unit 10) when Japanese troops drove the Chinese out of Korea, seized *Port Arthur* and seemed poised to capture *Peking* if necessary. The Chinese had no alternative but to sign a humiliating peace at *Shimonoseki* which gave Japan the island of *Formosa, Port Arthur* and a large indemnity money to be paid for the war.

The results of this war led to the *triple intervention* of *Russia, France* and *Germany* who told Japan that possession of Port Arthur might "disturb the peace in the Far East." Japan was forced to hand back the port and this caused deep resentment, especially as soon afterwards Russia received from China the monopoly of use of Port Arthur for trade. At the same time the Russians began to construct, with Chinese support, the *Chinese-Eastern Railway* across *Manchuria* to the Russian port of *Vladivostok*. Japan was determined to contest control of both Manchuria and Korea with the Russians. She gained an ally in Britain *(Anglo-Japanese Treaty, 1902)*, then won the Russo-Japanese War (See Work Unit 4).

THE TWENTY ONE DEMANDS

In 1914 *Japan* went to war with Germany as an ally of Britain. Her forces captured the Germany colony of *Shantung* and its port of *Tsingtao* Her government then used the European war as an opportunity to force concessions out of China. In 1915 China was presented with the *Twenty-One demands*, a comprehensive list including special commercial privileges for Japanese traders in Manchuria, acceptance of the Japanese control of *Shantung* and also of Japanese political, military and financial advisers. The Chinese accepted all but the last demand. The Twenty-One Demands aroused suspicion and resentment amongst Japan's allies, and even a backlash in Japan itself where it was felt that too much international goodwill had been sacrificed. They were also a turning point in relations between the USA and Japan; hitherto they had been friendly but now they drifted slowly but surely towards confrontation and war. (See Also Work Unit 10)

Another dispute came in 1917-18, after the Russian revolution. A Czech army, fighting against the Bolsheviks, reached Vladivostok. The Americans who were garrisoned nearby guarding war-supplies invited a Japanese division into *Siberia* to help the Czechs. The Japanese, however, sent in nearly 70,000 troops although by 1921 they found the cost of keeping such a force in the region too expensive and withdrew them. In 1921 the US tried to slow down Japanese naval re-armament at the *Washington Conference* (See Work Unit 18). Later US Restriction on Japanese immigration deepened the rift between the two countries. In the world in general, and Europe in particular, there was concern at the flood of cheap Japanese goods throughout the Twenties which led to demands from both manufacturers and trade unions that there should be protective tariffs.

THE MANCHURIAN INCIDENT

Japan tended to regard *Manchuria* not as a Chinese province - which it was technically - but as a battleground between herself and Russia. This was the reason that the Russo-Japanese war was fought in this region, and it was the reason that in the Twenties and Thirties the Japanese kept a powerful force, the *Kwantung Army* around *Port Arthur* By this time they were defending, not just the port, but investments in coal, iron, salt, and oil-shale and soya-bean cultivation. The Chinese refused to accept this situation and in September, 1931, an incident near *Mukden*, involving fighting between Chinese and Japanese troops and explosions on the South Manchurian Railway Line, led to a full-scale invasion of Manchuria by the Kwantung army.

In Japan itself there was confusion and differences of opinion about what had been entirely an army matter. The army itself was divided into two parties, the *Imperial Way Group* who favoured land expansion against Russia in Manchuria, and a *Control Group* who wanted to move southwards against China only.

Meanwhile, some Japanese newspapers and an ultra-nationalist party, the *Black Dragon Society*, applauded the action of the Kwantung army which by now had renamed Manchuria, *Manchokuo*, and set up the last Manchu emperor of China, *Pu Yi*, as its puppet head. The quarrel at home took a serious turn, with assassinations of opponents of the Imperial Way. Eventually, the Imperial Way overplayed its hand, staging a violent takeover with the murder of several cabinet ministers, and the attempted murder of the prime minister, *Admiral Okada*. Although this rising took place in the name of the emperor, *Hirohito* was horrified by such brutal murders. He condemned them, and this led to a counter-revolution by leading generals. Many of the officers who had taken part in the coup were arrested and some were shot. This failure left the Control Group free to continue expansion into China.

ATTACK ON CHINA

In 1937 the Japanese garrison stationed at *Fengtai*, south of the Great Wall, became involved in skirmishes with Chinese troops. In July, Japanese manoeuvres led to a more serious clash with them at the *Marco Polo Bridge*, near *Peking*. This incident widened into a full-scale invasion of China as the military again ignored the Tokyo government, this time led by *Prince Konoye*. The Chinese had just settled the differences between Communist and Nationalist and so were in a position to mount determined and national resistance to this latest aggression. By the autumn of 1937 a huge Japanese army was advancing on *Chiang Kai Shek's* capital, *Nanking*. The city was taken and there followed a brutal massacre of civilians. Next year *Hankow* and *Canton* fell in similar circumstances. But Chiang refused to give in, even when *Konoye* talked of Chinese co-operation in a Japanese-led *'New Order in Asia'*. What the Japanese called the *China Incident* became a major war which strained Japan's resources. This was still continuing when the Second World War began in Europe in 1939.

THE ROAD TO PEARL HARBOUR

Events in Europe soon affected Japanese plans. The conquest of *France* and *Holland* in May-June, 1940, and the desperate struggle being waged by Britain and Germany over the skies of southern England, left the Far Eastern possessions of all three countries at risk. In July the USA began to put pressure on Japan to stop expansion in China and the Far East; President Roosevelt laid a partial ban on the export of oil and iron. In September, 1940 Japanese troops were allowed to garrison *French Indo-China* with the permission of the local French governor. *Thailand* became a virtual dependency of Japan who built military bases in the country. Japan now dominated the *South China Sea*, threatening British-owned *Malaya*, the *Dutch East Indies* (now Indonesia) and US-run *Phillipines*. However, during 1941, the effects of the USA's economic blockade caused a financial crisis in Japan as her foreign exchange reserves were nearly exhausted. This meant that she would soon be unable to buy vital raw materials necessary for her military and naval plans.

TOJO TAKES OVER

The Japanese leaders debated whether to go for further expansion in Manchuria and China, or launch amphibious attacks on the Dutch and British possessions with their rice, rubber, coal, tin and oil resources. Until June, 1941, the problem was Russia, which had already successfully resisted Japanese encroachments into Manchuria in 1939. In that month, however, Hitler launched his armies against the Soviet heartland, leaving only the USA as an obstacle to Japan's ambitions. In October, 1941 *General Hidecki Tojo*, a hard-line militarist, took over as prime minister of Japan. Nicknamed 'the razor' because of his liking for 'sharp' solutions to problems, there was no doubt that he would not retreat before US pressure but would go to war. He demanded that the Americans give Japan a free hand in Asia. American public opinion was still isolationist, despite the aid Roosevelt was giving the Allies in Europe. Military conscription was passed by only one vote in Congress, and there was a widespread feeling that American lives should not be lost saving the British empire.

"THE DAY OF INFAMY"

Negotiations between the USA and Japan continued throughout the autumn of 1941. *Admiral Nomura*, the Japanese ambassador to the USA, was a peace-lover but he was out of touch with the war-party which was now running his country. Furthermore, American experts had cracked the Japanese war code and knew that Tojo and his cabinet were determined on war now that all supplies of oil had been stopped by the USA. Roosevelt made it clear that this economic stranglehold would only be loosened if Japan left China and other Far Eastern possessions she had seized. Whilst the two sides negotiated, a powerful Japanese carrier force left the *Kurile islands* north of Japan, and steamed across the Pacific to attack the US naval base at *Pearl Harbour* in *Hawaii*. On 26th November 1941, when this force was already on it way, Tojo broke off relations with the USA - a clear signal for war. Delay in decoding this message in *Washington,* the US capital, meant that Tojo's message was only known 6 hours before the attack which was launched on the morning of 7 December, 1941 - 'a day that will live in infamy', as Roosevelt called it. Surprise was complete and 8 US battleships were disabled or destroyed and 2,403 men killed. However, three US aircraft carriers - vessels which were to play a key role in the air-sea war which developed in the Pacific - were at sea that morning. In addition, Japanese dive bombers failed to destroy large stores of oil in the harbour.

President Roosevelt and most of the American people blamed the Japanese for attacking without warning. In fact, American mistakes helped make the disaster worse; radar station reports of planes sighted early that morning were dismissed as US planes on exercise and were ignored. *Pearl Harbour* destroyed isolationism at a blow. Roosevelt was able to declare war on Japan with almost unanimous support from Congress. Even so, Germany might not have been involved, at least at first, if Hitler had not decided to declare war on the USA. He was angry at the huge amounts of American munitions, weapons, ships and planes being supplied to Britain to keep her in the war, He regarded the Americans as decadent, and thought that the war with Russia was almost over. His decision saved Roosevelt difficulties with some anti-British Americans, and made the eventual defeat of Germany and Japan certain.

POST-WAR JAPAN

After her defeat and surrender in August, 1945, Japan was occupied by American forces and virtually ruled by *US General Douglas MacArthur*, the American supreme commander in the region. The *Emperor Hirohito* was allowed to remain on his throne, but he was no longer to be treated as a god. *Tojo* and other war leaders were tried and executed as war-criminals and the warlike *Shinto* was abolished as the state religion. Meanwhile, US aid poured into the country to clear up the appalling devastation wrought by nuclear and conventional bombing; altogether 5,000,000 homes were in ruins.

Although MacArthur was the dominant power in Japan until his removal in 1952, the US followed a policy of strengthening Japanese democracy. A more democratic *Diet* was re-established and *Yoshida*, an opponent of Tojo, was elected as prime minister. In 1952 Japan became independent again with the signing of the *Treaty of San Francisco*. On the whole American rule was beneficial, In 1946 the *Owner-Farmer Establishment Law* broke up the estates of large landowners and gave nearly 4,000,000 Japanese their own farms. Over-population was tackled in 1948 when the Japanese approved a *Eugenics Law*, making abortion legal and cheap. During the next 15 years the rate of population increase slowed dramatically, whilst agricultural efficiency and a booming economy meant that by 1976 Japan could feed its own population which stood at 112,000,000.

AN INDUSTRIAL GIANT

The economic boom was caused by US aid and also by the *Korean War* (1950-3), during which Japan was the main US base for its vast military effort. Pre-war industries, like cotton textiles, bicycles, sewing machines, started to decline and new industries were so successful that Japan became one of the world's economic and industrial giants. Iron, steel, lorries, ships, television, transistors and cars were produced on such a scale and were of such quality that Japan was able to flood the world with her goods. In ship-building Japan outstripped Britain by 1956 and by 1965 she was building 44% of the world's total tonnage. By the mid-1970's Japanese steel production was third in the world, beaten only by Russia and the USA.

Such dramatic success economically, equalled and even surpassed Japan's earlier modernisation achievements. Her commanding lead in many products caused concern in the rest of the developed world because of the Japanese policy of selling far more than they bought. In 1976 the *EEC* (European Economic Community) demanded that Japan import more European-produced goods but little was done to meet this request. The *Yom Kippur War* (1973) which led to a world shortage of oil, did cause unemployment and bankruptcies in Japan which is the world's largest importer of crude oil. But progress was still so steady that in the 1980's the USA put tariffs on Japanese goods, claiming that the Japanese did not compete fairly in the world markets.

SELF-ASSESSMENT SECTION

1. Who was the Shogun?

2. What were samurai?

3. What was the 'China Incident'?

4. What was bushido?

5. Who were the Genyosha?

6. Where was the Kwantung army stationed?

7. What were the aims of the Imperial Way Group?

8. Who was emperor of Japan at the start of the Second World War?

9. Who was nicknamed 'the razor'?

10. What was Manchukuo?

11. Put in correct details (by letter) against these names.

1. PRINCE KONOYE	A.	Japanese leader in Second World War.
2. ADMIRAL NOMURA	B.	Prime Minister nearly murdered in 1936.
3. GENERAL TOJO	C.	Headed Japanese modernisation programme.
4. COMMODORE PERRY	D.	US supreme commander in Japan.
5. EMPEROR MEIJI	E.	Headed Japanese government in late 1930's
6. GENERAL MACARTHUR	F.	Led expedition to open up trade with Japan
7. COUNT MATSUKATA	G.	Japanese ambassador to USA in 1941.
8. ADMIRAL OKADA	H.	Re-organised Japan's finances in late 19th Century.

12. "Japan is like a fish in a pond from which the water is gradually being drained away". This statement, by a naval officer to the Emperor Hirohito, refers to:-

    a) Lack of supplies for Japanese forces in China.
    b) Russian threat to Japanese supply lines in Manchuria.
    c) British, French and Dutch embargo on oil supplies to Japan.
    d) Total US embargo on trade with Japan.
    e) US naval blockade of Japanese trade routes.
    (TICK THE CORRECT ANSWER)

13. The Twenty One Demands were made in:-

       a) 1902   b) 1931   c) 1895   d)1904   e) 1915

       (TICK THE CORRECT ANSWER)

14. Which of these countries were allies of Japan during the First World War?

       a) France   b) Germany   c) Turkey   d) Austria
       e) Britain   f) The USA

15. In December, 1941 President Roosevelt said this in a radio broadcast to the American people.

> "In the past few years - and most violently in the past few days - we have learned a terrible lesson.... We must begin the great task that is before us by abandoning once and for all the illusion that we can ever again isolate ourselves from the rest of humanity ... there is no such thing as security for any nation ... in a world ruled by the principles of gangsterism. There is no such thing as impregnable defence against powerful aggressors who sneak up in the dark and strike without warning..".

    a)   Who were the powerful aggressors mentioned by Roosevelt?
    b)   What were the terrible lessons the Americans had learned in the previous years?
    c)   Who had sneaked up in the dark and struck without warning?
    d)   What do we call Americans who seek to isolate themselves from humanity? Why had their views changed?
    e)   What was the great task which lay before the USA?

16. Look at the two cartoons on the following page.

    a)   Explain the background to A.
    b)   Explain the background to B.
    c)   Describe the events which had led the British to change their attitude towards Japan between 1902 and 1931.

B. Punch Cartoon, 1931

THE HANDS OF THE LEAGUE;
OR, HER FIRST GREAT TEST.

A. Punch Cartoon, 1902

ALLIES.

"*Oh, East is East, and West is West . . . . ;*
But there is neither East nor West, Border, nor Breed, nor Birth,
When two strong men stand face to face, tho' they come from the ends of the earth!"
— RUDYARD KIPLING.

22

The Second World War
1939-1945

INTRODUCTION

The Second World War was fought by 56 nations and cost 50 million lives. This makes it the worst war in history. The First World War was Europe-centred. Its largest and fiercest battles were fought in a relatively small area of France and Belgium. For this reason it has a worse reputation amongst western Europeans, especially the British who lost three times as many men in 1914-18 as they did in 1939-45. The Second World War was a more truly global struggle, with widespread battles between Germans and Russians and a conflict which stretched from India across most of the Far East and Pacific. Even its 'sideshows' in the Mediterranean, North Africa and Italy, were on a scale which would have constituted major wars in previous centuries. It was fought also with technology far superior to that used in the First. The tanks, guns and aircraft pitted against each other widened the conflict to include civilians who died in nearly as great numbers as the fighting men. It is sometimes forgotten that the R.A.F.'s raid on Dresden in February, 1945, killed more people than those incinerated by atomic bombs at either Hiroshima or Nagasaki. These nuclear weapons, however, represented the final horror of a war dominated by scientific 'marvels' and mass-production.

The war was Europe-centred from 1939 until 1941. In some ways this was 'Hitler's War' because nazi forces overwhelmed country after country, until, by mid-1941, Hitler thought he had won. Only Britain, saved by her island situation, her airforce and her navy, held out but, without allies, she could not hope to defeat Germany. The time seemed ripe, in Hitler's view, for his long-anticipated drive east to secure 'lebensraum' from the despised Slavs. Operation Barbarossa, the code-name for the German invasion of Russia, was on a scale unique in history. Miracles of planning, organisation and logistics were performed by Hitler's armies as the Russians, caught unawares, lost millions of men and all their frontline airforce. Only desperate resistance gave them the time to let the winter set in and save the Soviet Union. A freezing winter for which the Germans were not equipped left them vulnerable to a Russian counter-attack in December. New Russian armies, supplied by the Americans, halted the German advance and saved Moscow, the Soviet capital. Next year, when the Germans struck south to capture the Russian oilfields, they suffered their first defeat at Stalingrad, a major turning point of the war.

Although fought on a gigantic scale, this war was still European - until 7 December 1941. On that day Japanese planes attacked the US naval base at Pearl Harbour in Hawaii. The USA declared war on Japan, whilst Hitler, angry at the aid Roosevelt was giving to his enemies, declared war on America. The entry of the USA had far-reaching implications. It meant that the entire Far East, including the possessions of Holland, France, Britain and Australia became a war zone. It also meant that the world's two super-powers were now involved, not only in the war, but in the peace which would follow - a fact which has affected world politics ever since.

The USA rightly judged Germany to be the greater threat and in spite of her own interest in the Pacific, chose to concentrate on the defeat of Hitler first. Consequently, as the war in North Africa was won by the Allies and Italy invaded, the US threw her enormous productive capacity into the contest. The Battle of the Atlantic, as the fight to get food and supplies into Britain was called, was fought by navies equipped with asdic and radar to offset the menace of the German 'U' Boats. The land war was affected by a US war machine superior to that of any other nation. It was said that Hitler would never have declared war on the USA if he had been round a Chicago factory. Certainly when he heard that Roosevelt had promised that America would produce 30,000 warplanes a year he said he was mad. The actual figure near the end of the war was 60,000.

Modern warfare is very expensive. Britain could not have afforded to fight after 1940 without US aid in money and supplies. Rich and powerful as Germany was, she had taken on two super-powers, Russia, whose manpower was almost inexhaustible, and the USA, whose industrial output was inexhaustible. Furthermore, after the technical achievements of 'D' Day, when thousands of Allied troops landed on open French beaches, supplied by a vast armada and a temporary harbour which had been towed across the channel, Germany was fighting Bismarck's nightmare - a two-front war. No amount of courage or military skill could alter the result after that. Germany was conquered by Allied and Russian troops so completely that this time there was no peace treaty for her nationalists to complain about. Japan, whose tentacles had spread all over the Pacific and Far East, was over-stretched. One by one her vital supply routes were cut, as the US's 'island hopping' tactics brought her troops steadily nearer to the Japanese homeland. Finally, the last and most terrible invention of the war destroyed two Japanese cities in a few minutes. This persuaded the Emperor to re-assert his authority and insist that his people give in.

The Second World War marked the end of Europe as the dominant force in world politics. It had destroyed itself by its own jealousies and rivalries and was forced to hand over its supremacy to the two super-powers.

THE 'PHONEY WAR'

The Polish forces were soon defeated by the Germans, who had overwhelming superiority in air power and tanks. The nazi victory was so swift that the Russians had to advance their own timetable. On September 17 the Russians began to occupy those Polish provinces promised them in the August agreement. When *Warsaw*, the Polish capital, fell on 27 September, the fighting was virtually over. This campaign was the first example of what became known as *'Blitzkrieg'* (German meaning, 'lightning war') which involved using tanks, assisted by aircraft, to break up and surround the enemy. Meanwhile, the Allies began a slow build-up for what they hoped would be a war of defence and attrition. A *British Expeditionary Force* (BEF) crossed to France and joined the French along the Franco-German frontier.

So little happened during the next 6 months that the period was nicknamed *'The Phoney War'*. It was, in fact, a time of build-up and re-grouping for the Germans. The British navy tightened its blockade of Germany and in a fierce battle in the South Atlantic chased the German 'pocket' battleship *'Graf Spee'* into *Montevideo* in Uruguay where its captain scuttled it when ordered to leave. A German 'U' Boat penetrated the Scapa Flow defences in Scotland and sank the British battleship, *'Royal Oak'*. The R.A.F. carried out raids over German cities, dropping not bombs, but leaflets calling on the Germans to surrender or overthrow Hitler. The Russians decided they needed territories to protect *Leningrad* and attacked *Finland*. After a 5-month *'Winter War'* (November, 1939 - March, 1940) they obtained the concessions they wanted. This aggression caused Russia to be expelled from the League of Nations.

In the spring of 1940 operations switched north. Britain considered invading *Norway* to help *Finland* and cut off Germany's supplies of Swedish iron ore. Hitler realised the danger and made a pre-emptive strike. Nazi forces overran *Denmark* and *Norway* in April. A British army sent to help the Norwegians was driven out. This gave the German 'U' Boats a long coastline for their bases. The German navy suffered severe losses during this campaign but sank two British destroyers and the aircraft carrier, *'Glorious'*. The failure of this expedition caused the fall of *Neville Chamberlain*, the British prime minister. He was replaced on 10 May 1940 by *Winston Churchill*, for long an opponent of the nazis, who headed a *Coalition* government of *Conservative, Labour* and *Liberals*. This replaced the Conservative ministry which had ruled throughout most of the Thirties.

THE FALL OF FRANCE

By a coincidence, the same day that Churchill became prime minister - 10 May - was chosen by Hitler to launch his blitzkrieg in the west; this was probably chosen because it was the anniversary of the signing of the Treaty of Frankfurt (See Work Unit 1). The Germans struck in two places, across *Belgium* and *Holland* in a 1914-style sweep (See Work Unit 12), and south in the *Ardennes*, a forest area where the French did not expect an attack because of the difficult terrain. Within days Holland and Belgium had been knocked out of the war, and the German *panzers* (armoured columns of tanks and other vehicles) had by-passed the *Maginot Line* and struck across France. This thrust cut the Allied line in two, splitting the BEF and the French, and reaching the French coast at *Abbeville* on 21

May. The BEF conducted a fighting retreat to *Dunkirk* where the British navy, assisted by small boats from southern England, managed to evacuate most of its troops, including thousands of French soldiers, to Britain (26 May - 4 June). This was called *'The Miracle of Dunkirk'* because, although it was a severe defeat, it saved the only army Britain possessed at that time.

The Germans now turned south, occupied *Paris* - which the French had declared an 'open city' and refused to defend - and began to round up the demoralised and scattered French divisions. On 25 June a new French government, led by *Marshal Petain*, signed an armistice which left most of northern France in German hands. Petain was allowed to form a satellite regime in the south, with its capital at *Vichy*. This government tended to be pro-German so when French naval units at *Oran* and *Mers-el-Kebir* declared for Vichy, Churchill sent British naval forces to destroy or disable them so that they could not be used by the Germans. A *'Free French'* army was formed in Britain. It was commanded by *General Charles de Gaulle*, who defied his superiors in France and vowed to continue the war until France was liberated.

THE BATTLE OF BRITAIN

Britain now stood alone. The threat of invasion was so serious that civilians, often older ex-servicemen, were formed into *Local Defence Volunteers* (LDV) to augment the regular army. This became the *Home Guard*. When the British defiantly rejected Hitler's peace offers, the nazi leader prepared for invasion. As a prelude he launched an all-out attack on British airfields and, later on *London* itself. This was the start of the *Blitz* - aerial bombing of London and other British cities which continued sporadically throughout the war, and caused heavy civilian casualties.

The Germans planned to get their troops across the Channel in barges and boats. This was a dangerous plan considering the superiority of the British navy, and impossible without command of the air. Goering promised Hitler an easy and swift victory but the RAF, equipped with *Spitfires* and *Hurricane* fighter planes, won the so-called *Battle of Britain* against the Luftwaffe operating at a greater distance and with slow-moving bombers which stood little chance once their fighter escort was destroyed. Of this battle, Churchill said, 'Never in the field of human conflict has so much been owed by so many to so few' and for this reason Battle of Britain pilots are known as the *'Few'*.

Hitler abandoned his invasion plans but sent his bombers over Britain throughout the winter, 1940-41.*London* was bombed on 50 consecutive nights and provincial targets like *Coventry* (where the cathedral was destroyed), *Liverpool, Portsmouth, Plymouth, Birmingham, Cardiff* and *Swansea* were also attacked and devastated. Thousands of civilians were killed in these raids and even more made homeless. Most city-dwellers had *Anderson* shelters in their gardens - installed before the war - and some had *Morrison* shelters in the house. These were designed to prevent victims being crushed when the building collapsed.

BATTLES IN NORTH AFRICA

Britain's empire, including the dominions, was also involved in the war and it was therefore possible to attack Italian North African possessions. (Italy had joined the war on Germany's side. See Work Unit 16.) British victory was so swift and complete that by 1942 the Germans had to send an elite force, the *Afrika Corps*, commanded by *General Erwin Rommel* to drive the British back. Rommel was so successful that his army at one time seemed poised to conquer *Egypt* and control the Suez Canal and Britain's links with the Middle Eastern oilfields. This danger was finally averted in October, 1942 when *General Bernard Montgomery's* Eighth Army won the *Battle of Alamein* and, aided by an Anglo-American force landed in *Morocco* and *Algeria*, finally drove the Axis forces out of Africa and invaded *Italy*.

LEND-LEASE AND THE ATLANTIC CHARTER

In early 1941 the USA was still not in the war but its president, *Franklin Roosevelt*, was anti-Nazi and promised 'all aid short of war'; isolationist feeling in the United States made it impossible for him to go further at that stage. Roosevelt also started his *Lend-Lease Scheme*, whereby goods as well as money could be 'loaned' to any country fighting Hitler; this meant Britain and, later in the year, Russia. In May, 1941 Britain confirmed her control of the seas by destroying the powerful German battleship, *'Bismarck'* after a maiden voyage lasting only a few days, although the British battleship, *'Hood'* was lost with nearly all hands.

In August, 1941 Roosevelt and Churchill met on a British battleship off *Newfoundland*.They signed the *Atlantic Charter*, promising freedom and aid to all peoples fighting Nazi tyranny, and guaranteeing certain basic human rights. This Charter was influential after the war in inspiring colonial peoples to resist imperialism. *The Battle of the Atlantic* against the 'U' Boats was affecting the USA as much as it had in the First World War. Roosevelt considered it vital that supplies should get through to Britain so he ordered his naval forces to 'shoot on sight' at German 'U' Boats even though Germany and the USA were not at war.

BALKAN INVASIONS

Germany became involved in the Balkans owing to the failure of the Italian invasion of *Greece*. Hitler had already overrun *Rumania* to ensure control of her oilfields. Now he conquered *Yugoslavia* and *Greece*. A British force which went to the aid of the Greeks was driven out. Most of the Italian fleet was destroyed in two battles, at *Taranto*, where a successful British attack was carried out with carrier-based torpedo-carrying aircraft, and in a fleet action off *Cape Matapan*. In May, 1941 a German parachute force took *Crete* from the British, who suffered heavy losses in naval battles around the island. In June and July, a British and Free-French army occupied *Syria* because its *Vichy* sympathisers had been helping the Axis powers.

OPERATION BARBAROSA

Hitler decided that the war in the west was over. The time had come for him to settle accounts with Russia. The campaigns against Greece, Yugoslavia and Crete, although they had delayed an invasion of Russia by a few months, had given him a safe right flank for the coming attack, which was code-named *Operation Barbarossa* (Redbeard). This had always been his chief ambition; the Nazi-Soviet Pact was merely to stop a two-front war developing whilst he dealt with France and Britain. On 22 June 1941 the Germans crossed the border into Russian-occupied Poland. The attack came as a surprise to Stalin who had ignored intelligence reports which warned him of a huge build-up of German tanks and troops. The German panzer armies fanned out into three main thrusts, against *Moscow, Leningrad* and *Kiev* (See map). The result was a catastrophe for the Red army; thousands of men were captured or killed and the Russian front-line airforce ceased to exist as a fighting force.

From the start the Germans treated the Poles and Russians with great brutality, so great that any chance of Russians who hated the Soviet regime helping them was wiped away. Stalin was able to appeal to the patriotic instincts of the Russian people and to declare all out war on the invader. As far as possible everything in the invader's path was destroyed; this became known as the *'scorched earth'* policy. In the north, helped by the Finns who saw a chance of revenge for the Winter War, the Germans moved into the suburbs of *Leningrad* and began an epic siege of that city. In the south they broke through to the *Crimea* and by December, 1941, their advance guard was nearing *Moscow*. The western Allied leaders, including Roosevelt, promised all possible aid to Russia, despite their dislike of communism. Fresh supplies of tanks in particular enabled the Russians to launch their first counter-attack and save Moscow. This was the first German setback of the war. By this time German troops were suffering the cold of a Russian winter for which they were not equipped because Hitler had gambled on a quick campaign.

STALINGRAD

In 1942 a German army moved south to capture the oilfields of the *Caucasus* and the key city of *Stalingrad*. The Germans battered their way into the city, reducing it to rubble in the process. In the house to house fighting which followed the Germans lost the superiority given them in tank battles. As the battle raged in the ruins, another Russian army surrounded the city, cutting off the Germans, whom Goering had promised he would supply by air. The Luftwaffe failed to do this, and after three months, the entire German force, including its commander, *Field-Marshal Friedrich von Paulus* were captured (Feb 1943). Apart from losing 140,000 dead, over 90,000 German surrendered, and this caused Hitler to issue a 'no surrender' order to his troops in Russia. Stalingrad was the turning point in the war between Russia and Germany, In 1943 the siege of Leningrad was lifted and the Germans were defeated in the biggest tank battle of the war at *Kursk*.

RUSSIAN CONQUESTS IN EUROPE

Russia was now aided by the USA, whose supplies arrived by sea at *Murmansk*, and by her own factories which had been dismantled and moved bodily to safety behind the *Ural mountains*. Altogether Russia received from abroad 10,000 tanks, 18,700 planes, 427,000 lorries and 1,100 locomotives. As a consequence of these supplies, and the courage of her troops, she began a steady drive west which did not end until her troops entered the ruins of *Berlin* in March, 1945. During 1944 the Russians defeated *Finland*, occupied *Bulgaria* and *Rumania* and penetrated into the *Baltic states, Hungary, Czechoslovakia, Yugoslavia* (where *Marshal Tito* had pinned down a sizeable nazi force) and reached *Austria* and *East Prussia*. In Poland they destroyed half the enemy forces facing them but when *Warsaw* rose in revolt against the Germans, Stalin was either unwilling or unable to enter the city before the nazis had wiped out the defenders. On 25 April 1945 the Red army met American troops advancing from the west - at *Torgau* near Berlin. This completed the conquest of Germany and led to Hitler's suicide, 30 April.

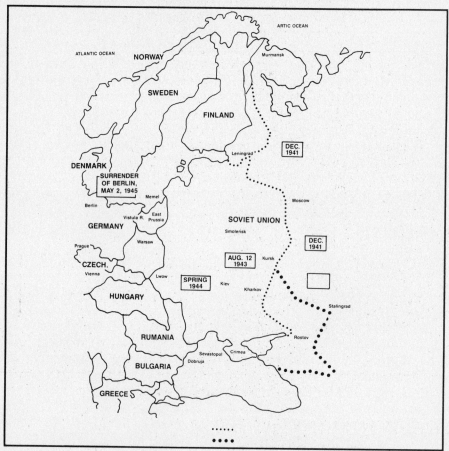

Soviet Advances, 1942-45

JAPAN AND THE USA ENTER THE WAR

On 7 December 1941 Japan attacked the US naval base at *Pearl Harbour* in *Hawaii*. Her troops also landed in *Malaya* and *Siam*. Roosevelt promptly declared war on Japan (See Work Unit 21). Germany then declared war on the USA. At first the Japanese advance was swift and dramatic. *Hong Kong, Malaya* and *Singapore*, Britain's chief base in the Far East, fell with little fighting. The *Dutch East Indies* (now Indonesia) were occupied, and by May 1942 Japanese troops had crossed *Burma* to threaten *India* and had occupied *New Guinea* to threaten *Australia*. The Americans were driven out of the *Phillipines* and other Pacific islands. These stunning Japanese successes were followed by their first setback. In June, 1942 a Japanese invasion of *Midway Island* was defeated at sea by an American carrier forces which inflicted heavy losses on the Japanese fleet and airforce.

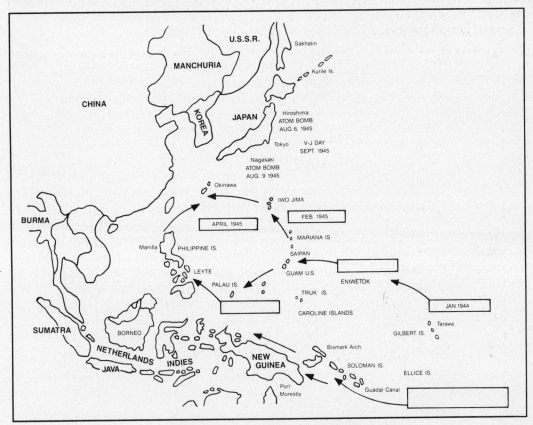

The War in the Pacific, 1941-45

"ISLAND-HOPPING STRATEGY"

Midway proved a sign of things to come. Between 1943 and 1945 US naval carrier forces established a superiority over the Japanese which meant that they could take back, one by one, the islands lost in the first few months of the war.

This strategy was called *'island-hopping'* and it involved the extensive use of amphibious forces. The *Soloman Islands, New Guinea* (with Australian troops involved), and the Phillipines were recovered, whilst the Japanese navy was virtually wiped out in the battles of the *Coral Sea* and *Leyte Gulf*. The British 14th army - nicknamed the 'forgotten Army' because priority always had to be given to the forces fighting in Europe - halted the Japanese drive on India, defeated them at *Kohima* and captured *Rangoon*, the Burmese capital.

HIROSHIMA

The Americans were soon within bombing range of Japan itself and their 'Super-Fortress' bombers began devastating fire-raids on largely wooden cities. *Iwojima* and *Okinawa* fell to the US marines but their losses were heavy owing to fanatical resistance. On 6 August 1945 an American Superfortress nicknamed *'Enola Gay'* dropped the first atomic bomb on *Hiroshima*, killing or injuring 160,000. Three days later *Nagasaki* was destroyed with a nuclear device. This caused the Japanese emperor, *Hirohito*, to insist that Japan surrender unconditionally. This saved the Americans attempting the invasion of Japan, an operation which the US military estimated would cost the lives of at least a million American soldiers. When American soldiers landed in Japan there was no resistance. Some Japanese leaders committed hara-kiri in consequence. *Russia* had declared war on Japan on 8 August and occupied *Manchuria*; this was part of an agreement reached with Roosevelt and Churchill at *Tehran* in November, 1943 (See later section).

THE ITALIAN CAMPAIGN

After the victory of the Eighth army at *Alamein* in October, 1942 and *General Dwight D. Eisenhower's* landings in *Morocco* and *Algeria*, the Germans and Italians were driven out of North Africa; there was a formal surrender of 250,000 men, including the Afrika Corps, in May, 1943. The Allies then invaded *Sicily*, a move which led to the fall and imprisonment of *Mussolini*. The new Italian government entered into secret negotiation with the Allies to change sides. Mussolini was rescued by German parachutists and taken to northern Italy where he was put in charge of a puppet regime run by the Germans. The Allied troops landed in Italy and began a drive on *Naples* which was halted by determined German resistance. A naval landing at *Salerno* was nearly driven into the sea and it was weeks before the city fell to British and American troops.

MONTE CASSINO

The next objective was Rome but the way was barred by rough terrain and well-entrenched German troops. A major obstacle was *Monte Cassino*, a mountain with an ancient monastery at the summit. Months of heavy fighting, and the destruction of the monastery by bombing, were needed before Mount Cassino was taken. Its loss led to the capture of *Rome* and the breaking of a line of defences called the *Adolf Hitler Line*, June 1944. Fighting continued in the north of Italy until April, 1945 because it was country ideal for defence. On 28 April 1945 *Mussolini* was captured and shot by Italian communist resistance fighters. His body was hung from a garage in a square in *Milan*, together with that of his mistress, Claretta.

OPERATION OVERLORD; THE INVASION OF EUROPE

From 1942 onwards Stalin made constant appeals for a *Second Front* to be opened in the west to ease the German pressure on Russia. This was a difficult operation because it involved sea-borne landings against heavily defended coastline, Hitler's so-called *Atlantic Wall*. A probing raid against *Dieppe* in 1942 by a largely Canadian force was a disastrous failure but its mistakes were useful lessons for the main invasion, code-named *Operation Overlord*, which began on 6 June 1944. D (Deliverance) Day was targeted at open beaches in the *Normandy peninsula* of France, mainly because Dieppe had shown how difficult it was to attack a defended port. Since it was estimated that it might be weeks before *Cherbourg*, the nearest major port, could be taken, an artificial harbour, *Mulberry* was towed across to the beach at *Arromanches* and oil was pumped from England by *PLUTO (pipeline under the ocean)*.

The five landing beaches were code-named *Utah, Omaha, Gold, Juno* and *Sword*. Some beaches were taken quickly but at Omaha the Americans suffered heavy losses when they became stranded by shallow waters and the tides. The overall commander of the invasion was *General Eisenhower*, with *General Montgomery* in charge of military operations. One hundred and thirty thousand men were landed on the first day and from then on the build-up continued steadily, aided by Allied control of the sea and air. Within 3 weeks *Cherbourg* was captured but determined German resistance kept the Allies trapped in Normandy until August, when, after the battle of *Falaise*, they broke out and threatened the Germans with encirclement. The Germans retreated and the way was open to *Paris* which was captured in August, 1944; *General de Gaulle* led his Free French troops into the city. A month earlier a group of German officers had tried to kill Hitler in order to end the war with favourable terms for Germany. The *Hitler Bomb Plot* failed to kill the dictator and he spent the rest of the war in investigating, arresting, torturing and executing anybody connected with it.

ARNHEM

With the Allies nearing Germany, *Montgomery* launched a bold attempt to seize the Rhine crossing at *Arnhem* in Holland and so gain access to the heart of Germany. The initial attacks were carried out by parachutists, whose job was to hold the bridges until land forces broke through from the south. *Operation Market Garden* proved a gallant failure. Reports of two German panzer divisions in the area were not given the importance they deserved, and defective judgement led to a landing at *Oosterbeke*. This involved a march into the town and caused delays. The land forces failed to get through in time, although the parachutists held out against a tank force for far longer than had been planned. Only about a quarter of the original airborne force made their escape.

BATTLE OF THE BULGE

The final stages of the European war saw Allied landings in southern France and Hitler's attempts to win the war with 'secret' weapons. In June, 1944 his *V1* rocket planes began to fall on London and, later in the year, his *V2* rocket bombs caused death and destruction. Neither altered the course of the war. In December, 1944, a final German offensive in the *Ardennes*, launched in thick fog, broke through the American lines to such a depth that the battle is known as the *Bulge*. Once the fog cleared Allied air power and re-inforcements drove the Germans back with heavy losses. In March, 1945 German engineers tried to blow up a bridge across the Rhine at *Remagen*. They failed and a few Americans were able to get across to secure the opposite bank. At the same time, British troops crossed in a glider-borne attack. Further south Allied troops had entered *Austria* and the link up with the Russians occurred at *Torgau*. Hitler committed suicide and Germany surrendered on 7 May, 1945.

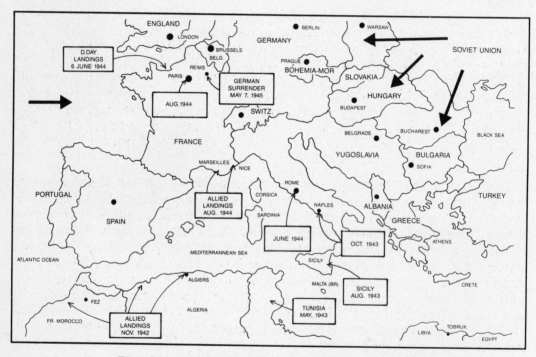

The Second World War in the West, 1942-45

THE WAR AT SEA AND IN THE AIR

The war between the 'U' Boats and the Allied navies went on without break from 1939 until 1945. A *convoy* system similar to that used in the First World War was necessary because a merchant ship on its own stood little chance against the 'unseen enemy'. Even convoys failed in the early days of the war because the British navy was short of ships. In May,1941 an armed merchant ship, the *Jervis Bay*, was the only escort for 37 merchant ships. Her captain engaged the German battleship, *Admiral Scheer*, in a suicidal conflict which led to the loss of the 'Jervis Bay', but allowed most of the merchant ships to escape. Later in the war aircraft, operating long-range from land, were able to join in the battle against the "U" boats.

The German reply was to form their submarines into groups. These *'Wolf Packs'* would stalk a convoy and attack when the time was ripe. Sometimes these tactics led to the loss of half the convoy. The Allies used asdic, radar and depth charges to counter the 'U' Boat menace. In 1941-2, 800,000 tons of Allied shipping were being sunk each month. Gradually, these losses were reduced and altogether the Germans lost 783 "U" Boats and 32,000 sailors during the war. US factories were able to replace the lost ships with hastily built, prefabricated *'Liberty' ships*. The importance of this sea battle cannot be over-estimated. Without command of the seas, Russia could not have received supplies, Britain might have been starved into surrender and 'D' Day would have been impossible.

BOMBING OFFENSIVES

In aerial fighting the Allies gradually obtained complete supremacy over the Luftwaffe and this was of enormous benefit to the land operations, notably in the 'D' Day landings. The *bombing* offensive against Germany was begun initially to offset the fact that Britain had no other way of assaulting Germany after the Fall of France. At first, these raids had two objectives: to destroy targets vital for the German war-effort and to break the morale of the German people and force them to surrender. After Russia's entry into the war, a third objective was added: to weaken the Luftewaffe and so ease pressure on the Red Army and air-force. After 1942 these campaigns involved the Americans, whose squadrons of heavy bombers, the *Flying Fortresses*, operated from British bases.

The driving force behind the bomber offensive was *Air Chief Marshal Arthur (bomber) Harris* who persisted in believing he could win the war with air power alone despite much criticism. In May, 1942 Harris launched the first *Thousand Bomber Raid* on *Cologne*. Germany was well-defended in the early stages of this offensive and air-crew losses were heavy. The attacks grew in number as the war progressed, and were continuous, with the Americans attacking by day and the British by night. Massive raids on *Hamburg* and other German cities caused 'fire-storms' due to the use of high explosive and incendiary bombs and these caused heavy loss of life amongst civilians. Finally, in February, 1945 the RAF devastated the city of *Dresden* in one night with appalling losses in a city crowded with refugees fleeing from the Russians.

A different approach to bombing was to attack specific targets to obtain maximum disruption. The most famous raid of this kind was the *Dambuster Raid* in May, 1943, led by *Wing-Commander Guy Gibson*, which breached the *Moehne* and *Eder* dams and flooded large parts of the *Ruhr*. It was in this raid that Gibson's *Lancaster bombers* used the *'bouncing bomb'* invented by *Dr. Barnes Wallis*. Bomber Command carried out attacks on the German battleships, *Scharnhorst, Gneisenau* and *Tirpitz* to prevent them leaving port and attacking convoys. The RAF also attacked 'U' Boat pens as part of the war in the Atlantic.

WARTIME CONFERENCES

The chief Allied leaders, *Churchill, Roosevelt* and *Stalin*, met several times during the war. At *Tehran,* Iran, in November, 1943, they agreed to open a 'Second Front' as soon as possible and to replace the League of Nations with a new world organisation as soon as the war against Germany was won. Russia also promised to enter the war against Japan as soon as Germany was defeated. The *Yalta,* Crimea, conference in February, 1945 was the most controversial. The three men agreed that German military power was to be destroyed and its leaders tried as war criminals. A new organisation, *The United Nations*, was to be founded at *San Francisco* in the USA, the principles of of the *Atlantic charter* were re-affirmed and Stalin was persuaded to allow free elections in territories liberated by the Red Army. Since that time Churchill and Roosevelt have been blamed for letting Soviet Russia take over eastern Europe and turn its countries into satellite states. In fact, the whole region was already occupied by the Red Army so there was little the Allies could do unless they were prepared to go to war with Russia.

POLAND AND MANCHURIA

Many arguments between Churchill, Roosevelt and Stalin concerned the fate of Poland, the country whose fate triggered off the war in the first place. Stalin made it clear that Russia must have a 'friendly' Poland as a buffer between Russia and Germany. He pointed out how often Russia had been invaded across the Polish territory. The Allies got him to agree to free elections and democratic parties in Poland but by 1947 the country was a communist satellite. At *Yalta* Stalin also asked that the verdict of the Russo-Japanese War be reversed. He re-stated his promise to declare war on Japan as soon as the war in Europe was over and demanded areas of *Manchuria* and *Sakhalin* which involved taking land from the Chinese as well as the Japanese.

The last war-time conference took place at *Potsdam*, near Berlin, and was attended by *Harry S. Truman*, the new President of the USA following Roosevelt's death, *Clement Attlee*, the new British prime minister after Churchill's defeat in the July, 1945 election, and *Stalin*. It dealt with the final plans for the defeat of Japan but Truman and Attlee mentioned only that they had "a super bomb", not its exact nature.

THE HOLOCAUST AND NUREMBERG

By 1942 Hitler's hatred of Jews made him decide on what he called the *Final Solution* - the mass murder of all Jews. The initial massacres were carried out by shooting. Later this method was abandoned in favour of *gassing* to save ammunition. Death factories were set up at *Treblinka, Auschwitz, Dachau* and *Belsen*. Victims arrived from all over Europe by cattle truck. They were told to strip for a shower and then led into specially-built chambers which could kill 2000 at a time. *Auschwitz*, in particular, was a vast industrial complex, covering 15 square miles, including gas-chambers and synthetic petrol and rubber works for the disposal and recycling of the bodies. Altogether, 6,000,000 Jews were killed in this way and it is known today as the *Holocaust* which means 'a destruction by fire'.

Many of the officials responsible for the holocaust, plus Nazi leaders including *Goering, Ribbentrop,* and *Seyss-Inquart*, were put on trial by the *Allies at* Nuremberg on charges of 'Crimes against peace' and 'crimes against humanity'. Some were sentenced to death and executed; Goering cheated the hangman by committing suicide. Goebbels had died with Hitler in Berlin in 1945.

SELF-ASSESSMENT SECTION

1. What was Lend-Lease?

2. What was Mulberry?

3. What was operation Barbarossa?

4. What was 'scorched earth'?

5. How did PLUTO get its name?

6. What was the purpose of 'island-hopping'?

7. What was the purpose of the Atlantic Wall?

8. What was Operation Market Garden?

9. Where was Sword Beach?

10. What was a V1?

11. Where were these battles fought and who won them?

a) Stalingrad	b) Midway	c) Taranto
d) Arnhem	e) Oran	f) Monte Cassino
g) Alamein	h) Crete	

12. Hitler invaded Norway:-

    a) to prevent an invasion by Britain.
    b) to prevent an invasion by Sweden
    c) to safeguard supplies of iron ore
    d) to cut off supplies to Russia
    e) to prevent an invasion by Russia
        (TICK THE CORRECT ANSWER)

13. The Second Front was a plan to:-

    a) invade Italy
    b) invade Vichy France
    c) invade Greece
    d) invade North Africa
    e) invade northern France
        (TICK THE CORRECT ANSWER)

14. Put in correct details (by letter) against these names.

1.	PETAIN	A.	US commander in chief
2.	DE GAULLE	B.	Victor of Alamein
3.	EISENHOWER	C.	Led bombing offensive
4.	MONTGOMERY	D.	Led Yugoslav partisans
5.	ROMMEL	E.	Captured by Russians
6.	HARRIS	F.	Leader of Vichy France
7.	PAULUS	G.	Commander of the Afrika Corps
8.	TITO	H.	Leader of the Free French

15. Look at the map below. Then answer the questions that follow.

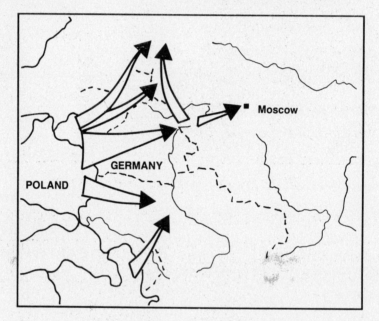

    a)   Who invaded Russia? What was this invasion code-named?

    b)   Why was this invasion launched in June, 1941, *and not before?*

    c)   What was Hitler's purpose in launching this invasion?

    d)   What were the long term results of this invasion?

16. The aerial photographs on the following page were taken over Germany in 1943.

    a)   What does A. show?

    b)   What had happened by the time B. was taken?

    c)   Explain what lay behind this operation and what were its results.

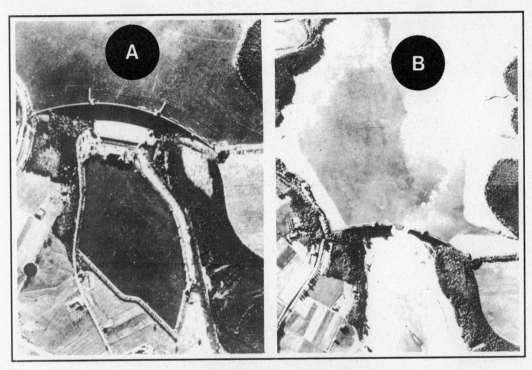

(Photographs: Imperial War Museum)

17. Put the correct captions (given on page 217) to the following photographs.

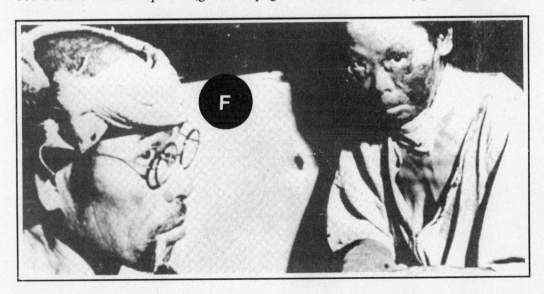

1. The Battle of Midway
2. The Dunkirk evacuation
3. The Battle of Britain
4. Hiroshima
5. The attack on Pearl Harbour

18. Imagine you are a soldier at one of these battles.

   a) Arnhem
   b) Stalingrad
   c) 'D' Day

From these notes, plus your previous knowledge, describe in as much detail as possible your experiences.

23

Stalin's Russia

INTRODUCTION

The original leaders of the Russian revolution underrated Stalin. When a Bolshevik asked Trotsky, possibly the most brilliant intellectual of them all, 'What is Stalin?', the great man replied. 'The outstanding mediocrity of the Party'. Yet this 'mediocrity' discarded Trotsky's ideas of world revolution, drove him from Russia, and, in 1940, had him murdered in Mexico. 'Trotskyite' became a label which could lead a person to death or imprisonment inside Russia.

It was true that Stalin was the odd man out in the Bolshevik leadership. Trotsky and Lenin were middle-class intellectuals, deeply influenced by western ideas, notably the writings of Karl Marx, the German founder of communism. Stalin was of peasant stock from the 'backwoods' region of Georgia. He spoke Russian with a Georgian accent, had no knowledge of foreign languages, and only visited Europe four times. This may well have given him a sense of inferiority and it certainly made him suspicious of everybody. It also seems to have given him a driving need to defeat his rivals and prove them wrong. It was not only Trotsky who roused his hatred. Seventeen leaders of the Russian revolution and half of the 139 members of the Party Central Committee were executed on Stalin's orders. In the country at large the death toll of those who dared to disagree with him rose to millions, a fact which he did not attempt to deny or cover up.

Stalin was a Russian first and a European second. In this respect he resembled some of the old Tsars who had preceded him. He did not believe that world revolution was possible or even desirable and preferred the opposite view. 'Socialism in One country' became the slogan of his industrialisation policies. He believed that Soviet Russia must become powerful enough to withstand the attack of the capitalist west, an attack he believed was inevitable. Whilst his opponents spoke of high ideals and explained their complicated theories, Stalin dealt in the 'nuts and bolts' of building an industrial economy. He was completely ruthless. He made terrible mistakes. But when he died Russia was the second industrial power in the world.

How did Stalin steal Soviet Russia from the men who had created it? How did he manage to rule as a dictator from 1929 until 1953? The key to his success was

218

sensed by Lenin who, in his last 'testament' of April, 1923, complained of Stalin's 'rudeness' and warned about the excessive concentration of 'boundless power' in his hands. It was a prophetic remark. Stalin was ready to do the dull, dirty work of organising the Party at provincial level. This may have been why Trotsky dismissed him as a 'mediocrity' but the results of such spadework were staggering. In 1924 ninety per cent of provincial party secretaries, key men in their areas, had been appointed by Stalin. Five years later most of the bosses at provincial level were Stalin's men. This in-depth control of the communist party power apparatus led to supreme power for Stalin. Occasionally action seems to have been taken at a lower level but he was always 'chairman of the board' and made the final decisions. By the time of the notorious purges of party officials and old Bolsheviks in the 1930's Stalin was in complete control and is known to have signed many of the death warrants himself.

The German attack on Russia in 1941, which Stalin had predicted for years, actually took him by surprise when it happened, and his mistakes at this time nearly cost Russia the war. When the tide of battle turned, Stalin took the credit for victories won by his generals. The 'personality cult' which resulted seems to have been believed by Stalin himself, who spent some of his later years watching films about Russian successes made by officials too terrified to tell him the truth.

Since his death in 1953 Stalin has been condemned by Russian leaders beginning with Khrushchev in 1956. The mistakes, the slaughter, the fake trials and confessions, have been revealed to the world by official accounts and the writings of one or two famous survivors. As a result his achievements have sometimes been ignored. Stalin was certainly an alcoholic and probably insane. He killed far more people than Hitler and set Russia's agriculture back at least half a century. But he made Russia a great industrial power, dragging her, with a great deal of kicking and screaming, into the mid-Twentieth century. We shall never know whether other Bolsheviks could have done the job better, although they could all have done it more humanely. We shall never know because Stalin made sure they never had the chance.

THE RISE OF STALIN

During the 1920's Russia made slow economic recovery after the ravages of the First World War and the civil war which followed. (See Work Unit 13) Lenin's *New Economic Policy*, with its leaning towards capitalism, was continued after his death, and peasants and traders were allowed to make profits. It was 1927 before Russian production reached the 1913 level. After Lenin's premature death in 1924 there was a power struggle between the Bolshevik leaders. *Joseph Stalin* - the word is Russian and means 'man of steel' - was at odds with *Kamanev, Zinoviev* and *Trotsky*. They were of middle class origin, he was working class.

Such personality differences were made worse by a serious rift about Soviet Russia's role in the world. As a convinced Marxist, Trotsky was aware that the communist revolution had occurred in a country unsuitable for it; Marx had envisaged a more industrialised country able to withstand the strains of changing from a capitalist to a communist economy. It was better, in Trotsky's view, to wait until revolution had spread to more industrialised countries, notably Germany. The weakness of this plan was that no other communist revolts were successful.

Furthermore, Trotsky's support of the *Communist International* and his talk of inevitable world revolution, merely increased the hostility of capitalist nations towards Russia. Communist Russia was alone, and so Stalin's opposite view, that Russia should consolidate its own revolution and prepare for the inevitable capitalist attack, seemed more realistic. This fact, plus Stalin's crucial position as General Secretary of the Communist Party's Central Committee, led to Trotsky's defeat. In 1927 he was expelled from the Party and in 1929 driven into exile. He continued to write powerful indictments of Stalin's brand of communism and became such an influential figure amongst the world's communists that Stalin arranged for him to be murdered by an agent in Mexico in 1940.

THE FIVE YEAR PLANS

Stalin and his supporters believed that Russian industry could be revolutionised by a series of plans, each spread over five years, and each calling for a specific increase in the production of coal, iron, timber, electricity, steel, concrete and tractors. None of these plans involved much increase in food, housing or clothing, although Stalin hoped to increase agricultural production by *collectivisation* - state control of farming. In his view this was essential if there was to be enough food for factory workers struggling to meet the targets of the *First Five Year Plan*. Throughout the late 1920's peasants, particularly wealthier ones called *kulaks*, had been hoarding grain to raise prices. This led in 1928 to the forcible requisitioning of grain by the government.

The first *Five Year Plan* proposed that 20% of all sown land should be collectivised. In key grain-growing areas this was done at such a rate that between June and October 1929 the number of peasants in collectives doubled. There was, however, considerable resistance from the peasants who took to killing their livestock and destroying implements rather than hand them over to the state. To deal with this problem, the government resorted to ruthless methods. Twenty five thousand officials, called 'workers' were sent into the countryside to speed-up the process. These *'twenty five thousanders'* expelled kulaks from their farms and seized their stock and tools. Altogether 5 million peasants, - men, women and children - were deported to barren regions, where they were left to fend for themselves or die. The numbers of Russian livestock halved between 1928 and 1932.

RAPID INDUSTRIALISATION

Meanwhile industrialisation proceeded at breakneck speed, urged on by officials who set impossible targets; the first Five Year Plan was actually supposed to be completed in four years. When such targets were not reached, or products proved of poor quality, it became the custom to blame 'sabotage' and imprison the engineers. There were trials of engineers in the *Shakhty* region of the *Donbass* and others, culminating in the trial of British engineers employed by Metro-Vickers in 1933. Foreign engineers were deported from the country after conviction;

Russian engineers were usually shot. In the meantime, industrialisation was proceeding quickly, even if not quite at the pace shown by government figures. Big increases in machinery, machine tools, turbines and tractors were achieved and areas like the *Ukraine*, the *Volga*, the *Urals* and *South-West Siberia* became industrialised. Extensive railway and canal building took place, and the *Dneiper Dam* supplied electric power for Ukrainian industry. Only agriculture showed a steep decline and in 1933 there was a serious *famine* leading to millions of deaths.

STAKHANOVITES

The *Second Five Year Plan* set more realistic targets which were reached and, sometimes, surpassed. Conditions on the land improved slowly because, although collectivisation continued, peasants were allowed their own plot of land and some livestock. Steel production trebled as the large factories set up by the first Five Year Plan developed into great industrial centres like *Magnitogorsk, Kuznetsk* and *Zaporozhe*. Coal and oil did not do as well and there was little increase in consumer goods, especially as more of the national budget was being spent on defence. Although the numbers of workers had decreased, output increased because of the *Stakhanovite* movement. *Alezksie Stakhanov*, a miner, cut 102 tonnes of coal in 30-31 August 1935, thus doing the work of 14 men. He had been given the easiest seams to cut, the best machinery and as much assistance as he needed. He became a national hero and his achievement was afterwards regarded as 'normal' production,

The *Third Five Year Plan* (1938-41) also emphasised the development of heavy industry but more productivity went on defence as the situation in Europe worsened. This plan was interrupted by Hitler's invasion of Russia in 1941.

THE PURGES

Until 1934 the only major trials in Russia had concerned sabotage of the economy. But in that year a communist who had criticised Stalin, *M.N. Ryutin*, was put on trial for his life. The *Poliburo* (Ruling Committee of Soviet Communist Party) opposed such extreme penalties and Ryutin and his supporters were merely expelled from the party. Since the accused included anybody who had read Ryutin's pamphlet, over a million members were thrown out. The significance of this trial was that it set the scene for what was to follow. *'Show' trials*, involving written confessions, bullying prosecutors and no proper evidence, were later used during the period of the great *purges*, 1936-8.

In January, 1935 *Zinoviev* and *Kamenev*, both old Bolsheviks, were arrested and charged with plotting to murder Stalin. They were linked with the absent Trotsky, who was charged with organising murders and sabotage inside Russia, and accused of working with the Nazi secret police. Both were found guilty and sentenced to terms of imprisonment. Next year the Supreme Military Tribunal re-tried them and they were shot, after making dramatic confessions which had been forced out of them.

221

The second show trials concerned more old Bolshevik leaders, *Bukharin, Rykov* and *Tomsky*, Tomsky committed suicide and when the others refused to confess, *Yagoda*, the official in charge of the investigations, was dismissed and replaced by *Ezhov*. During his time as *People's Commissar of Internal Affairs* thousands of people were executed, including *Marshal Tukhachevsky*, a brilliant soldier, eleven Deputy Commissars of Defence and eight admirals of the Soviet Fleets. All had been charged with being traitors. It was made clear that only by denouncing somebody else could a person remain alive; there were even targets of how many people had to be denounced in a given period. Finally, *Yagoda* himself was shot.

It seems that Stalin's aim in these trials was to eliminate all opposition to his power and his ideas. He was determined to destroy any chance of an alternative government to his own at a time when the rise of Nazi Germany posed a threat to communism.

RUSSIA'S SATELLITES

Russia's victory in the Second World War gave Stalin control of eastern Europe. By 1945 the Red Army had occupied 200,000 square miles of land containing 22 million people, and her border was 300 miles west of its 1939 position. Stalin had made it clear to his allies that he would not allow any of the countries of this area to be 'unfriendly'. He also admitted that 'any freely elected government would be anti-Soviet'.

In *Poland, Hungary, Bulgaria* and *Rumania* governments of *'National Unity'* were set up. The majority of members of such governments were communists who soon gained control and set up one-party states under Russian supervision. A 'dynasty' of Stalinist dictators - *Gomulka* in Poland, *Dimitrov* in Bulgaria, *Anna Pauker* in Rumania and *Rakesi* in Hungary - ruled under the watchful eye of the Soviet leader. *Yugoslavia*, which had not been 'liberated' by the Red Army, had its own Government of National Unity which was eventually dominated by the communist *Marshal Tito*. Tito, however, remained independent of Stalin, much to the latter's annoyance. Opponents of these governments were imprisoned, shot or exiled. Party elections did take place but there was never any doubt that the results would be overwhelmingly in favour of the existing regime.

THE CZECHOSLOVAKIAN COUP

Czechoslovakia, which had never been occupied by Russian troops. maintained a precarious independence until 1948. Its coalition government contained many communists who spent 1947 filling key posts with their supporters and proposing vote-catching schemes to deal with the economic crisis caused by a drought and consequent poor harvest. On 20 February 1948 the non-communist members of the government resigned, thinking that the communists' would do the same, thus leading to a general election. The communists, however, did not resign. Instead they staged huge demonstrations and called a general strike. This forced *President Benes* to resign and a new ministry of communists, led by *Klement Gottwald*, took power. *Gottwald* adopted Soviet methods to deal with the crisis and took Czechoslovakia firmly into the Russian orbit. (See Work Unit 30).

Winston Churchill, in a speech at Fulton, Missouri, in March, 1946, had already labelled the situation with an unforgettable sentence. 'From Stettin in the Baltic to Trieste in the Adriatic, an iron curtain had descended across the continent', he said. Ever since, the Russian satellites in eastern Europe have been known as *"Iron Curtain'* countries.

NATO AND THE GERMAN PROBLEM

[handwritten: Russia, not as STRONG as the WEST. HUGE WAR TIME LOSSES]

In spite of her commanding position in eastern Europe, Stalin's Russia was not as strong as the west, particularly the USA, seemed to think. Russia's war-time losses had been appalling: - 20,000,000 dead, 1,250,000 houses destroyed, 65,000 kilometres of railway line torn up and 17,000,000 cattle killed. On the other hand, her losses were balanced partly by her land acquisitions and the ending, temporarily at least, of the German threat which had plagued Russia for centuries. The USA had suffered far less and had emerged with a trump card, the atomic bomb, which had made her more powerful than all the other states in the world put together. Russia, like the smallest state, was vulnerable to the kind of devastation which had fallen upon Hiroshima and Nagasaki. Stalin had no bomb and no strategic airforce to deliver it on to the US mainland even if he had. His aim was to keep his conquests and make as much trouble for the USA as he dare without bringing the unthinkable, atomic war, down upon his people.

[handwritten right margin: USA ! No war damage PLUS Atomic bomb]

Germany presented a particular problem. After the German surrender, the country had been divided into four zones, administered by Britain, France, Russia and the USA respectively. Stalin did not want a powerful Germany but any hope of cooperation between the allies grew faint as the quarrel about the Iron Curtain states continued. A tricky problem was *Berlin* which was 100 miles inside the Soviet zone, with access only along narrow road and rail links, both vulnerable to land attack. In March, 1948 Stalin began a process aimed at easing the three allied military forces out of the capital. Trains were stopped frequently and searched. documents were demanded and examined at regular intervals. The reaction of the US military commander in Berlin, *General Lucius Clay*, was aggressive. He proposed to fire on any Russian troops who tried to board an American train but *President Truman* restrained him.

BERLIN AIRLIFT

[handwritten: March 1948 - Stalin attempts to rid Berlin of the US, French & GB zones]

On June 1948 the Russians cut off all supplies of food and fuel to Berlin, mainly because the Allies had begun to issue a new currency in their zones, a move which Stalin regarded as the first step to creating two Germanies. The Allied reply was a massive *Airlift* of supplies which lasted from June, 1948 until May, 1949. The three allied airfields in Berlin, *Tegal, Gatow* and *Templehof* were enlarged to take extra traffic carrying 8,000 tons of food a day. Stalin probably hoped that the cost of the airlift would force the Allies to give up their hold on Berlin. In fact, aided by a mild winter, a steady stream of planes - one every five minutes at Templehof - kept the citizens of the three western-controlled zones alive with supplies. Flying

[handwritten bottom: Allies, issued NEW CURRENCY in their zones]

NATO
↓
clear indication of USA's determination to STOP Russian expansion

conditions along the narrow 'corridor' allowed by the Russians were dangerous; 50 pilots lost their lives. But by May, 1949 it was clear that Stalin had lost. Berlin, complete with a wall round the Soviet sector, survives to this day as a divided city.

TRUMAN DOCTRINE AND MARSHALL PLAN

1949
↓
NATO

1955
↓
WARSAW PACT

The crisis over the airlift made a divided Germany certain. Russia formed her zone into the *German Democratic Republic*. The allies established the *Federal Republic of Germany* with its capital at *Bonn*. In the same year the west, led by the USA, formed the *North Atlantic Treaty Organisation* (NATO) consisting of the *US, Britain, France, Belgium, Luxembourg, Canada, Denmark, Iceland, Norway, Italy* and *Portugal*. In 1951 *Greece* and *Turkey* joined. Nato represented the most clear indication yet of the USA's determination to stop Russian expansion. The policy behind it was called *Containment*, not re-conquest, which would have been impossible. No attempt was to be made to weaken the Soviet grip on eastern Europe but, equally, Stalin must make no further moves west. Under the *Truman Doctrine*, the US gave food and supplies to states which appeared threatened by Russian, or communist, takeovers, notably *Greece* (where the communist had been beaten in a civil war, 1947-9) and *Turkey*.

At the same time, the *Marshall Plan* - named after US General *George Marshall* - or *European Recovery Programme* (ERP), provided massive aid to rebuild western Europe. Stalin refused to allow countries within the communist orbit to receive this aid. His counter-plan, called *Molotov*, after Russia's foreign Minister, did little to help; Russia was too much in need of the money and materials herself.

LAST YEARS

COMINFORM - 1947
Stalin's retaliation to USA's T.D. + M.P.

Stalin spent the post-war years re-creating the terror of the Thirties. Mass expulsions from the party, mysterious disappearances, trials, and shootings again poisoned Soviet life. Russian prisoners-of-war returning home were often marched on to prison camps; Stalin did not want them to tell of their experiences. The *Leningrad Affair* in 1949 resulted in false accusations, trials and the shooting of leading politicians in the city. The Communist Party, despite these purges, grew larger and its recruits were often engineers, technicians, agriculturalists - the people needed to rebuild a ruined economy. A *Fourth Five Year Plan* (1946-50) was the instrument of this reconstruction.

On 13 January 1953 *'Pravda'*, the official Russian newspaper, announced the discovery of a *'doctor's plot'* to murder Stalin and other Soviet leaders. They were, it seemed, members of an American-Jewish organisation; Stalin was anti-semite. On 23 February all further news of this plot stopped, mainly because the dictator had suffered a stroke which disabled him on the night of 1-2 March. Stalin's personal physician was not at hand to help him because he had been sent to the Lubyanka prison as a suspect, chained up and beaten regularly to get a 'confession'. Stalin died on 5 March 1953 and soon afterwards it was announced that there had been no plot.

Stalin's achievements had been considerable. He had turned Russia into the second most powerful country in the world but it had been done at enormous cost in human life and happiness. Long before his death he had been treated to what was later called *'the cult of personality'*. Russian propaganda portrayed him as a sort of god, a hero who had saved Russia and carried on the work of the only man who might be his equal, Lenin. Many towns were named after him and there was usually a statue of him in a town or village. On his 70th birthday, a special building was erected to house the numerous presents he received from a 'grateful people'. Yet millions had been executed by him and millions more were in *prison camps*, the *gulags* described by Alexander Solzhenitsyn, the Russian novelist.

TWENTIETH PARTY CONGRESS

At first three men, *Georgi Malenkov, Nikolai Bulganin* and *Lavreti Beria*, succeeded Stalin. Malenkov lost the power struggle when an *East German national* rising took place in June, 1953. (See Work Unit 30). *Beria*, who was chief of police and associated with Stalin's terror, was shot. Bulganin retired and by 1956 *Nikita Khrushchev* was sufficiently in control to condemn aspects of Stalin's rule at the *Twentieth Party Congress*.

Poland and *Hungary* were restive under communist rule. The Poles dismissed their Stalinist leaders and similar action in Hungary led to demonstrations by students and workers demanding greater freedom and better living conditions. The Soviet forces stationed in *Budapest*, the Hungarian capital were too small to deal with the trouble so the Russian commander signed an armistice with the rebels and allowed *Imre Nagy*, a moderate communist, to be head of government. Nagy wanted Hungary to have the same neutral status as Austria.

His bid for freedom from Soviet control came at the worst possible moment; the Americans were about to have a Presidential Election and the British had just invaded *Egypt* (See Work Unit 35). A rival 'government', headed by *Janos Kadar*, appealed for Russian help and Red Army units attacked *Budapest* on 4 November 1956. There was bitter fighting as Nagy's supporters called a general strike but the result was the death of Nagy and hundreds of his men. About 200,000 Hungarians escaped across the border into Austria, The Red Army had destroyed a 'worker's government' and shown the limits of Khrushchev's 'liberalism'.

SELF-ASSESSMENT SECTION

1. What was a Stakhanovite?

2. Who coined the phrase the 'Iron Curtain"?

3. What does NATO stand for?

4. What was the Doctor's plot?

5. What is 'Pravda'?

6. What does 'Stalin' mean in Russian?

7. Who was chief of police when Stalin died?

8. Who led the Hungarian revolt in 1956?

9. Who called Stalin 'a mediocrity'?

10. What was the NEP?

11. 'Socialism in one country' was a slogan of:

    a) Stalin
    b) Kamenev
    c) Lenin
    d) Trotsky
    e) Zinoviev
    (TICK THE CORRECT ANSWER)

12. The 'Twenty five thousanders' were:-

    a) an elite unit of the Red Army
    b) specialised farm workers
    c) scientists and technicians
    d) advisers to the peasantry
    e) specialists sent to speed up collectivisation
    (TICK THE CORRECT ANSWER)

13. Put in correct details (by letter) against these names.

1. PAUKER	A. Old Bolshevik
2. TITO	B. Communist leader of Poland
3. KADAR	C. Czech communist leader
4. GOMULKA	D. Russian marshal shot for treason
5. GOTTWALD	E. Communist ruler of Rumania
6. ZINOVIEV	F. Russian leader after Stalin's death
7. MALENKOV	G. Yugoslav leader who defied Stalin
8. TUKHACHEVSKY	H. Led counter-revolution in Hungary

14. In 1948 General Lucius Clay wrote to President Truman:

> "Obviously, the full consequences of this action must be understood. Unless we take a strong line now, our life in Berlin will become impossible. I do not believe that the Soviets mean war now. However, if they do, it seems to me that we might as well find out now as later. We cannot afford to be bluffed."
>
> (Quoted in 'The Berlin Blockade' by Ann and John Tusa. Hodder and Stoughton, 1988).

a) What was 'this action' referred to in the source?
b) In what way would the Allies' life in Berlin have become impossible?
c) What had sparked off the Soviet action?
d) Why were the Russians unlikely to have wanted war with the USA at that time?
e) What 'strong line' was taken by the Allies? What were its long term results?

15. Study Sources A,B,C,D, and E and then answer the questions.

A. "You're against the collective farm because you can't see anything beyond your own cow, and your chicken coop of a hut. It's snotty but it's my own! The Communist Party is pushing you into a new life and you're like a blind calf; lead it to the cow's udder and it kicks and shakes its head. But if the calf doesn't suck at the teat it'll never live to see the light of day. And that's all. I shall sit down this very day to write that I want to join the collective farm and I call on others to do the same. But those who don't want to shouldn't interfere with those that do".

> (A peasant, Maidannikov, speaking in Mikhail Sholokhov's novel, 'Virgin Soil Upturned' published in Russia in 1932).

B. A Soviet picture of 1931, showing crowds of peasants applying to join collective farms.

(Photograph by Novosti Press Agency)

C. "In 1930, 10,000 families (60,000-70,000 people, as families then went) passed through Tomsk, and from there were driven farther, at first on foot,... although it was winter .. then upstream along the *(river)* Vasyugan - still over the ice ... In the upper reaches of the Vasyugan and the Tara they were marooned on patches of firm ground in the marshes. No food or tools were left for them. The roads were impassable, and there was no way through to the world outside,

227

except for two brushwood paths. Machine gunners manned the
barriers on both paths and let no one through from the death camp.
They started dying like flies ... Rather late in the day, when the rivers
unfroze, barges carrying flour and salt were sent ... but they could not
get up the Vasugan ... They died off - every one of them".

(From Alexander Solzhenitsyn's 'The Gulag Archipelago'
Vol 3 Collins/Fontana.)

D. "This was why I dreamed of a cow. Thanks to the vagaries of our
economic system, a family could support itself for many years by
keeping a cow ... Some of the milk had to be sold to buy hay, but
there was always enough left over to add a little richness to the
cabbage soup. A cow gives people independence, and without over-
exerting themselves, they can earn a little extra to buy bread. The State
is still in quandary about this relic of the old world; if people are
allowed to buy hay to feed their cow, then they only do the very
minimum of work on the kolkhoz *(collective farm)*; if on the other
hand, you take their cow away, they will die of hunger. The result is
that the cow is alternatively forbidden and then permitted again".

(From 'Hope against Hope' by Nadezda Mandelstam,
translated by Max Hayward. Collins Publishers.)

E. RUSSIAN LIVESTOCK (million head)

	1928	1929	1930	1931	1932	1933
cattle	70.5	67.1	52.5	47.9	40.7	38.4
pigs	26.0	20.4	13.6	14.4	11.6	12.1
sheep & goats	146.7	147.0	108.8	77.7	52.1	50.2

Questions

a) Which of these sources would have been approved of by Stalin? Give
reasons for your answer.

b) What caused the decline shown in E.? How was this connected with
sources A, B, C, and D?

c) Sources A and C were written by Russian novelists. What reasons can
you think of for C being more reliable as a source than A.?

d) What part of Stalin's collectivisation programme is described in C.?
Why did Stalin think it necessary to treat people in this way?

e) The writer of C. had been a prisoner in a labour camp. Would this make
his evidence more, or less, reliable? Give reasons for your answer.

f) Using your own knowledge, and these sources, describe what life was
like for a Russian peasant at this time.

16. In February, 1931 Stalin wrote:-

> "To slow down the tempo means to lag behind. And those who lag behind are beaten. The history of old Russia shows ... that because of her backwardness she was constantly defeated ... Do you want our Socialist fatherland to be beaten? ... If you do not want this you must put an end to this backwardness as speedily as possible ... There are no other ways ... We are fifty to a hundred years behind the advanced countries. We must make good this lag in ten years. Either we do it or they crush us".

> (Joseph Stalin 'Problems of Leninism', Moscow, 1945)

a)   What methods did Stalin use to deal with Russia's backwardness?
b)   Why were 'the advanced countries' likely to try and crush Russia?
c)   What event proved Stalin's prophecy true?
d)   How far did Stalin achieve his aims?

24

The United Nations

INTRODUCTION

There are two principal reasons why the United Nations has been more successful than its predecessor, the League. First, its founders knew of the mistakes made by the League and learnt from them In particular, they decided that the UN must have the power to raise armed forces to carry out its resolutions. Second, unlike the League, the UN has been supported by all countries of the world, including the two most powerful, Russia and the USA. And whereas Italy, Germany and Japan left the League for good, the one or two 'walkouts' from the UN have been only temporary. These factors have helped the UN police a world as tense and dangerous as the one the League presided over between 1918 and 1939.

There are also two reasons for its failures. First, few of its founders in 1945 could have predicted the intensity of the Cold War which developed between Russia and the USA in the 1950's. This confrontation has dominated world affairs and rendered some of the UN's peace-keeping initiatives ineffective. Soviet and American conflicts within the Security Council, with frequent use of their power of vetoes, has, at times, paralysed a vital part of the organisation. And because of the Cold War, neither great power would allow the UN to mediate in any matter which it thought affected its vital interests. The Berlin Airlift, 1948-49, the Cuban missile Crisis, 1962 - when the world came near to nuclear war - and the US involvement in Vietnam, 1965-73, were never referred to the UN. The Middle East problem, where Russia supports the Arabs and America, Israel, has seen sporadic but ineffective UN action for the same reason.

Second, an organisation which began with 50 members and now has over 150 may truly represent the nations of the world but such size leads to block voting which sometimes makes a mockery of the ideals of the UN charter. The large number of new states who joined in the 1950's and 60's were nearly all Asian or African ex-colonial territories. Their leaders, who had sometimes suffered at the hands of their ex-masters, were deeply suspicious of US 'economic imperialism' and often hostile to their original western rulers, usually British, French or Dutch. Such states were also poor and in need of every kind of aid. Soviet Russia, who had never ruled any of them and whose own subject peoples enjoyed no such independence, was able to pose as the enemy of imperialism and friend of Third

World states. Consequently, she could often be assured of a block of votes in her favour on a matter which did not interest them, in return for benefits which did.

Nevertheless, the UN's record in smaller wars and disputes is impressive. The Congo, Kashmir, Indonesia, Palestine and Cyprus have all been affected by UN mediation, and the only large-scale war fought by the UN in Korea led to the defeat of aggression. The UN remains a vital world agency, doing good work on many fronts besides the political. It cannot alter the power balance in the world, and it cannot be better than its members will allow. But it is still an influence for good in a world full of evil.

SIGNING THE CHARTER

The United Nations developed from the wartime alliance of nations fighting Germany, Italy and Japan. Its principles were based on the *Atlantic Charter* (See Work Unit 22), issued by Churchill and Roosevelt in 1941. On 1 January 1942, 26 nations signed a *Declaration of United Nations*, setting out plans for a future organisation. Two years later the four major powers fighting the war against the Axis powers met in conference at *Dumbarton Oaks*, near Washington, USA, and signed the *Charter of the United Nations*. The *United Nations Organisation* (UNO) was founded on 24 October 1945, a date celebrated as *United Nations Day*. The first meeting of its *General Assembly* was held in *London* in January, 1946. Later, the American *Rockefeller* family made a gift to UNO of the site on which the headquarters now stands in *New York*. There is a 39 storey building for the General Assembly and Secretariat, and a smaller building for the *Security Council*

AIMS

The UN was founded to replace the League of Nations, keep world peace and give all peoples the right to self-determination. Its *Charter* banned war except for defence of UN principles, treaty obligations or self-defence. It also allowed for the use of international force to stop aggression, an important difference from the League which had no such power. It allowed for regional defence pacts between member nations and a few, notably *NATO* and the *Warsaw Pact*, have been signed since 1946. It also exists to encourage cultural, economic and political cooperation between nations.

STRUCTURE

UNO's structure resembled that of the League but with procedural differences. A *General Assembly* of all member states meets each September. Each state has one vote but can send up to 5 delegates. Voting is by simple majority, or in important cases, by a 2/3rds majority. This is a great improvement on the league system which required a unanimous vote for action. A *Security Council*, consisting of delegates from *Britain, France, Russia, the USA* and *Nationalist (now Communist) China*, is in continuous session to deal with crises. Each Security council member had the right of veto over UN decisions until 1950. Owing to the confrontation which developed between Russia and the USA, far too many vetoes were applied and at times the council was paralysed. After 1950 it was decided that in such situations the *Assembly* could send UN observers to the crisis area to decide what action was necessary. Now no one member-state can hold up the work of the Assembly by using its veto.

The *Security Council* also has 10 non-permanent members whose seats are shared between the West, Latin America, Africa and eastern Europe respectively. The Council also has a military staff and the power to raise armed forces under UN control. This has been done with respect to *Korea*, the *Congo* (now *Zaire*), *Palestine, Kashmir* and *Cyprus*. The Security Council elects the UN's chief, the *Secretary-General*, who holds office for a period of 5 years. These are chosen from small and neutral states and since 1945 there have been five -*Trygve Lie* of *Norway, Dag Hammarskjold* of *Sweden, U Thant* of *Burma, Kurt Waldheim* of Austria and *Perez de Cuellar* of Peru.

MAIN AGENCIES

The UN has an *Economic and Social Council (ECOSOC)* which appoints *commissions* to look after *Asian and Far Eastern Affairs, Human Rights* and *Population Control*. Apart from these commissions, it has *Agencies* including the *Food and Agricultural Organisation* (FAO), the *World Health Organisation* (WHO), the *International Monetary Fund* (IMF) and the *International Bank for Reconstruction and Development* (IBRD). Not every member of UNO belongs to all of these agencies. The FAO has its headquarters in *Rome*, Italy. It specialises in dealing with pest and disease control, and teaches irrigation and improved farming techniques. Altogether, it has set up over 380 food-farming projects to help eliminate starvation and malnutrition.

The *WHO* combats disease world-wide. It deals with the provision of doctors, medicines and medical supplies for epidemics, and tries to increase health-awareness and medical skills in under-developed countries. The *IMF* was formed to help countries who have a balance of payments problem. Member nations put a quota of their own currency into the fund and they are allowed to draw up to four times that amount in gold if they are in difficulties. The *IBRD* (International Bank for Reconstruction and Development), usually known as the *World Bank*, makes loans for development to under-developed countries. This is done with money which it raises by the sale of stock to member countries, and the issuing of bonds in the world's money markets.

I.L.O. AND I.C.J.

UNO took over the *International Labour Organisation* (ILO) from the League. Its aims are to improve worker's conditions worldwide by advocating maximum hours, minimum wages, paid holidays and guaranteed employment. The ILO Assembly meets at *Geneva* each year. Its membership is made up of two government delegates, one employers' delegate and one workers' delegate from each member state. The *International Court of Justice* was also taken over from the League. It still meets at the *Hague, Holland*, and consists of 15 judges, all from different countries, who are chosen by the General Assembly and Security Council voting separately. The Court gives judgements on particular matters if requested, and it also gives legal advice to the Assembly and Council. Its decisions are reached by a simple majority.

The *Secretariat* (or civil service) of the United Nations has about 5,000 staff who range from scientists, lawyers, technicians, broadcasters, artists, accountants to clerks and typists. They prepare all the numerous reports on the activities of UN and its agencies. The Secretariat works in five languages - *Chinese, Russian, Spanish, French* and *English.*

U.N.E.S.C.O.

The United Nations Educational, Scientific and Cultural Organisation (UNESCO) was founded to spread literacy, numeracy and knowledge, and to increase goodwill and understanding between nations by educational and cultural means. UNESCO grants scholarships for student travel and study, and publishes hundreds of books in many languages. It deals with problems associated with the mass media - newspapers, television, film and radio and also studies the effects of various geographical conditions, i.e. drought, floods etc on human life. In recent years some member states, notably *Britain* and the *USA*, have felt that UNESCO was being used for anti-western propaganda and have refused to pay their share of its financing. UNESCO's headquarters is in *Paris*, France.

The *International Children's Emergency Fund* (UNICEF) was founded to improve the conditions of children throughout the world by helping those affected by war, epidemics, hunger and preventable diseases. It has set up over 40,000 health centres and sometimes works with WHO.

THE UN AND SOUTH AFRICA

The UN has taken a leading part in the battle against *apartheid* in *South Africa.* (See Work Unit 27). In 1953 it appointed a commission to consider the racial situation in that country. This commission reported that conditions were bad, and harmful to international relations. In succeeding years the UN Assembly has regularly passed resolutions calling on the white South African government to review its policies in the light of the principles of the *Atlantic Charter.* After the *Sharpeville* killings in 1961 (See Work Unit 27), the UN Secretary-General, *Dag Hammarskjold*, went to South Africa to negotiate with the Afrikaaner regime but its leader refused to change their policies of racial segregation.

Next year the UN called on its members to break off diplomatic relations with South Africa, close their ports and airfields to South African ships and aircraft, suspend exports to South Africa and boycott all South African imports. The UN then set up a sanctions committee to monitor the situation. African members were prominent in all these Un decisions because they saw no other way of combatting a power with such military and economic strength.

Britain and the USA condemn apartheid but do not agree that it is a threat to world peace. They have usually been opposed to sanctions as a weapon against South Africa, believing that they would be ineffective and, at best, merely hurt the poorest sections of the South African community, i.e. the blacks and the coloureds. This view was strengthened after the failure of sanctions against *Rhodesia* (now Zimbabwe), a country far weaker economically than South Africa. (See Work Unit 26). Britain's economic involvement with South Africa - two thirds of South Africa's gold reserves are handled through London banks - has been cited by her enemies as the real reason for her stand against sanctions. Another reason may be the importance of the *Simonstown* naval base in South Africa to western navies in time of war. Whilst one side continues to claim that only strong sanctions will bring the South African leaders to the conference table to make genuine concessions, the other maintains that a total blockade would carry the danger of war and anarchy in South Africa.

NAMIBIA

In 1946 the UN formed a *Trusteeship Council* to carry on the League's work on mandated territories. The work of this Council decreased as the number of colonial territories diminished but with regard to *South West Africa*, a mandated territory taken over by the South Africans from the Germans after the First World War, there was continuous controversy. The UN claimed that *South Africa* had violated the terms of its original mandate by introducing apartheid into the territory, and called on her to withdraw. A legal battle, conducted by various African states through the *International Court of Justice*, failed to get a favourable decision, so in 1966 the Assembly voted almost unanimously that South Africa's mandate should be terminated, In 1968 it set up its own Council to rule *Namibia* - the new name for the territory. In 1988 South Africa agreed to withdraw from the region after Russia promised to stop backing the Cuban troops in neighbouring Angola.

POLITICAL ACTIVITIES

Unlike the League, the UN has been very active in world affairs. This involvement has varied according to the circumstances, from sending observers and mediators to small peace-keeping forces and sizeable armies. In 1946 the UN conducted the negotiations which led Russia to evacuate its troops from *Persia* (Iran) which it had sent in for strategic reasons during the war. In *Greece*, where there was a strong communist movement after the German withdrawal in 1944, British troops first stopped a communist coup and then, when another rebellion occurred, withdrew their forces. The UN was unable to settle this problem which culminated in a *Greek Civil War*, 1947-49, in which the communists were defeated with US help. When *India* and *Pakistan* quarreled over ownership of *Kashmir* province, at the time of the partition of India in 1947 (See Work Unit 33). UN observers were sent to the disputed border region where they remained for 20 years.

In 1948 the British gave up their mandate of *Palestine* because of the continuing violent clashes between Arab and Israeli settlers. They handed the matter over to the UN, who proposed a *partition* plan, dividing the country between Jew and Arab. This was accepted by the Jews but rejected by the Arabs. *Count Bernadotte*, a Swede, was sent into Palestine as a UN mediator but was murdered by Jewish terrorists. The Israelis then set up their own state (May 1948), and , in the war with the Arab states which followed, won their independence. Bernadotte's successor, *Dr. Ralph Bunche*, arranged the armistice which ended the fighting between the two sides.

KOREA

When *North Korea* invaded the South in June, 1950 (See Work Unit 29), the Security Council had no Russian representative; he had walked out in protest when the USA used its veto to block Communist China's application for membership. This fact was crucial because North Korea was a 'client' state of Russia, and Russia's certain veto would have prevented what followed. The Security Council voted for military action and called on the USA, whose forces were based in nearby Japan, to take the lead in fighting aggression. The *Korean War* 1953 involved 15 states but America provided the bulk of the land, air and sea forces. During the fighting *China* invaded *South Korea* to assist the communist North Korea. When the war ended the frontier between the two states was virtually the same as when it started. Although this was a clear victory for the UN, it had been achieved by forces under the direction of an American President. Since that time the UN has been careful to use neutral troops in any peace-keeping action, not the soldiers of a major power.

During the *1956 Suez crisis* (See Work Unit 35) a UN peace-keeping army was invited into Egypt after the USA had insisted that the French, British and Israeli forces be withdrawn. Obviously this force could not have defeated these armies militarily; its job was to separate the combatants, patrol the seas around Egypt and clear sunken ships from the Suez Canal. A few days later the *Hungarian Rising* occurred (See Work Unit 23) but attempts by the UN to intervene were foiled by the Russians and their Hungarian allies, who refused to even allow *Dag Hammarskjold* to land in *Budapest*, the Hungarian capital, for negotiations.

ZAIRE

In 1960, a crisis in the *Congo* (now Zaire), following premature independence (See Work Unit 26) led to the UN to send an army into the country. Over the next four years a grand total of 100,000 troops of many different nations took part in this mission. In 1961 the UN supervised elections but when the province of *Katanga* attempted to secede (break away) from Zaire, a civil war broke out in which UN troops played a leading part, *Dag Hammarskjold* was killed in a plane crash in Africa whilst on his way to negotiate with the rebel Katangan leader, *Moishe Tshombe*. The Katangan rebellion failed but some member-states objected to what they regarded as interference in Zaire's internal affairs and refused to help pay for the operation.

In 1965 a UN peace-keeping force was sent to *Kashmir* where fighting had again broken out between India and Pakistan. In the same year the UN imposed economic sanctions on Rhodesia (now Zimbabwe) after the country's white settlers, led by *Ian Smith* defied the British government when it attempted to set up a multi-racial state and issued a *Unilateral Declaration of Independence* (UDI), thus perpetuating white supremacy. This UN move was not successful owing to a great deal of 'sanctions busting' and support from South Africa.

RESOLUTION 242

In 1967 *President Nasser* of Egypt ordered the UN troops stationed between the Arabs and Israelis in *Sinai* to leave. This withdrawal allowed Egyptian troops to seize *Sharm-esh-Sheik* and close the *Straits of Tiran* to Israeli shipping. This precipitated the *'Six Day's War'* in which Egyptian forces were annihilated in a matter of days by air-strikes. This war left Israel in possession of a great deal of Arab territory and Britain, France, Russia and the USA took the intiative in the UN to pass *Resolution 242/67* which called on Israel to give up its conquests and the Arabs, for their part, to recognise Israel as a sovereign state. This was agreed to by all the Arab states concerned, except *Syria*, but rejected by the Israelis who regarded these conquests as essential for their security. After the *Yom Kippur War*, 1973 between Egypt and Israel, a UN peace-keeping force was placed between their armies in January, 1974.

DISARMAMENT

The period since the Second World War has not been one of disarmament, instead, there has been an arms race between the super-powers, and re-armament by many other countries. Much of this development has taken place in more than usual secrecy, mainly because of the nature of nuclear and other sophisticated weaponry. The immense expense of scientific research, and the rewards of getting a clear advantage over one's opponent, have meant that the major nations have regarded secret re-arming as necessary for their national security. For this reason the UN has been ineffectual in persuading any significant arms reductions, and all treaties limiting weapons have been done independently by the great powers, notably in the *SALT* talks and the agreements signed between *Michael Gorbachev*, the Russian leader, and *President Ronald Reagan* in 1987-8.

The *UN Atomic Energy Commission*, formed in 1946, had put forward the so-called *Baruch Plan*, sponsored by the USA, which offered to destroy all its nuclear weapons and hand over rights of inspection to this commission. Russia rejected this plan because it would have left the USA with the technical knowledge to make such weapons, whilst prohibiting Russia from carrying out the necessary research. It would also have involved giving up the power of veto which Russia was not prepared to do.

The UN played an important role in the signing of the *Nuclear Test Ban Treaty*, 1963 which followed on the Cuban Missile Crisis (See Work Unit 35). Russia and the USA agreed to stop nuclear tests in the atmosphere, outer space and under water. This was partly due to both countries feeling that they had nothing to gain by further research of this kind. It is significant that *France* and *China* who are both developing nuclear capabilities refused to acknowledge this Treaty and continued testing.

SELF-ASSESSMENT SECTION

1. What is the title of the chief executive of UNO?
2. What is the UN Secretariat?
3. How many delegates can each member-state send to the Assembly?
4. Where was the UN charter signed?
5. What is the significance of the 24 October in UN's history?
6. Name the countries with permanent seats on the Security Council.
7. What does IMF stand for?
8. Where does the International Court of Justice meet?
9. Where is the UNESCO headquarters?
10. Which plan for nuclear disarmament was rejected in 1946?

Cartoon A

(Source: The Herblock Book. Beacon Press, 1952)

11. Look at cartoon A on the previous page. Then answer the following questions.
    a) Who is banging China's head against the wall? Why is he doing this?
    b) Who had bricked up the door so firmly, and why?
    c) 'The long exclusion of Communist China with its 600 million people is ridiculous. UNO cannot be truly described as a 'world organisation' if one fifth of the world's population is denied membership'.
       ('The League of Nations and UNO' by Gibbons and Morican. Longman, 1970)
       Do you agree, or disagree, with this comment? Give reasons for your answer.

12. Which of these crises did not involve the UN? Explain why.

    a) Korean War
    b) Suez
    c) Congo (Zaire)
    d) Cuba
    e) Kashmir

13. Look at this cartoon. Then answer the questions.

(Source: Low cartoon. Evening Standard.)

    a) This cartoon appeared in 1950 and was entitled "History doesn't repeat itself". What part of history was the cartoonist referring to?
    b) Who is holding the hand of the lady representing the UN? What is the significance of this figure in the cartoon?
    c) To what part of the world were the two figures rushing, and why?
    d) Did history repeat itself in this instance or was the cartoonist's optimism

238

justified? Give reasons for your answer.

14. During the late 1940's Russia complained frequently that the UN member-states were just puppets of the USA and voted as she wished. In what way had the situation changed by the 1970's and why?

15. Describe in as much detail as possible the work of one of these UN agencies.

   a) WHO   b) FAO   c) UNESCO   d) IMF

16. Explain the background to the UN's involvement in ONE of these disputes.

   a) Palestine b) Suez   c) Congo (Zaire)   d) Kashmir

   (Look at Work Units 25, 32, 33 and 34 if you need help)

17. Imagine you are an inhabitant of a Third World country. Describe the ways the UN has helped you achieve a higher standard of living and a better life.

25

Twentieth Century Africa
Part One

INTRODUCTION

The colonial powers drew lines across Africa without thought for tribal, ethnic or religious differences, producing artificial territories which suited their own interests, or represented a compromise with another power. The results divided tribes, languages, religions and cultures. The Yoruba tribe, for example, became British in Nigeria and French in Dahomey. The Makone tribe of Tanganyika became first German, then British. Borders often reflect commercial interests, not social, economic or political reality. Gambia is long and thin because the British aim in taking it over was to control the Gambia river and promote their own trade at the expense of the French. It was as if a conquering power in Europe were to create a country consisting of half France, part of Switzerland and a section of Austria.

Independence when it came in the second half of the Twentieth century turned these artificial geographical entities into 'nation states', some almost too large and diverse, others too small, according to the size decided by their former colonial masters. The consequence has been some deeply divided countries, and, in several cases, civil war. In Nigeria, the Ibo tribe proclaimed their independance and formed a separate state called Biafra. This break-away movement was only subdued after a bloody civil war from 1967-70. In the Congo (now Zaire) the Kasai tribe seceded to become a state called Katanga and this secession was only defeated after another war. The idea of a union of all African states, promoted by the Organisation of African Unity after its formation in 1963, has seldom been more than an idea. Tanganyika and the island of Zanzibar united to become Tanzania in 1964, but other unions, like that of Guinea and Ghana, were failures.

Western-style democracy has not taken root in the new African states where opposition parties have tended to consist of one tribe. Such tribal divisions are more dangerous than differences of opinion among similar people so most African states have developed one-party systems in which electors choose different candidates from the same party. The weakness of this kind of democracy has been illustrated by a number of military takeovers, Soldier-dictators have seized power, supported by the army. Such leaders are often corrupt and brutal; the worse case was the regime of General Idi Amin in Uganda between 1971 and 1979. These men often come to power promising to wipe out corruption and restore law and order. They usually behave no better than their predecessors. Like Nkrumah of Ghana, they become corrupted by their own power and popularity and adopt luxurious life-styles whilst their people remain in poverty. Even so-called benefits have sometimes backfired. Better health facilities leading to a declining death rate have led to over-population. This has put a heavy strain on weak economies, whose governments have had to feed, clothe and find work for the extra people. Industrialisation has created comparatively wealthy elites, like the copper miners of Katanga and railway workers of Tanzania. It has caused a drift away from the countryside into the towns and produced the slum shanty towns which surround many African cities.

No poor country can hope to finance its own development. Most African industry, therefore, has been established with foreign capital usually supplied by multi-national companies. This produces economic imperialism, in which company directors and shareholders, rather than colonial governments, influence state policy. Most of the original imperial powers are now members of the European Economic Community. The EEC grants aid to Third World countries, including those in Africa, under an agreement known as the Lome Convention, 1975. This convention gives states the right to use aid in any way they like, and also gives trade concessions, such as duty free access to European markets, in some cases. This goes some way to offset the effects of economic imperialism. The problem of how to help states during crises caused by disease, drought or a drop in world prices, is tackled by what is known as the Stabex system. This pays compensation to countries affected in this way.

The colonial powers, for good or ill, brought Africa into the Twentieth century. But they created more problems than they solved. They left five main languages, English, French, Arabic and Swahili (a form of Arabic), plus the Afrikaans spoken by white South Africans. These cut across true African languages in many cases. They left religious differences between Moslem and Christian, and Christian churches of all denominations. They left different monetary systems and a railway network designed to serve only the former colony; few lines actually connect the new states and many have different gauges (widths) which hampers integration. The feelings of guilt about all this has led to deep divisions in the west and controversies over such matters as apartheid, racism and aid. The Scramble for Africa happened quite quickly. Its effects may take centuries to work themselves out.

AFRICAN MANDATES

After the First World War Germany's colonies were taken away and shared out between the Allies. *South West Africa* (now Namibia) was administered by *South Africa*, whose troops had conquered it from the Germans, whilst *Britain* took over *Tanganyika* and Belgium took over *Ruanda-Burundi*. The *Cameroons* and *Togoland* became French colonies. Such colonies were held under the supervision of the League of Nations and were not supposed to be colonies in the normal sense of the term. The *Covenant* of the League (See Work Unit 16) envisaged trusteeship whereby the colonial government would prepare the natives for self-rule. This was called a *mandate*, so these former German colonies were called *mandated territories*. The idea of preparing colonial peoples for self-rule and then granting them independance was extended later to all colonies, although it was many years before it was accepted by some of the ruling powers. In fact, some countries actually increased their empires during the early years of the century, notably Italy with Mussolini's invasion of *Abyssinia* in 1936 and *Libya* in 1939. (See Work Unit 15).

AFRICAN NATIONALISM

The First World War had involved African troops in campaigns against the Germans. There had also been both disruption and development due to the war. For example, the economies of some colonies had benefited by supplying vital war materials to their parent countries. Nationalist movements, demanding some kind of independence, arose as the full meaning of Woodrow Wilson's idea of self-determination became known. After all, if Europe's frontiers could be redrawn on nationalistic lines, why not those of Africa? A key factor in this battle was education, without which the Africans would never be able to run their own affairs, and many of the new nationalist leaders were university-educated, sometimes in the USA. Nationalist feeling was particularly strong in *Algeria, Morocco* and *Tunisia*, whose people shared a common religion, *Islam* (Moslem) and a common language, Arabic.

The colonial authorities looked on nationalist politicians, however moderate, as dangerous revolutionaries who advocated too rapid improvement of education and citizenship. In the mother country there were plenty of people who realised that the days of empire were drawing to a close - particularly Labour and Liberal supporters in Britain - and that some sort of self-rule would have to replace imperialist control. A more important point, perhaps, was the financial burden of empire now that *Britain* and *France* has suffered so grievously in the war.

In this respect Britain's approach had combined being cheap with trying to preserve local culture. This system was called *Indirect Rule*, in which a British-appointed *governor*, representing the Crown and answerable to *Parliament*, had overall charge of the territory but the local administration was continued through *tribal chiefs* who were advised by British *District Officers*. There were also some moves towards democracy with a *Council* and *Legislature* (law-making Assembly) elected by a few carefully chosen voters. In *Nigeria, Lord Lugard*, the British administrator who virtually 'created' the country, called this cooperation between local chiefs and colonial officials, a *Dual Mandate*. Nationalists condemned this kind of rule from which they were often excluded anyway.

FRENCH COLONIAL ATTITUDES

French policy was different from British. It was called *Assimilation*, that is, trying to make the natives "French" by promoting the French language and culture.

Such a policy involved controlling each colony directly from France, and French officials were in charge at every level of administration. France built up her colony's economies with only French needs in mind - raw materials for France in return for a guaranteed market for French-made goods. Such tight rule provoked serious resistance at times, especially in Moslem *North Africa*. In 1925 a revolt in neighbouring *Spanish Morocco* by the warlike *Rif* tribe spread to French territory where a rebel chief, *Abd el Krim* declared an independent *Rif Repubic* with its own elected Parliament. Like many later Moslem leaders who fought colonialism, Abd el Krim was not a modern nationalist-style revolutionary. He had no desire to modernise the country but rather wished to preserve traditional Moslem religion and culture. The rebellion was crushed in 1926 but it was a taste of what was to come in the French empire later in the century.

EFFECTS OF THE SECOND WORLD WAR.

The Allies fought the Second World War against two racist regimes, that of Germany and Italy, and one imperialist regime, Japan. Consequently, their leaders took an anti-racist stand which naturally influenced colonial peoples throughout the world. In 1941 *President Roosevelt* of the USA and *Winston Churchill*, prime minister of Britain, produced their famous *Atlantic Charter* - so named because they met on a British battleship off the American cost - which proclaimed the right of all people to choose their own form of government. Churchill was, in fact, an imperialist, who was thinking of the European peoples conquered by the nazis. Roosevelt, however, was anti-imperialist and was certainly thinking of colonial peoples in the British empire in particular. This Charter was seized on by nationalists everywhere, particularly in *India* and *Africa*. Such ideals also impressed African soldiers who returned to their homeland after quite extensive travels during which they had glimpsed the freedom enjoyed by non-colonial peoples. These factors, plus improving education, caused many to question the ideas of empire accepted by their parents.

DE-COLONISATION

Both *France* and *Britain* had been greatly weakened by the war, both materially and in other ways. *France* had been conquered by the Germans and her prestige amongst colonial peoples was never the same again. *Britain* had performed well and made a brave stand for freedom. But she had won at great material cost; after 1940 she could not have afforded to fight the war without US financial aid. She was now far too weak to carry the heavy burden of empire, and a policy of gradual independence was a necessity. British socialists had always been against imperialism and their party, *Labour*, was now in power. *The Labour Government*, elected with a large majority in 1945, made the key move in 1947 when it granted independence to *India*, Britain's largest and richest possession and the so-called 'Jewel in her crown' (This referred originally to Queen Victoria) (See Work Unit 32). The *Conservative* party which came to power in 1951 continued the policy of disengagement and granted independence to many African territories, beginning with *Ghana* in March, 1957.

What might be termed Britain's last imperial move, the attack of *Suez*, had ended abruptly the year before when the USA forced the British and French to withdraw their forces (See Work Unit 34). The French carried on with *assimilation* and made all their colonial people French citizens. But a long civil war in *Algeria*, made worse by the presence of a large number of French *colons* (white settlers) led to French army revolts and the fall of the *Fourth Republic, General Charles de Gaulle* became first President of a *Fifth Republic* in 1958. He and his successors granted independence to all African French possessions in the years which followed. (See Work Unit 30)

GHANA

The *Gold Coast* colony's economy was based on the export of *cocoa*. The colony had few tribal divisions, although the north tended to fear domination by the south. Its nationalist leader, *Kwame Nkrumah*, was educated at *Achimota College* and after graduation he taught for a time in the USA. Returning to Ghana in 1949, Nkrumah formed the *Convention Peoples Party* (CPP). The CPP's aim was immediate independence through *'Positive Action'*, that is, strikes, boycotts and non-cooperation with the authorities. Such activities landed Nkrumah in jail in 1950 but the CPP's policies had convinced the British governor that self-rule was desirable. This feeling was strengthened by elections to the Legislature which showed that Nkumah had popular support. Consequently, in 1952 Nkrumah was elected prime minister of the colony. With independence imminent, Nkrumah's party campaigned for a *unitary state*, whilst northern politicians pressed for a federal system which would have given their regions autonomy. In 1957 the CPP won 72 out of 104 seats in the National Assembly. This gave Nkrumah the mandate he needed to establish a unitary state. It was called *Ghana* and Nkrumah became its President. This new state included *Togoland*.

Ghana's history since independence has been unhappy. Between 1957 and his overthrow in 1966, *Nkrumah* became pleasure-loving and dictatorial, and his officials corrupt. Nkrumah's Ghana had some achievements to its credit - the *Volta River complex* and *Tema port*, improving social services and better education. Nkrumah was overthrown by the army, whose rule was replaced in 1969 by *Dr. Busia*, an old opponent of the President, who took charge of a civilian government. By this time corruption and crime were running at a high level so Ghana expelled foreign workers because she said they were adding to the crime rate (In June, 1983 the Nigerian government sent all its Ghanains home for the same reason). Busia's all-party democracy was replaced by another military regime, that of *Colonel Acheampong*. Acheampong tried to reduce Ghana's dependance on a single crop. He also initiated a campaign of self-sufficiency with the slogan, *Operation Feed Yourself!* This was not successful, and since 1979 Ghana has been ruled by military men, led for most of the time by *Flight Lieutenant Jerry Rawlings*.

THE CONGO (ZAIRE)

Until 1906 the *Congo* was the personal property of *King Leopold*, the *Belgian King*, who brutally exploited the rubber plantations. When these outrages became known, *Leopold* was forced to hand over the administration to the Belgian government. *Belgium* ran the Congo in an orderly fashion but made no attempt to prepare its people for self-rule. In 1959-60 riots and unrest suggested that a civil war similar to that in *Algeria* might break out. With foreign capital being withdrawn from the country as a consequence, the Belgian government panicked and granted immediate independence. This sudden change left the Congolese unprepared to run their country; they lacked skilled workers in every department. *Patrice Lumumba*, leader of the *Mouvement National Congolais*, became prime minister 18 days after independence.

Lumumba was faced by army mutinies, massacres of white settlers and the secession of the rich copper-producing province of *Katanga*. Katanga's leader, *Moise Tshombe*, was backed by the mining company, *Union Miniere*. Lumumba appealed to both the UN and Russia for help. A UN peace-keeping force arrived in the country but at first it was ineffective in what was a war situation. *Dag Hammarskjold*, the UN Secretary-general, was killed in an air-crash whilst on his way to the Congo as part of a peace initiative. Lumumba was murdered by mutinous army units. Heavy fighting continued for several years and it was 1963 before Katanga was subdued by UN troops. In 1965 the army took charge of the country, led by *General Mobutu*. Mobutu had crushed a revolt by white mercenaries led by a Belgian named *Jean Schramme* in 1967 and two further revolts in Katanga (now named *Shaba* province). Mobutu renamed the Congo, *Zaire*, and built up a personality cult. In 1974, for example, *Mobutuism* replaced Roman Catholicism as the state religion.

NIGERIA

Nigeria is deeply divided by tribal and religious differences. In the Moslem north, the dominant tribes are the *Fulani* and the *Hausa*. In the mainly Christian south, the western part is mainly *Yoruba* and the east, *Ibo*. The British authorities favoured establishing a unitary state upon independence because it made more sense economically. But regional rivalries were too strong, and when *Nigeria* was granted independence in 1960 it was a *federal state* divided into 12 autonomous regions. A northerner, *Sir Abudakar Balewa*, was prime minister of this federation, with a southern, *Dr. Tafawa Azikiwe*, as Governor- General. For a few years there was a precarious balance between the rival forces. Then in 1965 there were charges of a rigged election in favour of the north and these accusations led to riots and massacres of Hausa and Ibo. In 1966 *Colonel Ojukwu* declared the oil-rich eastern region a separate state called *Biafra*. A three year civil war followed which was won by the Nigerian army led by *General Gowon* (1967-70).

Gowon tried to re-organise Nigeria after the war. His rule proved a failure. Nigeria's large profits from oil exports were squandered through incompetence and corruption. Shortages, inflation and poverty in the countryside grew worse. In 1976 Gowon was overthrown by *General Muhammed*. Muhammed embarked on a programme of thorough reform. He dismissed the 12 provincial governors and over 10,000 other officials suspected of corruption and inefficiency. He divided the country into 19 provinces to give a greater degree of autonomy. But when he tried to reduce the size of the army he was murdered. His replacement, *General Obasanjo*, tried to slow down inflation by cutting defence expenditure which accounted for three-quarters of Nigeria's budget at that time. The slump in oil prices after the *Yom Kippur War* in 1973 (See Work Unit 34) hit the national economy hard because oil-exports accounted for 95% of Nigeria's foreign earnings. In 1979 Nigeria was forced to raise loans in Europe.

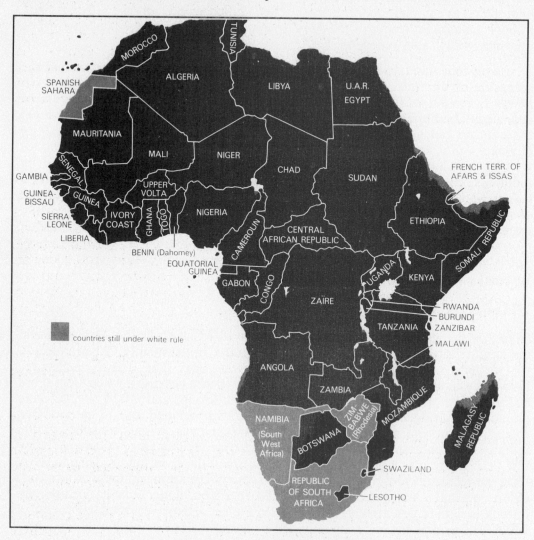

Independent States in Africa, 1977

TANZANIA

Tanganyika (the name of the territory before it united with Zanzibar) had a smooth progress to independence. This was because it was an ex-German colony and was therefore, first, a *mandated territory*, under the *League*, and, finally, a trustee territory under the*United Nations*. *Julius Nyerere*, the nationalist leader and founder of the *Tanganyika African National Union* (TANU) in 1954, took a strong anti-racist stand and this helped prevent trouble between Africans, Europeans and Asians. *Nyerere* became prime minister when independence was granted in 1963 and the next year *Tanganyika* joined the island of *Zanzibar* to form *Tanzania*.

Nyerere rejected as far as possible a capitalist economy for his country. In 1967 his so-called *Arusha Declaration* set out a socialist alternative. This envisaged a government elected and run by 'peasants and workers', with communally-owned villages called *'Ujamaa'*, a Swahili word meaning to work together as a family. Nyerere's *African Socialism* involved nationalising banks and business, and giving education a rural rather than urban bias. The *Five Year Plan* which followed the Declaration was only partially successful. Some sites chosen for the new villages were unsuitable, many peasants did not want to move from their old homes, and some still preferred to own their own land.

KENYA

Kenya had a large and influential white settler population who owned businesses and farmed the so-called *White Highlands*, a region which had originally been owned by the *Kikiyu* tribe. The settlers at first opposed all moves towards independence and, until 1944, there was no African representative on Kenya's Legislative Council. In 1952 a mass movement of the Kikiyu, built around a secret society called *Mau Mau*, began to raid white farms, kill settlers and murder Africans who supported British rule. Although the British launched a military campaign against these terrorists, the authorities, both in Kenya and Britain, recognised that genuine grievances lay behind the uprising. At a political level they began to make concessions, allowing two nationalist parties, the *Kenyan African National Union* (KANU) and the *Kenyan African People Union* (KAPU) to contest elections. KANU represented the Kikiyu and KAPU the smaller Kenyan tribes. At the same time the British imprisoned KANU's leader, *Jomo Kenyatta*, on a charge of inciting the Mau Mau rising. Kenyatta always denied this charge.

In 1961 KANU won a majority of seats on the *Legislative Council*. Its leaders refused to take part in the government until Kenyatta was released. The British gave in, and *Kenyatta* became prime minister and then *President* of the new *Republic of Kenya* in 1963. He proved to be a moderate and respected leader who persuaded many of the white settlers to stay and contribute to the economy. Both agriculture and industry have boomed since independence, although Kenya's capitalist economy is largely owned by foreigners. In later years Kenyatta himself became dictatorial as 'father figure' of his country. In 1969 the KAPU opposition party was banned, and its leader, *Oginga-Odinga*, imprisoned for 'fermenting unrest between tribes'. In 1975 an outspoken critic of the government was murdered, possibly with the help from the police. By the time of Kenyatta's death in 1978 a growing population was causing unemployment.

SELF-ASSESSMENT SECTION

1. What is the Stabex system?

2. What was Zaire's former name?

3. Which African state had a Biafran civil war?

4. What was "assimilation" when applied by the French?

5. Who proclaimed a Rif Republic in 1926?

6. What was Britain's 'jewel in the crown'?

7. What was a colon?

8. Who built the Volta river complex?

9. Which country gave Zaire its independence?

10. Name one African mandated territory.

11. What do these initials stand for?

> KAPU   CPP   KANU   TANU

12. The Arusha Declaration was:-

   a) a declaration of Tanzanian independence
   b) a programme of capitalist planning for Tanzania
   c) a declaration of war against Uganda
   d) a programme of socialist planning
   (TICK THE CORRECT ANSWER).

13. Indirect rule was:-

   a) rule by tribal chiefs
   b) rule by colonial officials
   c) rule by district officers
   d) rule by a governor and local chiefs
   (TICK THE CORRECT ANSWER)

14. Using the two lists below, match the men (letters) to the countries (numbers).

   a) AMIN   b) NYERERE   c) TSHOMBE
   d) LUMUMBA   e) LUGARD   f) NKRUMAH
   g) MOBUTU   h) GOWON

   1) KENYA   2) ZAIRE   3) NIGERIA
   4) GHANA   5) UGANDA   6) TANZANIA

15. Compare and contrast the British and French systems of ruling colonies. Give reasons, and examples, to show which system you think to have been the more successful.

16. Explain the problems facing African states after independence. Give examples and describe what you consider to be a successful and an unsuccessful state.

26

Twentieth Century Africa
Part Two

INTRODUCTION

Afrikaaner domination of South Africa arose from a feeling of being threatened by the English, not the coloured population. The coloured man's subjection was taken for granted. But the English had first imposed an alien culture on the Boer, and then, when he objected, beat him into submission. After defeat in the Boer War, Afrikaaners felt that their separate identity as a nation was at risk from 'Englishness'. In these circumstances they created a myth out of the troubled past. This centred around the Great Trek and involved the vision of brave pastoral people who passed through the wilderness like the Israelites of old, enduring hardship and overcoming attacks by bloodthirsty natives.

A secret society, the Broederbond, encouraged an Afrikaaner economic and cultural revival. The language itself was developed from a speech known as "Kitchen Dutch'. Dictionaries of this tongue were published, European classics translated into it and a new Afrikaaner literature created. At first this strong anti-British stance was softened by leaders like Jan Smuts, a man with a Cape background, English education and links with international statesmen. This very 'Englishness' led to his eventual rejection by hard-liners who, in 1938, were able to turn the centenary of the Great Trek into a national pilgrimage, complete with ox-wagons, to the site of the Boer victory at Blood river. After the Second World War, during which some Afrikaaner leaders refused to condemn or fight the nazis, Smuts and his party were defeated and from 1948 the Nationalist Party ruled South Africa.

Having won the battle for a separate identity against the British, it seemed natural to the Afrikaaner to erect barriers to exclude other 'foreign' influences - negro, coloured and Asian. In particular, the Nationalists asserted their right to be a free white nation at the expense of the majority South Africa's peoples. 'Throughout Africa today, African peoples are claiming the right to express their own personality and nationhood... the white nation in South Africa has the same right' states an official government pamphlet. Clearly, this is not acceptable, even if the majority population in South Africa were treated fairly. But with apartheid, the Afrikaaner has turned racial discrimination into a rigid system of laws and penalties, a prison from which there is no parole and no escape.

The reasons for apartheid are not entirely racial, although racism plays a large part. Another reason is economic, stemming from the fact that South Africa's rich, booming industries have been built on cheap black labour. The combination of social superiority, allied to economic privilege makes apartheid very attractive to most Afrikaaners. To quote Stephen Robinson writing in the 'Daily Telegraph' in 1988, 'apartheid is a system which has always had more to do with economic privileges than racial bigotry... In essence, apartheid gave each and every Afrikaaner - however stupid and unemployable he or she might be - an inalienable right to a well-paid and undemanding job in the public service. The right to travel in a separate train compartment or call a black man 'kaffir' was never more ... than icing on the Boer cake'.

World wide condemnation of apartheid, constant resolutions at the United Nations, attempts at sanctions and even terrorism, have come up against a rock-like obstacle in the Afrikaaner's 'laager' mentality. When attacked by their enemies, the Voortrekkers turned their wagons into a laager (circle) and fought off all comers. Obviously apartheid is a sort of laager inside which the Afrikaaner defies his modern enemies. It also enables him to feel that, though the world condemns him, this is because the world is wrong and he is right. It is these attitudes which have led to a dangerous stalemate in South Africa . An Afrikaaner farmer said on BBC TV in 1979, 'We developed the country, We worked for it. South Africa , the country we got, was a bare piece of ground...'. The African replies, quite simply, 'Let my people free'. Only some form of violence, it seems, can change the situation.

THE CENTRAL AFRICAN FEDERATION

In 1953 Britain formed a union from the three colonial territories of *Southern Rhodesia, Northern Rhodesia* and *Nyasaland*. It was called the *Central African Federation* (CAF). The aim was to give the new state economic strength. For example, the *Kariba dam* project would not have been possible without the CAF and the thriving copper belt of Northern Rhodesia benefitted from the prosperous farming community in Southern Rhodesia. The local point of view was different. Nationalists in Northern Rhodesia and Nyasaland particularly disliked union with Southern Rhodesia, a country with a strong white settler community and farms run in South African style. They felt that the prime ministers of Southern Rhodesia and Northern Rhodesia, *Sir Geoffrey Huggins* and *Sir Roy Welensky*, saw the Federation mainly as a way of strengthening white supremacy in the region.

In view of this dissatisfaction, Britain appointed a *Commission of Inquiry*, headed by *Lord Monckton*, to look into the matter. *Monckton* reported that the CAF was a financial success but that few Africans were prepared to accept it. Consequently, in 1964 Britain broke up the CAF into *Zambia* (Northern Rhodesia) and *Malawi* (Nyasaland). Southern Rhodesia's white settlers now demanded their independence but Britain refused to recognise what would have been a white-minority government. The settlers, led by *Ian Smith*, then issued a *Unilateral* (one-sided) *Declaration of Independence* (UDI) in 1965. Britain refused to recognise Smith's regime and joined with the UN in banning trade with Southern Rhodesia. These sanctions were ineffective because of South African help and 'blockade busting' through supply routes from South Africa and Portuguese *Mozambique*.

LANCASTER HOUSE AGREEMENT

Until 1974 all attempts to persuade the Smith regime to move towards majority rule failed. In 1974 a revolution in *Portugal* produced an anti-imperialist government ready to give up its colonies. *Mozambique* was granted its independence and its Marxist government soon made it a haven for African 'freedom-fighters' operating against Smith's Rhodesia. Both the USA and South Africa now put pressure on Smith to come to an agreement with the *Patriotic Front*, a guerilla organisation led by *Joshua Nkomo* and *Robert Magabe*. In 1976 Smith reluctantly agreed to black majority rule. Three years later *Abel Muzerewa* and *Ndabaningini Sithole*, two leaders in favour of peaceful progress, won an election. The *Patriotic Front* claimed this election was a fraud and continued with the guerilla war. At a conference at *Lancaster House* in London a new agreement was negotiated whereby British officials took temporary charge of Southern Rhodesia whilst another election was held. British troops were sent to the country where they supervised those guerillas who came out of hiding. In February, 1980 *Robert Magabe* won a resounding electoral victory and became prime minister of an independent *Zimbabwe* with *Joshua Nkomo* in the cabinet. In later years, Nkomo was forced to retire and Magabe founded a one-party state.

UGANDA

In *Uganda* various ancient African kingdoms, the largest of which was *Buganda*, favoured a federal system when independence came. The *Kabaka* (king) of *Buganda* was exiled in 1953 because he opposed a unitary state, a system favoured by Britain and some nationalist leaders. In 1961 the *Democratic Party* won an election, mainly because most Bugandans had refused to vote. It was decided that Buganda should have a federal relationship with the rest of the country when it became independent. As a sign of his importance, the Kabaka was made *President*; *Milton Obote* became prime minister.

In 1966 army units led by *Idi Amin* attacked the Kabaka's palace and he fled from the country. Obote now became President and *Buganda* lost its federal status. In June, 1971 Obote was accused of extravagance, corruption and nepotism and overthrown by *Idi Amin* in a military coup. Amin's regime began a reign of terror, with particularly brutal suffering for the *Ankoti* and *Langi* tribes. In 1972 *Uganda* expelled most Asians and confiscated their property. This caused drastic deterioration in Uganda's economy. In 1979 Ugandan exiles, supported by the Tanzanian army, invaded Uganda and overthrew *Amin* who fled to *Libya*

SOUTH AFRICA

The first Dutch settlers in South Africa believed they were chosen by God to be leaders over the natives. Consequently, they introduced racial segregation almost at once. When the English colonial administration gave the slaves their freedom in 1834, the Boers left the Cape in disgust, and began the *Great Trek* to the north to found what became the *Orange Free State* and the *Transvaal*. Such racial attitudes hardened over the years. One of the conditions written into the *Treaty of Vereeninging* which ended the Boer War, was that no African should be given political rights. The *Union of South Africa*, formed in 1910, perpetuated white supremacy; the Boers only agreed to it after making sure that no non-white could vote for the new Parliament in *Pretoria*. During and after the First World War, South Africa's leading politician and soldier, *Jan Smuts*, favoured racial tolerance. Such moderation pleased neither side. The *African National Congress* (ANC) pressed for the *pass laws*, which required all Africans outside the tribal areas to carry identity cards, to be repealed. White resistance, spearhead by *General Hertzog*'s *Afrikaaner National Party,* made sure there was no repeal. In 1927 Smuts was forced against his will to pass the *Immorality Act* which made mixed marriages (between white and coloured) illegal. In 1934, *Smuts* and *Hertzog*, leaders of the English and Afrikaaner groups respectively, united to fight the economic effects of world depression. Their *United Party* did not please extreme Afrikaaners who formed the *National Party* led by *Dr. D.F. Malan*.

BEGINNINGS OF APARTHEID

There were three major groupings in South Africa -*black Africans, Cape Coloureds* (the name given to people of mixed race) and South African-born *Indians*. Of these, the largest group were the black Africans. The Afrikaaner aim was to confine the coloured population to special *'reserves'*, totalling about 13% of the land. *The Native Land and Trust Bill*, (1936) made these reserves the permanent home of black Africans and denied them the right to own land elsewhere. Another aim was to protect the jobs of white workers. This was done by barring black people from towns and cities without a permit. *Segregation* was achieved by making separate zones for blacks and whites in every area where they might meet, on trains, in cafes, on beaches, in parks and public buildings. The *Immorality Act*, produced the deepest and most lasting segregation of all, and sometimes led to the forcible breakup of families where trace of a different colour was detected in a husband or wife's ancestry.

NATIONALIST VICTORY

Another Afrikaaner aim was to eliminate English culture and replace it with Afrikaaner language and customs. The *Broederbond*, a secret society, worked towards this end, and, during the Thirties, succeeded in becoming influential in economic as well as cultural matters. During the Second World War many Afrikaaners sympathised with the nazis because of their racist views. However, South African troop played a distinguished part in the war, fighting in North Africa and Europe. After the war, Smut's long grip on government, shaken at times but still strong, was brought to the end. His English education and friendship with British politicians like Winston Churchill, his less than total commitment to racial segregation, led to his defeat in the *1948 General Election*. The *Nationalist Party* campaigned for what it called *separate development* (apartheid) free from English influences. This also meant separate, and far superior, living conditions for the white, as opposed to the coloured and black peoples.

APARTHEID

Daniel Malan led the *Nationalist Party* to victory in 1948 on a programme of white supremacy. This victory was historic because it has never been reversed and the Nationalists have ruled South Africa ever since. *Malan's* aim was to systematically 'Afrikaanerise' the civil service, armed forces, industry and business. By this time South Africa was the richest state on the continent owing to a booming economy and high gold prices. South Africa supplied gold, diamonds and uranium to Europe and the west. She had a rich and varied agriculture and an industrial base comparable to a modern European state. This development had been made possible by abundant capital and cheap labour.

The black people who constituted 72% of the population, had to do all the manual work but were denied all social or political rights. In 1950 the *Population Registration Act* classified people as *European, Coloured* (mixed race) and *African* (Bantu). Families which resulted from marriage between people of these groups were to be broken up. At the same time, the *Suppression of Communism Act* made it illegal to oppose apartheid and also classified 'communism' as anything which caused hostility between Europeans and non-Europeans. The *Group Area Acts* of 1950 and 1957 provided that the ownership and occupation of any particular area should be for one specified group only. The majority of land was reserved for the Europeans. Bantus were granted their own *'homelands'*, or *Bantustans*, to which they were often complete strangers until transported there by government order.

The *Separate Representation of Voters Act*, (1953) removed coloured voters' names from the electoral roll. The *Promotion of Self-government Act*, (1959) abolished all African representation in the South African Parliament. The African National Congress (ANC) spearheaded native protest and staged demonstrations against these laws. At a protest meeting at *Sharpeville* in 1960 the police opened fire on demonstrators, killing 60. After Sharpeville, the *ANC* and the *Pan-African Movement* were banned, and the leader of the ANC, *Nelson Mandella*, was imprisoned on a charge of terrorism. Mandella's long imprisonment made him the focus of world-wide protest against apartheid. Streets, parks and public buildings in various parts of the world were named after him and he became the world's most famous political prisoner.

BANTUSTANS

In 1960 South Africa became a *republic*. Although there are republics within the Commonwealth, notably *India*, such a move calls for an application to remain in it.

When South Africa's application was opposed in the aftermath of the Sharpeville shootings, the South African prime minster, *Dr. Hendrik Verwoerd*, withdrew his country's application and South Africa left the Commonwealth. *Verwoerd*, and his successor, *Johannes Vorster*, tried to present apartheid in a better light. Whilst trying to establish friendly links with Black African states, and in the case of *Malawi*, succeeding, they presented apartheid as a new concept of a multi-racial society. Under such a system, they claimed, each black group would be treated as a separate racial entity entitled to its own culture and homeland. Since the best land and industry is in Afrikaaners hands, these *Bantustans* cannot support themselves and are economically dependant on South Africa.

The first Bantustan to be granted 'home rule' was the *Transkei* in 1963. Since that time 10 have been founded covering 13% of South Africa's territory. Some Bantustans are large: five, *Xhosa, Zulu, Seped, Tswana* and *Seshoeshoe*, are bigger than many independent African states. Some are situated in fertile land near the *Drakensberg mountains*; others are in the dry interior. Some are not in one piece. *Bophutatswana*, for example, is in 7 parts and *Kwazulu* in 40. The South African government envisages what it calls complete independence for these areas eventually, and this happened to the *Transkei* in 1976. The Transkei's inhabitants have no legal rights outside the Bantustan and are classified as foreigners in the rest of South Africa.

OPPOSITION TO APARTHEID

There has been both black and white protest inside South Africa to apartheid, and world-wide condemnation outside. Many countries have banned sporting links with South Africa, whose rugby and cricket teams have been excluded from international competition since the early 1960's. Calls for *sanctions* against the South African regime have come from many countries and organisations, including the *United Nations* (See Work Unit 24). These have not been successful. Large amounts of western capital are invested in South Africa's rich economy and her trade links with the outside world remain strong. Opposition within the country has been contained and often crushed by an efficient police, armed as a para-military force.

In 1956 *Father Trevor Huddleston*, an outspoken critic of apartheid, was forced to leave his ministry in *Sophiatown*. *Alan Paton*, the South African novelist and chairman of the *Liberal Party* which advocated a multi-racial society, had his party banned in 1968. *Helen Suzman*, leader of the *Progressive Party*, has campaigned for the vote for all citizens but has had little success. *Pass-burning* was a recognised form of black protest from 1952, when it became the law for all Africans to carry such documentation, until the abolition of such laws by *P.W. Botha*, prime minister from 1978. In 1976, in a move to gain tighter control of education, the government closed many Bantu schools or took them over. This flared up into a serious riot at *Soweto*, near *Johannesburg*, where black students resented having part of their lessons conducted in Afrikaans. Many pupils were arrested and imprisoned, including a protest leader, *Steve Biko*, who died while in police custody.

NEW SOUTH AFRICAN CONSTITUTION

Botha's more moderate policy was influenced by industry's demand for better educated workers, and the need to create trade links with black African states. He abolished much social segregation, allowing multi-racial theatres, hotels and restaurants, and introducing some multi-racial sport. In 1983 the white South African electorate voted for a new *Constitution*. This provided for a segregated three-chamber Parliament, one for *whites* , one for *coloureds* and one for *Asians*. The voting system was arranged in such a way that the white chamber could overrule the other two chambers. This new Constitution, marking as it did a step forward, was resented by blacks who were excluded from the arrangements. On the other hand, such 'liberalism' by Botha's ministry, led to a white backlash. Extremist Afrikaaners formed a *Conservative Party* which has campaigned against the Nationalists at election, especially after the *Mixed Marriages* and *Immorality* Acts were repealed in 1985.

South Africa remains at the centre of the world stage. Geographically, she has a key strategic role to play in western defence, commanding the sea-route round the Cape of Good Hope. Her gold reserves and industry make her important in world economic affairs. Her anti-communist stance pleases some western states, and her control of *Namibia* until 1989, where she fought the African freedom organisation SWAPO *(South West Africa's People's Organisation)*, led her to intervene in the communist takeover of *Angola* by Cuban troops. The change of *Mozambique* and *Angola*, from official territories to communist regimes, forced South Africa to rethink its foreign policy as regards Africa.

SELF-ASSESSMENT SECTION

1. What did the Immorality Act forbid?

2. What is a "coloured" in South Africa?

3. Which was the first Bantustan?

4. What is the Broederbond?

5. Which other African state helped to overthrow Idi Amin?

6. What did the Monckton Commission report?

7. Which country ruled Mozambique before it gained its independence?

8. Who was the prime minister of Southern Rhodesia in the 1950's?

9. What is a laager?

10. What happened at Sharpeville?

11. Put in correct details (by letter) against these names.

    1. NELSON MANDELLA   A.   Took South Africa out of the Commonwealth

    2. STEVE BIKO   B.   Imprisoned ANC leader

    3. HELEN SUZMAN   C.   Proclaimed UDI in 1965

    4. HENDRIK VERWOERD   D.   Forced out of Sophiatown

    5. JAN SMUTS   E.   Died in police custody

    6. TREVOR HUDDLESTON   F.   South African soldier and statesman

    7. IAN SMITH   G.   Leader of South African Progressive Party.

12. What do these initials stand for?

         CAF   UDI   ANC   SWAPO   PF

13.

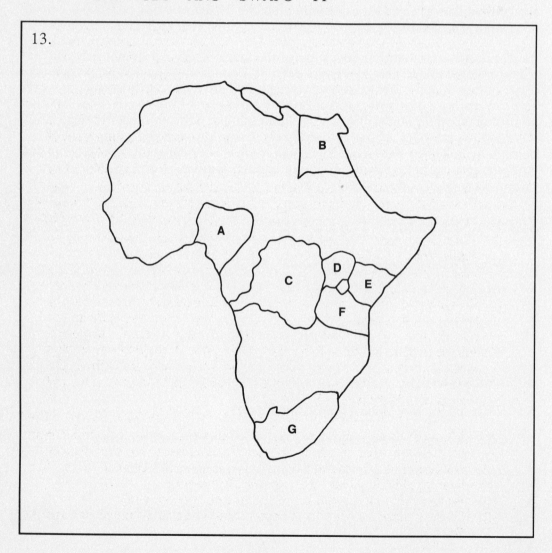

13. Look at the map on the previous page. Then write down the correct African state indicated by the letters. They are Nigeria, Uganda, Congo (Zaire), South Africa, Tanzania, Egypt and Kenya.

14. "Apartheid is a system which has always had more to do with economic privileges than racial bigotry ... In essence, apartheid gave every Afrikaaner ... the right to a well paid and undemanding job in the public service. The right to travel in a separate train compartment ... was never more than icing on the Boer cake"

> Stephen Robinson, 'Daily Telegraph', 1988

Explain this statement in the light of P.W. Botha's reform of apartheid in the 1980's. Give reasons why you think it is a correct or incorrect assessment of the situation.

15. Read these two Sources, then answer the questions.

A. "In all three territories, Africans gained little from Federation. The idea of 'partnership' was forgotten. Africans did not share in the economic boom that lasted for the first three years ... They were taxed on things they bought in the shops such as clothing, footwear and dried milk, and they were charged high prices by white and Asian traders. ... There were many instances of racial discrimination. The Lusaka City Council tarred the road to the European hospital but not the 180 metres to the African Hospital. A white man killed his African employee and was gaoled for a year, but when an African robbed his employer he was gaoled for five. At Ndola and Mufulira, restaurants refused to serve tea to African politicians; when they did they charged £5".

> (From 'Iron Age to Independence' by D.E. Needham, E.K. Mashingaidze and N. Bhebe. Longman, 1974 and 1984.)

B. "The Organisation of African Unity celebrates its 25th birthday in Addis Ababa today with neither the continent or the organisation in the best of health. Against a background of bloody war and worsening famine in Ethiopia, the host country, African heads of state have little for which to give thanks. Of the 30 African leaders present when the body was founded in 1963, two-thirds have been assassinated or overthrown by military coups, and many states remain unstable. Africa is also falling into economic despair. A major issue at this week's summit include the conflict between Chad and Libya, the future of the western Sahara, which is still under Moroccan rule, and the perennial problem of South Africa.."

> Report by Jeremy Gavron, Daily Telegraph, 25 May 1988.

a) Which of these sources do you think was written from the African point of view and which from the Western? Give reasons for your answer.
b) Do you think any of the facts in these sources is incorrect? If not, how do you think they have been used by the writers?
c) Write a report similar to B. about other parts of the world.
d) Write a report similar to A. about conditions in an inner city area of Britain.

16.   "Many historians now argue that too much attention is paid to the conflict between the British and Boer whites; the Boer War was less significant in the long run than the common attitude of whites towards blacks that was typified in the Treaty of Vereeninging."

Elizabeth Campling. 'Africa in the Twentieth Century', Batsford, 1980.

Using material in Work Unit 6 as well as 25 and 26, write an essay explaining what Elizabeth Campling means by this comment.

17.

(Source: Paul Popper Ltd.)

a) Why is this sign in two languages?   b) What system does the sign illustrate? Why has it caused worldwide condemnation?   c) How far has this system been modified in recent years? Why do think it has been modified?

27

The United States 1945-1988

INTRODUCTION

In the USA contrasts between the rich and poor, between what is said and what is done, are starker than elsewhere. This is because, to quote Alistair Cook, "America didn't inherit a nation - it invented one that was supposed to be better than everything that had gone before". The American Dream *(See introduction to Work Unit 3)* brings comfort to those who believe in it, but it also brings disillusionment to those who wake up and find it was only a dream and that their country is no more moral than other countries. And many Americans are disillusioned by a country, founded on principles of justice, fairness and simple living, which is now rich, crime-ridden and almost overwhelmed with material possessions.

The USA emerged from the Second World War the most powerful nation on earth, with an industrial base which had supplied most of the nations fighting Germany and Japan, made the atomic bomb, and given a new-found prosperity to millions of workers. The US economy produced goods at such a rate and in such quantities that it needed consumer-spending on a grand scale to make it work. As Wendell Wilkie, a Presidential candidate in the 1940's remarked, "The American economy is not going to be able to prosper after the war unless Americans regard as necessities what other people look on as luxuries". It was an attitude, immoral to some, which gave birth to the 'consumer society' in Europe and Japan as well as the USA.

US prosperity has not been seriously eroded, despite inflation, war and strong international competition. The spectre of another 1930's style Depression has been avoided. But it has had two noticeable effects on American life. First, it has produced a small but well-publicised group of people who have 'opted-out' of the 'rat-race'. The hippies of the late 1960's, and the various communities established since, have grown out of a genuine disgust at such luxury and extravagance in a world of poverty. Second, and more important, it has produced bitter feelings amongst those too poor to share in it. In particular, this has involved the black population who have found themselves at the bottom of the pile in contempory America. Since 1945 there has been a continuous battle for negro rights fought at

259

many different levels - Supreme court rulings, Congressional Acts, peaceful and violent protest. This battle has now ranged over the whole spectrum of the problem, from arguments about racial segregation in the South to job opportunities and the quality of life for negroes in the North.

The USA has suffered one national trauma since 1945 - the defeat in Vietnam. No event since the Civil War has so divided American opinion. To some, the USA's involvement in Vietnam was a necessary defence of democracy against communist aggression. It was fought to prevent the fall of one country causing the collapse of another - the so-called 'domino theory'. To others, it was a brutal interference in the internal affairs of a country, 10,000 miles away; a war which led to atrocities being committed by US troops. To many, both inside and outside the USA, it demonstrated that not even America's huge destructive power could beat a well-organised peasant army fighting in terrain unsuitable for modern weaponry. The whole tragic story, with riots, demonstrations and 'draft-dodging' ended, eventually, in the most humiliating military defeat. This was a psychological blow to a people who had, until 1973, never lost a war. It is significant that for some years after Vietnam, Americans, who have usually made a fuss of their ex-servicemen, largely ignored the men who had fought in 'Nam'.

Since 1945 America has been the leader of the free world, standing for the virtues of freedom and capitalism against the harsh regimentation of communist states. At least that is how most Americans see their country. To their surprise, such a stand has given them more brickbats than bouquets. Not only the USA's enemies, but her allies, have sometimes condemned her 'war-mongering'. To be top dog, as the British found out before the Americans, rarely makes you popular.

THE TAFF-HARTLEY ACT

On 12 April 1945 *President Roosevelt* died at the start of his fourth term as President. He was succeeded by his Vice-President, *Harry S Truman*. Within months, the USA was at peace. The expected slump, as the US shifted from a wartime to a peacetime economy, did not materialise, because of continued full employment. This was encouraged by the Truman administration through the *Committee for Economic Development* (CED) which worked on the basis that if industry wished to avoid further government controls it must keep up levels of employment. However, currency inflation led to unrest; in 1946 there were 5,000 strikes involving nearly 4,600,000 workers. Congress and the administration reacted to this state of affairs by passing the *Taff-Hartley Act*. This act banned unions operating a 'closed shop', made it illegal to use union funds for political purposes and ordered an 80-day 'cooling off period' if the proposed strikes seemed likely to damage the economy. The same year a strike threat by US steel workers led *Truman* to announce that all strikers would be called up for the army, thus making them liable to military law. The steel workers had no alternative but to give way.

TRUMAN'S FAIR DEAL

Truman won the 1948 Presidential election for the Democrats and introduced, in place of the *New Deal*, his own *Fair Deal* programme. The *Fair Deal* proposed to build on the foundations of the older programme, and many of its measures were similar - government funding of public works, more low-cost housing and better social security, including higher old age pensions. It wanted subsidies for public (state) schools, aid to agriculture and government sponsored medical insurance together with a higher minimum wage. This programme was opposed, not only by Truman's Republican opponents in Congress, but by some conservative-minded politicians of his own Democratic party, Some aid was given to farmers through subsidised prices based on the cost of living and there were rises in wage levels and social security benefits. By 1949 the economy was beginning to slow down, and unemployment was rising, but the start of the *Korean War* (See Work Unit 28) led to re-armament which boosted industry.

COMMUNIST SPYING

Fear and dislike of communism was strong amongst many sections of the US community after the Second World War. This was caused by the Russian takeover of *eastern Europe*, the development of the 'Cold War' (See Work Unit 29) and the Communist victory in *China* (See Work Unit 10). There was a feeling that a great deal of this communist success had been achieved with the help of traitors and so, in 1948, the government set up the *Un-American Activities Committee*. At first this committee was supposed to look for Nazi sympathisers but it soon began to find communists. Evidence of Soviet spying was not hard to find. In 1950 *Klaus Fuchs*, a leading nuclear scientist, was imprisoned in Britain for giving atomic secrets to the Russians. In *Canada* the police rounded up a spy-ring. In America itself, a high-ranking State Department official, *Alger Hiss*, who had been an adviser to Roosevelt at *Yalta*, was convicted of perjury after denying that he had passed secrets to the Russians, and two other spies, the husband and wife team of *Ethel* and *Julius Rosenberg*, were executed for espionage. It was not surprising that when the Russians exploded their first *atomic bomb* in September, 1949, many Americans were certain that treachery had speeded up this development.

McCARTHY'S WITCH HUNT

The outbreak of the *Korean War*, following an invasion of the south by communist Korea, encouraged *Senator Joseph McCarthy* to take over and misuse the Un-American Activities Committee. McCarthy was only interested in winning votes and gaining higher political office. His methods consisting in claiming that an unspecified, or specified, number of people were 'communists', although he never produced any evidence to back his charges. For example, he accused 205 civil servants at one time, later reducing the number to 57 - the so-called *'Heinz Variety Figure'*. Many innocent people had their reputations smeared, and their careers ruined, by this *'Witch-hunt'*. Anybody who had vague left-wing leanings, and some who had none. were liable to be denounced as 'communists' and 'enemies of the state'.

Among McCarthy's most distinguished victims were *Robert Oppenheimer*, an atomic scientist, who was sacked from his government posts, and *General George Marshall*, one of the most senior and respected figures in the US army. Whether

McCarthy could have ended Marshall's career will never be known because about the time of that particular accusation he made his first TV appearance; hitherto only his voice had been heard on radio. The sight of McCarthy's blustering and bullying of witnesses, exposed his true character to the American public. In 1954 he was removed from his post and censured by the Senate.

CIVIL RIGHTS

Ever since the *American Civil War* (See Work Unit 3) coloured people in the USA had been treated as second-class citizens and usually denied the rights given to white people. *President Truman* tried to get a *Civil Rights Bill* through Congress which would have ensured that blacks in the Southern states would be able to exercise their voting rights. In many areas these existed only on paper because of intimidation or legal trickery. This bill was rejected but Truman, in his capacity as commander-in-chief, did end segregation in the army, where there had been separate black regiments. *General Dwight D. Eisenhower*, who won the Presidency for the Republicans in 1952, continued this aspect of Truman's policies. He appointed the liberal-minded *Earl Warren* as *Chief Justice* of the *Supreme Court*. Warren used the Court's right to interpret the Constitution to rule in 1954 that segregated schools, common in many southern states, were unconstitutional. This ruling was resisted in many parts of the South. In 1957 nine black children tried to enrol in the all-white school at *Little Rock, Arkansas*, as a test case. When the riots which followed were not put down by the state governor, Eisenhower sent in regular army units to escort the children to school.

MARTIN LUTHER KING

The *Civil Rights Movement*, which aimed to gain rights for blacks by peaceful protest, was led by the *Reverend Martin Luther King*. In 1955 at *Montgomery, Alabama*, King led blacks in sit-ins on buses, in stores and restaurants which were reserved for whites. He also organised and led *protest marches* through the South, during which some of his supporters were injured or murdered. King's slogan was *'We shall overcome'* and this sentiment, set to music, became the theme song of black protest. In 1957 *Eisenhower* managed to get another *Civil Rights Bill* through Congress. This made it illegal to put obstacles in the way of black people voting. Meanwhile the traditional 'black' South and 'white' North situation was changing as large numbers of blacks moved into northern cities looking for work. They proved to be no more welcome than they were in the south and there were race riots at *Baltimore, Detroit* and *Cleveland*.

BLACK POWER

These riots were caused partly by bad treatment and discrimination. They were also the work of the *Black Power* movement whose members rejected King's peaceful methods. This movement was spearheaded by a fanatical *Black Moslem* group who were anti-white and wanted a separate black state in America. The issues in the North were different from those in the South. In the North there was no segregation in public places or education, but there was discrimination against blacks in jobs and housing. The riots of the mid-1960's were very serious. In 1965 the *Watts* district of *Los Angeles* was nearly destroyed and there were many deaths and a great deal of damage in *Chicago, New Jersey* and *Newark*. In 1968 *Martin Luther King* was murdered by a fanatic and this was seen as further proof by the militants that peaceful protest did not work.

KENNEDY'S NEW FRONTIER

In 1960 *John F. Kennedy* regained the Presidency for the *Democrats*. Kennedy came from a rich and influential Irish-American family in Boston. His comparative youthfulness, and his inspiring speeches seemed to point to a better future for the USA. His *New Frontier* programme suggested that modern problems were to be beaten in the same way as the old pioneers had tamed the west, with courage and tenacity. In fact, the New Frontier's ambitious plans for foreign aid, better housing, schools and medical care were often blocked by a hostile Congress. Kennedy continued the *Civil Rights* policies of Eisenhower and Truman. When *James Meredith*, a coloured student, attempted to enrol at a whites-only college in *Oxford*, Mississippi, and there were riots, Kennedy sent army units to restore order when the state governor refused to deal with the situation. Kennedy also appointed the first black judge, the first black ambassador and the first black captain of a US warship.

MURDERS OF JOHN AND ROBERT KENNEDY

At this time the *Congress of Racial Equality* (CORE) was founded by blacks disatisfied with the slow progress of reform. Kennedy's policies on Civil Rights were continued by his successor, *Lyndon B. Johnson*, after Kennedy himself had been murdered in *Dallas* in November, 1963. (At the time *Lee Harvey Oswald* was arrested for the killing but he was killed a few days later by *Jack Ruby*. Since 1963 various suggestions have been made as to the killers, including opponents of Civil rights, Cuban exiles and the Mafia.) In 1964, Johnson signed the most effective *Civil Rights Act* passed by Congress since the Civil War. It provided for complete de-segregation in public places, equal opportunities for employment and education and a guarantee of the right to vote. Some blacks were grateful for this, and Johnson's victory in the 1964 Presidential election was helped by negro voters in Arkansas, Florida, Texas and Virginia. But others turned to the *Black Power* alternative, notably *Stokely Carmichael*. There were serious riots through until 1968, some initiated by whites and some by blacks. The murder of *Luther King* in that year sparked off nationwide riots and disorder and in *Washington* there were 40 fires burning at one time. The murder of *Robert Kennedy*, President Kennedy's brother, in 1968 was seen as a blow to the Civil Rights movement because as US Attorney-General Robert Kennedy had fought for coloured workers' rights.

KENNEDY AND CUBA

Kennedy's domestic policies had been frustrated by an alliance of Republicans and southern Democrats. His foreign policy was more successful. In 1961 he founded the *Peace Corps*, a force of American men and women who volunteered for service to humanity. Peace Corps members were trained thoroughly and received only living expenses and a small sum at the end of two years' service. Their job was to live with the people they went to help, to teach English and practical skills. They were ready to turn their hand to any work, from laying sewage systems in Bolivia to building a town in Pakistan. The Peace Corps appealed to idealistic young men and women, mostly just out of college, and the number of countries requesting such help rose from 12 in 1961 to 47 in 1968.

Partly to meet the threat of *'Fidelismo'*, the attitudes of *Fidel Castro*, the revolutionary leader of *Cuba* and ally of the Russians, Kennedy initiated the *Alliance of Progress* in 1961. This was signed between the President and the leaders of every Latin American state except Cuba. The *Alliance* planned a long-term effort to build up the living standards in Latin America. Over a 10 year period, the USA proposed to help Latin American countries with schools, housing and public health programmes. It was also planned to diversify certain economies, stabilize prices and currencies, institute fairer methods of taxation and, in general, seek to reduce poverty and social injustice. The Alliance was only partially successful. In some countries, notably *Chile, Columbia* and *Venezuela*, it accelerated reform for a time. In others, it was regarded as too revolutionary by right-wingers, or a cloak for US 'imperialism' by left-wingers. In general international matters, Kennedy tried to encourage more *free trade*. He initiated the *Kennedy Round* of talks whereby nations who belonged to the *General Agreement on Tariffs and Trade* (GATT) agreed to progressively reduce their tariffs.

MAN ON THE MOON

Kennedy's worst mistake in foreign affairs was to approve a *Central Intelligence Agency* (CIA) plan to let Cuban exiles opposed to Castro invade the island. The *Bay of Pigs* landing proved a fiasco; Castro's troops were alerted and few Cubans joined the invaders. His most solid achievement was probably the signing of the *Nuclear Test Ban Treaty* in 1963. (See Work Unit 24). In two areas he committed the USA to heavy expenses in the future - the American involvement in *Vietnam* and the *Space Programme*, aimed at putting Americans on the moon by 1970. This was achieved in July, 1969 by *Neil Armstrong* and *'Buzz' Aldrin*.

VIETNAM

The US gradually became more involved in the attempt to stop *North Vietnam* conquering the south (See Work Unit 28). Inside the USA this led to protests and riots when students and others objected to the *draft* (call-up) being used to man the armed forces for this undeclared war. Because there was a relatively high proportion of black troops in Vietnam, the issue also had a racial aspect. Opponents of the war claimed that America was wrong to interfere. They also condemned the heavy bombing raids being carried out by the US airforce in Vietnam, saying the USA was waging an aggressive, imperialist war. There were anti-war demonstrations and riots all over the US, and some men fled abroad or went to prison rather than be called up for service.

Johnson's *Great Society* scheme for bettering the conditions of the people was a casualty of this disorder, because the colossal expense of armaments for the war fuelled *inflation* and led to a severe balance of payments problem. The *dollar*, hitherto the world's strongest currency, was weakened, until in 1971, *Richard Nixon*, Johnson's Republican successor, devalued it. The *Oil Crisis* in 1973 (See Work Unit 34) left the German *mark* and the Japanese *yen* stronger currencies.

THE HIPPIE SIXTIES

During the *Johnson* and *Nixon* years (1963-74) there were other protests, notably by blacks, hippies and women. Hippies felt that the USA was in the grip of *Big Business* - corporations - and the technology associated with it. They *'dropped out'* of society, living in communes, growing their own food and sometimes making their own clothes. Other youngsters became involved in the vague forms of protest associated with *pop-music* and the misuse of *drugs*. In August, 1969 a *Rock Concert* was due to be held in a field near *Woodstock* in New York State. The concert was not held at Woodstock, but it became famous by that name when 400,000 instead of the expected 50,000 turned up to hear 'protest' singers like *Joan Baez* and *Jimi Hendrix* and groups like *Family Stone* and *Jefferson Airplane*. Women's groups, called *feminists*, demanded greater equality with men. Feminism was helped by the new 'freedom' given to women by the *contraceptive pill* and easier access to legal *abortion*.

WATERGATE

In 1972 *Richard Nixon* was alarmed when the *New York Times* published secret information about the US involvement in Vietnam. This material could only have been obtained from sources within the government and they became known as the *Pentagon Papers* after the headquarters of the US armed forces in *Washington*. Nixon set up a *Special Investigation Unit* to close such leaks - nicknamed the *'plumbers'*. He also became obsessed with possible treachery and disloyalty and won the 1972 Presidential Election with the aid of a campaign group called the *Citizen's Committee for the Re-Election of the President* (CREEP). Afterwards it emerged that CREEP had burgled the *Watergate Hotel* in Washington to find out the rival Democratic Party's plans. The burglary was discovered, and in a series of court cases, many of Nixon's highest officials were imprisoned for complicity.

The President himself denied that he knew anything about the Watergate break-ins. At the same time, he refused to hand over tape-recordings made when discussing Watergate with his staff. In February, 1972 the investigations reached a crisis with the charging of *John Mitchell*, Nixon's top legal official, with conspiracy, perjury and obstructing the course of justice. This affair forced the President to hand over the tapes which were published and became best-sellers, especially when it became clear that they showed that Nixon did know about the burglaries. Nixon was now threatened with *impeachment* - a form of trial of the President which had only once been threatened before, to *Andrew Johnson* in 1868, and never actually carried out. Nixon then resigned, the first US President to do so. His successor, *Gerald Ford*, pardoned him and thus saved the ex-President from further humiliation.

CARTER AND IRAN

In 1976 the Democrats regained the Presidency when it was won by *Jimmy Carter*, an ex-naval officer and farmer from Georgia. Such a choice of an 'outsider' may have been caused by disgust at Watergate and the activities of Washington 'insiders' but it gave the US a President with no influential group of supporters in Congress. During Carter's Presidency the US's balance of payments problem grew worse and the dollar weaker. Inflation more than doubled between 1976 and 1979. Carter played the peace-maker in the Middle East (See Work Unit 34) but showed weaknesses in the face of the Soviet invasion of *Afghanistan* in 1979 and the Cuban-backed takeover of *Angola*.

When the *Shah of Iran*, a US client ruler, was driven out by a Muslim Fundamentalist revolution led by the *Ayatollah Khomeini*, the backlash against the Americans became violent. The US Embassy in *Tehran*, the Iranian capital, was stormed by Iranian Revolutionary Guards and its staff taken hostage. Carter first tried *sanctions* to free the hostages, and then launched an ill-fated air-strike which broke down in the desert hundreds of miles from Tehran. Such a humiliation made the election of a Republican, in this case *Ronald Reagan*, an ex-film actor, certain in 1980.

REAGAN'S PRESIDENCY

Reagan cut federal spending but this increased unemployment, especially amongst disadvantaged groups like *blacks* and *hispanics* (Americans originating from the Latin American countries). Consequently, Reagan reversed this policy in 1982. The federal government then began to spend more than it collected in taxes. This increased employment, but the US *budget deficit* grew to 211 billion dollars in 1985. These deficits were covered by borrowing, both inside America and overseas. To obtain such credit, the US administration was compelled to pay higher interest rates, and this forced foreign countries to do the same. In 1985 the *USA, Japan, West Germany, Britain* and *France* - the *Group of Five* - agreed to cooperate to stabilise the exchange rate between different currencies.

In 1987, some of Reagan's leading military men on the *National Security Council*, in particular *Admiral Poindexter*, and other officers, notably *Colonel North* were investigated for a secret deal with Iran, apparently involving weapons supplied in return for the release of American hostages held in Iran and Lebanon. President Reagan denied knowledge of the scheme but his muddled answers led to the affair being dubbed *Irangate*. Reagan retired in 1988 and was succeeded by his Vice-President and fellow Republican, *George Bush*.

SELF-ASSESSMENT SECTION

1. Who appoints judges of the US Supreme Court?

2. What are Civil Rights' Bills concerned with?

3. Who said, 'We shall overcome'?

4. What was the 'Heinz Variety Figure'?

5. Who initiated a programme called the Great Society?

6. Name a foreign currency stronger than the dollar in the 1970's.

7. What does the word, 'Woodstock' refer to?

8. What is an hispanic?

9. What is the NSC?

10. What did the Group of Five hope to achieve?

11. The Kennedy Round was concerned with:-

    a) Protectionism
    b) Free Trade
    c) Isolationism
    d) The Space Programme
    e) Nuclear Test banning
        (TICK THE CORRECT ANSWER)

12. Put the correct party (Democrat or Republican) beside the names of these US Presidents.

    Franklin Roosevelt   Harry S. Truman
    Dwight D. Eisenhower   John F. Kennedy
    Lyndon B. Johnson   Richard M. Nixon
    Gerald Ford   Jimmy Carter
    Ronald Reagan   George Bush

13. The idea that the overthrow of a non-communist country in South East Asia would lead to the overthrow of others is called:-

    a) Fidelismo
    b) Defeatism
    c) The Domino Theory
    d) The Kennedy Doctrine
    e) Revisionism
        (TICK THE CORRECT ANSWER)

    It was put forward in connection with:-

    a) US involvement in Korea
    b) US involvement in the Phillipines
    c) US involvement in Europe
    d) US involvement in Vietnam
    e) US involvement in Cuba
        (TICK THE CORRECT ANSWER)

14.

(Source: U.S. Information Services).

Look at this photograph. Then answer the questions.

  a)   This was a famous incident in what campaign?
  b)   Where did it take place, and when?
  c)   What are the soldiers doing in this photograph?
  d)   Why was this action necessary?
  e)   Who ordered this action? What particular constitutional power allowed him to do this?

15. Fill in the gaps in this extract from the words listed over the page:-

"Mitchell resigned as attorney-general in 1972 in order to run the ......
(known by the acronym ......) and, as a resident of the ..... apartment block
in ..... was a neighbour of the ..... offices there. These were ..... during
the election campaign, apparently as part of a ...... plot to spy on their
opponent. He denied having had any part in such a conspiracy but a tape-
recorded conversation between ...... and John Erlichman, his domestic
counsellor, held in March, 1973 has the following exchange: 'John says he
sorry he's sent those ...... in'. Nixon, 'That's right'. At that point Mitchell
chimed in, 'you are very welcome, sir' and laughter was heard".

(From an obituary notice on John Mitchell,
11 November, 1988, in the 'Daily Telegraph'.)

    1. Democratic Party
    2. Campaign for the Re-Election of the President
    3. Watergate
    4. CREEP
    5. Republican
    6. burgled
    7. Washington
    8. Nixon
    9. Burglars

16. Name and describe *two* activities of which an American might be proud during this period, and *two* of which he might be ashamed.

17. Imagine a conversation between a negro living in the South and one living in the north, in which each describes his/her own particular experience of racial discrimination..

28

The Far East since 1945: Korea, Malaysia and Vietnam

INTRODUCTION

The term South East Asia refers to the countries between India, China and Australasia. Although the teeming millions of these regions differ in race, religion and culture, they were all, with the exception of Thailand, ruled by foreigners before 1941. Consequently, when Japan invaded, her troops were able to pose as liberators come to free fellow Asiatics from their European masters. The reality, of course, was far different, and the unfortunate Asians soon found they had exchanged one colonial master for a worse one. Japanese propaganda backfired on them. It accelerated the people's desire for independence by reminding them of their colonial status, and, at the same time, gave them a colonialist regime to fight. Before the war ended the Japanese were struggling against guerillas who could claim to be fighting on the side of their colonial masters. After Japan's defeat, the old imperialist powers, Britain, France and Holland, returned to find well-organised resistance movements, some nationalist and some communist.

These powers reacted in different ways. The French and Dutch tried to restore their empires in Indo China (Vietnam) and Indonesia respectively. In both cases this led to military defeat and expulsion brought on by local resistance and outside pressure; the USA, in particular, helped force the Dutch out. Britain was ruled by an anti-imperialist Labour government which gave India and Burma self-rule and helped the Malayans to be free of both imperialism and a communist takeover.

The USA, meanwhile faced a dilemma. Traditionally, Americans, as successful rebel colonists in the first place, are against empires. They had also just fought the Korean War and were disinclined to engage in further Asian adventures. But America was in a turmoil of anti-communist hysteria; this was the time of the McCarthy witch-hunts. Their leaders, notably President Eisenhower and his Secretary of State, John Foster Dulles, distrusted communism in general and communist China in particular. The victories of the Chinese in 1949 and the North Vietnamese in 1954, made Eisenhower and Dulles believe that unless a stand was made, one Asian country after another would succumb to communist takeovers, like a row of falling dominoes. With this 'Domino theory' in mind, the two Americans set out to overturn the Geneva agreement which had virtually handed South Vietnam to Ho Chi Minh's communist regime in the north.

At first the Americans interfered in South Vietnam, Laos and Cambodia secretly, by subversion and political intrigue. Their efforts in South Vietnam were unsuccessful and the country lurched from one corrupt dictatorship to another. Then they started to send advisers and military equipment to be used against a communist army supplied by the Russians. Finally, in 1964, the Americans took the fatal step of intervening openly in the fighting with planes and ground troops. For the next five years their forces were sucked into a military quicksand.

By this time Lyndon Johnson was US President. Johnson seemed to have believed initially that the USA could win the war by air-power alone. This proved a costly mistake. The Russians supplied the north with anti-aircraft guns to defend Hanoi, the North Vietnam capital. The US airforce wasted its bombs, scattering them in vain over acres of dense jungle. To the outside world and to many Americans, the war seemed a 'David and Goliath' battle with America cast as the defeated giant. As early as 1966 Johnson began to bid for peace. Yet, as the negotiations dragged on, the American involvement grew larger and so did the protest within the US, where TV pictures of dead or wounded US troops and of US raids causing devastation were shown daily. In 1968 it became clear that the war could not be won militarily. General Giap, the North Vietnamese commander, was able to attack every major US base during the Tet religious festival at a time when there were half a million US combat troops in Vietnam.

In 1973, a new President, Richard Nixon, elected partly on a promise to 'bring the boys home', concluded an ignominious peace which left Ho free to conquer the South during the next two years. It was the worst defeat in US history and the first war they had lost. South East Asia was freed from imperialism, American or otherwise, and, although it had plenty of communist governments, traditional rivalries prevented them uniting into a vast communist block. For example, China attacked Vietnam and Vietnam invaded Cambodia in the years following the American withdrawal. The only country to gain a cheap victory was Russia, which had inflicted a severe defeat on its great rival without using its own troops.

THE PARTITION OF KOREA

Korea is a peninsula on the southern eastern corner of *Manchuria*. Over the centuries it had been conquered, first by the Chinese, and then, in 1910, by the Japanese (See Work Unit 21). During the Second World War its future independence was guaranteed by the *Cairo Declaration* in 1943 - a joint statement by *Churchill, Roosevelt* and *Chiang Kai-Shek*, the leader of Nationalist China. By the time of the Japanese surrender in 1945, *Russia* had entered the war against Japan, and the country was occupied by Soviet as well as US troops. The country became divided almost by accident, as Japanese soldiers to the north of the 38th parallel surrendered to the Russians, and Japanese troops to the South to the Americans. The actual 38th parallel border was fixed by quite junior officers of the two victorious armies. In the long run this produced two different regimes, a communist government in the north headed by *Kim Il-sung*, and a US-sponsored government in the south led by *Syngman Rhee*.

In 1947 the USA took the problem to the *United Nations* who appointed a *commission* to go to Korea and supervise free elections to decide the country's future. These commissioners were not allowed into *North Korea* and so the elections resulted in a government for *South Korea* only. Russia set up the North Korean government officially in 1949 when both occupying troops withdrew. In January, 1950, *Dean Acheson*, a high official of Truman's administration, defined what was called a *defence perimeter*, that is, an area of South East Asia which the USA might feel compelled to defend against aggression. This perimeter excluded *Korea* and *Taiwan*. Consequently, when the North Koreans, backed by the Russians, invaded *South Korea* on 25 June 1950 in a bid to unite the country by force, they did not expect opposition from the USA.

UNITED NATIONS ACTION

The invasion of Korea came at a time when Russia was boycotting the *UN Security Council* in protest against the USA's refusal to allow Communist China membership. The USA was able to get the Council to condemn the invasion and to agree to send a UN army to defeat it, something which would have been vetoed by the Russian delegate. The UN force was really a US one, because the Americans had large army, navy and airforce units in nearby Japan. Fifteen other nations including *Britain*, sent units to take part in the war. *China* condemned the UN decision as illegal interference in the internal affairs of Korea. The situation was an embarrassment to China, whose leaders had only just won the civil war and were looking for a period of peace to consolidate their power.

At first the South Korean forces were driven back into a small area around the southern port of *Pusan. General Douglas MacArthur*, the US commander, then hit back with an amphibious landing at *Inchon* behind the North Korean front. This cut the North Korean supply lines and resulted in a battle which left 140,000 North Koreans killed or captured. MacArthur drove forward, crossing the 38th parallel, and reaching the *Yalu river* border with China. *Mao Tse Tung*, the Chinese leader, regarded this as a clear threat to China, which had been invaded through Korea in 1931. He warned the UN that the advance must stop. Truman flew to *Wake Island* in the Pacific to congratulate MacArthur on his victory and also to ask him whether he thought there was danger of Russian or Chinese intervention. MacArthur assured him there was no danger.

CHINESE INVASION

MacArthur was right about the Russians but wrong about the Chinese. *Mao* knew that the Americans were friendly with his nationalist enemy, Chiang Kai Shek; they had supplied him throughout the civil war and supported him in *Taiwan*. He decided that *China* was in danger, and in November, 1950, sent the *Chinese 4th Field Army* across the *Yalu* This took the UN forces by surprise. They were driven back over the 38th parallel and retreated in confusion. MacArthur managed to stabilise the situation and then proposed the counter-attack by carrying the war into China. Truman was against such an action, which might lead to a protracted land and war and the possible use of the atomic bomb. He was also convinced that the real danger from communism was in Europe. In April, 1951 he dismissed MacArthur, who returned to the USA to be greeted as a national hero. The war became a stalemate, with fighting continuing for two years until an armistice, signed at *Panmujon* in 1953. No peace treaty has so far been concluded between the two Koreas, and a de-militarized zone marks the border.

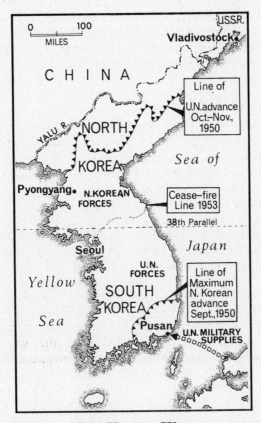

The Korean War

INDONESIA

In 1942 the Japanese conquered the British colony of *Malaya*, including *Singapore,* the *Dutch East Indies* (now Indonesia) and *French Indo-China* (now Vietnam). In all three regions they encouraged nationalist leaders in their fight against western imperialism, largely because they hoped for local support for their own policies. In *Indonesia* they gave *Sukarno*, leader of the *Nationalist Party*, some part in their administration. They also promised the Indonesians independence once they had won the war. When *Japan* surrendered, *Sukarno* proclaimed *Indonesia* an independent state. British forces arrived and persuaded the Dutch, by the *Linggadjati agreement* (November, 1946) to recognise Sukarno's republic in *Java, Madura* and *Sumatra*, and to organise *Borneo* and the smaller islands as part of a *Federation of the United States of Indonesia* which the Dutch hoped would be united with *Holland* by 1949. When it became clear that the Dutch intended to treat both these republics as colonial possessions, fighting broke out between their forces and the nationalists which was only stopped for a short time by the *Renville Agreement*, 1948.

HAGUE CONFERENCE

By this time both the UN and the USA were putting pressure on the Dutch to concede independence to the islands. In January, 1948 Holland was allowed to rule the region until a plebiscite has been held,. This was 'stage-managed' by the Dutch officials who then set up administrations for the islands. A communist rising in the Republic was put down by Sukarno's forces but in December the Dutch attacked him, bombing *Jakarta*, the capital of Indonesia. The UN and the USA condemned the Dutch action and the USA cut off much-needed economic aid to Holland. A conference held in August, 1949 at the *Hague* in Holland patched up a peace between the two sides, based on the idea that Indonesia and Holland were equal partners. In 1954 this 'union' was dissolved and three years later all Dutch citizens were expelled from Indonesia. Finally, i. 1963, *West Irian* (part of *New Guinea*) was handed over to Indonesia; the Dutch had clung to this region on the grounds that the inhabitants were not Indonesian and would not get a fair treatment from Sukarno's government.

SUKARNO'S RULE

Sukarno stayed in power until 1965, supported by Russian aid in spite of his opposition to the communist force on the islands. In 1963, when *Sarawak* and *North Borneo* (now Sabah) joined *Malaysia*, Sukarno objected, and the ensuing confrontation led to fighting between Indonesia and British and Australian troops; Australia and Britain had been asked for help by Malaysia. Potentially, Indonesia is one of the world richest's countries. She possesses 40% of the world's *rubber*, 30% of its *pepper* as well as large amounts of *copra, palm oil, tea, sugar, coffee* and *tobacco*. Sukarno squandered this wealth by mismanagement, particularly after he expelled Dutch experts. The country became bankrupt as large sums of money were spent importing food for its 100 million people. Politically, *Sukarno* performed a balancing act between the army and a powerful communist party. In 1965 a false report of his death led to a communist rising which was put down after a great deal of bloodshed; about a half a million communists, including the leader, *K.N. Audit*, were killed. In 1967 Sukarno was over-thrown and replaced by *General T.N.J. Suharto*. Suharto put many of his opponents in jail but the economy prospered with a growth rate of 7% in the 1970's.

MALAYA AND SINGAPORE

During the Second World War the Chinese population of *Malaya* formed an efficient communist guerilla movement to fight the *Japanese*. In 1948 the British authorities proposed a *Malayan Union* in which citizenship would be obtained by any person who had lived ten years in the country. This was an attempt to deal with the antagonism between Malay and Chinese, but it failed because the Malays claimed it would give more political power to the Chinese. The British then put forward a modified plan for a *Malay Federation* with restricted citizenship for the Chinese. The Chinese communists in Malaya began a rebellion which lasted for 12 years and which involved the British moving large numbers of people into resettlement areas where they would be free from intimidation by the rebels. In August, 1957 the British granted *Malaya* independence but *Singapore* refused to join the federation, largely because its predominantly Chinese population feared a Malay government hostile to them. In 1965 *Singapore* became independent, led by *Lee Kuan Yew*. In 1963 the ex-British colonies of *Borneo, Sabah* and *Sarawak* joined Malaya and it became the *Federation of Malaysia. Brunei* remained outside this federation.

VIETNAM

Modern *Vietnam, Cambodia* and *Laos* were ruled by the French and known as *French Indo-China* until 1941 when all three regions were conquered by the Japanese. A resistance movement developed, which in the north of Vietnam led to the creation of an independent communist state under the leadership of *Ho Chi Minh*. After Japan's defeat in 1945, the French returned with the idea of re-establishing a colonial regime. At first, they recognised Ho's government but in 1947 set about re-conquering the north with the aid of military equipment from the USA. The USA gave help because its leaders believed in the so-called *Domino Theory*, the idea that if one Asian state fell under communist control, others would follow. The French hoped to set up a puppet state in the south under *Bao Dai*, the ex-emperor of *Assam*, but he refused to cooperate because he was a nationalist. North Vietnamese troops, called *Vietcong*, fought a guerilla war of infiltration and surprise; hiding by day and fighting by night.

DIEN BIEN PHU

These tactics were successful against regular forces operating in the conventional way. The Vietcong commander, *Vo Nguyen Giap*, in particular, was a master of ambush and surprise. The French might hold a town by day but they usually lost it during the night. They reacted by fortifying and guarding towns, bridges, canals and roads. This was expensive and scattered their forces. In 1954 the French retired behind the defences of *Dien Bien Phu*, hoping to lure the Vietcong into a pitched battle where their superior equipment would give them an advantage. They also calculated that if Giap's forces concentrated for battle they would run out of supplies, especially as they had no heavy artillery to destroy *Dien Bien Phu*. Their calculations were proved wrong. Eighty thousand peasants, carrying food, weapons and ammunition, surrounded the town. Others dragged heavy guns into position around its perimeter. The French troops were battered into surrender (7 May 1954) and at the *Geneva peace conference*, held in July, France agreed to give up Vietnam.

SOUTH EAST ASIA TREATY ORGANISATION

President Eisenhower, and his Secretary of State, *John Foster Dulles*, were strong anti-communists and firm believers in the Domino Treaty. Both were dissatisfied with the results of Geneva, particularly the provision of elections for 1956, elections which they believed would be rigged in North Vietnam where the majority of the population lived. South Vietnam also refused to accept the Geneva decisions. The USA, although so often anti-imperialist in the past, regretted the expulsion of the French because it removed a useful defence against communist expansion. Eisenhower and Dulles decided to buttress South Vietnam. To do this they created a NATO-style alliance against the Chinese.

The *South East Asia Treaty*, established by the *Manila Pact*, was an alliance of the *Phillipines, Thailand, Pakistan, the USA, Australia, New Zealand, Britain* and *France*. All these countries promised joint military action against open aggression and cooperation and consultation against any 'subversive' activities. The plan envisaged the defence of an even wider area than that covered by the members of the alliance - *Vietnam, Cambodia* and *Laos*, as well as the *South-West Pacific*. SEATO was never as successful as NATO. Some of its members, like Pakistan, were too far away to render effective resistance; she only joined to get US help against India. France soon lost interest, and Britain became less involved after her commitments to Malaysia ended. Above all, most of the signatories were determined to stay away from involvement in *Vietnam*, especially as they knew this was the USA's main interest in forming the alliance. SEATO was dissolved finally in 1975.

HO CHI MINH

Ho Chi Minh was under economic as well as political pressure to complete the conquest of *South Vietnam*. The agricultural South virtually fed the North so the 17th parallel division had more than geographical significance. Furthermore, *Ho*, a convinced Moscow-trained communist, shared the traditional Vietnamese distrust of the Chinese and knew that the industrialisation programme he was initiating in the North needed Czechoslovakian and Russian expertise. He therefore increased guerilla activity in the south and prepared to renew the war. In 1955 the Americans supported a plot which overthrew *Bao* because he was believed to be 'soft' on communism and replaced him with *Ngo Dinh Diem*. *Diem*, a Catholic, became unpopular because he persecuted Buddhists and refused to hold the promised elections. Meanwhile, Ho's supporters in the south formed the *National Liberation Front* whose guerilla arm was the *Vietcong*. The Americans replied by sending equipment, aid and experts to the country.

In 1963 Buddhist opposition to *Diem's* brutal and corrupt rule was shown when Buddhist monks burnt themselves to death in public. The authorities replied by looting and damaging pagodas and torturing monks. The Americans cut off aid to *Diem*, who was overthrown and killed in November. He was succeeded by a series of short-lived military dictatorships who were now supported, not just by advisers, but by US planes and soldiers. *Ho* decided to send his regular troops into Vietnam to help the Vietcong and the war became one between North Vietnam and the USA. The number of US troops involved grew steadily, from 23,000 in 1964 to 550,000 by 1968.

In August, 1964 North Vietnamese torpedo-boats opened fire on the US warships in the *Gulf of Tonkin* and Vietcong guerillas attacked the US base at *Bien Hoa*, near the South Vietnamese capital, *Saigon*. Russian aid for North Vietnam came along the so-called *Ho Chi Minh Trail* through *Laos* and *Cambodia*. *President Johnson* ordered the bombing of North Vietnam, particularly the capital, *Hanoi*. These raids grew in intensity and led to world-wide condemnation of America. Vietnamese peasants were ill-treated by both sides. The Americans destroyed their villages by air and land and occasionally committed atrocities; the worst was the *My Lai massacre*, 1967, for which the US officer responsible was punished. The Vietcong slaughtered the headman of any village suspected of cooperating with the Americans. Inside the USA protest and disillusionment reached crisis proportions (See work Unit 27). American troops in Vietnam became demoralised, frequently taking drugs and sometimes killing their officers. In late 1968 *President Johnson* ordered a temporary halt to the bombing of the North and peace negotiations began in *Paris* between the *USA, North* and *South Vietnam* and the *Vietcong*.

PARIS PEACE SETTLEMENT

Richard Nixon, who succeeded Johnson as US President in 1968, worked hard to extricate the USA from Vietnam, scaling down both troops and supplies. He was assisted in this by *Henry Kissinger*, his chief adviser on foreign affairs, who travelled the world on so many missions that his technique was called *Shuttle Diplomacy*. In January, 1973, a *peace settlement* was signed in *Paris*. This agreement arranged for a special international commission to supervise the ceasefire until Vietnam could become one country. Everybody knew that this was not peace, but a temporary truce to allow the Americans to leave. The US withdrew its troops, although at the time Kissinger estimated that were at least 145,000 North Vietnamese troops in the South supporting the Vietcong. The war continued until 1975 when communist troops captured *Saigon*. During the last offensive the North Vietnamese received massive Russian aid, whilst the US Congress made sure the US airforce was not allowed to bomb enemy supply lines.

KHMER ROUGE

Vietnam was the worst military defeat suffered by the USA. At home it led to deep disillusionment and division. Abroad, the Domino Theory seemed to have worked because communist regimes took over *Laos* and *Cambodia*. In *Cambodia*, renamed *Kampuchea*, a particularly brutal and fanatical group called the *Khmer Rouge* seized power, emptied the major cities and murdered at least a million people. The Vietnamese overthrew the Khmer Rouge, probably because it was Chinese-sponsored. This caused China to invade Vietnam in 1979 to punish the Vietnamese government. The Chinese suffered heavy losses at the hands of the well-equipped and veteran North Vietnamese army and withdrew. Inside Vietnam persecution of its ex-enemies in the south led many refugees to flee from the communist regime. As they fled by sea they became known as *'The Boat People'*.

SELF ASSESSMENT SECTION

1. What was the "defence perimeter"?
2. What did the Cairo Declaration guarantee?
3. What happened at Panmujon?
4. What is the modern name of the Dutch East Indies?
5. Why did Singapore wish to be independent of Malaya?
6. Who were the Vietcong?
7. Who were the 'Boat People'?
8. What happened at Dien Bien Phu?
9. What was the significance of the Gulf of Tonkin incident?
10. What was the Ho Chi Min Trail?
11. The Domino theory was:-
    a) a theory regarding the balance of power in Asia.
    b) a theory that if one non-communist nation experienced a communist takeover others would follow.
    c) a theory that communism would triumph in Asia.
    d)   a theory that China would take over most of Asia.
    e) a theory that non-communist states could help each other if attacked by a communist state.
    (TICK THE CORRECT ANSWER)

It was a belief of:-

a) General Giap
b) President Johnson
c) Dean Acheson
d) President Eisenhower
e) Ho Chi Minh
(TICK THE CORRECT ANSWER)

12. Which of these countries was NOT in SEATO?

Phillipines	Thailand	India	Pakistan
The USA	Australia	Canada	New Zealand
Britain	France		

13. Put in the correct details (by letter) against these names.

1. KIM IL SING   A. Planned successful landing at Inchon.
2. RICHARD NIXON   B. Ruler of North Korea
3. HO CHI MINH   C. Ruler of South Korea
4. DOUGLAS MACARTUR   D. He brought the boys home
5. SYNGMAN RHEE   E. Ruler of Indonesia
6. AHMED SUKARNO   F. Ex-emperor of Assam
7. BAO DAI   G. Ruler of North Vietnam

14. One of Mao Tse Tung's generals once described his tactics in the following way; They were used by the Vietcong in South Vietnam. Read this and then answer the questions.

"There are those who cannot imagine how guerillas could survive for long in the rear of the enemy. But they do not understand the relationship between the people and the army. The people are like water and the army is like fish. How can it be difficult for the fish to survive when there is water?"

a) What are guerillas?
b) Is it true to say that the people were always on the side of the Vietcong? What other methods did the guerillas use to obtain cooperation?
c) Where was the final battle fought between the two sides?
d) In what ways is this statement more true of the war in China (1946-9) than that in Vietnam?

15. Read these two sources, then answer the questions.

A. "Most of the non-Communist nations of Asia cannot, by themselves and alone, resist the growing might and grasping ambition of Asian Communism. Our power, therefore, is a vital shield. If we are driven from the field in Vietnam,then no nation can ever again have the same confidence in American promises or American protection. In each land the forces of independence would be considerably weakened"

(Television broadcast by L.B. Johnson, 28 July 1965, quoted in 'In our time' by Godfrey Hodgson. MacMillan, 1977)

B. "Vietnam is thousands of miles away from the US. The Vietnamese have never done any harm to the US. But contrary to pledges made by its representatives at the Geneva Conference, the US government has ceaselessly intervened in Vietnam; it has unleashed and intensified the way of aggression in South Vietnam with a view to prolonging the partition of Vietnam and turning South Vietnam into a neo-colony and a military base for the US.."

(Ho Chi Minh, writing to President Johnson, 15 February 1967.
Quoted in 'Documents on World History 2'
by J Wroghton and D. Cook. MacMillan, 1976)

a) When and how did the partition mentioned in B. occur?
b) Why did Ho Chi Minh favour the Geneva agreement?
c) What country had received American guarantees?
d) Why did the USA feel she must take on the responsibilities described in A.? What particular event had made her worry about the 'growing might' of Asian communism?
e) In what part of Asia has the USA been successful in halting the spread of communism?
f) Which of these two arguments (A or B) do you find the more convincing? Give reasons for your answer.

16.

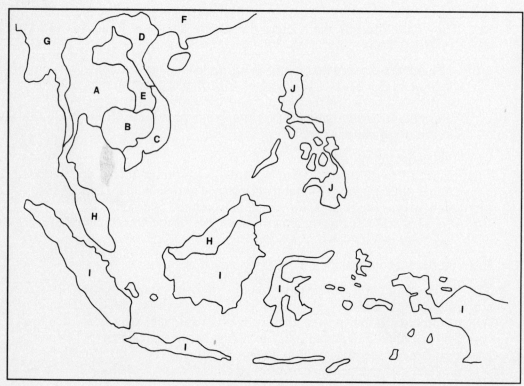

a) Name the countries A to J.
b) Name the ruler of country I after independence.
c) Which country was part of the Dutch empire?
d) Which country was part of the French empire?
e) Which country was part of the British empire?
f) Which country was ruled for some years by the USA?
g) Which country was NOT part of any of these empires?
h) Which country experienced a war from 1950-3?
i) Which country experienced a war from 1945-75?
j) Which country experienced a revolution after 1949?
k) Of what countries are the following cities the capital?

Saigon   Seoul   Rangoon   Jakarta   Manila   Hanoi

29

The Cold War: Europe since 1945

Had suffered HEAVY LOSSES from these previous invasions. BITTER, wanted PROTECTION felt it was only fair that the East European countries should have pro-Soviet Govts.

INTRODUCTION

If Poland had not been hostile to the USSR's communism Russia would not have been able to have been invaded

Was Soviet expansion into eastern Europe after the Second World War part of the traditional Russian policy of occupying territory as a buffer against invasion? Or was it part of a worldwide Marxist conspiracy, a battle for the hearts and minds of men and women? To a certain extent it was both. Stalin could not afford to allow freedom to Russia's satellites because in most cases it would have produced hostile governments. Russia had been invaded twice in 30 years through Poland and had suffered almost immeasurable devastation and loss of life. Democratic states on Russia's borders would have threatened the stability of the Soviet regime, built as it was on the principle of a one-party state and distorted into a system of terror by Stalin. These countries had to be 'communized' and so a Soviet sphere of influence became, inevitably, a victory for Marxism.

Feared the "DOMINO THEORY"

The top men in the US administration in the late 1940's were convinced that communism by its very nature must aim for world conquest. Roosevelt had been inclined to be soft towards Stalin. Had he lived he might have accepted Russian control of eastern Europe. His successor, President Truman, however, agreed with his advisers. 'The Russians are planning world conquest'. he said once. Later he remarked, 'Unless Russia is faced with an iron fist and strong language another war is in the making'. The truth was not quite so simple. Stalin knew his country was weak and exhausted. It was doubtful whether he thought in terms of further expansion. Although he was deeply concerned to keep Germany weak, and constantly demanded reparations from her, he seemed to have wanted two things from the Allies. First, he wanted recognition of Russian's legitimate right to security; this meant accepting what had happened in eastern Europe. Second, he hoped to get American aid to help rebuild the shattered Russian economy.

Roosie ↓ Soft towards Stalin BUT Truman ↓ Tougher, more SUSPICIOUS more ANTI COMMUNIST

The Americans were not prepared to help Russia whilst such a 'sphere of influence' existed in Europe. Their leaders felt this, and so did some of their multi-national electorate; the 7 million Polish-Americans, for example, agreed with John Foster Dulles when he complained that in eastern Europe, 'countless human beings were abandoned to despotism and godless terrorism'. The Cold War which

Stalin
i) Germ. should be kept WEAK so that USSR is protected
ii) REPARATIONS to rebuild USSR's economy

Stalin
i) Recognition of Russia's legitimate RIGHT to security, ie, control of E. Europe
ii) American help to rebuild SHATTERED USSR's economy.

KRUSCHEV → "Peaceful co-existance"

followed was a state of confrontation and open hostility which lasted from 1946 until at least 1963. It involved active subversion and political intrigue, and its effects spread over the world. Actual fighting, when it did occur, was done indirectly by one or other of the super-powers. For example, US-equipped Israelis fought Russian-equipped Arabs, and Russian-equipped North Koreans fought a US army officially employed by the United Nations, as both Russia and the USA interfered in local quarrels.

U.S.A's Containment Policy:

The US policy during the Cold War was called Containment; if Russia could not be thrown back, she must be held. Essentially, this policy consisted of the Truman Doctrine, which promised aid for countries threatened by a communist takeover, the Marshall Plan, which poured aid into war-torn Europe and revived the Germany economy and NATO, a military alliance to defend Europe against Soviet attack. The final parting of the ways came over Germany. Stalin did not object to a united Germany, but he wanted it kept permanently weak and open to communist influences. The Allies refused to accept this and, after the Berlin Airlift, built their own capitalist Germany out of the US, French and British zones. Stalin's response was to create an East Germany in his own image. The division of Germany became as permanent as any human arrangement can be.

i) Truman Doctrine
ii) Marshall Plan
iii) NATO

Stalin
↓

Wanted a WEAK Germ, a) so that she could never be strong enough to threaten USSR again, & b) so as to keep her, as a result of her WEAKNESS, open to COMMUNIST INFLUENCES

In the 1950's Dulles aimed at 'liberation' - the vague idea that if the USA showed itself sufficiently hostile to Soviet power there might be revolutions behind the Iron Curtain. At times his hostility reached the stage where it was dubbed 'Brinkmanship' by his opponents, who thought he was bringing the world to the brink of war. Yet when risings did occur in Poland, Hungary and Czechoslovakia they were crushed by Soviet armed force whilst the USA looked on helplessly. On the other hand, no Soviet military move was made against the west. If Russia had a sphere of influence in Europe, so did the USA.

The Cold War gradually 'warmed up.' In the early 1960's Nikita Khrushchev, Russia's new leader, suggested 'peaceful co-existence' between the super-powers. Since nuclear war was unthinkable, and the capitalist system doomed anyway, he suggested peaceful competition instead of confrontation. In 1972 the Helsinki Final Settlement recognised Soviet gains in Europe. In the 1980's Mickhail Gorbachev's policy of 'glasnost' (openness) seemed to offer hopes of a more liberal regime inside Russia.

G.B., U.S.A., + France Zones
↓

THE IRON CURTAIN *Own CAPITALIST Germany - One Zone*

By 1946 Europe was divided by the so-called *'Iron Curtain'* which separated Russia's satellites from the west. The USA, looking for ways to combat the spread of communism, announced the *Truman Doctrine*. This promised US aid to countries threatened by a communist takeover. In particular, Truman had in mind the situation in *Greece* where a strong communist movement was only held in check by British troops who had entered the country at the end of the war. Truman was determined to restrict Russia to the *Black Sea*, safeguard the *Straits* and make sure she did not turn *Turkey's* flank by entering Greece. In 1947 Britain told the USA that she could no longer afford to 'police' these areas and the USA took over responsibility for them, pouring in 400 million dollars-worth of aid to help the

US POLICY → CONTAINMENT *if U.S.S.R. could not be THROWN BACK they must be HELD.*

Truman Doctrine → gives aid to TURKEY, thereby keeping her armed forces MOBILISED, + ∴ strong enough to RESIST

Turkish army stay mobilised, and the Greek government win the civil war against ~~its communists (1947-49).~~ The Truman Doctrine was one of the first signs of the <u>Cold War</u> between the USA and Russia.

threat of Communism from USSR

Greece ↓ Royalists versus Communists ↓ British troops in Greece to fight for royalists AGAINST communism ↓ By 1947, could no longer afford it ↓ U.S.A. helps w/ TRUMAN DOCTRINE

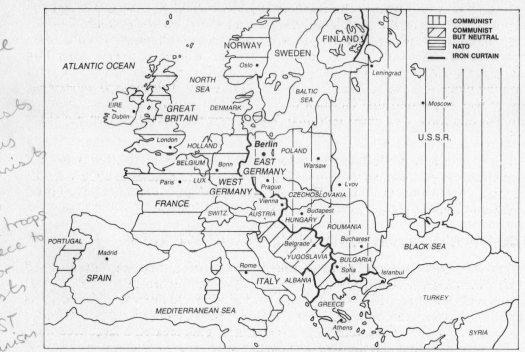

Europe during the Cold War

MARSHALL AID

The USA's plans to rebuild the European, and in particular, the Germany economy were built around the *European Recovery Programme*, nicknamed the *Marshall Plan* after the US Secretary of State. Russia at first took some part in organisations struggling to aid European recovery. She sent delegates to various relief organisations but soon decided that the US plans involved American domination of Europe. She then refused to take part in the work of the *United Nations Relief and Rehabilitation Agency* (UNRRA), and later made sure that none of her satellites received Marshall aid. Every other war-affected country, including neutrals like *Switzerland* and *Sweden* and ex-enemies like *Austria* and *Italy*, was given help. This led to economic prosperity in Europe by the early 1950's. (See also Work Unit 23)

N.A.T.O.

The *Berlin Airlift* (See Work Unit 23) marked the final break with Russia over Germany. In June, 1948 the *Brussels Treaty* was signed between *Britain, France, Holland, Belgium* and *Luxembourg*. Each of the signatories promised armed support in the event of an attack from the east. In 1949 the *USA, Canda, Italy,*

U.S.A. → determined to RESTRICT USSR to BLACK SEA
→ SAFEGUARD the STRAITS
→ keep TURKEY free from communism by keeping GREECE a NON-COMMUNIST country.
CONTAINMENT

Portugal, Norway and *Iceland* joined this alliance which became the *North Atlantic Treaty Organisation* (NATO). The essence of this pact was Article 5 which stated, 'an armed attack against one or more (of the member states) shall be considered an attack against all'. Furthermore, the NATO was to keep integrated forces permanently on the alert. This represented the tightest war organisation ever set up in time of peace. The huge costs of modern armaments made such cooperation essential and the USA, who supplied the bulk of the money needed for financing the alliance, usually supplied the leading military men. The only stumbling block was the question of a rearmed Germany. This aroused widespread fears. It was suggested that German troops should be used only in a 'European army' but this force was never recruited. *West Germany* finally entered NATO in 1955.

Russia already had a fully integrated system of defence with the Red Army and her satellite forces. This military organisation was made official in 1955 with the formation of the *Warsaw Pact*. This consisted of *Russia, Albania, Bulgaria, Czechoslovakia, Hungary, East Germany, Poland* and *Rumania.*

EUROPEAN COAL AND STEEL COMMUNITY

In 1944 *Belgium, Holland* and *Luxembourg* formed a customs union called *Benelux* for closer economic cooperation. In 1948 the organisation of European Economic Cooperation (EEC) was formed to administer and distribute Marshall Aid fairly. Three years later *France, West Germany, Italy* and the *Benelux* countries formed the *European Coal and Steel Community*. This created a large free trade area for the production and transport of coal and steel. These organisations were the brainchild of two men, *Jean Monnet* and *Robert Schuman,* both French, who developed these international schemes out of the need to carry on the modernisation of France. They realised that in the world which was evolving, no country, except a super-state, could afford to 'go it alone' in production, research and sales of vital commodities. *Britain* refused to join the ECSC because it would have meant losing control of her two major industries . Since British coal production in 1950 was half of Europe as a whole, and her production of steel, one third, this was a blow to the new organisation. However, the outbreak of the Korean War in 1950 created such a demand for steel that the Community was able to overcome its teething troubles during a boom period.

EUROPEAN ECONOMIC COMMUNITY

The ECSC was so successful that it was used as a blueprint for wider cooperation. In 1957 its member countries formed a *European Economic Community* , or *Common Market*. This proposed a common market and common tariff for member countries, to be arrived at in 12 or 15 years. These common policies were to cover agriculture, transport, mobility of labour and other important aspects of the economy of member states. The EEC had a similar structure to the ECSC - a *Commission* of nine members, a *Council of Ministers* and an *Assembly* recruited from the Parliaments of the *Six*. There was also a *Court of Justice* and an *European Atomic Energy Commission - Euratom -* to coordinate and finance research into the development of nuclear power. *Britain* did not join for several reasons. She valued her strong links with the Commonwealth, the USA and Scandinavia in trade matters and wished to protect her subsidised agriculture. She proposed, instead, that there should be a free trade area covering western Europe but that each member state should retain its links with non-member states. This would have allowed Britain to continue preferential arrangements with the *Commonwealth.*

EUROPEAN FREE TRADE ASSOCIATION

Some of the Six favoured the British scheme but *France* was opposed to it. She feared that Britain's industrial products would swamp her own manufactures at a time when she was facing stiff competition from *West Germany.* There was also a general feeling that the British did not favour the political integration which lay at the heart of the EEC. When Britain's plan was rejected she turned to a European *Free Trade Association* (EFTA) consisting of *Britain, Norway, Sweden, Denmark, Switzerland, Austria* and *Portugal.* By 1960, however, the EEC was so successful that Britain decided to · seek entry for herself and her EFTA partners. After lengthy negotiations, Britain's application was rejected, largely because of the opposition of *Charles De Gaulle,* the French leader.

De Gaulle was willing to consider British entry if Britain joined with *France* to produce a nuclear deterrent. But Britain's decision to buy Polaris, the submarine weapon, from the USA and to be supplied with research and 'know-how' by the Americans, made De Gaulle regard Britain as a 'Trojan Horse' of American influence in Europe. *De Gaulle* also knew that *Britain* if accepted for membership, would threaten *France's* leading position in the Community. It was to counter-balance this French influence that some of the other EEC members would have liked Britain to join.

In 1972, after De Gaulle's death, *Britain* was admitted to the EEC, together with *Norway* and *Denmark,* although Norway left later when a national referendum produced a 'no' majority. The remaining EFTA countries, plus *Iceland* and *Finland,* carried on with their own cooperation but signed free trade treaties with the EEC.

COMMON AGRICULTURAL POLICY

Divided feelings amongst the British public about Common Market membership led *Britain* to stage the first *referendum* in her history on the subject in 1975. This resulted in a majority of two to one to stay in the EEC. But trade union distrust of a 'rich man's club' of capitalists, working against the interests of workers, a strong aversion to giving up any part of Britain's sovereignty and a dislike of the way the EEC's *Common Agricultural Policy* (CAP) worked, remained strong in Britain. The *CAP* aims to make Europe self-sufficient in food production. In practice, this had led Dutch, German and French farmers to make sure that their governments obtain high guaranteed prices from the EEC. This policy has led to over-production, with surplus products stored in, either *'Lakes'* or *'Mountains'.* Such surpluses are often sold cheaply to Russia and eastern European countries. *Britain* as a food-importing country, opposes the CAP but the French, German and Dutch Governments refuse to antagonize their farmers. By 1986 the CAP policies threatened the EEC with bankruptcy.

WESTERN POLITICAL UNITY

European political unity has proved more difficult to achieve than economic unity. *Winston Churchill* wanted a sort of 'United States of Europe' to be formed. He saw it as a way of preventing further European wars, and also as a counter-balance to the Eastern Bloc. Although Churchill was not in office after the war, the idea of European unity was favoured by the Labour government (1945-51), also in May, 1948 the *European Movement*, as it was called, was launched, and from this developed the *Council of Europe*, a 'parliament' of delegates from member-states. These representatives were not elected, but appointed. The Council had no law-making powers, and its meetings, held four times a year at *Strasbourg* were really debates, Eventually its membership widened to include *Denmark, Norway, Italy, Sweden, Eire, Greece, Iceland, Turkey, Austria, Cyprus, West Germany* and the *Benelux* countries. In 1978 elections for delegates were held for the first time; successful candidates became MEP's - members of the European Parliament. Seats were allocated according to a country's population. The MEP's sit as Liberals, Conservatives, Socialists etc., not as British, French, German or Dutch. *Britain* held its first European election in 1979 when its electors voted for 81 out of a total 410 seats. The British Conservative party, already ruling in Britain, won 60 of the seats.

WEST GERMANY

The dominant figure in West Germany's politics after the war was *Konrad Adenauer,* an anti-nazi who progressed from Mayor of Cologne and President of the Prussian Council of State, to leader of the *Christian Democratic Union* (CPU), a conservative party which won power in the *Bundestag* after the first elections held in 1948. Under Adenauer's leadership, the German people grew accustomed to democratic forms of government, involving a two-party rivalry between the CPU and the SPD (Socialist) Party. During the first 20 years of its existence, the Federal Republic elections regularly showed an 80% turn-out, indicating a high level of interest amongst the electorate.

THE ECONOMIC MIRACLE

German political stability was the result of industrial growth on such a scale that it was dubbed the *'Economic Miracle'*. This was masterminded by *Ludwig Erhard,* a professor who began his political career as adviser to the Americans, and who succeeded Adenauer upon his retirement from the Chancellorship. West Germany's success was due to several factors. First, there was the tremendous initial boost provided by *Marshall Aid*. Second there was the fact that Germany had no nuclear weapons, no navy or airforce and only a small army. Thus her industries, when they were rebuilt on the most modern lines,could concentrate on profitable production. Third, there was the effect of low interest rates which made investment in industry attractive. Finally, and probably most important, there was the sheer hard work and discipline of the German people who, literally, 'dug themselves out of the rubble' with few strikes and only moderate pay demands.

In the years after the war, half a million houses were built each year, factories and mines-re-equipped and cities rebuilt. In 1950 there were 15 million unemployed in West Germany. Ten years later there was a labour shortage. Despite having lost the *Silesian* mining and industrial complex to Poland and the East, West Germany's production in 1960 equalled the whole of German production in 1936. She had become the world's third largest producer after the USA and Russia.

DE GAULLE AND ADENAUER

Adenauer's political policies were not so successful. He could not reunite his country, although a visit to *Moscow* in 1955 secured the release of German prisoners of war still held by the Russians. His close alliance with the Allies and western capitalism only roused hostility in the Soviet leaders. He made sure that West Germany was as fully integrated as possible with the West, joining the various groupings which led to the European Community. He also tried to re-establish friendly relations with France after centuries of war and rivalry.

In 1963 *France* and *West Germany* signed a *Treaty of Cooperation* which, apart from guaranteeing political cooperation, aimed to encourage cultural and educational exchanges between the young people of the two countries. These friendly relations were founded on personal links between *De Gaulle* and *Adenauer*. They cooled slightly after Adenauer's retirement in 1963, when West Germany adopted a more friendly attitude towards Britain, an attitude symbolised by the visit of the British Queen to West Germany in 1965.

TITO'S YUGOSLAVIA

From 1947 *Russia* controlled *East Germany, Poland, Czechoslovakia, Rumania* and *Bulgaria*. In each country, *Stalin* installed leaders who had often spent the war in Moscow and were out of touch with the people. *Yugoslavia,* although staunchly communist under the leadership of *Josip Broz*, known as *Marshal Tito*, had liberated herself from the Germans without the aid of the Red Army, which had only passed through the northern provinces towards the end of the war. Tito and his partisans, helped by British Military Missions, had fought a successful war, and Tito himself was regarded as a national hero by many Yugoslavs. From the start, therefore, Tito took an independent line with Moscow, complaining, for example, about the behaviour of Red Army troops when they were in Yugoslavia. Even this mild criticism annoyed Stalin who by this time demanded unquestioning obedience from his satellites. Consequently, in 1948 Stalin expelled *Yugoslavia* from the *Cominform*, a communist information bureau with headquarters in *Belgrade*. He also cut off all aid and imposed economic sanctions. This breach led to purges of 'Stalin men' in Yugoslavia and purges of leaders accused of 'Titoism' in Russia. In other satellite countries Stalin saw to it that at the first sign of independent thinking, communist leaders were sacked or shot.

EAST GERMANY

East Germany (The Germany Democratic Republic) remained poverty stricken from the effects of the war, and Russian occupation. The Soviet authorities took industrial machinery and other materials away to Russia to assist their own rehabilitation programme. They forced the East Germans to work harder for less pay, reducing them to the level of slave labour. Many tried to flee to the west and this led to the building of defences along the actual borders of the *Iron Curtain*.In June, 1953, soon after the death of Stalin, the East German government announced even higher targets for workers, who were already suffering from a poor diet, rationing, food queues and over-crowded housing. The workers of the Soviet Zone in *Berlin* reacted by taking to the streets for a huge demonstration involving at least 50,000 people. They also seized control of factories, set up their own management committees and staged 'sit-ins' behind temporary barricades.

BERLIN WALL

News of this *Rising* was broadcast by western radios to the rest of East Germany. This caused similar disturbances in other cities, where the Red flag was burned, pictures of *Stalin* and *Walter Ulbricht* the East German prime minister destroyed and security guards and party officials beaten up. But the people's demand for *'Bread and Freedom'* was met by Soviet tanks, arrests and executions. Only later did the new leaders in Moscow make concessions, such as cancelling further reparations payments.

A later eastern European disturbance, the *Hungarian Rising, 1956* is dealt with in Work Unit 23.

The 'Iron Curtain' of barbed wire and watchtowers along the frontier between the two Germanies, grew more permanent with every year that passed. In 1961 East Germany blocked up a major loophole, the crossings inside *Berlin* itself. The building of a *Berlin Wall* across the city by the East German government aroused an outcry in the west, particularly as people who have tried to cross have been arrested or shot. Such events have often been photographed by television and film crews and this has increased the distaste felt in the free world about a regime which needed to lock its people in. In 1969 *Willy Brandt*, the West German Chancellor, went so far as to recognise *East Germany as a sovereign state*. Both Germanies are members of the United Nations.

CZECHOSLOVAKIA,1968

Czechoslovakia was ruled for many years by *Antonin Novotny*, a hard line communist. In 1968, *Novotny,* a Czech who detested Slovaks, was overthrown and replaced by *General Jan Svoboda* and *Alexander Dubcek*. For some time there had been discontent inside the country for economic reasons. Czechoslovakia was the most highly industrialised of all the Soviet satellites and, as such, needed western supplies and technical knowledge to keep its industries running. This was not possible whilst tied to the Soviet bloc. Discontent over this situation led gradually to demands for greater freedom from Moscow's control. *Dubcek* in particular, thought the time had come to liberalise a communist state.

THE 'PRAGUE SPRING'

Under the terms of the *Action Programme* (April, 1968), drawn up by Dubcek and his supporters, there was to be freedom of speech, free elections to a genuine parliament, autonomy for *Bohemia* and *Slovakia* and an end to press censorship. It was even suggested that Czechoslovakia should sign some sort of treaty with *West Germany*. The Russian leaders were deeply disturbed by these developments which threatened, not only to spread to other satellite states, but also to take a key strategic 'piece' i.e. Czechoslovakia, out of their Iron Curtain European defences. In June, Warsaw Pact forces were due to carry out manoeuvres in Czechoslovakia. These had been arranged a long time before what became known as the events of the *Prague Spring* (Prague is the capital of Czechoslovakia). But the forces which arrived were much larger than planned and the Red army tanks seemed in no hurry to go after the manoeuvres finished. Throughout the summer there were feverish negotiations - both sides seemed to have realised the dangers - and then, on 20 August 1968, the troops of *Germany, Poland, Russia, Hungary* and *Bulgaria* invaded Czechoslovakia ' to prevent a counter-revolution'.

RUSSIAN OCCUPATION

The Czechoslovakian army offered no resistance, Dubcek had promised that it would not. Dubcek was arrested and flown to Moscow where he may have been tortured. Later he was re-instated but gradually demoted. Czechoslovakia was reduced to obedience, first by being forced to agree to Russian troops being permanently stationed in the country, then by the dismantling of all reforms. A new premier, *Gustav Husak,* was installed. He proceeded slowly, obviously because the Russian leaders wished to minimise the damage done in the outside world by their armed aggression against a supposed ally. The western world did little except condemn the Soviet action; it was clear that the west recognised Czechoslovakia as part of the Soviet sphere of influence.

POLAND

In the past *Poles* and *Russians* have been divided by territorial quarrels, aggravated by religious differences; the Poles are *Catholics* and the Russians *Orthodox*. Since 1945 there had been a clash between a deeply Catholic Poland and an atheistic state, Soviet Russia. The strength of the Church in Poland is such that in moments of crisis, even communist party officials have been ready to negotiate with priests. In 1970 there was rioting in many Polish cities because of rising prices. A crowd burnt the Communist Party headquarters at *Gdansk*(formerly Danzig). The Polish leader from 1956, *Wladyslaw Gomulka*, was replaced by *E. Gierek* to try to defuse discontent. Gierek tried some liberalisation but without any great success. In 1978 the election of a Pole, *Cardinal Wojtyla*, as *Pope John Paul II* - the first Pole to be so honoured - inspired the Poles to form a number of free trade unions under the general name of Solidarity.

SOLIDARITY

Solidarity's leader was *Lech Walesa,* an electrician in the Gdansk shipyards. In 1980 there were strikes in favour of legalising *Solidarity* which involved hundreds of thousands of workers in the *Gdansk* shipyards and the coalfields of Polish *Silesia. Gierek* was forced to yield to some of the demands for greater freedom and better conditions. He recognised *Solidarity* but was promptly ousted by army hard-liners led by*General Jaruzelski. Jaruzelski* imposed martial law, banned Solidarity once again and imprisoned most of the union's leaders. In 1983 the Pope stated that he would only visit his homeland if martial law was lifted and Solidarity members released from prison. Jeruzelski agreed and the Pope made a triumphant return to Poland. In 1986 *Walesa* was let out of prison and allowed to return to his work in the shipyards. Solidarity remains both a focus of opposition to Russian influence, and a political force demanding general freedom, not just trade union rights. This was shown when *Margaret Thatcher,* the British prime minister, visited Poland in 1988 and insisted on meeting Walesa and going to *Gdansk.*

SELF-ASSESSMENT SECTION

1. What is the more usual name for the EEC?

2. What is Polaris?

3. What does Euratom do?

4. Which country voted to leave the EEC?

5. What is an MEP?

6. What have 'Lakes' and 'Mountains' to do with the EEC?

7. What is the Bundestag?

8. By what name was Josip Broz better known?

9. Whose slogan was 'Bread and Freedom' in 1953?

10. What happened during the 'Prague Spring'?

11. What two countries signed a treaty of cooperation in 1963?

    a) France and East Germany
    b) France and Russia
    c) Austria and West Germany
    d) France and West Germany
    e) Russia and East Germany
        (TICK THE CORRECT ANSWER)

12. The Action Programme contained policies suggested by:

    a) Alexander Dubcek
    b) Clement Gottwald
    c) Walter Ulbricht
    d) Lech Walesa
    e) Wladyslaw Gomulka
        (TICK THE CORRECT ANSWER)

13. What do these initials stand for?

CAP   EEC   CPU   EFTA   ECSC

14. Read these documents, then answer the questions.

A. "At the present moment in world history every nation must choose between alternative ways of life. The choice is too often not a free one. One way of life is based upon the will of the majority, and is distinguished by free institutions, representative government, free elections, guarantees of individual liberty, freedom of speech and religion, and freedom from political oppression. The second way of life is based upon the will of a minority forcibly imposed upon the majority. It relies upon terror and oppression, a controlled press and radio, fixed elections, and suppression of personal freedoms. I believe that it must be the policy of the United States to support free peoples who are resisting attempted subjugation by armed minorities or by outside pressure".

> Truman, speaking to US Congress, 12 March 1947
> (Source: Public Papres of the Presidents, Harry S Truman, 1947)

B. "It is logical that the United States should do whatever it is able to do to assist in the return of normal economic health in the world, without which there can be no political stability and no assured peace. Our policy is directed not against any country or doctrine but against hunger, poverty, desperation and chaos. Its purpose should be the revival of a working economy in the world so as to permit the emergence of political and social conditions in which free institutions can exist..."

> George Marshall, speaking at Harvard University, 5 June 1947.
> (Source: Department of State Bulletin, XVI, 15 June 1947)

C. "It is becoming more and more evident to everyone that the...Marshall Plan will mean placing European countries under the economic and political control of the United States...this Plan is an attempt to split Europe into two camps and, with the help of the United Kingdom and France, to complete the formation of a bloc of several European countries hostile to the interests of the democratic countries of Eastern Europe and most particularly to the interests of the Soviet Union...An important feature (*of the Plan*) was to make use of Western Germany and German heavy industry (the Ruhr) as one of the most important economic bases for American expansion in Europe..."

> Andrei Vyshinsky, speaking to the United Nations assembly,
> 18 September 1947 (UN Gen Ass records)`

D. To achieve lasting peace, we must study in detail how the Russian character was formed - by invasions of Tartars, Mongols, Germans, Poles, Swedes and French; by the intervention of the British, French and Americans in Russian affairs from 1919 to 1921; by the geography of the huge Russian land mass situated strategically between Europe and Asia...Add to this the tremendous emotional power which Marxism and Leninism gives to the Russian leaders - and then we can realise that we are reckoning with a force which cannot be handled successfully by a 'Get tough with Russia' policy...."

Henry Wallace, US Secretary of Commerce
addressing a rally in New York, 12 September 1946
(Source: Vital Speeches of the Day, XII i October 1946, reprinted in LaFeber)

(All these quotations reproduced in 'Origins of the Cold War'
by Martin McCauley, Longman, 1983)

a)   Which Source is against the Truman Doctrine?
b)   Which Source is against the Marshall Plan?
c)   Which Source suggests a fear of a re-armed Germany?
d)   Which particular Sources are summarised in these statements?

(1) The Marshall Plan was used to widen US markets.
(2) The Truman doctrine aimed to save people from communist control.
(3) The US administration did not understand Russia's fears about security.
(4) The Marshall Plan was designed partly to give people greater freedom.

e)   Do you agree with the arguments in D? Give reasons for your answer.
f)   Which source in your opinion shows least prejudice? Give reasons for your answer.
g)   Using these Sources, explain the attitudes which led the two super-powers to embark on the Cold War.

15. Study the map on the following page.

a)   Name the countries which are part of the Soviet bloc.
b)   Name the country which defied Russia in 1948.
c)   Name two neutral countries i.e. not involved in the Cold War.
d)   Name three countries which have rebelled against Soviet control since 1945.
e)   Which two countries were created as a result of the Second World War?

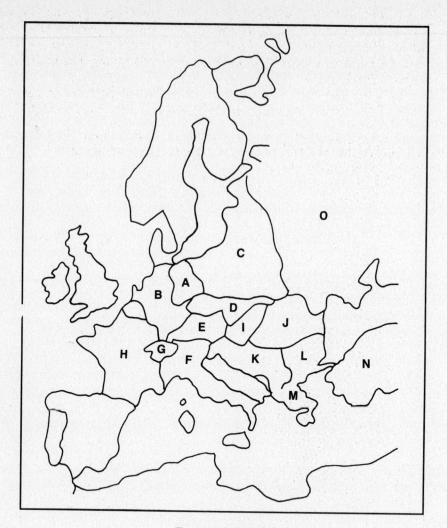

Europe, 1945-88

16. Read these documents, then answer the questions.

A. "In our view, participation in a political federation, limited to Western Europe, is not compatible either with our Commonwealth ties, our obligations as a member of the wider Atlantic community, or as a world Power".

Sir Stafford Cripps, Labour Minister, to House of Commons, 26 June 1950
Hansard vol 476, col. 1947-8
Quoted in Mowat, 'Ruin and Resurgence' Blandford Press, 1966

B. "No Socialist Party...could accept a system by which important fields of national policy were surrendered to a supra-national European representative authority, since such an authority would have a permanent anti-Socialist majority and would arouse the hostility of the European workers".

National Executive Committee of the British Labour Party pamphlet 'European Unity' May 1950. Also quoted in Mowat

Using these two sources, explain the main fears of the Labour Party regarding European integration. How far have they been proved wrong or outdated in the years since the formation of the EEC.

30

France since 1945

INTRODUCTION

Post-war politics in France were dominated by Charles de Gaulle, the leader of the Free French forces during the Second World War. He first came to power when he returned to France with the victorious Allied troops in 1944. With fighting still going on in Paris and bullets whistling overhead, de Gaulle led a triumphant walk down the Champs Elysee in Paris, "History gathered in these stones and these squares, seemed to be smiling down on us", he wrote later. De Gaulle took charge of a provisional government which ruled until 1946. He presided over France's recovery from the immediate devastation of war and from the deep division left by the Vichy regime and the victories of the communist resistance.

The parting of the ways came when he disagreed with the constitution of the new Fourth Republic. De Gaulle believed that France should have a President with extra powers in time of crisis; a focal point of stability around which the nation could rally. He thought this was the only way to avoid the constant changes of government of the Third Republic, pointing out that between 1875 and 1940, whereas Britain had had 20 governments and the USA 14, France had had 102. Some saw this as a bid for dictatorship so de Gaulle retired to found the Rassemblement, more a political movement than a party. His influence was still strong and 'Gaullist' became a recognised label in French politics.

De Gaulle came to power again in 1958 as a consequence of the Algerian war. Although he was obsessed with French history and determined to restore France to her former greatness in the world, he seems to have regarded the Algerian colony as expendable. The army officers and colons (French colonists) who supported both de Gaulle and the Fifth Republic he founded, did not realise this. They thought he stood for imperialism, for 'assimilation' and 'integration'. De Gaulle played a double game, misleading the 'Paras' (elite French paratroopers and their officers) and the colons until he was sure of enough public and military support inside France. Then he acted decisively, giving Ben Bella and his FLN nationalists the independent Algeria for which they had fought so hard. The rebels cried 'traitor' but it was too late. Attempts on de Gaulle's life failed, and he survived to be President under a constitution which gave him the powers he had wanted in 1946.

This left de Gaulle free to tackle three major problems as he saw it. These were the question of France's relationship with NATO, her relationship with a re-armed Germany and her attitude towards the Common Market and Britain's application for membership. On the first issue, de Gaulle wanted equality with Britain and the USA in the alliance, particularly in the exchange of technical information about nuclear weapons. When these demands were not met, he refused to have NATO rocket sites in France, reduced France's military commitment to NATO and began developing France's own nuclear deterrent. Finally in 1966, he took France out of NATO.

De Gaulle's attitude towards West Germany grew out of his feelings about Britain and the Common Market. De Gaulle never really wanted Britain in the Market. He regarded her as too closely involved with the USA to be truly 'European'. There was only one circumstance which would have made him say 'Yes' to Britain's entry - if Britain had joined France in making a nuclear weapon independent of the Americans. When the British tied themselves even more firmly to the US nuclear defence by buying 'Polaris', the submarine missile, he became determined that Britain would never enter the EEC whilst he lived. It was then that de Gaulle signed a treaty of friendship with West Germany, declaring that it was 'a vital and fruitful development'. In fact, he wanted West Germany to guarantee French domination of the Common Market. Most German politicians, except Adenauer who had negotiated the treaty, realised this. Their reception stopped short of rejection, but they hedged their acceptance with demands for closer cooperation with the USA and NATO.

The Paris upheavals of 1968 were dealt with by de Gaulle at the time but he could not stop the inevitable consequences. Within months, international business was taking its money out of France. The franc was weakened and wage increases de Gaulle had granted to placate the workers were soon lost by inflation. France found herself forced to accept foreign loans to keep going. This burst the bubble of Gaullism, showing that France was no longer powerful enough to 'go it alone'. The history de Gaulle had sensed that day in the Champs Elysee was just history. France could not pretend to be a super-power in the modern world. De Gaulle retired in 1969 and died the following year. He left France two legacies. One was inspirational; the moment when he went to London in 1940, made himself the guardian of the national spirit and vowed to fight on. The other was practical; the constitution of the Fifth Republic which has given France political stability.

THE FOURTH REPUBLIC

Although communists had taken a leading part in resisting the nazi occupation, their political power in France was handicapped by a strong right-wing and the development of the *Cold War*. At first, moderates and right-wingers rallied around *Charles de Gaulle,* who headed a provisional government from 1944 until 1946. This was a period of recovery, assisted by Marshall Aid, and also of the founding of the *Fourth Republic* (the Third Republic was deemed to have ended with the Fall of France in 1940). De Gaulle resigned in 1946 after disagreements on various matters. He was annoyed that an old-style Assembly had been formed under the new constitution, thinking that France needed a more Presidential style of government to prevent the instability of the Third Republic. He was particularly annoyed when the Assembly tried to defeat his proposed budget for the army.

De Gaulle's stand was seen by many as a threat to democracy; military heroes had become dictators more than once in Republican French history. De Gaulle did not wish to be a dictator. He believed that French history showed they were a disaster in the long run. De Gaulle retired from active politics and founded the *Rassemblement du People Francais*, a right-wing, anti-communist movement for 'the regeneration of France'. When de Gaulle called for the National Assembly to be dissolved, the other political parties united against him. The President, *Vincent Auriol* called on *Robert Schuman*, who formed a government which was both anti-communist and anti-de Gaulle.

ROBERT SCHUMAN

Schuman inherited a serious situation. The large communist party and its allied trade unions were still powerful in the streets and were staging nationwide strikes which paralysed industry. Schuman called up army reservists to help keep public order and passed a law which virtually made strikes illegal. Armed with such powers, his Minister of the Interior, *Jules Moch*, suppressed the disorders ruthlessly. Thousands of workers were imprisoned after street battles. This led to counter violence in which strikers at *Marseilles* attacked the Law Courts. Another strike at the state-owned *Renault* works was suppressed. At the same time, *Jean Monnet,* reorganised key industries and agriculture under government direction. War-time rationing was abolished, a move which broke the flourishing black market.

In foreign affairs, France joined *NATO* in order to receive US aid, accepting that this would mean the eventual re-arming of Germany. The French government, urged by army leaders and the right-wing, decided to keep their empire; they had suffered enough humiliation and defeat during the war and were not prepared to retreat anymore. This move led to confrontation and war in *North Africa*, and a war in *Vietnam* which France finally lost at the battle of *Dien Bien Phu* in 1954 (See Work Unit 28).

FRENCH COLONIES

During the Second World War France's North African territories - *Algeria, Tunisia* and *Morocco* - had been used, either as theatres of war or bases for military activity. The Fall of France, the principles of the *Atlantic Charter* and the presence of strong US military and civilian administrations in the region, strengthened the hands of the nationalists; President Roosevelt, in particular, was anti-imperialist. In *Tunisia,* for example, *Habib Bouguiba*, head of the *Neo-Destour* (Nationalist Party) was released from prison in 1943 and allowed to go to the USA for a time. In 1947 the newly-formed *Arab League*, pledged to fight for Moslem unity and Arab nationalism, set up a *Maghrib Bureau* (Maghrib is Arabic for west) to coordinate Arab nationalist activity in Morocco, Algeria and Tunisia.

MOROCCO AND TUNISIA

The French, followed their usual policy of *assimilation* (See Work Unit 5). They suggested a *French Union* between these colonies and the homeland. This offer was rejected by the countries of the Maghrib Bureau who claimed that in all three, Arabs were, in fact second class citizens. Sporadic guerilla activity against French rule increased after the French defeat in Vietnam. This humiliation set off a chain reaction; arson, murder, sabotage and rioting spread across North Africa. The French reacted with repression. In *Morocco,* the Sultan, *Mohammed V* was exiled because he supported the nationalists; this made him a national hero. In *Tunisia* , *Bourguiba* was imprisoned on an island and riots followed. Matters were made worse by a white settler organisation, the *Red Hand*, which murdered Arab nationalists and their white supporters. The British decision to evacuate Suez in 1954 was followed by a nationalist revolution led by *Colonel Nasser* (See Work Unit 34) in *Egypt*. This made Egypt the focus of Arab resistance to the French. *Pierre Mendes-France* and later *Guy Mollet* both socialist prime ministers, offered *Morocco* and *Tunisia* a form of self-government inside the French Union which turned into complete independence by 1956.

ALGERIA

France gave independence to Tunisia and Morocco partly to be free to concentrate on holding Algeria. Algeria was a different case from the other two North African territories. It was France's oldest colony in the region, having been colonised in 1830, and its 9 million population included 1 million Europeans, half of them French. Many of these *colons*, as they were called, had been born in Algeria and looked upon it as their home. They played an important part in the Algerian economy, holding key posts as civil servants, railway workers, shopkeepers and businessmen. The Algerian economy was booming, first, because of *Monnet's* policies, which had increased investment in communications, schools, hospitals and farms, and second, because of the discovery of *oil* in the *Sahara* in 1954. The colons did not intend to give up their privileged position and they had strong support from the army. Army officers felt that this time they must not fail. This feeling was particularly strong amongst the *paras*(paratroopers) who had borne the brunt of the fighting in *Vietnam*.

THE F.L.N.

The Algerian nationalist leader was *Ben Bella* who led an army called the *Front de Liberation Nationale* (F.L.N.). The FLN was supported by the *Arab League* and supplied from Nasser's *Egypt*. Fighting began initially in the *Aures District* and gradually spread throughout the entire colony. The French public was divided about the war. Successive socialist governments were inclined to give Algeria independence. They gave way when threatened by an army mutiny which might lead to civil war inside France. The war itself was prosecuted with excessive brutality on both sides; torture became a normal method of extracting information or terrorizing the enemy. There was widespread condemnation of the French by foreigners; French journalists who wrote critical articles were sometimes imprisoned without trial. The war had become a threat to French democracy and the stability of the Fourth Republic.

In 1956 *Guy Mollet* the French prime minster, suggested free elections to decide Algeria's future. He ordered *General Catroux* as Minister to Algeria but the general refused to leave France. An all-out effort to settle the war militarily, involving 400,000 troops, led to a stalemate. Both *Sultan Mohammed* of Morocco, and *President Bourguiba* became worried in case the war spilled over into their territories. In February, 1958, for example, the French bombed an FLN base at *Sakiet* in Tunisia, killing 75 people. The two Arab leaders held a conference with the FLN at *Tunis*. This led to an unfortunate incident. The French pilot carrying *Ben Bella* and some of his supporters back from this meeting disobeyed orders and landed at *Algiers* where the French authorities imprisoned them. This deeply offended the Sultan, whose guest Ben Bella had been only a few hours before. Although the French pilot was guilty of mutiny, the French government did not punish him through fear of trouble at home.

ARMY REBELLION

After the failure of the *Suez operation* (See Work Unit 34), an expedition undertaken partly to cut off FLN supplies from Egypt, the French began to think seriously of ending the Algerian war. This caused an *army rebellion* in Algeria, led by *General Raoul Salan,* the French commander-in-chief . It began on 13 May 1958 and spread to the island of *Corsica*, a useful stepping stone for any landings in France. At this time it was believed that half the military commanders of regions in France were prepared to join the rebels when the coup, planned for 30 May, occurred in *Paris*. The French government ordered the fleet to recapture Corsica but the admirals at first made excuses and then did nothing. On 28 May the last prime minister of the Fourth Republic, *Pierre Pflimlin* resigned and the President, *Rene Coty*, turned to the only man with enough prestige to influence the army,*Charles de Gaulle*. De Gaulle flew to Algeria where he managed to calm the rebels and get them to agree to stay their hand. *Salan* was left in command of the troops but deprived of his civilian authority. Other senior officers were sent away from Algeria.

THE FIFTH REPUBLIC

At home de Gaulle called for a new *Constitution* for a *Fifth Republic*. This constitution gave executive power to a President who would rule for 7 years - previous Presidents were only figure-heads - and gave him the power to select his own ministers who were not be members of the *Assembly*. There would also be a prime minister but in a crisis the President could dissolve the Assembly and rule by decree. This US-style Presidency was accepted by the French people in a national referendum. Armed with such powers, de Gaulle turned to the Algerian problem. He offered the Algerians three choices; independence, integration or association with France, the choice to be made within 4 years from the end of fighting. This led to a second revolt by the European settlers in January 1960. This was crushed by de Gaulle who now had much stronger support inside France, where war-weariness was aggravated by tales of the bad behaviour of the French army in

Algeria. Repeated Gaullist successes at elections between 1958 and 1960 showed this. The Algerians, meanwhile, demanded immediate independence, not a wait of 4 years.

ALGERIAN INDEPENDENCE

De Gaulle kept up the military pressure on the FLN but at the same time negotiated with them at meetings at *Melun* and *Evian*. This led to a final revolt by the French generals in Algeria in April, 1961. This revolt was crushed after 4 days and *General Salan* and *Jouhaud* were sentenced to death - they had fled after the failure - and other officers to long terms of imprisonment. By now the colons regarded de Gaulle as a traitor. An *Organisation Secrete* (OAS) began a terror campaign in France, including several unsuccessful attempts on de Gaulle's life. The OAS frightened many settlers into thinking there would be reprisals if they agreed to Algerian independence and so led to a mass exodus of colons from the country. At first the FLN rejected de Gaulle's proposals because they included French occupation of the *Sahara* and the port of *Mers-el-Kebir* (for 15 years only) after independence. In July, 1962, however, Algeria became independent of France under the leadership of *Ben Bella*. The departure of the colons deprived the new state of much-needed expertise and capital.

DE GAULLE AND EUROPE

De Gaulle saw himself as the personification of the spirit of France from the day he fled to England in 1940, defied his own government and formed the *Free French* government in exile. This symbolic act revitalised the French at a time of disaster, helping many of them to regain their self-respect after such an humiliating surrender. The *Vichy* regime and its supporters (See Work Unit 22) detested de Gaulle for doing this. When de Gaulle became President in 1959 he applied his strong nationalist views to the problems of Europe. One aspect of the *EEC* and *NATO* which he did not like was the principle that small nations had the same voting rights as large ones. De Gaulle would have preferred a Europe dominated by *France* and with *West Germany* and *Italy* as partners. He did not want *Britain* to join the Common Market and vetoed her application on several occasions.

De Gaulle believed *Britain* was too subservient to the USA, especially after the conclusion of the Polaris agreement left Britain dependant on American nuclear weapons. His decision to build a French atomic bomb and set up a special French 'Strike Force' was condemned by the British and Americans, who regarded his 'puny' weapon as no deterrent to the Russians. De Gaulle, on the other hand. never believed that the Americans would risk a nuclear war to save Europe, and therefore maintained that Europe must have its own defences. For him, the possession of a nuclear bomb was an important way of making France a major power again. The *Cuban Missile Crisis* (See Work Unit 35) confirmed de Gaulle in his view about the USA, for the Americans went into that nuclear confrontation without consulting any of their European allies.

FRANCE, USA AND WEST GERMANY

De Gaulle believed that NATO was out of date after Cold War tension lessened as a result of the Cuban Crisis in 1962. He claimed that advanced weapons' technology, particularly long range missiles, meant that the Americans no longer needed Europe strategically; the US presence in Europe was a political, rather than a military, necessity. After the Americans refused to share weapons' research with France, de Gaulle withdrew the French fleet from NATO's Mediterranean forces, refused to have NATO rocket sites on French soil and, in 1966, took France out of NATO altogether.

In 1963, after a visit to Germany de Gaulle concluded a *Franco-German Treaty* with *Adenauer*, the Chancellor of West Germany. The treaty was a failure, Whilst everybody was pleased that France and Germany seemed to have buried their age-old enmities, the West German Parliament refused to take de Gaulle's anti-American line and altered the treaty. They realised that it arose from de Gaulle's desire to create a different European system from that evolved after the war with Europe dominated by France and Germany but excluding Britain. Many Germans, by contrast, actually wanted Britain in Europe as a counter-balance to what they saw as excessive French influence. The Russians condemned the treaty because they realised it would lead to the re-arming of West Germany.

THE STUDENT REVOLT, 1968

In 1968 France's universities were caught up in the wave of discontent and violence which was sweeping Europe. There were many causes for this   inner-city deprivation, the war in Vietnam and a general feeling of discontent among the youth of the time. In France, this discontent centred on the universities, particularly those around Paris, where there was over-crowding, out of date syllabuses and too much bureaucracy. The trouble flared up first at the *Sorbonne* where the students began an occupation of the university buildings. The university authorities called in the police who behaved with such brutality that the citizens of the capital joined in on the students' side. On government orders, the police moved in to prevent occupation of the *Left Bank* area of Paris and a fierce battle continued all night. At the same time workers went on strike in Paris and other French cities. occupying factories and setting up action committees.

EDUCATIONAL REFORMS

De Gaulle returned from a state visit to Rumania to take control. His prime minister, *George Pompidou*, talked of another 'French Revolution' and begged him to resign. De Gaulle, having made sure that the army chiefs were on his side, soon restored order. There was little real unity between the workers and the students. Their aims were different; the students wanted education reform, whilst the communist trade union leaders were looking for shorter hours and more pay for their members. *De Gaulle* appointed *Edgar Faure* to carry out extensive reforms of higher education. The size of French universities was to be kept at a maximum of 20,000 students; this created 65 universities. Faure also introduced teacher-student management committees. However, although de Gaulle won another election soon afterwards, he quarrelled with his associates by proposing to abolish the French *Senate*. When he held a referendum on the subject he was defeated and at once resigned. He died in 1969.

In 1968 France exploded her own *hydrogen bomb* in the Pacific. In spite of this, France had little real nuclear capability and was still dependant on the USA and NATO for its defence. In other ways, Gaullism was exposed as unworkable. The financial effects of the 1968 upheaval were serious. Financiers began to take their money out of the country and the franc was threatened with devaluation. De Gaulle refused to contemplate devaluation but he did have to accept foreign loans. The workers who found their pay increases lost in inflation and the students who grumbled that the educational reforms had not happened, or were coming too slowly, began to realise that France was dependant upon the political and industrial power of the USA like every other country in the western alliance.

DE GAULLE : SUMMARY

De Gaulle was autocratic; a law unto himself who rarely consulted his ministers. He justified this by saying that he had become President at a time of national crisis, which was true. But he continued to rule in the same way long after the Algerian war. He exercised control through a rigid censorship of the government-run radio and TV and also by 'special courts' which, although set up to deal with terrorism, reminded people of nazi and Vichy methods during the Second World War. His main political ideas regarding Europe and France were opposed by most other parties in France but he carried them out with the aid of referendums which bypassed the normal machinery of democracy. He fell from power finally when his attacks upon the *National Assembly* and the *Senate* alarmed the French people. After his resignation, a new President, *George Pompidou,* did not object to *Britain's* entry into the *Common Market in 1972.* France remained outside NATO.

SELF-ASSESSMENT SECTION

1. Where did France explode her first hydrogen bomb?

2. Who founded the Rassemblement?

3. What was the Vichy Government?

4. Why was a Fourth Republic set up in France?

5. Who instigated strikes in France after the war?

6. Who became ruler of Morocco upon independence?

7. What island was taken over by the French army rebels in 1958?

8. Why did the French want to keep the Sahara region?

9. What is the Sorbonne?

10. Who carried out education reforms in 1968?

11. Write two or three sentences about EACH of these organisations. Which one was successful in its aims?

   FLN   OAS   RED HAND

12. Put the correct details (by letter) against these names.

   1. PIERRE PFLIMLIN   A. Led an army revolt in Algeria
   2. HABAB BOURGUIBA   B. Leader of the FLN
   3. RAOUL SALAN   C. Reorganised the French economy after
                                 the war.
   4. BEN BELLA   D. Leader of independent Tunisia
   5. GEORGE POMPIDOU   E. Last prime minister of the Fourth
                                 Republic
   6. PIERRE MENDES-FRANCE.   F. Suppressed post-war strikes
   7. JULES MOCH   G. Socialist prime minister of France
   8. JEAN MONNET   H. De Gaulle's last prime minister and
                                 successor.

13. Here are listed four of de Gaulle's aims in his foreign policy. Sort them into order of importance, A being the most important, B and C being of secondary importance and D relatively unimportant.

   a) To make France into a world power again.
   b) To form an alliance with West Germany
   c) To give Algeria its independence
   d) To keep Britain out of the EEC
   e) To make France the dominant power in the EEC

14. Here are some sources which illustrate de Gaulle's career. Examine them and then answer the questions.

   A. "I, General de Gaulle, now in London, call on all French officers and men who are at present on British soil....to get in touch with me...I realise I now speak for France. In the name of France I make the following solemn declaration; It is the bounden duty of all Frenchmen who still bear arms to continue the struggle".

   B. "I know what happened here. I know what you wanted to do. The road you have thrown open in Algeria is the road of renewal and fraternity...France considers that the whole of Algeria there is only one category of inhabitants - only complete Frenchmen, having the same rights and duties."

   C. "I promise you that we shall continue to fight until sovereignty is re-established over every inch of our soil. No one shall prevent our doing that. We shall fight beside the Allies, with the Allies and as an ally and the victory we shall win will be the victory of liberty and the victory of France".

D. "De Gaulle was to become.....a rallying point for those anxious to preserve their colonialist privileges in Algeria; for those anxious to overthrow theRepublic in France; for those thinking in terms of an authoritarian or presidential regime; even for those (mostly in Algeria) who were planninga military-Fascist dictatorship in France."
(Alexander Worth 'The De Gaulle Revolution' Robert Hale Ltd, 1960)

E. "Frenchmen of Algeria, how can you listen to the liars and conspirators who tell you that by giving Algerians a free choice, France and de Gaulle want to abandon you, to withdraw from Algeria, and to surrender to the rebellion? Is it abandoning you, is it wanting to lose Algeria, to send and maintain there an army of five hundred thousand men....?"
(A,B,C and E. from 'de Gaulle' by Aidan Crawley. Collins 1969)

a) Put these dates to sources A, B,C and E

1940   1958   1960   1944

Put places to sources A,B,C and E.

England   Normandy   Algeria

b) What year is the writer of D discussing?

c) Which source helped make de Gaulle famous? Which source illustrates a triumphant moment in his life?

d) "De Gaulle played a double game over Algeria".

Which sources illustrate this? Explain why.

e) How many of the predictions in D came true, and how many did not? Explain your answers.

f) Sources A,B,C, and E were speeches made for special occasions. How reliable/unreliable can such sources be to the student?

(Source: 'De Gaulle' by Adrian Crawley, Collins 1969).

g)   Look at this photograph. One source is directly related to it. Say which one, and give the reasons for your choice.

15.   Explain why de Gaulle opposed Britain's entry to the Common Market. How did reflect his own attitude to the western alliance?

16.   Explain how EITHER a Vichy supporter OR a communist resistance fighter would have felt about de Gaulle's stand during the Second World War. You may need to refer to Work Unit 20 to help with your answer.

31

China since 1949

INTRODUCTION

There is some truth in the saying that Mao Tse Tung was the Lenin and Stalin of China. Like Lenin, he both led a successful revolution and added to the philosophy of communism. Like Stalin, he drove his people ruthlessly into the 20th century, modernising the country at great cost in human life and suffering. But the Russian dictator never initiated a movement like the 'Cultural Revolution' which Mao unleashed in 1966. Mao told the young Red Guards who carried out this revolution, 'To rebel is justified' Revolutions, he maintained, would always break out because, 'junior officials, students, workers, peasants and soldiers do not like big shots oppressing them'. These were strange remarks from the biggest shot of them all, a man treated like an old-style Chines emperor.

In his early years of power Mao copied the Soviet system. A Five Year Plan, aided by Russian technicians and Russian finance, aimed to build up heavy industry and collectivise farming in a Stalinist way. The split with Russia arose from two factors. Mao objected to Khrushchev's 'de-Stalinisation' policy. Whilst he was aware what a monster Stalin had been, he felt that his achievements in modernising Russia should not be dismissed. Furthermore, as senior Communist leader after Stalin's death, Mao thought that Khrushchev should have consulted him before producing such a 'U' turn in communist and Soviet policy. On the Russian side, Mao's second Plan, called the 'Great Leap Forward', seemed economically unsound and therefore likely to cost the Russian taxpayer a lot of money. Being communists, this quarrel between the two leaders was translated into arguments about whose brand of Marxism was the purest. By 1960 the rift was open and Russia cut off all technical aid, thus dealing a severe blow to China's modernisation programme.

The Great Leap Forward did prove a failure. There were several reasons for this but basically it arose from Mao's belief that the Chinese people were uniquely gifted and capable of performing near miracles. It was a belief which led Mao to quarrel with his Party officials who knew that it was wishful thinking on his part. This quarrel intensified as the years went by and caused Mao to enlist the support of the army. Led by Lin Piao, the army became a sort of school of Mao's thoughts and ideas. This development coincided with a change in the Chinese leader's attitude to intellectuals. Mao's 'Hundred Flowers' campaign invited criticism of his rule but some intellectuals were too outspoken. Although China could not be modernised without an adequate supply of scientists and technicians, Mao chose this moment to turn against educated 'elitists' and to declare,'Of course some things can be learned at school, I don't propose to close all schools, What I mean is that it is not absolutely necessary to go to school'.

This remark by an ex-school teacher set the scene for the Cultural revolution. Mao maintained that revolutions are never won once and for all; they must be fought for again and again. The Red Guards appointed to carry out this new revolution were told to attack the 'old monsters' - capitalists, landlords, rich peasants, foreigners, even 'bad elements and Rightists'. With so many enemies to choose from it is not surprising that they wrought havoc in China. Universities and schools were closed and their teachers and students sent to work on the land, factories disrupted and production disorganised. A backlash of workers against these moves produced a state of near civil war in China, as pitched battles between Red Guards and their opponents were fought in many Chinese cities. The chaos only died away after Mao's death in 1976.

Since that time the mistakes of the Cultural Revolution have been blamed on the so-called 'Gang of Four', a group of politicians led by Mao's unpopular wife. In fact, Mao must be blamed for most of what happened. Mao invented 'Maoism', a creed which delayed China's modernisation, temporarily ruined her education and levelled down rather than up. Mao's achievements are similar to Stalin's. He inherited a fragmented country, occupied and humiliated by foreigners. He made many mistakes for which the Chinese people suffered. But when he died China was strong enough to face the world as a major power, and to recover sufficiently from his 'revolution' to follow the path of moderate capitalism in recent years.

CHINESE-AMERICAN HOSTILITY

On 1 October 1949 *Mao Tse Tung* proclaimed the *Chinese People's Republic* in Peking after winning the civil war (See Work Unit 10). The *Koumintang* forces led by *Chiang Kai Shek* retired to the island of *Formosa* (now Taiwan) where they set up a rival government. Soviet Russia signed a military security pact with China and sent technical and financial aid. The USA refused to recognise communist China and began re-equipping Chiang's forces on Taiwan. The Americans had supported the Koumintang throughout the civil war, and their hostility towards Red China increased when the two clashed in *Korea* the following year (See Work Unit 28). In the United Nations, the American veto kept communist China out; the Koumintang representative sat in China's place.

'REVISIONISM'

After Stalin's death in 1953, Mao saw himself as the communist world's 'elder statesman' and China's brand of communism as the only true one. Russia's new leaders, particularly *Nikita Khrushchev*, talked of *'peaceful co-existence'* between themselves and the west. This seemed to Mao to be the wrong line to take towards capitalists, especially when Khrushchev attempted to increase Russia's material prosperity and to give aid to non-communist leaders like *Nehru* of India. Mao believed this was a contradiction of Lenin's theories. He called it 'revisionism' i.e. a revising and distortion of Marxism. He also believed that Russia was too friendly with, and too afraid of, the USA, a country he dismissed contemptuously as a *paper tiger*'! Khrushchev replied that the 'tiger' had 'nuclear teeth'.

SINO-RUSSIAN DISPUTES

In 1960 Russia withdrew all its technicians from China and cut off technical aid. The quarrel took on the traditional aspect of disputed frontiers. Russian and China share a 9,000 kilometre border, much of it seized during the last 150 years by Russian settlers. Fighting certainly took place between Russian and Chinese troops during these years, although the remoteness of the area and excessive secrecy make it difficult to know the extent or the result of the battles. In 1962 the Chinese leadership accused Khrushchev of 'cowardice' at the time of the *Cuban Missile Crisis* (See Work Unit 35). The following year China refused to sign the *Nuclear Test Ban Treaty* agreed between other nuclear powers. In 1965 Mao also refused to join a united front of socialist states against American intervention in Vietnam mainly because of Russian support for the North. The downfall of Khrushchev led to better relations between Russia and China. Relations also improved between China and the USA after the visit of *President Nixon* to the country in 1971. The USA dropped its UN veto against Red China, which was allowed to join. *Nationalist China* was expelled.

TIBET AND INDIA

In 1950 China annexed *Tibet*, a country over which she had traditionally claimed sovereignty. In 1956 Tibet became an autonomous region of China. Three years later Tibet's spiritual leader, the *Dalai Lama*, fled the country after an unsuccessful rebellion against the Chinese. Until the occupation of Tibet, *India* had been friendly with Red China. *Nehru*, the Indian leader, was one of the first world statesmen to recognise the People's Republic; this was as part of his 'non-aligned' policy of neutrality in the Cold War. Nehru had also acted as peacemaker between the Chinese and Americans during the truce negotiations ending the Korean War. But India and China did disagree about their borders. In the *Himalayan* mountains the Indians preferred the *MacMahon Line* drawn originally by the British when they ruled India. This gave India land up to the crest of the mountain range.

China preferred a line set down in the valley which would have given her a further 32,000 square miles of territory. She also claimed a region known as the *Askai Chin* which the Chinese wanted as a route from Tibet to *Sinkiang province* (See map). In 1962 Chinese troops attacked, defeating the Indians and taking over *Ladakh* and other regions. Three years later, when *India* was fighting *Pakistan*, (See Work Unit 33) China increased her difficulties by making hostile moves against *Sikkim*, an Indian protectorate. China seemed to want to assert her supremacy over the only eastern nation likely to threaten her leadership in the region.

HONG KONG

Every Chinese leader since 1949 has laid claim to *Hong Kong* - taken by Britain after the *Opium Wars* (See Work Unit 10). To avoid serious trouble, and probably because the port gives China access to western markets, the Chinese have not seized it, although it would be a simple matter militarily. In 1983 *Britain* signed an agreement with *China* by which Hong Kong will go back under Chinese rule in 1997. In 1988 the *Anglo-Hong Kong Trust* was set up privately in Britain. Its aim was to ensure that both business and cultural links between Britain and the island continue after 1997. However, large numbers of firms and individuals decided to leave the island before the handover date.

MAO'S CHINA

In 1949 China was ruined and devastated after two decades of civil war. Industrial production was halved and there was high inflation accompanied by shortages. The communist government nationalised heavy industry, gas and electricity supplies, railways and banks, imposed strict press and radio censorship, broke up large estates and distributed the land amongst the peasants. They also passed acts to emancipate women from ancient restrictions, and to seize all European investments except those belonging to Russia. It was a time for settling old scores. Thousands of landowners were murdered by peasants who took the law into their own hands. Thousands more were executed by government order. Communist indoctrination of their opponents was so thorough that a new phrase,'*brain-washing*' came into fashion to describe the wholesale propaganda campaign and prison regimes set up to 're-educate' 'enemies of the people'.

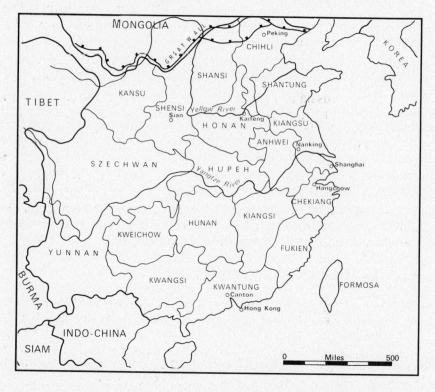

FIRST FIVE YEAR PLAN

A *Five Year Plan*, introduced in 1953, aimed to build up China's industry in the same way as Stalin had done in Russia. Peasants were organised into *collectives*, where 10 or more families pooled their resources to increase agricultural production. This met with similar resistance to that experienced in Russia; peasants were angry at losing property they had just gained from the communist victory. When there were riots and local risings, Mao gave way to the extent of allowing peasants to own some land of their own. He also broke up the collectives into smaller units. In 1957 Mao announced the *'Hundred Flower campaign'* in which critics were invited to air their grievances. The results did not please Mao and some of those who spoke out were punished. This experience probably led Mao to take an anti-intellectual stance later.

"GREAT LEAP FORWARD"

The Second Five Year Plan was called the *'Great Leap Forward'*. It envisaged large scale increases in production, partly by unorthodox methods. Mao summed the scheme up as *'walking on two legs'*, that is, using both large and small industry. For example, the steel industry was to be, not only a matter of factory complexes, but also of thousands of 'backyard furnaces'. In this way every peasant would become a part-time steel worker. *Collectives* were organised in the opposite way. They were turned into much larger communes, comprising thousands of families. Communes were to be self-sufficient, with schools, hospitals, communal dining-rooms, dormitories and nurseries. They also had their own building teams and militia units for defence.

The *'Leap'* proved a failure. Some peasants resented being part of a large team, often transplanted to a strange area. Their reaction was so hostile that production dropped as it had in Russia under Stalin. Food output, targeted for 375 million tons in 1962, only achieved 175 tons. Most 'back-yard' steel was of poor quality and of little use to industry. A succession of droughts and floods, combined with the cutting off of Russian aid in 1960, forced Mao to modify his plans. In some communes peasants were given their own property. Industrially, however, China continued to advance. New industries, making cars, machine-tools and aircraft, did well. Established ones, like coal, steel and chemicals, grew steadily. China became the world's second largest coal-producer, and her steel industry equalled that of Russia and the USA. In 1964 Chinese scientists exploded their first nuclear weapon, and three years later, a hydrogen bonb was tested.

THE CULTURAL REVOLUTION

Mao believed in *'continuous revolution'*, an idea which appealed particularly to the young, both in China and abroad where it was taken up by the so-called *New Left*. The Chinese leader was afraid that after his death certain of his close associates, notably *Chou En-Lai* and *Liu Shao-chi*, might move towards a Soviet system with too much emphasis on industrial development and not enough on the ideals of communism. In 1966 he made his move, assisted by Defence Minister, *Lin Piao*. China's youth was roused by a massive propaganda campaign which stressed the

311

wisdom of Mao's ideas in a '*Little Red Book*' of his thoughts. They were told that nothing was too difficult if this was used as their guide. Gangs of youngsters, calling themselves *Red Guards*, were encouraged by Mao to look upon themselves as the 'shock troops' of this new revolution. They were seen roaming through China's cities, attacking people wearing western-style clothes or lipstick.

Mao, whose original victory had been due to the support of the peasants, urged people to return to the land. As a result, schools and colleges were shut by the Red Guards and their teachers, lecturers and students forced to go and work in the countryside. The *Cultural Revolution,* as it was called, gradually became more violent, as Red Guards clashed with workers who saw the confusion and disorder slowing down production and causing unemployment. Hitherto revered leaders like *Liu Shao-chi, Peng Chu* and *Teng Hsaio-ping* were humiliated by unruly youngsters and forced to resign. Mao associated himself with all this activity in a rather unusual way. In a symbolic act he plunged into the river *Yangtze* and swam 14 kilometres. Thousands of Red Guards copied this *Great Long Swim*, whilst other trekked along the route of the original *Long March* in 1934. (See Work Unit 10).

DEATH OF MAO

Workers often resisted the Cultural Revolution when factories were closed as a result. There was serious fighting between workers and Red Guards in *Wuhan* and *Shanghai*. For a time most intellectual life was similarly paralysed. *Lin Piao* seems to have realised the seriousness of the situation and may have used the army to try to stop it the worst excesses of revolutionary enthusiasm. Mao found out about Lin's 'treachery' and the famous general died mysteriously whilst apparently escaping from China by plane in 1971. Fighting and disruption continued until 1973 when the army and *Chou En-Lai* seemed to have restored order. *Teng Hsiao* was re-instated as communist Party General-Secretary, and when both Chou and Mao died in 1976, *Teng* became the ruler of China.

CHINA SINCE MAO

At a Chinese Communist Party meeting in 1978 *Teng* announced that the class struggle was over. He suggested more private ownership and foreign investment and less hostility to western ideas and fashions. Maoists who objected to these policies were defeated after further fighting. *Madam Mao*, the leader's much younger wife, and her friends, nicknamed the Gang of Four, were tried and imprisoned for their activities during the Cultural Revolution. These actions represented a momentous change, equivalent to Khruschev's 1956 denunciation of Stalin, because it announced to the Chinese people that Mao had made mistakes.

Since 1978 there has been steady industrial advance, but also inflation, corruption and over-investment. The large communist bureaucracy, which Mao himself had defied during the Cultural Revolution, remained as influential as ever. China improved economically (under *Teng*) but not politically.

People with a better standard of living found that their political situation had not improved. Marxists also point out that a communist party which has ceased to believe in the class struggle has lost its reason for existing. *Teng* was 84 in 1988. He faced as many problems as Mao in 1949 - some of them created by Mao himself.

SELF-ASSESSMENT SECTION

1. What was China's Second Five Year Plan called?

2. Who was China's Defence minister until 1971?

3. What is the official name of Red China?

4. Name an 'old monster' Red Guards were told to fight.

5. Where did the Koumintang government go after its defeat in 1949?

6. Who was a 'paper tiger' according to Mao?

7. Whom did Mao accuse of 'revisionism'?

8. What did Nehru mean when he talked of 'non-alignment'?

9. Where is the Askai Chin? Which two countries quarrelled over it?

10. In what year is Hong Kong due to return to Chinese rule?

(Camera Press. Reproduced in J. Robottom's 'Modern China', Longman, 1967)

11. Look at the photograph on the previous page.

    a)   Who is the man holding the paper?
    b)   What is he announcing?
    c)   Give the date of this historic event.
    d)   Explain, briefly, the significance of this event in China's history.

12. 'Walking on two legs' meant:-

    a)   Using both small and large industry.
    b)   Modernising China without outside help.
    c)   Forming both collectives and communes.
    d)   Using only 'backyard furnaces' to produce steel.
    e)   Using both foreign and Chinese labour.
    (TICK THE CORRECT ANSWER)

13. Read these sources, then answer the questions.

    A. "When there were eight households working jointly in a labour group for mutual help, it meant that one of the households had its land sowed roughly eight days earlier than the last household's....This led to a lot of argument....finally we said, 'Let us try cultivating it altogether and then just sharing produce...'"

    B. "I have had the job for eight years now. It is a heavy responsibility......the leaders of the labour groups are responsible for the day-to-day work but my task is to coordinate all the work and see that all goes smoothly and that we stick to our plans... planning, supervising, training, solving problems, finding out members' views and listening to them..."

                                       (Two farmers in Liuling village, Shensi, quoted in Hookham, 'A Short history of China,' Longmans, 1969)

    C. "The first thing to do is to find out exactly who's who in the village and how the village works: who profits, who suffers. You generally choose to live with the poorest peasant you can find and you live with him - not eating or sleeping any better than he does. You do that until he sees you really mean it - until he gives you his confidence".

    D. "Sometimes I was alone and the people would be shouting at me all they thought I had done wrong; sometimes they would have several of us at these meetings and the crowd would be larger...The people were sometimes very angry. I didn't understand any of it at first; I didn't know they had any special grievance against me. They then added up all the money they thought I owed them, so they said that the land I owned was really theirs now, for they had worked for years for too little".

(Source: R. Payne "Journey to Red China' William Heinemann Ltd., London)

a) Why was the writer of D. unpopular? What was likely to happen to him?

b) Which two sources are concerned with collective farming? Give reasons for your answer.

c) Which source was written by a Communist Party Official? Give reasons for your answer.

d) Which source gives a clue as to why the communists were successful in getting the peasants on their side?

e) Which two sources imply that collective farming was introduced at the request of the peasants? What evidence is there to suggest that this was not always the case?

f) How reliable are any of these sources considering the nature of communist rule? Explain your answer.

14. Explain the main reasons for the rift between China and Russia in the later 1950's and 1960's.

15. Give examples of Chinese expansion since the communist victory in 1949.

16. Why was the USA hostile towards communist China for some years? What events caused this attitude to change?

32

The British Empire: Dominions and India

INTRODUCTION

The British empire approached the end of the First World War with its supporters in confident mood. Its peoples had fought loyally with the mother-country; its different methods of government had survived the stresses and strains of war. In 1917 Jan Smuts, the ex-Boer leader, said," All the empires we have known in the past and that exist today are founded on the idea of assimilation, of trying to force human material into one mould. Your (*the British*) whole idea is different. You do not want to standardize the nations of the British empire; you want to develop them into a fuller, greater nationality" He went on to suggest that the dominions should become 'autonomous nations of an Imperial Commonwealth' with India as an important portion of the same'.

Part of Smut's confidence was justified. By 1926 the six dominions, Canada, Australia, New Zealand, South Africa, Newfoundland and the Irish Free State (now Eire), were independent countries in fact and in 1931 this independence became legal by the Statute of Westminster. It was, however, as some critics said, 'A whiteman's club'. India, which comprised three quarters of the empire's population and boasted a history longer than that of Britain, had not been granted dominion status. In 1917 Edwin Montague, British Secretary of State for India, promised that Indians would soon participate in every branch of administration as India developed 'self governing institutions'. These vague words were translated into the Montagu-Chelmsford reforms of 1919 which fell far short of satisfying India's nationalists.

The Indian nationalist movement had gained a powerful recruit in the 1920's with the arrival from South Africa of Mohandas Gandhi. Gandhi was a strange mixture of saint and salesman. He wanted dominion status within the Commonwealth rather than the complete break desired by Jawarharlal Nehru and others. What transformed such moderate aims was his methods. Gandhi's campaigns of passive resistance and civil disobedience roused the masses in a way no other nationalist leader managed to do. This bony figure, clad in little more than a loincloth, appealed to the under-privileged and brought them for the first time into the battle. His practical achievements were small. India did not gain the freedom he twice claimed would come within a year of him starting a campaign. His spiritual significance was immense. Gandhi brought India to the brink of revolution, only stopping at telling peasants to rebel and Indian soldiers to mutiny. This frightened both his friends and enemies. When the Government of India Act of 1935 gave the Indians control of their own home affairs, Gandhi's followers found that their own nationalist leaders crushed them even more ruthlessly than the British.

From the 1930's until independence in 1947 three themes dominated Indian history. First, there were the various schemes for a federated India, a sort of 'United States' for the sub-continent. Federation would have suited the British, the semi-independent Indian princes and the majority Hindu population. On the other hand, a strong central government was just what the minority Moslem population did *not* want. They preferred a weak central authority which would give them a great deal of freedom. Consequently, federation never materialised due to their opposition. Second, the danger of social revolution, as we have seen, frightened all authorities, Muslim, Hindu and British. When Gandhi's campaigns paralysed India's major cities and brought second-class citizens, such as the lower castes and women, into the fray, moderates feared anarchy. By 1939 the Indian National Congress, supposed leader of Indian resistance to British rule, was actually acting in partnership with the Raj (nickname for British rule)to keep order.

Finally, and most important in the long run, was the growing tension between the Hindu and Moslem communities. Only Gandhi, a Hindu, ever bridged the gap between the two; the other leaders lined up on one side or the other. No sooner were British members of a council replaced by Indians than the question arose. 'Which Indians?' Should they be Hindu or Moslem, or what each regarded as a fair proportion of the two? Where the Moslems were in the majority they were usually satisfied. Where they were in the minority their discontent created the drive, and produced the leaders for, a separate country, Pakistan. When independence came in 1947 it proved a poisoned gift. The sub-continent was not only divided into two hostile states. It became a slaughterhouse as thousands of refugees fled from the rule of one authority or the other.

THE DURHAM REPORT

In 1900 the *British Empire* comprised one-quarter of the world's land surface and one fifth of its population. It consisted of *colonies* and *dominions*. Colonial rule was direct and imperialistic (See Work Units 5 and 26). Dominion status was different. The idea of self-rule by some parts of the empire had been suggested by *Lord Durham* who was sent to Canada by the British Government in 1837 to report on the situation following disturbances involving the French population. The *Durham Report*, 1839 suggested the Canada should become self-governing in all home affairs, a condition Durham christened 'dominion'. He claimed this would prevent the sort of successful rebellion and breakaway staged by the American colonists in 1774. This idea was accepted in principle and in 1867 by the *British North America Act*, the four provinces of *Ontario, Quebec, New Brunswick* and *Nova Scotia* became the *Dominon of Canada*.

317

OTHER DOMINIONS

In 1900 *Australia's* six states joined in a US-style federation dominion. Each state has its own Assembly but each sends representatives to a Federal Parliament of two Houses, the *Senate* and *House of Representatives*. *New Zealand* refused to amalgamate with Australia and in 1907 became a separate dominion. *South Africa* achieved dominion status in 1910 not long after the Boer War (See Work Unit 6). In 1914 Britain's declaration of war against Germany was understood to include the dominions and apart from an unsuccessful rebellion in South Africa, this was accepted by its peoples. *Irish nationalists* staged a rebellion against British rule in 1916, and after much fighting and disorder, the 26 southern Catholic counties were granted dominion status as the *Irish Free State*. Six northern, Protestant-dominated counties refused to join and remained part of the United Kingdom. This led to trouble and terrorist activity which since 1969 has made a British army presence in Northern Ireland necessary. The *Irish Free State* took no part in the Second World War - the only dominion not to do so - and in 1949 left the Commonwealth, becoming an independent state called *Eire*.

THE IMPERIAL CONFERENCE

After the First World War the imperial bonds seemed as strong as ever. At the Versailles Peace Conference, for example, Britain represented the dominions. But in the early Twenties some dominions began to take a separate line in foreign policy. When Lloyd George's pro-Greek attitude led to a crisis with Ataturk's troops at *Chanak* in 1922, his appeal for dominion troops to help was refused. Next year the dominions refused to sign the *Treaty of Lausanne* (See Work Unit 8) and in 1925 the *Locarno Treaty* (See Work Unit 19}, indicating that they were not prepared to be connected with treaties which they had no part in framing.

By this time the dominions were independent in all but name and in 1926 *Mackenzie King*, the prime minister of Canada, suggested that such freedom should become legal. He did this at the *Imperial Conference*, a landmark in Commonwealth history. At this meeting the Commonwealth was defined as a 'group of self-governing communities'. They were united by a common allegiance to the Crown. Each dominion was to have a Governor-General whose position was to be equivalent to that of the monarch in Britain. A committee of experts was set up whose job was to put these decisions into legal form. This was done by the *Statute of Westminster* in 1931. *Canada* and *New Zealand* did not use their new rights for many years. *Newfoundland,* the smallest and poorest dominion, voluntarily reverted to being a crown colony in 1933.

IMPERIAL PREFERENCE

Attempts to create an economic union were not so successful. *Imperial Preference*, a plan to give preferential treatment to empire imports, was rejected by the British electors at the 1905 General Election. In 1932 it was again rejected by Commonwealth leaders at the *Ottawa Conference. Neville Chamberlain,* a British cabinet minister, put a 10% surcharge on all imports except Empire ones, hoping that the dominions would follow suit and thus produce an *Empire Free Trade* area. The idea was that the dominions would supply food and raw materials to the British 'workshop'. The dominions were affected by the world depression and refused to give similar concessions to British exports in case they harmed their own industries. No general agreement resulted from the conference.

INDIA

In 1885 middle class Indians - lawyers, doctors and journalists - formed the *Indian National Congress,* one of the oldest and largest political parties. The Congress's policy at this time did not aim at the ending of British rule. Congress members demanded an equal share of representation on legislative councils, a better chance of good jobs and a fair opportunity for Indian industry and commerce to compete in the outside world. By 1908, the existence of more 'white' dominions led Congress to demand dominion status. A clear warning of the dangers to come appeared in 1909. When the *Morley-Minto Reforms* gave some Indians the vote for the first time it became clear that Muslims would be outnumbered. The British introduced a separate voting register for Hindus and Muslims but this problem grew as the years passed.

MONTAGU-CHELMSFORD REFORMS

The ideas and events connected with the First World War, notably the *Russian Revolution* and Woodrow Wilsons' *'self-determination',* acted as a spur to Indian nationalism. After the war Britain tried to show its gratitude for the large part played in the fighting by Indian troops. In 1919 the *Montagu-Chelmsford Reforms* set up a dual system of government which was called *dyarchy.* Under this scheme health, education, industry and finance were run by Indians and police, law and order and finance by the British appointed *Viceroy* and his half-Indian, half British *Central Executive Council.* These elected councils gained further power by the *Government of India Act* of 1935. This granted wide powers to elected Indian representatives. In 1937 elections held under this Act led to Hindu domination of the regions where they were in the majority. This naturally increased the discontent felt by the minority Muslim community. Muslin discontent focused on the *Muslim League*, founded in 1906, and led in later years by *Mohammed Ali Jinnah*. Jinnah started his career as a member of the Indian Congress but by 1913 he was heading the Muslim League.

GANDHI

A leading figure in the Indian nationalist movement was *Mohandas Karamchand Gandhi*, later called "*Mahatma*" or "Great Soul". Gandhi had been educated as a lawyer in England and had spent 20 years in South Africa fighting racial prejudice. Gandhi admired Britain and the British but after his return to India in 1914 he worked hard to gain dominion status for his country. Gandhi was a pacifist who rejected both western education and technology. He worked through mass movements, not political parties, and called his inspirational methods *satyagraha* (soul force). Satyagraha took the form of passive resistance by non-cooperation and civil disobedience. In 1920 Gandhi mobilised the lower castes in provinces which had not previously been politically active. Because he opposed Britain's treatment of Muslim *Turkey* during the *Chanak* crisis, he won the support of Muslims as well as Hindus. Using Congress as a launching pad, he started a campaign of civil disobedience, promising his followers that they would gain self-rule of a dominion type within a year . His plan involved *hartals*, days of fasting and prayer without work, boycotts of British goods and refusal to pay taxes and obey laws. This campaign failed and Gandhi was sentenced to 6 years in prison in 1922.

A violent incident in *Amritsar* where certain wartime regulations were still in force, led to British troops firing on an 'illegal' gathering, killing 379 and wounding 1,000. *General Dyer*, the British officer responsible, was censured and retired from the army but the memory of the *Amritsar Massacre* (1919) helped fuel Gandhi's campaign by stirring up ill-feeling against the British.

SIMON COMMISSION

In 1927 *Britain* appointed a commission, headed by *Sir John Simon* to consider revision of the *Montagu-Chelmsford Reforms*. Many nationalists boycotted it because it did not have a single Indian member. *Simon* proposed more self-rule for Indians but this at once raised the problem of Hindus versus Muslims. In the *United Provinces and Bombay,* for example, Hindus were in the majority and would rule Muslims; in *Bengal* and the *Punjab* the opposite would be true. Many high-caste Hindus also disliked the idea of rule by people of a lower caste; they would have preferred even the British to that. In the early 1930's *Gandhi* launched another campaign, bringing many cities to a standstill with strikes and civil disobedience. Various conferences were held in England to try to solve the problem. In 1930 *Jawarharlal Nehru*, English-educated nationalist, refused to attend a London meeting because the British would not promise immediate dominion status. In the same year *Nehru* proclaimed Indian 'independence' and this day. 26 January, is still celebrated as Indian independence Day.

GOVERNMENT OF INDIA ACT

A *Round-Table Conference* about India took place in London in 1931. *Gandhi* called off his campaign to attend but he returned home dissatisfied with the slowness of British acceptance of Indian self-rule. In Britain the ruling Conservative Party was split on the issue, with an influential group led by *Winston Churchill* and *David Lloyd George* claiming that dominion status for India would be a "a betrayal of empire". They were opposing the *Government of India Act* of 1935. This gave Indians entire control of their provincial councils with voting rights for Indians who owned a certain amount of property.

This did not satisfy *Gandhi* or *Nehru* who complained that it still left the *Viceroy* supreme ruler of India. The first elections held under this act in 1937 put Muslims for the first time under Hindu rule after the British authorities had forcibly shared out the seats because the two communities could not agree. This led to riots and further accelerated the move towards two states on the sub-continent. *Jinnah*, head of the *Moslem League* evolved the idea of a separate Muslim state called *Pakistan*. This word meant 'land of the pure' and it contains letters representing some Muslim peoples territories, *P for Punkab, A for Afghan, K for Kashmir* and *S for Sind*. The Hindu leaders and Congress were totally opposed to the scheme, but riots and killings every year made division more likely when independence came.

SECOND WORLD WAR

The Second World War provided a boost to the Muslim campaign. Congress refused to cooperate with the British war effort and started a *'Quit India'* campaign against British rule. The *Muslim League* did not take this line and this pleased the British authorities who started to treat *Congress* as a Hindu organisation and the *Muslim League* as the spokesman for all India's Muslims, although this was not strictly true. When the 'Quit India' leaders were put in jail, *Jinnah* was free to organise the Muslims as a truly separate force in India.

The entry of *Japan* into the war in 1942 divided Hindu opinion. A minority argued that the Japanese were only interested in driving the British out of the sub-continent and would not remain after they had won the war. One Congress leader, *Chandra Bose* even recruited an *Indian National Army* from Hindu soldiers in Japanese prisoner of war camps to fight for Japan. In 1942 Britain sent *Sir Stafford Cripps,* a Labour politician, to India to enlist Indian support for the British war effort. The *Cripps Mission* issued a report promising India dominion status after the war and the right to leave the Commonwealth if she wished.

Muslim officials, meanwhile, were sharing government with the British in the *Punjab*, and Muslim officials took over key positions in *Bengal, Sind, Assam* and the *North West Frontier Province*. In the 1945-6 the *Pethick-Lawrence Mission* offered India dominion status, but stated that autonomy would be granted to certain Muslim states in a federal India. *Congress* and the *League* quarrelled over the right to appoint Muslim representatives to the proposed government. It was clear that when Britain granted independence to the sub-continent, India would have to be partioned between Muslims and Hindus.

LORD MOUNTBATTEN

In spite of what had happened during the war, *Jinnah* felt that the British authorities favoured Congress, and so he began a *Direct Action* campaign which led to riots and killing, between Muslims and Hindus during 1946-7. *Lord Wavell,* the British Viceroy, advised the British government that a united, independent India was not possible for at least 10 years. He suggested dividing power between the Indian provinces. The British rejected Wavell's advice and replaced him with *Lord Louis Mountbatten*. They announced that India would become independent by June, 1948 and planned to partition India between Hindu and Muslims, leaving the princely states free to join whichever country they wished. Lord Mountbatten reported that partition and independence must be brought forward to August 1947 or communal violence, already very severe, would become uncontrollable.

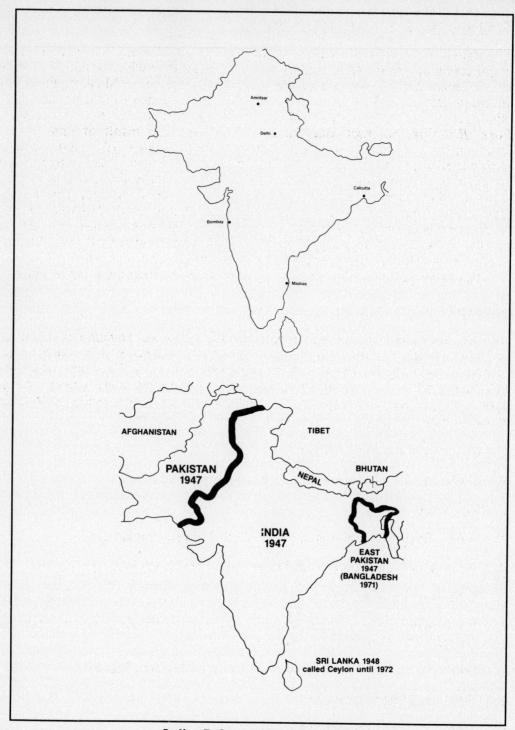

India - Before and After Partition

RADCLIFFE COMMISSION

The British Government accepted *Mountbatten's* assessment of the situation. A major problem was possible borders for *Pakistan*, a state which would have to be in two separate parts because of the geographical spread of Muslim and Hindu communities. Both *West* and *East Pakistan* would contain large minorities of Hindus anyway. The British set up a committee of two Hindus, two Muslims and *Lord Radcliffe* to mark out the new frontiers. The result of this hurried arrangement was that when independence came in August, 1947, thousands of terrified refugees fled from the rule of either India or Pakistan. These refugees were attacked by their enemies and in the space of two months about 2 million men, women and children were slaughtered. Three states ruled by princes, *Travancore, Hyderabad,* and *Kashmir*, considered independence. Both *Travancore* and *Hyderabad* became part of India, although Hyderabad was actually invaded and blockaded by the Indian army. Muslim *Kashmir* was invaded by Pakistani troops to prevent the Hindu ruler giving it to India. An Indian army entered the country to stop this happening and the country has been divided between the two ever since.

NEHRU AND JINNAH

Jawarharlal Nehru became prime minister of *India*, a post he held until his death in 1964. *Jinnah* was made Governor-General of *Pakistan* and President of the National Assembly. He was bitterly disappointed by the actual frontiers of the new Pakistan. *East* and *West Pakistan* were 1600 kilometres apart, whilst the rich agricultural districts of *East Punjab, Calcutta* and *West Bengal,* had gone to India, Jinnah died in 1948 and was succeeded by *Liaquat Ali Khan*.

SELF-ASSESSMENT SECTION

1. What was the title of the chief British official in India?

2. What was dyarchy?

3. Which British general was involved in the Amritsar massacre?

4. What is the significance of 26 January in Indian history?

5. What was Imperial Preference?

6. What was the Irish Free State's title *after* 1949? How was its position different after that date?

7. Name the country which was the subject of the Durham Report?

8. What does 'Pakistan' mean?

9. Who was prime minister of Canada in 1926?

10. What was the name of the commission which set the boundaries of India and Pakistan.

11. Dominion status is:-
    a) Complete independence.
    b) A system of dual political control.
    c) Independence within the Commonwealth.
    d) Alliance with other empire countries
    e) Rule by British Crown
       (TICK THE CORRECT ANSWER)

    It was first suggested by:-
    a) Winston Churchill
    b) Jawarharlal Nehru
    c) Mohammed Ali Jinnah
    d) Lord Durham
    e) Mohandas Gandhi
       (TICK THE CORRECT ANSWER)

12. The Statute of Westminster:-
    a) Gave empire possessions self-rule.
    b) Gave the dominions self-rule.
    c) Legalised the actual position of the dominions
    d) Gave self-rule to India
    e) Forbade dominion status for India.
       (TICK THE CORRECT ANSWER)

13. Certain letters in the word Pakistan refer to the first letters of the names of Muslim territories. Complete this list -

    A for ....
    K for ....
    S for ....
    P for ....

    Which of these territories has been disputed by India and Pakistan since 1947?

14. Explain, briefly, the different attitudes to the granting of Indian independence of:
    a) Lord Wavell
    b) Lord Mountbatten.

15. Look at this map. Then answer the questions that follow.

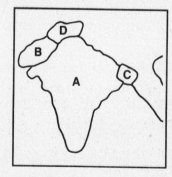

a) Which letter indicates India
b) Which letters indicate East and West Pakistan
c) Name the province disputed between India and Pakistan.
d) Using this map, and your knowledge of the subject, explain in what ways the partition of India was unsatisfactory to

    (i) India and
    (ii) Pakistan.

16. Read these sources, then answer the questions.

A. "I wish to bring about a state of affairs in which every Englishman would look upon every Indian as his equal. I want to bring down the Englishmen from the superior heights from which he talks and to make him think of even the most ordinary Indian labourer as his equal........".
Gandhi (Quoted 'History Today' magazine, 83/84 Berwick St, London W1V 3PJ October 1969)

B. "Personally, I owe so much to England in my mental makeup ever to feel wholly alien to her. And, do what I will, I cannot get rid of the habits of mind and the standards and ways of judging other countries as well as life generally, which I have acquired at school and college in England.....if I have become what is called an uncompromising opponent of British rule in India, it is almost in spite of myself"
Nehru (History Today Magazine, 83/84 Berwick St, London W1V 3PJ , October 1969)

C. "I have been authorised on behalf of His Majesty's Government to state clearly that in his judgement... the natural issue of India's constitutional progress.... is the attainment of dominion status."
Lord Irwin, Viceroy, 1929
(Quoted in 'History of the 20th Century' Purnell, Issue 46)

D "Take the instance of South Africa.... General Hertzog (*the South African Prime Minister*) has returned from London (*where he attended the Imperial Conference*) completely converted, knowing that if he wants to declare independence today he can get it. I should not be satisfied with any constitution that we may get from the British Parliament unless it leaves that power with us also, so that if we choose to declare our independence we could do so..."
Gandhi, 1926
(Quoted Purnell, as above)

a) What indications are there in B. that the British had ruled India for a long time? What does B. tell you about the *way* they had ruled India.
b) Which source suggests that the Imperial Conference had deeply effected Indian nationalists. Give reasons for your answer.
c) Regarding A. what other people, besides the British, were likely to look down on the Indian labourer?

d) Regarding D. what dominion did leave the Commonwealth?
e) Source C. did not please India's nationalists. Can you think of reasons why this was so?
f) What does EITHER A or B tell you about the characters of GANDHI or NEHRU.? Only deal with one of these men.
g) What important problem regarding Indian independence is NOT mentioned in any of these sources? Can you think of a reason why it was ignored?

17. Imagine you are a Muslim OR Hindu refugee in 1947. Describe the *background* to your experiences, and how you managed to survive them.

33

The Indian sub-continent since 1947

INTRODUCTION

When Mahatma Gandhi was murdered in January, 1948 by a Hindu fanatic who blamed him for the partition of India, Nehru said in a national broadcast, "the light has gone out of our lives and there is darkness everywhere". Nevertheless, however much Nehru may have admired Gandhi as a person, his policies as ruler of India were far different from those favoured by the Mahatma. Gandhi lived the life of a Hindu holyman, even if it was accompanied by worldwide publicity. He represented, in spite of his western education, the traditional India. Nehru was a convinced socialist who believed that India must not glorify poverty but wipe it out. He set about industrialising the country with a series of Five Year Plans.

Most Indian nationalists, obsessed with the battle against Britain, made the mistake of thinking that once the British were gone India's problems with the outside world over. Nehru, who had more international experience, should have known better. India after 1947 was alone in a big world with some big powers in it, one of them, China, sharing her borders. In spite of this, Nehru kept India neutral, or as he put it, 'non-aligned' in the Cold War, hoping to gain the world's respect and perhaps help keep the peace. At times he condemned Britain, the USA and Russia for their actions, for example, over Cuba, Suez and Hungary. Whenever possible, as in Korea and Vietnam after 1954, he played the peacemaker.

The flaw in this policy was that it ignored the most important job of any government - to safeguard national security. A country can live in 'splendid isolation' if it is strong and safe. India was neither. In 1962 Nehru's non-alignment was shattered by a Chinese invasion of northern India. Border incidents between Chinese and Indian troops should have warned him; signs of Chinese interest in the region were clear. Nehru, who could sense the danger of war in most parts of the world, seemed unaware of the danger on his own doorstep. He had refused to make alliances and had taken an opposite line to Britain and the USA on many issues. Faced with a national disaster he was forced to beg military aid from Britain and the USA. Finally, the Chinese saved him by halting their troops when they had occupied the territory they wanted. It was a tremendous blow to Nehru's prestige and his policies.

Nehru's shortsightedness where China was concerned was due partly to his obsession with Pakistan, a state which neither he nor his people thought should haved existed. Whilst as Indian premier he preached reasonableness and peace to the world, he looked upon Pakistan with cold hostility. During his lifetime, and since his death, India has fought successful wars against its hated Muslim rival, first over Kashmir, and later when India helped East Pakistan gain its independence from West Pakistan. Certainly the contrast between the two countries since independence seems to suggest that partition was a mistake. India remains, despite intense pressure inside and outside the country, the world's largest democracy. This is a fine achievement in a country whose teeming population is divided by race, religion and language. Pakistan has a history of instability and has been under military rule for most of its existence. This is partly due to its economic weakness which became worse after it lost its chief market, East Pakistan.

Pakistan has been plagued by ethnic differences; for example, in Sind where the people are divided between the native Sinds and Muslim migrants from India called Mahajirs. Its' tax system is unfair - landlords and farmers do not pay taxes - and most of its income is from US aid. A great deal of this money is spent on defence, particularly as between 1979 and 1988 the USA saw Pakistan as a defence against communist infiltration following the Russian invasion of Afghanistan. Corruption has been rife and the only prolonged period of civilian rule under Zulfikar Al Bhutto ended in disaster when General Zia ceased power and executed him. A second period of civilian government was started in 1988 when the army allowed free elections following the mysterious death of Zia in an aircrash. Bhutto's daughter, Benazir, became prime minister of a country she admitted was 'bankrupt'.

NEHRU'S POLICIES

Nehru ruled the world's largest democracy - 170 million people in 1947. His *Congress Party* won elections regularly. Its only serious opponents was the *communist party* which actually achieved power in *Kerula* province. Elswhere it has sometimes polled 10% of the votes at elections. In 1950 *Nehru* declared India a *republic* but requested that she remain a member of the *Commonwealth*. This was a significant move for the future of the Commonwealth; since that time quite a number of ex-colonies have become republic but remained part of the Commonwealth.

Nehru was a socialist so he approached India's vast problems of poverty and technical backwardness with left-wing solutions. The first of his *Five Year Plans* started in 1951. India's major industries were nationalised, using loans from both eastern and western bloc countries. The emphasis was on state planning, with new industries and scientific development given priority. Nehru also tried to encourage birth control to limit the growth of population. But the main problem, *poverty,* was not solved. Most Indian peasants manage to grow only the minimum amount of food to feed themselves and their families. Such *subsistence farming* leaves no safety margin to deal with emergencies, like the birth of another child, or the arrival of the monsoon rains late or early. Some progress was made but there is need for more *irrigation* to improve agricultural production.

SOCIAL PROBLEMS

Nehru outlawed the Hindu *caste system* which divides people into four castes, or classes, determined by birth. They ranged from the highest, the *Brahmins*, to the lowest, the *untouchables*, whose jobs were of the most menial kind. This Hindu custom seemed wrong for a state which contained so many Muslims, and, in fact, Nehru also made India a *secular state*, that is, a country without a state religion. His battle against poverty came up against a *rising birth-rate*; by 1976 India's population had topped 600 million. Another problem was *language*. At least 60 different languages are spoken in India and some people are prepared to kill for the right to speak their tongue. Those who speak Hindi, for example, tried to make it the official language of India. This was opposed by the *Bengalis* and *Tamils*. In Bombay there was bloodshed between the *Marathi*-speakers, who are the majority, and those who speak *Gujarati*. Some saw the solution of this problem in the division of India into provinces which all spoke the same language, that is, *Linguistic states*. This is not practicable on a nationwide scale but one such province, *Andhra*, was set up in 1953.

MRS GANDHI'S INDIA

Nehru died in 1964. His successor, *Lel Bahadur Shastri* offered the post of prime minister to Nehru's daughter, *Mrs Indira Gandhi*, (no relation of the Mahatma) but she refused. Shastri, however, died suddenly in 1966 and Mrs Gandhi then stood for election against *Mororji Desai*. This contest was the first sign of a split in the *Congress Party* which had ruled India since 1947. *Mrs Gandhi* won the election (355 seats to 169) and continued her father's policies with an *Economic Development Plan*. This was designed to increase India's wealth by 6% a year, create millions of extra jobs and lead to a big rise in income for the average Indian. Such plans were hampered by *famine*, particularly bad in *Bihar* province, and the *Orissa floods* of 1971. India's success in the *Second Indo-Pakistan War* of 1971, kept Mrs Gandhi in power until the mid-1970's when *Desai's* opposition, *Janata* (Peoples) *Party* began to gain political strength.

STATES OF EMERGENCY

In 1975 a High Court ruled that *Mrs Gandhi* had acted dishonestly during some elections. She was banned from holding political office for 5 years. Her reaction was to declare a *state of emergency* which involved imprisoning hundreds of her opponents and imposing press censorship. More positively, she embarked on an ambitious modernisation scheme, building new power stations, increasing the area under irrigation and promising the peasants more land. To tackle the problems of the still rising population, her government offered bonus payments to men and women prepared to be sterilised. The minimum marriage age was set at 18 for women and 21 for men. Her son, *Sanjay*, assisted her in this policy and was accused by his enemies of ordering the forcible sterilisation of men in some provinces. Such accusations affected Mrs Gandhi's popularity and in the 1977 General Election Desai's *Janata Party* decisively defeated the Congress Party. Consequently, *Mr Desai* became prime minister. The *Janata* was little more than a loose alliance of politicians and people opposed to Mrs Gandhi. It soon collapsed into quarrelling groups. Mrs Gandhi's 'misconduct' was still under investigation and she spent a short time in jail for refusing to give evidence. In 1980 her section of the Congress Party regained power.

DEATH OF MRS GANDHI

The constant *Sikh* campaign for a separate state - *Sikh Khalistan* - came to a head in June, 1984 when Sikh extremists occupied the *Golden Temple* at *Amritsar*, the Sikh's most holy shrine, and began to store weapons and equipment there for an armed rising. Mrs Gandhi sent Indian troops to storm the Temple, a move which horrified even moderate Sikhs who had not agreed with the original occupation. In October *Mrs Gandhi* was assassinated by a Sikh soldier of her own bodyguard. She was succeeded by her son, *Rajiv Gandhi*, hitherto an airline pilot not a politician; her eldest son, *Sanjay*, had been killed in an air crash. *Rajiv* also had trouble with *Sikh* separatists. In 1988 he managed to defuse another violent seizure of the Golden Temple without making a direct attack. He also sent Indian troops into Sri Lanka (formerly *Ceylon*) to assist the government in its civil war with the *Tamils*.

INDIA, PAKISTAN AND CHINA

Nehru refused to take sides in the Cold War between the super-powers. He complained about the behaviour of both at different times, but tried to remain on friendly terms with them. Nehru failed to see the danger from *China* even after the Chinese occupation of *Tibet* in 1950 (See Work Unit 31). The *Sino-Indian War* of 1962 (See Work Unit 31) humiliated India and was a serious blow to Nehru's prestige both inside and outside India. His last years were spent seeking aid from Britain and the USA, moves which were contrary to his policy of non-alignment. During his rule, *France* gave up its small Indian possessions - *Pondicherry, Karikal, Mahe and Yanan* - which she had held from the 18th century. *Portugal* tried to hold on to *Goa, Danan and Dia* by declaring them part of metropolitan Portugal but in 1961 Indian forces occupied them, thus ending centuries of Portuguese colonial rule.

THE KASHMIR PROBLEM

For many years Nehru was concerned about *Pakistan*, symbol of a partition which most Indians believed should never have happened. Bitterness about partition itself was fuelled by the quarrel over *Kashmir* (See Work Unit 32), the use of the waters of the *River Indus* and compensation for the 17 million people who fled from one country or the other in 1947. *Kashmir* proved to be the most persistent problem. *Hsri Singh*, its Hindu ruler in 1947, appealed for Indian help when the *Poonch* province of this mainly Muslim region was occupied by Pakistani tribesmen. India gave help on condition that Kashmir became part of India. Indian troops arrived just in time to prevent a complete Pakistani takeover but they also overthrew *Hari*.

Nehru promised a plebiscite to find out the wishes of the *Kashmiri* people and in 1948 referred the dispute to the *United Nations* (See Work Unit 24). In 1949 the UN managed to get a ceasefire between the two sides, and in reality Kashmir was divided between a western part, consisting of *Poonch, Baltistan* and *Gilgit* ruled by Pakistan, and the rest of the country ruled by various Sheiks who were Indian puppets. By 1957 *eastern Kashmir* was a fully federated member of the Indian union. By this time Nehru had gone back on his promise of the plebiscite for the region because *Pakistan* had entered into a military alliance with the USA in 1954. He was furious about this treaty which he believed violated the non-alignment principles he had laid down for the sub-continent. *Kashmir*, which also had a border with *China*, later became a factor in the the *Sino-Indian War*.

INDO-PAKISTAN WAR

In 1965 *Pakistan* decided to settle the Kashmir dispute by force. In August her troops crossed the UN ceasefire line but in the fighting which followed the Pakistan attack was halted, and then thrown back by an Indian invasion of Pakistan itself. During this campaign India took over a strategic part of Pakistan, the vital military road which runs through the *Vale of Kashmir*. Pakistan felt let down by the USA during this war. After Nehru's death, India's leaders began to move away from his strict non-alignment. They decided that India could no longer afford to have no friends with an enemy like China was on her borders. *Mrs Gandhi* made a treaty with Russia, partly to offset the US-Pakistan alliance.

PAKISTAN

Pakistan proved a weak state, both politically and economically. Its two parts were separated, not only by geography, but by linguistic and racial differences. The people of *East Pakistan*, for example, have more in common with their Indian Bengali neighbours than those of West Pakistan. Jinnah's death so soon after Pakistan's foundation left the state without its founding father, and *Liaquat Ali Khan*, who succeeded him, was murdered in 1951. Several years of short-lived governments, disorder and corruption, followed. This was due to the difficulty of balancing the needs of *East and West Pakistan*, and when the *Muslin League* was badly defeated in East Pakistan elections, the government of West Pakistan showed its hand by sending *General Iskander Mirzal* as military governor of East Pakistan. This proved to be the beginning of military rule for both parts of Pakistan. From 1958 political parties were banned and *General Ayub Khan* ruled as head of state.

THE AWAMI LEAGUE

East Pakistan was now being treated like occupied territory by the West Pakistanis and a strong secessionist movement,. the *Awami League*, grew up in East Pakistan. In 1969 *Ayub Khan* resigned and his successor, *General Yahya Khan*, tried to re-introduce a one-man, one-vote democracy. In the elections which followed, the *Awami League* won a decisive victory in East Pakistan, whilst in West Pakistan, *Zulfikar Ali Bhutto's People's Party* gained power. *Bhutto* realised that *Sheik Mujibar Rahman*, the Awami League Leader, voiced the genuine discontent felt by the Bengalis of East Pakistan. They outnumbered the West Pakistanis but were under virtual occupation by a not very well behaved West Pakistani army. Bhutto held talks with *Mujibar* to try to solve the problems but these failed. Mujibar began to act like the ruler of a separate state.

SECOND-INDO PAKISTAN WAR

Bhutto imprisoned various Awami leaders, including *Mujibar,* and this led to fighting as a result of which about 10 million refugees fled from East Pakistan into India. India felt that this was a problem which must be solved decisively. In 1971 her troops invaded both parts of Pakistan. The Pakistani army in the east was forced to surrender; that in the West was defeated and forced to give up territory known as the *Rann of Kutch* and another part of *Kashmir*. Mujibar became ruler of an independent country called *Bangladesh* (Bengali-land). Bhutto was left to rule a state which had lost half its territory and population, a great deal of its raw materials and manufacturing industry and foreign markets which had been supplied by East Pakistan. In 1972 *Bhutto* and *Mrs Gandhi* met at *Simla* and worked out an agreement on Kashmir's frontiers and also on the repatriation of prisoners -of - war.

BANGLADESH AND PAKISTAN

Bangladesh's history was troubled. In 1975 *Mujibar* was murdered during quarrels between warring sections of his army. The country's economy was in ruins. There were deep divisions between Hindus and Muslims, and between Bengalis and Biharis. Inflation, food shortages and disastrous floods increased Bangladesh's problems. Two generals, first *Ziar Rahman* and then *Ershad*, have exercised an army dictatorship and attempts at democratic elections have either been abandoned amidst claims of ballot-rigging, or their results have been overruled by the military.

In *Pakistan* Bhutto was overthrown in any army coup led by *General Mohammed Zia-ul-Haq*. Two years later Bhutto was condemned to death for murder and hanged. Zia often promised free elections but in fact retained a tight military grip on the country. In 1983 and 1985 he held elections and also allowed *Miss Benazir Bhutto*, the executed President's daughter and leader of the opposition, to return to Pakistan. A referendum held in 1984 gave *Zia* office for 5 years. His position was strengthened after the Russian invasion of *Afghanistan* in 1979 because Pakistan became a bulwark against any further Soviet expansion in that region. Millions of Afghan refugees were allowed across the border and Zia equipped and supported the *Muhajeen* fighters in their battle with the Russians and their Afghan government.

BENAZIR BHUTTO

In 1988 Russia announced that she would carry out a phased withdrawal of her troops from *Afghanistan*; the actual civil war between the communist government and the Muhajeen continued. *Zia* was killed in a suspicious air-craft explosion in 1988. Elections were held in November, 1988, and these gave Miss Bhutto's party enough seats for her to be made prime minister - the first woman ruler of a Muslim state. Her room for manoeuvre was restricted by the army who still retained the final word in any political matter.

SELF-ASSESSMENT SECTION

1. Who was the first prime minister of India?

2. In which Indian province did the communists gain power?

3. What is 'non-alignment'?

4. Which Pakistani prime minister was hanged?

5. Where is the Golden Temple? What is its significance to Sikhs?

6. Who was Mrs Gandhi's opponent in the 1966 election?

7. Why was Mrs Gandhi murdered?

8. Name the province disputed between India and Pakistan since 1947.

9. What was the aim of the Awami League?

10. Who invaded Afghanistan in 1979?

11. Briefly explain these terms:-

    secular state;   subsistence farming;   linguistic state;   Caste system

12. Put the correct details (by letter) against these names

1.	ALI JINNAH	A.	Killed in air crash
2.	INDIRA GANDHI	B.	Ruler of Kashmir in 1947
3.	SANJAY GANDHI	C.	Governor of East Pakistan.
4.	HARI SINGH	D.	Leader of Awami League
5.	ISKANDER MIRZA	E.	Founder of Pakistan
6.	AYUB KHAN	F.	Murdered prime minister of India
7.	RAJIV GANDHI	G.	Military ruler of Pakistan
8.	MUJIBAR RAHMAN	H.	Prime minister of India in 1980's

13. The Sino-Indian War was between:-

    a) India and Pakistan
    b) India and Tibet
    c) China and Pakistan
    d) East and West Pakistan
    e) China and India
        (TICK THE CORRECT ANSWER)

333

14. Bangladesh was formerly:-

    a) West Pakistan
    b) Bengal
    c) Kashmir
    d) East Pakistan
    e) Sri Lanka
    (TICK THE CORRECT ANSWER)

15. Read these two sources, then answer the questions.

    A. 'In the next few years there were a number of incidents leading to Chinese complaints of Indians crossing into Tibet and India complaints of Chinese troops found south of the frontier. These (*accusations*) could be accounted for by the difficulty of knowing exactly where one is in such a country, and the Indians in particular, anxious to prove that India and China could co-operate peaceably in Asia, were not on the lookout for more serious or sinister explanations'.

    Peter Calvocoressi: World Politics since 1945
    Longman, 1968.

    B. 'India claimed these lands (*the Aksai Chin and North East Frontier Agency*) on the grounds that in 1914 Britain...had negotiated these frontiers with Tibet...successive Chinese governments refused to recognise these arrangements - in fact, the Chinese Communists had built a military road right through the middle of the Aksai Chin...They (*the Chinese*) naturally assumed that the Indians accepted both this and the Chinese occupation of the NEFA to the north of the MacMahan Line. Prime Minister Nehru had never raised serious objections and had always been friendly towards the People's Republic. Thus the Chinese were very surprised when Nehru ordered his troops to adopt a 'forward' policy in both sectors in 1962'.

    Brian Catchpole. A Map History of China.
    Heinemann Educational 1976

    a) Which source favours the Chinese explanation of what happened?
    b) Which source favours the Indian view of the matter. (In both a and b give reasons for your answer).
    c) What reasons does Source A give for border encroachments by both the Chinese and Indians? Do you agree with this explanation, bearing in mind Source B? Give reasons for your answer.
    d) On what matter regarding Indo-Chinese relations do both sources agree?

16. Explain the troubles which have beset Pakistan since independence. How far could they have been forseen in 1947?

17. Imagine you are an Indian peasant. Describe some incidents in your life between independence in 1947 and 1988.

34

The Middle East:
Israel and the Arabs

INTRODUCTION

Few political problems are as controversial as the Jewish-Arab confrontation in the Middle East. To Arabs, the state of Israel is a western colony, an imperialist power which drove out the native Palestinians. To many Jews, Israel is the long-desired home of a people who have been persecuted throughout the ages, a welcome return to their original homeland after an appalling massacre of Jews by the nazis. Foreign countries take sides, many of them, including Russia, for the Arabs. Israel's most powerful supporter, however, is the USA which maintains, finances and on at least one occasion in 1973, probably saved the country. The USA does this because of the large and influential Jewish-American community in her own country. Repeated wars between Israel and various Arab states have increased the problem, as one victory after another has given the Israelis, not only security for their own borders, but more land and power. What began as a tiny state, formed as the result of the Zionist dream, is now a nationalist mini-empire, sworn enemy of the Arab nationalism around it. And because Russia supports the Arabs and the USA, Israel, the Middle East remains a flashpoint between the super-powers.

The story begins with what both Jew and Arab regard as broken promises. Before the First World War, Palestine was part of the Turkish empire. In 1917 the British promised the Arab population self-government if they helped drive out the Turk. In the same year the Jewish settlers were promised "a national home" by a British government anxious to increase Jewish-American help for their war-effort. When the war ended, neither promise was kept, Britain took over Palestine as a League of Nations' mandated territory and held it until 1948. By that time the battle-lines between Jew and Arab had been clearly drawn. Jewish immigration into Palestine, allowed by the British as part of their promise of a national home, increased year by year, especially as a result of Hitler's persecution of German Jews in the 1930's. The Arabs would not agree to share power with the expanding Jewish population in a bi-national state, or accept a partition of the country between themselves and the Jews. General strikes, several Arab rebellions and Jewish and Arab terrorism made Palestine ungovernable and Britain gave up her mandate in 1948, handing the problem back to the United Nations. The UN suggested dividing the country between Arab and Jewish settlers but this partition plan was rejected by the Arabs. In the war which followed the British withdrawal, the Israelis won a resounding victory and set up their own independent state.

Most of the controversy about the rights and wrongs of the problem stem from this war. The Israelis maintain that there was a concerted plan by several Arab states to drive them into the sea, thus strangling the infant Zionist state at birth. The Arabs point out that, in fact, the various Arab states - Egypt, Transjordan (now Jordan), Syria and Iraq - were unprepared for war and had different aims. Their side also contained a "traitor" in the person of King Abdullah of Transjordan who, whilst officially on the Arab settlers' side, secretly planned to conquer Arab Palestine and add it to his own kingdom. This scheme contravened the UN partition plan but it was known to the British and supported by their Foreign Secretary, Ernest Bevin. The British case is that Bevin warned Abdullah, whose elite Arab League was commanded by an Englishman, Glubb Pasha, not to cross the frontier lines of the new Jewish state.

Finally, this 1948 war led to the most lasting problems of all, that of the Palestinian refugees. Many Israelis argue that the Arabs fled of their own free will. Over the years evidence has accumulated that these people were uprooted ruthlessly and driven from their farms and villages by terrorist methods. Thus Jewish nationalism triumphed at the expense of Arab nationalism, and, as one Jewish historian has written, "The refusal to recognise the Palestinians right to self-determination and statehood proved over the years to be the main source of the turbulence, violence and bloodshed that came to pass". Other territories occupied by victorious Israeli armies can, and have been evacuated. The Palestinians remain a homeless and dispossessed people whose state would have to be planted inside Israel.

ZIONISM

After the Romans crushed their rebellion in AD 70, many Jews remained in *Palestine* but many more were scattered over Europe and the Middle East. This is called the *diaspora*, or dispersal. Throughout the Middle Ages, Christian hostility towards Jews as the enemies of Christ was widespread and they were discriminated against by law and custom. It was natural that some Jews should wish to return to their original homeland. The idea of establishing a separate Jewish state in Palestine is called *Zionism*. A pioneer Zionist was *Theodore Herzl*, an Austrian Jew, who organised the *First Zionist Conference* in 1897. Herzl tried to interest both the Tsar of Russia and the Kaiser of Germany in his schemes, because both regarded the Jews within their borders as a "problem". Later *Herzl* formed the *Jewish Colonial Trust* , a bank to finance Jewish settlement in Palestine. Not all Jews were Zionist. Some believed that the establishment of such a state would only increase anti-semitism (hatred or dislike of Jews).

WARTIME PROMISES

During the *First World War* influential Zionists gained the support of *Lloyd*

George and *Woodrow Wilson*. In 1917 Britain issued the *Balfour Declaration*, a letter written by a cabinet minister, *Arthur Balfour*, which claimed that the British would work for "the establishment of Palestine as a national home for the Jewish people". *Britain* at the same time promised the Arabs self-government if they helped the British to defeat their Turkish masters, In one British government letter concerning the matter, vague wording led the Arabs to believe that one of their new states would be *Palestine*, then part of *Syria*. After the war, neither the Jews nor the Arabs received self-government (See Work Unit 15).

PALESTINE UNDER THE BRITISH

Palestine, which contained a large Arab and Jewish population, was taken over by *Britain* as a League of Nations mandate. The country was soon seething with discontent. The Arabs would probably never have agreed to a Jewish state but matters were made worse in their opinion by the flood of Jewish refugees from Europe let into the country by the British authorities as a result of the Balfour Declaration. In 1929 a quarrel about the *Wailing Wall* in *Jerusalem*, a spot sacred to both Jews and Arabs, caused riots between the two communities. The Jewish settlers answer was to form their own defence force, *Hagannah.*

In 1937 there was an *Arab Revolt* against British rule which had to be put down with troops. Sabotage by Arabs and counter-terror by Jewish organisations like *Irgun* and the *Stern Gang* reduced the country to a state of civil war. During the *Second World War*, Britain tried to restrict Jewish immigration but after 1945, when the details of the nazi holocaust became known (See Work Unit 22), world-wide sympathy for the Jews made it it became difficult to cut down their entry. The Arabs showed their anger and frustration by attacking Jewish *Kibbutz* (settlements).

FOUNDATION OF ISRAEL

Britain's Labour government (1945-51) was anti-imperialist; for example, it gave India its independence (See Work Unit 33). It did not want to inherit a Palestine torn by terrorism at a time when Britain was weak from the effects of fighting the war, When the *United Nations* suggested a *partition plan*, dividing Palestine into Arab and Jewish areas, the Arabs rejected the plan outright. The Jews accepted it, although some historians think the Jewish leaders were not sincere and really intended to take over the Arab regions.

The rejection of this plan caused the British to announce that they would withdraw from *Palestine* and hand it back to the UN in May, 1948. Zionist leaders at once set up the state of *Israel*. A war followed in which members of the *Arab League - Jordan, Egypt, Syria* and *Iraq* - attacked the Jewish state. The Arab leadership was divided in its aims, *King Abdullah* of *Jordan* wanted to add Arab Palestine to his own dominions. By 1949 the Israelis had won the war. About 750,000 Palestinians either fled from the country, or were driven out by the Israelis. They settled in makeshift camps in neighbouring *Jordan, Syria* and *Egypt.*

During this first *Arab-Israeli war* the UN representative sent to try to arrange a truce, *Count Bernadotte,* was murdered by Jewish terrorists. The final truce arranged for *Jerusalem* to be divided between *Israel* and *Jordan* (it is a holy city to both Muslim and Jew). Although Israel claimed the *Gaza Strip* (see map) she allowed Egypt "temporary" possession of it. *Russia* turned against Israel when she realised that the new state was a "client" of the USA; this was at the beginning of the Cold War.

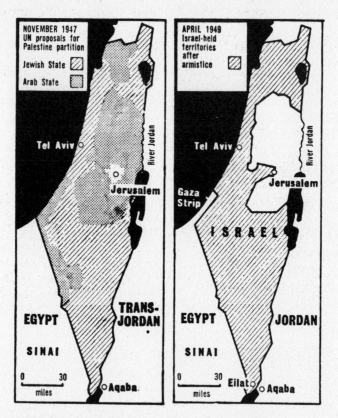

SUEZ AND THE SECOND ISRAELI WAR

David Ben Gurion, Israel's first prime minister, was soon faced by a "new" *Egypt.* In July, 1952, *Gamel Abdul Nasser* overthrew the corrupt *King Farouk* and arranged for the final evacuation of British troops. *Nasser* planned to modernise Egypt and unite the Arab countries in a firm alliance against Israel. As part of his modernisation schemes, he planned to build the *Aswan High Dam,* an important project which, by irrigating the *Nile Valley* would increase the cultivable land by 25% and help feed Egypt's rising population. Nasser asked the World Bank for funds to build the Dam but the Bank was under US influence and the US administration was suspicious of *Nasser* because of his open hostility towards *Israel.* His radio broadcasts condemned Israel on every occasion and he also allowed *fedayun* (an Arabic word meaning "self sacrificers") raiders to train in camps in the Gaza strip for attacks on Jewish kibbutz.

338

SUEZ NATIONALISATION

In 1955 the Israelis hit back with a large scale raid on these camps. The *Gaza Raid* destroyed a military encampment and killed 26 Egyptian soldiers. *Nasser* appealed to *Britain*, *France* and *the USA* for weapons to defend Egypt, claiming that his country was militarily weak against such aggression. They all refused for different reasons, the French because Nasser was supporting Algerian rebels (See Work Unit 30). *Nasser* then bought arms from *Czechoslovakia* and *Russia*. The US government declared this to be a pro-communist move and promptly cut off all aid to Egypt. This produced a crisis. Nasser nationalised the Anglo-French owned *Suez Canal Company*; the canal itself was under Egyptian control anyway and Israeli ships were excluded from using it. This action boosted the Egyptian leader's popularity with his own people and might have led to extra finance through dues on tankers using the canal.

OPERATION KADESH

Anthony Eden Britain's Conservative prime minister, believed *Nasser* to be a threat to peace in the Middle East. He likened him to Hitler and was determined not to use "appeasement" in Nasser's case; he had resigned from the Government over Chamberlain's appeasement policies in the 1930's. In September, 1956 *Eden* held secret meetings with the French prime minister, *Guy Mollet* and *David Ben Gurion* at which it was decided to assist Israel militarily when the Israelis attacked *Egypt* in order to deal with the fedayun menace. On 29 October 1957 the Israeli army opened its *Operation Kadesh*. This campaign involved capturing the *Sinai* peninsula, the *Gaza Strip* and *Sharm-el-Sheik*, the Egyptian base on the shores of the *Gulf of Akaba*. By 5 November the Israeli army had achieved all its objectives and captured large amounts of Russian and Czechoslovakian equipment from the Egyptians.

FRANCO-BRITISH INVASION

The Israeli success in the *Sinai Campaign* was partly due to the actions of Britain and France. Both countries pretended that the canal was in danger. They issued an ultimatum to both Israel and Egypt to stop fighting and, when this was ignored, landed troops at *Port Said* and captured *Ismailia*. At the same time they gave vital air support to the Israelis who were vastly outnumbered by the Egyptian airforce. In fact, as the British and French knew, it was no part of the Israeli plan to go anywhere near the Canal which in any case was blocked by *Nasser* with sunken ships. It was clear that there had been *collusion* (secret collaboration) between Britain, France and Israel. The British and French aim was to use the Israeli invasion as an excuse to overthrow Nasser.

U.S. INTERVENTION

In Britain there was an outcry from both the Labour opposition and Eden's own Conservative party. *Russia* demanded that the Franco-British force be withdrawn and talked of military action if they stayed. *President Eisenhower* was furious that the USA had not been consulted about the Suez invasion. He threatened to stop financial aid to Britain unless she withdrew her troops. Britain was facing a money crisis so she had to obey. Eden was forced to resign and British troops were brought out of Egypt. The French considered carrying on alone but eventually allowed a UN peace-keeping force to move into *Sinai* and *Sharm-el-Sheik*.

Nasser's position in the Arab world was strengthened by this fiasco. His troops had been badly beaten and none of his Arab allies had come to his aid. But Britain and France had been humiliated. Later French leaders, particularly *General de Gaulle* when he came to power, did not forgive the USA for Suez. It was one of the reasons why France withdrew her troops from NATO and made her own nuclear weapons . (See Work Unit 30). Israel, however, had gained an enormous amount of military prestige. She had also secured and enlarged her borders.

THE SIX DAY WAR

After *Suez*, Nasser still remained a dominant figure in the Arab world. He tried various unions between *Egypt* and *Syria* and *Egypt* and *Iraq* but both were shortlived. He interfered in the internal affairs of other Arab states, notably with the murder of *King Feisal* of Iraq in 1958. He also supported the *Palestine Liberation Front* (PLO), led by *Yasser Arafat*. The PLO aimed to return Palestine to the Arabs and create an Arab state. This underground force hi-jacked aircraft, planted bombs with devastating effects (the *Lydda Airport Massacre*) and murdered Israeli athletes at the *Munich Olympics* in 1972.

Fighting continued along the Israeli-Syria border with the Syrians shelling Israeli settlements from the *Golan Heights* and Israeli troops raiding inside Syria. In 1967 Nasser decided to make a decisive move to assert his pre-eminence in the Arab world. He ordered the UN peace-keeping force out of *Sinai* and *Sharm-el-Sheik* and closed the *Straits of Tiran* to Israeli shipping. Then he massed a large Egyptian army on the Egypt-Israel border. He gambled that Russia would veto any UN attempt to get the Straits reopened, and that the whole Arab world would join him if Egypt was attacked.

The Israeli reply was a devastating attack on *Egypt, Jordan* and *Syria*. Most of the Egyptian airforce and two-thirds of its army were destroyed in a matter of days. The Jordanians were driven out of *Old Jerusalem* and the Syrians off the *Golan Heights*. At the end of this *Six Days War* all three Arab countries surrendered. *Jordan* lost the *West Bank* region, *Syria* the *Golan Heights and Egypt* all lands east of the *Suez Canal*. Israel has since refused to give up these lands on the grounds of security. The United Nations, in its *Resolution 242* ordered her to do so but added that Israel was entitled to "secure and recognised frontiers".

Sporadic fighting continued on the *Suez Front* particularly after the Russians supplied the Egyptians with up to date anti-aircraft missiles and fighter planes. *King Hussein* of Jordan drove the PLO out of his country because its raids on Israeli territory were inviting Israeli retaliation. Because this happened in September, 1970, the PLO formed a fanatical branch of terrorists called *"Black September'*. It was this group which carried out the massacre at the Munich Olympics.

YOM KIPPUR WAR

In 1970 *Nasser* died and was succeeded by *Anwar Sadat*. *Sadat* sent Russian advisers home but demanded that Israel evacuate the *Sinai*. At the same time *Syria* campaigned for the return of the *Golan Heights*. When both these demands were rejected by Israel, *Israel, Syria, Jordan and Iraq* invaded Israel on 6 October 1973, the Jewish festival of *Yom Kippur* (The Day of Atonement). The Egyptians broke through the Israeli *Barlev Line*, whilst the Syrians captured a vital observation post, *Mount Hermon* on the *Golan Heights*. It was a critical moment for Israel, with her enemies triumphant and Russian supplies pouring in to make up Arab losses. After an initial hesitation, the USA began a massive airlift of equipment and supplies. This helped the Israeli army when it began its counter-strike. The Syrians were beaten and driven back towards *Damascus*, their capital. An Israeli army crossed the Suez Canal and got behind the Egyptians in a region known as the *Bitter Lakes*. With an entire Egyptian army trapped west of the canal and about to be wiped out, *Sadat* was forced to sue for peace. The war ended on 25 October when Israeli commandoes recaptured *Mount Hermon*.

The *Yom Kippur War* had lasting and world-wide repercussions. *Saudi Arabia, Kuwait, Libya, Bahrain and Iraq,* all leading members of the *Organisation of Petroleum Exporting Countries* (OPEC}, decided to use oil as weapon to force the west to put pressure on Israel to give up her conquests. OPEC quadrupled world oil prices, thus increasing inflation and balance of payment problems in the west. These economic effects continued throughout the 1970's.

EGYPT-ISRAELI PEACE TREATY

In 1977 *President Sadat* made peace with the Israelis after visiting Israel and speaking to the *Knesset* (Israeli Parliament). This agreement was organised and financed by the USA who hoped to safeguard her Middle Eastern oil supplies by a peace treaty which made a general war between Israel and the Arabs unlikely; without *Egypt*, the Arab states stood no chance of victory against the Israeli forces. In return *Egypt* received large amounts of US aid for her weak economy. She also agreed to allow Israeli shipping free access through *Eilat* (see map). *Israel* evacuated *Sinai* and promised to leave the *Gaza Strip* at a later date. The whole Arab world was dismayed by this treaty, partly the work of *President Jimmy Carter* of the USA. They condemned Sadat as a traitor and later he was murdered by his own troops in a sudden attack at a military review.

LEBANON AND PALESTINIAN UPRISING

In *Lebanon,* where civil wars raged between Christian and Muslim groups, both *Israel* and *Syria* intervened. In 1976 Syrian troops entered the country and defeated PLO forces who were supporting the Muslim groups. In 1982 Israel invaded Lebanon and drove the PLO out. In doing so their troops clashed with Syrians in the north of the country. Strong international pressure was put on Israel to withdraw. She did so after the US sent in a peace-keeping force of Americans marines. After suicide raids on the marine base in *Beirut*, the Lebanese capital, in which hundreds were killed, *President Reagan* ordered his men home. *Syria* then moved in troops to try to keep peace between the warring factions. This was not very successful and fighting continued.

In 1988 Palestinian bitterness at Israel's occupation of the *West Bank* and *Gaza Strip* led to riots and strikes. This was known as the Palestinian uprising or *Intifada*. Such unrest was dealt with brutally by Israeli troops, and TV pictures of several incidents caused an international outcry against the Israeli occupation. In December 1988 *Yasser Arafat* proclaimed the creation of a *Palestinian state* and called on Israel to negotiate a settlement. When he attempted to speak at the UN headquarters in *New York*, the US government refused him a visa on the grounds that he was a terrorist. Later *Arafat* addressed a special meeting of the UN assembly in *Geneva*.

SELF ASSESSMENT SECTION

1. Who organised the First Zionist Conference? Why did it meet in Europe?

2. What was the purpose of the Jewish Colonial Trust? How far was it successful?

3. What was the origin of "Black September" terrorism?

4. Which US President negotiated the peace treaty between Egypt and Israel?

5. What was Haganah?

6. Who is the leader of the PLO?

7. What is a Zionist?

8. What were the fedayun?

9. Name the UN peace negotiator killed by Jewish terrorists in 1948.

10. Who succeeded Nasser as ruler of Egypt? What happened to him?

11. Write short notes on these subjects:-

    Six Day War; UN Partition Plan; Yom Kippur War.

12. The Balfour Declaration stated that after the First World War,

    a)   Arabs could have self rule.
    b)   all Arab states, except Palestine, could have self rule.
    c)   The Palestinians could have a separate homeland.
    d)   the Jews could have their own state.
    e)   the Jews could have their own homeland.

It was issued to influence:-

a)   Turks.
b)   Germans.
c)   Americans.
d)   Arabs.
e)   British Jews
     (TICK THE CORRECT ANSWERS)

13. Explain the significance of UN Resolution 242. In what ways does it try to be fair to both Jew and Arab?

14. Read these sources, then answer the questions.

   A. "There may have been mistaken judgements in carrying out our policies, but the test is the motive.... What were out motives? We had objectives........First, we had a special part to play in preventing a general outbreak of war in the Middle East. Second, Nasser was a menace and must at least be checked. Third, the Canal had to be brought back under some kind of international control.......Right to the end of his life Eden believed that the Government he had led had done what was right. Because Hitler was not checked, 20 million people died, Eden was determined to see that it did not happen again".

   From "Suez, 1956 by Selwyn Lloyd,
   Foreign Secretary at the time of Suez. Published in 1978)

   B. "For the army officer all along was the one man who had no doubts. Ever since last spring *(of 1956),* colonels at selection boards, majors at TA drill halls, retired majors at Old Comrades' Association dinners, have been quite certain that the first international priority was to "give that pip-squeak Nasser a damn good kick in the pants".

   (British soldier engaged in the Suez operation.
   Quoted in "Suez and Sinai" by Harry Browne, Longman 1971).

   C. "Israel and Egypt are locked in conflict in that area *(Suez)*. The first and urgent task is to separate the combatants and to stabilize the position. That is our purpose. If the United Nations were then willing to take over the physical task of maintaining peace in that area, no one would be better pleased than we..."

   (Sir Anthony Eden in the House of Commons
   1 November 1956 Hansard

   D. "We were not successful in our wider objective; we did not bring about Arab-Israeli peace or restore control over the Canal...some successes were gained. The military weakness of the Egyptian forces were exposed..This had important consequences. From the day of Egyptian defeat in the Sinai desert the chances of a Nassar empire were scotched, not killed. Even so, the Sudan did not hesitate to resist the grasping demands which Nasser later made upon her northern boundary. It is unlikely that Nasser or any other Arab leader will readily undertake a war of extermination against Israel in the immediate future, without support from the outside".

(Sir Anthony Eden. 'Full Circle' Houghton Mifflin.)

E. "What he (*Nasser*) did was not to try to reduce the temperature in the cold war; what he did was to exploit it for Egypt's purposes. Therefore, Nasser's hands are not clean by any means...We must not believe that because the Prime Minister (*Eden*) is wrong Nasser is right. That is not the view of this side of the House (*the Labour opposition*). What has deeply offended us is that such wrongs as Nasser has done and such faults as he has have been covered by the bigger blunders of the British Government...We are satisfied that the art of diplomacy would have brought Nasser...to agree about the free passage of ships through the Canal"

(Aneurin Bevan's speech in House of Commons, 5 December 1956, Hansard).

a) Which sources are nearest the truth about the purposes for which Eden launched the Suez operation? Give reasons for your answer.
b) A and D were written years after the events. In what ways is such a view an advantage or a disadvantage?
c) Explain how sources A.C.D. and E might be biased.
d) Is source D correct in its assessment of the future in the Middle East? Explain how events since 1956 have confirmed, or contradicted,what Eden predicted.
e) What events in the years leading up to 1956 would have given British people the attitude to Nasser shown in B?

15.

A   The British Cabinet considers what to do about Palestine in February 1947.

7 February 1947: The Foreign Secretary reported that it was clear that the Arabs were opposed to Partition. The Arabs also demanded that there should be no further Jewish immigration into Palestine.
The Jews claimed that the Balfour Declaration meant that Britain had promised that a Jewish State would be established in the whole of Palestine.

The Cabinet then adopted a plan which would establish self-government in Palestine after a period of five years.

14 February 1947: The Foreign Secretary reported that both the Arabs and the Jews had refused to consider the plan agreed in the Cabinet on 7 February 1947. It was agreed that Britain should refer the problem to the judgement of the General Assembly of the United Nations.

Cabinet Papers

B.

THE UNCOVERED WAGON

('Vicky' Cartoon in News Chronicle, 28 April 1948.
Creech Jones was the British Colonial Secretary.
Ernest Bevin, the Foreign Secretary, is on the donkey).

 a)   How far is B. fair or unfair to the British government at the time? Use
   A. to explain your answer.

 b)   How satisfactory or unsatisfactory do you consider a political cartoon to
   be when dealing with a complex subject like the Palestine problem?
   What aspects of the problem has the artist left out?

16. Imagine you are EITHER a Jewish refugee trying to reach Palestine in 1946
OR a Palestinian refugee leaving the country in 1948. Describe your
experiences, and explain why you are leaving one country and fleeing to
another.

35

Russia since 1945

INTRODUCTION

A vital aspect of the Cold War was the weapons' technology race between the two super-powers. Put simply, which country had the best and most effective means of delivering nuclear weapons? The US led this race until 1953, when the Soviets exploded their first hydrogen bomb, and 1957 when they put the first man-made earth satellite, the Sputnik, into orbit. Any rocket which could do this was obviously powerful enough to deliver bombs to any part of the USA. From that moment the USA believed it was faced by the so-called 'missile gap' - the possibility that the Russians might have gained nuclear superiority. Russian Intercontinental Ballistic Missiles (ICBM's) might be able to destroy the missiles and B52 bombers on which the USA relied for her defence, Both President Eisenhower and his successor, President Kennedy, regarded this as a crisis and began to increase US expenditure on rocket research and defence.

The estimates of Russian strength, and the American reaction to them, were based on false information. The US strike capacity far exceeded that of the Soviets at the time. But the fact that the US leaders believed their country was at a disadvantage is the background to an understanding of the Cuban Missile Crisis of 1962. The fact that the Russian leader, Nikita Khrushchev, knew that his country was inferior is also a factor. Khrushchev's policy of peaceful co-existence, which calculated that capitalism would collapse from its own 'rottenness', had been accompanied by a decrease in Russian armament expenditure between 1955 and 1960. By 1960 Russia was ringed with US missile bases in Europe and the Middle East. In these circumstances, Khruschev saw the bitter quarrel between the USA and Castro's Cuba as an opportunity to redress the imbalance and perhaps score a propaganda victory. Castro had just defeated a US-backed invasion by Cuban exiles in the 'Bay of Pigs'. He appealed to Khrushchev for weapons to defend his island and his regime.

Khrushchev decided on a gambler's throw. He would do far more than supply Cuba with some weapons for her defence. Indeed, Cuba was merely a pawn in the game he was going to play. He decided to set up missile sites in Cuba capable of launching surface to air anti-aircraft missiles (SAM's). This would give the Soviets a base within a 100 miles of the American mainland and a foothold in Latin

America, traditionally regarded by the USA as her own sphere of influence. What the Russian leader did not expect was the rapid and hostile reaction of President Kennedy. The 'Bay of Pigs' humiliation was not something the US leader intended to repeat. This time he would be tough towards communist expansion. The US navy was ordered to blockade Cuba and stop all Russian merchant ships which might be carrying equipment for the missile sites. Krushchev warned Kennedy not to stop a ship. The world stood on the brink of nuclear war. After a few tense days, the Russian leader gave way. The missile sites were dismantled.

It seemed a great US victory, although it dismayed America's European allies who were not consulted about Kennedy's actions. It was probably the end of the Cold War because the two super-powers had been too near the brink. A 'hot-line' was set up so that future Russian and American leaders could talk to each other if a crisis seemed to be brewing. Since that time there has been a clear progress on disarmament , from the Test Ban treaty of 1963, through the SALT.talks and the reducing of weapons, men and tanks by Gorbachev's Russia in 1980's.

This progress has been accompanied by radical changes inside Russia itself. Khruchchev was succeeded by Leonid Brezhnev who presided over a static period in Soviet history. Life was just a repressive as under Stalin but not so dangerous; fallen leaders were not shot. In the mid-1980's Mickhail Gorbachev proposed, not only a new political system, but a Russia where Christians were not second class citizens, telephones were not tapped and a TV programme called 'May I Speak?' would allow Russians to do just that. However, as one of his supporters said, 'There would be chaos and anarchy if we decided to create other parties'. A free Russia was to remain a one-party Russia. Lenin would have expected no less.

NIKITA KHRUSHCHEV

Stalin's long reign of terror ended in March, 1953, with his death. Towards the end his grip of Soviet life and politics was complete. The purges continued and the Communist Party Congress did not meet between 1939 and 1952. Stalin's departure was followed by a *triumvirate* (rule by three). Of these *Nicolai Bulganin* was little more than a figurehead. The other two, *Georgi Malenkov* and *Nikita Khrushchev* battled for power until 1957 when victory went to Khrushchev. Khrushchev was a communist official and agricultural expert who had become Stalin's favourite by carrying out his policies ruthlessly. There was only one important casuality of the changeover. *Laurenti Beria* , the Chief of Police, was shot, probably because of his unpopularity with the army.

DE-STALINISATION

In 1956 Khrushchev made a long speech at the *Twentieth Congress* of the communist party. In it he denounced many of what he called Stalin's 'mistakes' as far back as the death of Lenin. This speech was never published in Russia but its main points became known both inside and outside the country. It caused a stir in Soviet satellite countries and may have helped to lead to risings in *Poland* and *Hungary* (See Work Unit 29), for no public criticism of the dictator had been heard for at least 20 years. Khrushchev's speech began a process of downgrading

Stalin from the high position his 'personality cult' had given him. A number of towns named after him had their names changed and his body was removed from its position beside Lenin in Red Square, Moscow.

SPUTNIK

Khrushchev set about improving Russian agriculture. He knew that Stalin's *collectivisation programme* had caused, not only misery, but inefficiency. He began to exploit new lands in *Kazakhstan* but the results were not encouraging. Fortunately for the new leader, it was at this time that the effects of Stalin's industrialisation began to bite. Russian industry scored a major 'first' with a successful space programme which startled the world. The Russians, helped by German rocket scientists captured at the end of the Second World War, put the first artificial satellite round the earth in 1957. This *Sputnik* was followed by an even greater triumph when *Yuri Gagarin* became the first human being to orbit the earth in 1961. Such rocket power, which could also be used for launching nuclear weapons, shocked the USA. Successive American administrations conducted an expensive space research programme which led in 1969 to the US putting the first men on the *moon*.

PEACEFUL CO-EXISTENCE

Khrushchev was anxious to improve living conditions for the Russian people. He knew this could be done only by reducing expenditure on armaments. As a convinced communist, he believed that the capitalist system was doomed to collapse through its own 'rottenness'. Before the inevitable happened, he proposed that communism and capitalism should peacefully 'co-exist' in peaceful competition. The policy of *peaceful co-existence* faced up to the facts of nuclear war because both powers now possessed hydrogen weapons of awesome power. Peaceful co-existence also had good propaganda value, because it pleased many Russians, Europeans and Americans and also impressed non-aligned countries who took it as a sign of Soviet good intentions.

U2 SPY PLANE

In 1959 Khrushchev initiated a *Seven Year Economic Plan* which depended on using money saved from armament expenditure. He travelled to the USA where he met *President Eisenhower* . Later he put a plan for general disarmament to the UN Assembly. In 1960, however, a summit meeting between Khrushchev and other world leaders in *Paris* was broken up when news came that a US spy aircraft, on a regular photographic mission over Russia, had been shot down and its pilot, *Gary Powers*, captured. Whether Khrushchev knew this would happen, or was taken by surprise will never be known. He walked out of the conference at the news, condemning the US for such activities. *Powers* was put on trial and imprisoned for a time.

CUBAN MISSILE CRISIS 1962

In the opinion of US leaders, their *containment policy* regarding Russia (See Work Unit 29) depended on having a superiority over the Soviets in strategic weapons and defence in general. This had led to an *arms' race* which by the late 1950's the Americans believed they were losing. This sprang partly from the success of *Sputnik* , which suggested rocket power capable of dropping nuclear devices on most major cities in the USA and wiping out the American's own nuclear strike force. In such circumstances the hostile attitude of *John Foster Dulles* , the US Secretary of State towards Russia was nicknamed *brinkmanship* by his opponents because he seemed to be bringing the world to the brink of war, especially when he talked of 'liberating' the people of eastern Europe. In fact, by the early 1960's the US strike capability was far superior to that of Russia and Khrushchev was worried at the imbalance of forces in the US's favour.

CUBAN REVOLUTION

It was this fact which led him to a most dangerous exhibition of brinkmanship in 1962. When *Castro* won his revolution in *Cuba* and drove out the US-sponsored *Batista* (See Work Unit 9) the US reaction was hostile. They had been supporters of Batista in the civil war which had raged since 1952 and American 'Big Business' was deeply involved in the island economy. Their first move was to support the invasion of Cuba by anti-Castro forces; this was the ill-fated *Bay of* Pigs expedition (See Work Unit 27). Castro, who until then had been a typical Latin American nationalist, now announced that he was a *Marxist-Leninist ,* probably to get help from Russia in face of such a powerful enemy to his north. From that time events drove Cuba into the Soviet camp. In February 1962 *Cuba* was excluded from the *Organisation of American States* after strong pressure from the USA. Next month, *President Kennedy* put an embargo on US trade with Cuba and this led to a rapid deterioration in Cuba's economic situation.

SAM MISSILES IN CUBA

By May, 1962 Castro had signed a trade agreement with Russia and in August, after a visit to Moscow by his brother *Raul* US intelligence sources reported that there were Soviet SAM missile sites being constructed on the island. This meant that *Cuba* was being given a nuclear strike capability within 100 miles of the US coast. Khrushchev's aim seems to have been to improve Russia's overall strategic position although he later claimed that Russia could hit American cities from their own homeland if necessary. The move may also have been a bid for prestige and power in an area always regarded as its own sphere of influence by the USA. Both *Castro* and *Khrushchev* claimed that these missiles were only for defence against another possible invasion from the US mainland.

U.S. BLOCKADE

In October *Kennedy* announced that the US had evidence of *Russian missile sites* in Cuba, as well intelligence indicating that Russian merchant ships were sailing towards the island with aircraft, weapons and equipment. He ordered US regular troops to *Florida* the nearest American state to Cuba, and put a naval blockade around the island to stop the Russian ships. *Khrushchev* at first denied that there were any rocket sites on Cuba. Then he changed tack and warned the Americans not to stop Russian ships.

In this crisis, the two leaders acted more sensibly behind the scenes. *Khrushchev* ordered the ships to slow down and *Kennedy* began to talk privately to the Russian leader. Kennedy was sensitive on any matter concerning *Cuba* after the Bay of Pigs failure. He also calculated that his Democratic party might lose the 1962 Congressional Elections if the missiles were installed so near US territory. Khrushchev may have hoped to get the missiles operational before they were discovered by the Americans. He certainly did not expect such a strong reaction from the US President.

TEST-BAN AND 'HOT-LINE'

On 27 October 1962 Kennedy promised not to invade, or sponsor an invasion of *Cuba* . The following day Khrushchev ordered the missile sites to be dismantled. The Cubans, and Castro, felt let down by the Russians. Such a serious crisis led to a lessening of tension in the Cold War. In August, 1963 Russia and the USA signed a *Test Ban Treaty* which stopped all nuclear tests except those held underground. A direct *communications* link, the so-called *Hot-Line*, was set up between *Moscow* and *Washington* to try to avoid an accidental firing of nuclear weapons due to a failure in communications. Both sides claimed victory in the Cuban Crisis, Kennedy by standing firm against Russian threats and Khrushchev in managing to keep the peace in the face of American 'war-mongering'.

THE CZECH CRISIS

The regime of *Alexander Dubcek* in Czechoslovakia became too liberal for the Russians. *Leonid Brezhnev* and *Alexie Osygin*, the two Russian leaders after Khrushchev's fall in 1964, were worried in particular about the new press freedoms which they feared would be used for criticism of other communist-bloc countries. At a meeting of the *Warsaw Pact* allies in 1968, *Poland, East Germany, Hungary,Rumania and Bulgaria*, issued a Russian-inspired *'Warsaw Letter'* , calling upon the Czechs to suppress 'anti-socialist' forces in the country.

When this was ignored, 200,000 Warsaw pact troops *invaded Czechoslovakia* on 20-21 August. The Czechs had promised not to put up military resistance; in any case it would have been of little use against such a well-organised occupation. The people resorted to widespread demonstrations, secret radio broadcasts and anti-Russian slogans daubed on walls, to show their feelings. *Dubcek* was arrested and taken to Moscow but later returned to Czechoslovakia where he was progressively demoted. Russia had maintained her grip on a vital strategic area at the expense of showing the world that the Soviets were not prepared to allow eastern European countries to change their political systems. (See also Work Unit 29).

SALT AND DETENTE

After 1969 the USA and Russia entered into negotiations to limit the spread of nuclear weapons and reduce their numbers. *Strategic Arms Limitation Talks* (SALT) continued well into the 1970's. This slowness to reach agreement was due partly to the fact that improvements in weapons' techniques often posed new problems of control and, in particular, inspection. At the same time, *Brezhnev*, now sole leader of Russia, started negotiations to get the western European countries to accept the boundaries established at the end of the Second World War.

The so-called *Final Act* of the SALT agreement was signed at *Helsinki* in 1975. It started an era of what was dubbed *Detente*, that is, a relaxation of tension between east and west. Detente involved recognising the "Iron Curtain" boundaries established in 1945 in Europe in return for a promise by the Soviets that they would show a greater concern for *human rights*. In spite of this promise, the persecution of people who criticised the Russian system, called *dissidents*,continued under Brezhnev. The only badly treated racial group allowed to leave Russia during the 1970's were the *Jews*; 100,000 left the Soviet Union with official permission, although many more remained in labour camps or under other forms of detention.

Brezhnev's *Five Year Plan* (1971-5) tried to shift the balance of the Russian economy slightly away from heavy industry and towards the production of consumer goods. It was not successful due to inefficiency, bureaucracy and widespread corruption by state officials. It was also hampered by serious failures in 1971-2 when first, *frost* and then *drought* , killed off the main crops. The Soviets were forced to buy grain from the USA and Canada and this caused a drain of Russian gold reserves which led to *inflation*. When Brezhnev died in 1983 he was succeeded by Andropov, a KGB official who had helped Khrushchev crush the Hungarian rising. He seemed to be a reformer but died before he could prove himself.

GORBACHEV

After a short interlude with the aged *Chernenko*, the position of Party Secretary was taken over by *Mickhail Gorbechev* who instituted a new era in Soviet history. First, he announced that his policy was *glasnost* , a Russian word meaning 'openness'. Russia would cease to be the closed society of the Stalin age; free discussion, TV and radio coverage, would be allowed as in western countries. Second, the Soviet economy, stagnating because of bureaucratic methods, was to be revitalised by *Perestroika* (economic reform). Both policies led to what appeared to be a liberalisation of life inside Russia and an attempt to reduce tension between the Soviet Union and the outside world. Gorbachev announced a phased withdrawal of Russian troops from *Afghanistan* - invaded in 1979 to support a communist regime - and in successive agreements with the USA, removal of intermediate weapons from central Europe, and a reduction in Soviet forces attached to the Warsaw Pact, 1988.

NEW POLITICAL SYSTEM

Gorbachev set about tackling the problems of Russia, summed up by one Russian writer as, 'a poorly developed country encircled by missiles - just some sort of political monster, no more'. This man was allowed to speak on TV; in itself this was a sign of glasnost,. In 1988 Gorbachev announced that a new Parliamentary body elected more fairly, was to be set up to counter-balance the power of the party. It would have a President and would elect a 400-500 strong inner Parliament to legislate effectively; Stalin had increased the size of Congress to about 5,000 and communist party membership to 18,000,000 thereby making them too large to be effective. Gorbachev acknowledged the extreme diversity of nationalities within the Soviet Union, promising each one more political and cultural freedom. This encouraged demonstrations in *Armenia*, where there was racial strife, and *Estonia*, where there were demands for independence. Gorbachev also agreed to give the Russian Church back some of the property confiscated in 1917 and allowed it to celebrate its millennium in 1988. In March 1989, Russia held its first 'open' election in which voters were given a free choice of communist party candidates. This resulted in victory for a number of reformers including *Boris Yeltsin*, who defeated the communist 'old guard' opposed to "glasnost". Such extraordinary results may prove a turning point in Russian, and world, history.

SELF-ASSESSMENT SECTION

1. What was the "missile gap"?

2. What does "glasnost" mean?

3. Name the first man to orbit the earth.

4. Who was Gary Powers?

5. What is the "hot-line"?

6. What was the significance of the "Warsaw Letter"?

7. Name a Russian state affected by racial tension in recent years.

8. Which country did Russia invade in 1979?

9. What was the Russian Church allowed to do in 1988?

10. What was a Sputnik?

11. Put the correct details (by letter) against these names.

1. LAURENTO BERIA.	A.	Russian figurehead
2. NICOLAI BULGANIN	B.	Signed Final Act in Helsinki
3. NIKITA KHRUSHCHEV	C.	Russian Chief of Police
4. FIDEL CASTRO	D.	Initiated reforms in Russia
5. LEONID BREZHNEV	E.	Favoured peaceful co-existence
6. MICHAIL GORBACHEV	F.	Ruled with Khrushchev for a time
7. GEORGI MALENKOV	G.	Ruler of Cuba after revolution

12. What do these initials stand for? Write a sentence or two describing ONE of them.

ICBM   SALT   OAS

13 Detente was:-

    a)   An alliance between Russia and the west.
    b)   An easing of tension between Russia and the west.
    c)   A means of limiting the spread of nuclear weapons.
    d)   A proposal for complete disarmament.
    e)   A proposal to limit NATO and Warsaw Pact forces.
        (TICK THE CORRECT ANSWER)

14. The 1963 Test Ban treaty banned:-

    a)   All nuclear tests.
    b)   Weapons research.
    c)   Space programmes.
    d)   Nuclear tests on the surface or in the atmosphere.
    e)   Underground nuclear tests.
        (TICK THE CORRECT ANSWER)

15. Explain why it is easier to find out about life in Russia now than it was in the time of Brezhnev or Krushchev.

16. Imagine you are a Russian aged 60. Describe the changes you have experienced in your life.

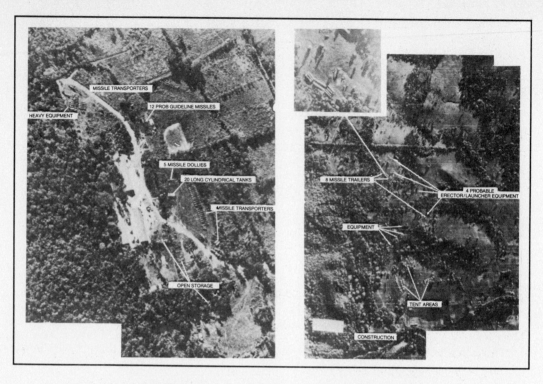

17. The above photographs were issued by the United States Embassy in London on 23 October 1962 and published in the "Times" the following day.
Look at them carefully and then answer the questions.

    a)   Where were these photographs taken?
    b)   What do they show?
    c)   Why did they cause alarm in the USA?
    d)   Describe the course of events which followed shortly after the publication of these photographs.

Answers

Note. In the answers requiring several sentences of explanation possible scores are indicated by *levels of response 1,2 and 3*. These can be only a rough guide but indicate that level 1 would be a less satisfactory answer than one awarded level 3. Simple factual answers, designed to test how much the reader has learnt from the Work Unit, which could merit only level 1, are unmarked. Level 2 and 3 answers are indicated by (2) and (3) printed after them. Of course, the actual marks awarded would depend on the marking scheme adopted for the particular paper. Readers should aim to improve on the author's answers with level 4 and 5 responses! Essay-type answers cannot be demonstrated in the confines of a book this size. They should be attempted by reference to the appropriate Work Unit(s) and also from the reader's previous knowledge of the subject.

WORK UNIT 1

1. Because Bismarck had made a speech saying that policies could not be carried through by speeches but by 'blood and iron'.
2. Because the Prussian army was well trained and efficient and had been devastatingly successful against Austria in 1866 (2).
3. Austria-Hungary.
4. Albrecht von Roon.
5. Helmut von Moltke.
6. Railways.
7. The Six Weeks war between Austria and Prussia.
8. The Spanish had exiled Queen Isabella because of her misgovernment.
9. Because Leopold was a member of the Hohenzollern royal family of Prussia. His accession to the Spanish throne would have placed Hohenzollerns on two of France's frontiers, the Spanish and German, instead of one, and so encircled France with potentially hostile countries (2).
10. Sedan, where Napoleon III surrendered with this troops.
11. B.
12. B.
13. 1C 2E 3A 4H 5F 6J 7I 8G 9B 10D
14 a) Germany's victory over France.
    b) Because Paris had been besieged by the Germans and its inhabitants had suffered bombardment and starvation (2).
    c) Bismarck aimed to isolate France and deprive her of allies. In essence, this meant concluding treaties with Russia and Austria, the only continental countries powerful enough to help France (2).
    d) The German annexation of the French provinces of Alsace and Lorraine which remained both a material loss and a deep humiliation to France (2).
15-19. Essay answers.

WORK UNIT 2

1. 'Progress, liberalism and recent civilisation'.
2. The German states.
3. Catholics who refused to accept the Doctrine of Papal Infallibility.
4. Ferdinand Lasalle.
5. The Centre Party.
6. Social Democratic Labour Party (the Socialists).
7. The National Labour Party.
8. Werner von Siemens.
9. A group of industrialists who fixed prices and established quotas to prevent over-production.
10. The Doctrine states that the Pope cannot be wrong when he speaks on doctrinal and spiritual matters because of divine guidance.
11. A.
12. B.
13. 1C 2A 3D 4H 5F 6E 7I 8G 9B.
14. a) Bismarck.
    b) The Kaiser. He is shown wearing a crown.
    c) The German empire.
    d) The Kaiser disagreed with Bismarck's policies, in particular his friendship with Russia and his determination not to build a powerful navy in case it roused the hostility of Britain. By contrast, the Kaiser wanted a large navy and planned to offset Russian influence in the Balkans by strengthening ties with Turkey. He also favoured less persecution of socialists.(3).
15-17. Essay answers.

WORK UNIT 3

1. George Washington.
2. Founding Fathers.
3. President Thomas Jefferson.
4. South Carolina.
5. Abraham Lincoln.
6. Northern officials sent to administer the southern states during the so-called Reconstruction period. Southerners claimed they were penniless adventurers who arrived with little more than they could carry in a carpetbag. (2).
7. Andrew Carnegie.
8. In the Middle West.
9. A doctrine proclaimed by President Monroe which stated that no European power was to interfere in the affairs of North or South America.
10. Theodore Roosevelt. To gain control of the land on which to build the Panama Canal, vital to move American warships quickly between the Pacific and Atlantic oceans. (2).
11. C.
12. C, D, A, B.
13. B.
14. a) It was probably written by a southerner because it represented the distinctly southern view that secession (disunion) was better than freeing the slaves.

b) By wanting to create 'free' states from new territories thus giving the north power and influence in Congress.

c) The language is emotive and extreme i.e. 'horrors' and 'the incendiary's torch', and is designed to frighten the reader and stir his/her prejudices about the consequence of emancipating the slaves (3).

d) Yes, because the writer states that disunion is preferable to the 'horror' of emancipation.

e) Burn down the houses of white people and engage in murder, robbery, and by implication, rape. The last word was too emotive for even this writer to use. (3).

15. a) Its subject is the occupation of the southern states by Northern armies during the Reconstruction period after the Civil War.

b) The Southern States.

c) The solid vote by the south for the Democratic party. This was a factor in US politics for many years and was due to the Republican Party being the government. which fought and won the civil war. (2).

d) The bag which envelopes most of the figures in this drawing refers to the nickname 'Carpetbaggers' (See answer to Question 6). The soldiers and weapons make the point that it is only military power which keeps the Carpetbag administrations going in the south. (2).

e) The artist was against the Reconstruction policy. He/she shows the south as a women being burdened by men - a clear emotive point - and shows the armed men marching through a desolate landscape, ruined by the war and, therefore, by definition, by the North. To complete the condemnation, the main figure sitting in the bag is General (later President) U.S. Grant, the North's most successful soldier during the Civil war (3).

16. a) Japan.

b) The point was probably that the Filipinos were Catholics and this Church was disliked and condemned by most Protestants. Both writers of these Sources appear to be Protestants, or to favour the Protestant viewpoint. (2).

c) Two reasons are given, that the Filipinos were not fit to govern themselves, and the islands were essential for the rich trade with China. Clearly the latter reason was the most important to US businessmen who had been trying to 'open up' China and Japan to trade for most of the 19th century. (2).

d) Part 4 of Source A. and the final sentence of Source B.

e) Source A. The point is that McKinley, as President, was responsible for the annexation of the Phillipines and needed to justify it to the American people and the world. The writer of Source B, had far less responsibility, and may have been expressing a personal viewpoint or trying to please his voters. (3).

17-19. Essay answers.

WORK UNIT 4

1. He was called the 'Liberator' because he freed the serfs.
2. Tsarist secret police.
3. Students and other intellectuals who went to live in the countryside to try and gain the support of the peasants for their liberal programme. The word is Russian and means 'To the People'.

4. Bolshevik.
5. An organised massacre of Jews, usually with official approval. The word means 'destruction'.
6. Poles, Finns, Ukrainians.
7. 'Big Bulgaria' was split into three by the decisions of the Congress of Berlin - a smaller independent Bulgaria, Eastern Rumelia and a province returned to Turkey.
8. The Japanese fleet commanded by Admiral Togo.
9. President Theodore Roosevelt of the USA.
10. Austria.
11. 1D 2C 3B 4E 5F 6G 7A.
12. D.
13-15. Essay answers.
16. a) Russia.
    b) Britain. She did not want the 'dogs' i.e. the smaller Balkan states, to drive the Turk out of Europe, nor did she want a large Bulgarian satellite state of Russia in the Balkans. This increase in Russian influence would threaten her vital interests in the Straits, Mediterranean and Middle East. The policeman's distinctive British-style helmet probably refers to the 'keep the peace' role adopted by the British fleet when it anchored off Constantinople as the Russian advance neared the city. (3).
    c) Bosnia, Herzegovina, Serbia and Montenegro - the names are on the collars.
    d) Turkey, the traditional enemy of these peoples, who had ruled them with varying degrees of brutality for centuries. The figure is wearing the traditional dress of a 19th century Turkish official. (2).
    e) Austria.
    f) Austria played a key role in the events following the war. Her main interest was to restrict Russian influence in the Balkans where several independent states, notably Serbia, were opposed to her multi-national empire, including, as it did, many Balkan peoples. At the Congress of Berlin, whose decisions overthrew the terms of the Treaty of San Stefano, Austria took over the administration of Bosnia-Herzegovina, a mainly Serbian region, and so infuriated Serbia. (3).
17-19. Essay Answers.

WORK UNIT 5

1. Because this was the section of the Triangle of Trade which involved transporting negro slaves to the West Indies and the southern states of America. Over-crowding on the ships led to much disease and many deaths.
2. Ghana.
3. Sir Garnet Wolseley.
4. Tripoli and Cyrenaica.
5. The British Government, following a private move by the British prime minister, Benjamin Disraeli.
6. The Mahdi.
7. A British army led by Lord Kitchener.
8. Because they found wind conditions in the Red Sea variable and difficult.

9. Arabi Pasha.
10. Sir Evelyn Baring, later Lord Cromer.
11. B.
12. Essay answer.
13. Uganda (A) Eritrea (D) Madagascar (B) Cameroon (C) Tanganyika (C) Egypt (A) The Congo (E).
14. 1D 2E 3H 4A 5C 6B 7F 8G.
15-16. Essay answers.
17. a) Source A. The writer implies that the canal is not vital to British interests. He also reminds his audience that Britain ruled India long before the canal was built.
    b) Britain intervened commercially, to protect her general Middle Eastern trade, and strategically, to safeguard the sea-routes to India, Ceylon and Burma, Australia and New Zealand (2).
    c) Source C. It uses the same arguments as Source B. but it is couched in stronger and more unequivocal terms. (2).
    d) Underlying all the sources is the importance of India to Britain.
18-19. Essay answers.

WORK UNIT 6
1. The Dutch.
2. To break free from British rule; the Cape had been taken over by Britain as part of the general peace settlement after the Napoleonic wars ended in 1815 (2).
3. European businessmen and their workers engaged in gold mining around Johannesburg.
4. Marthinus Steyn.
5. The Voortrekkers (Boers).
6. A despatch sent by Lord Milner, British High Commissioner, to the Colonial Secretary, Joseph Chamberlain, claiming that the Uitlanders were little more than 'helots' - the Greek word for slaves in Sparta.(2).
7. Kaiser William of Germany.
8. He fled into Portuguese controlled territory.
9. Lobengula.
10. To enter the country after the Uitlanders had rebelled, using the rebellion as an excuse to restore law and order.
11. Essay answers.
12. 1C 2D 3B 4G 5I 6H 7A 8F 9E.
13. a) A British officer carrying out the official party policy of destroying farm houses believed to be used by Boer commandos for their raids on the British army and its installations. (2)
    b) That of Lord Kitchener. the British commander in South Africa, whose task was to destroy Boer guerilla resistance and force them to surrender.
    c) Suspects may have used it, but it was also policy to destroy farms so that they could not be used later.
    d) The Boers certainly did not forget the burnings or the concentration camps in which their women and children were detained. Whole generations were infected with a dislike of all things British and a determination to gain their independence. (2).

14-15. Essay answers.
16. a) The British army authorities.
    b) Boer women and children whose homes had been destroyed by the British.
    c) They were used to house the homeless after such destruction.
    d) Essay answer.
17. A.
18. Essay answer.

WORK UNIT 7

1. The Senate (or Upper House) and the Chamber of Deputies (or Lower House).
2. The Senate.
3. Ferdinand de Lesseps.
4. The old French monarchy and its system of government.
5. Bordeaux.
6. The Catholics had to form Associations of Public Worship if they wished to run their cathedrals and churches and this was the French name for them.
7. He was offered the crown but refused to have the tricolour as his flag, preferring the old royal flag.
8. Jean Juares.
9. A French novelist who wrote a pamphlet, 'J'accuse' in which he attacked the conviction of Dreyfus and poured scorn on the judges and the accusing officers. He was sentenced to prison for this but fled abroad. (2).
10. Jules Ferry, who was an anti-clerical determined to free French education of all Church influence. (2).
11. A.
12. 1G 2D 3E 4A 5C 6B 7I 8F 9H.
13-16. Essay answer.
17. a) The Communards.
    b) The tricolour was the flag of Republican France. The Red Flag was a symbol of workers' revolution. (2).
    c) Women were fighting as well men, mainly because it was a battle fought inside the city.

    d) The writer was strongly opposed to the Communards. He accuses them of sacrificing all noble feelings and ideal - justice, charity, humanity, prudence, decency and common sense - and allows them by implication only the virtue of courage. Their beliefs are condemned as mere 'party spite' and their motives are ascribed to vanity and fanaticism. The Republican soldiers are described as 'regular troops' and their progress through the city as an occupation, not an invasion or seizure. The utter devastation left by these 'regular troops' is not mentioned. (3).
18. Essay answers.

WORK UNIT 8

1. Sebastopol.
2. Russia and Austria.
3. The Ottoman empire (Turkey).

4. Because of the Turkish massacres of Christians following a rebellion in Bulgaria. The Tsar proclaimed his intention to drive the Turk out of Europe. (2).
5. France.
6. Franz-Joseph of Austria and Tsars Nicholas I, Alexander II and III and Nicholas II.
7. As an outlet on to the Aegean Sea and so to the Mediterranean.
8. A group of army officers who rebelled against the Sultan in 1908 and tried to establish a slightly more democratic government in Turkey.
9. Christians, Catholics, Muslims, and Jews.
10. An agreement between Britain and the Nationalist regime of Turkey which recognised the latter as the legitimate government.
11. 1C 2F 3A 4H 5G 6D 7E 8B.
12. D.
13. Essay answer.
14. a) A. is Austria, B is Russia and F is Turkey. Turkey wanted to hold on to her European territories. Russia wished to dominate the Balkans in order to gain easy access to the Mediterranean and Middle East, Austria to offset Russian influence and decrease nationalist tension amongst her own subject peoples. (2).
    b) Bulgaria.
    c) Because it had been partitioned into three parts at the Congress of Berlin.
    d) Bosnia-Herzegovina, which was taken over by Austria in 1908.
    e) Austria (A) and Serbia (D) quarrelled about freedom for the Serbs under Austrian rule and also in economic matters, notably the 'pig war'. (2).
15. a) The Balfour Declaration.
    b) Both Arabs and Jews thought that they would get at least self-government after the Allied victory. The Jews worldwide, particularly in the USA, were more inclined to help the Allied cause, and the Arab staged a revolt against Turkish rule. (2).
    c) The League's scheme of mandated territories. This made Britain the ruling power in Palestine. In 1948-49, after the final British withdrawal, the Jews defeated the Arabs and founded the state of Israel. The Palestinian Arabs became stateless and, in many cases, homeless (2).
16-17. Essay answers.

WORK UNIT 9

1. Ferdinand VII.
2. Brazil.
3. Because he led successful liberation movements in several Latin American provinces.
4. Chile.
5. Fulgencio Batista.
6. Emperor Maximilian.
7. Emilio Zapata.
8. Luis Drago, Foreign Minister of Argentina, declared that no nation had the right to collect debts from other nations by force, as the US maintained it could do.

9. Theodore Roosevelt, the US President , announced that, as a corollary (follow-up) to the Monroe Doctrine, the USA might have to act as 'policemen' if Latin American states were guilty of 'wrongdoing' or 'impotence'. (2).
10. A Latin American description of the USA.
11. Essay answer.
12. a) The author was probably American. He says he looked 'in vain' for Americans and American ships and financial institutions. It is clear that this is what he wanted to find. On the literary side, the source gives away the author's nationality when he uses the word 'sidewalk' instead of pavement; the former is the American word for such walkways. (3).
    b) Because, as the author remarks, the British had played a major part in Argentina's economic development, supplying inventions, money and manpower to build her factories, mines and railways. (2).
    c) Cattle
    d) Refrigerated ships, which meant that meat could be shipped to Europe in good condition. Hitherto only hides had been exported. (2).
    e) The USA, following the closure of its frontier in the west, and with its industries well-developed, began to invest heavily in Argentina and other Latin American states. Britain, meanwhile, was weakened economically by the First World War and had to sell off many of her investments in Latin America. (3).
13. 1H 2G 3F 4A 5B 6C 7D 8E
14. C.
15. a) The warships and the arsenal of weapons on display refer to the USA's military involvement in the Panama region, where a canal was considered vital for the concept of a 'two-ocean navy' which could move quickly between the Atlantic and Pacific oceans. The shovels refers to the plan to continue work on the canal project, which had been started by European investors but had run into practical difficulties involving difficult terrain and disease, mainly malaria. (3).
    b) Roosevelt's 'doctrine' maintained that the USA had the right to interfere in Latin America affairs (See answer to question 9). Such a doctrine would supply the 'gangplank' for US involvement in Panama. (2).
    c) It refers to the Isthmus of Panama, and, probably, to the new state of Panama, formed after the rebellion against Columbia.
    d) It seems certain that the artist was against Roosevelt's policy, probably because he was a supporter of the rival Democratic party; the ship has the trunk and outline of an elephant's head and the elephant is the symbol of the Republican Party of which Roosevelt was then the leader. The Republicans are also pinpointed by the 'GOP' flag, 'Grand Old Party' being a Republican nickname. The words 'Coup d'etat', placed near the US flag, are probably a reference to the USA's swift support of a rebellion against a lawful government. (3).
16. Essay answer.

WORK UNIT 10

1. The Chinese empire.
2. All non-Chinese peoples.
3. To trade in opium which they brought from India.

4. Conquerors from Manchuria, who supplied both emperors and a ruling class for China from 1644 until 1911.
5. The 'Arrow' was a British Ship seized by Chinese officials on suspicion of smuggling. This incident caused the British to take military action against the Chinese. (2).
6. Chinese labourers forced to work abroad for the European powers with bases in China as part of the peace settlement imposed on the Chinese after the Second Opium War, 1856-8 (2).
7. Empress Tze Hsi.
8. Any concession made by the Chinese government to one foreign nation automatically applied to all the others with interests in China.
9. Attempts were made to carry out economic, educational and social changes in China.
10. From their physical training and their name, 'Society of Righteous and Harmonious Fists'.
11. C.
12-13. Essay answers.
14. a) Koumintang or Nationalist.
    b) Chiang Kai Shek, the commander of this army.
    c) It was defeated by the communists and driven off mainland China on to the island of Formosa (Taiwan).
    d) The Manchu imperial government.
    e) The theme of both sources is the corruption and inefficiency which was a major cause of the Koumintang defeat in 1949.
    f) Because its main opponent for the previous 8 years had been the Japanese, and they surrendered on VE Day.
15. 1B 2H 3E 4G 5C 6I 7F 8D 9A.
16. a) Chinese communists, known as 'Long Marchers' because of their long and dangerous journey to reach this spot.
    b) They provided deep shelter for the communists against air attacks from the Koumintang airforce.
    c) Because of its remoteness. More accessible regions were dominated by the Koumintang.
    d) Without its survival in this spot, the communist army and administration might well have been destroyed, thus altering the future history of China. Yenan gave Mao's armies a respite at a time when they seemed to be facing defeat, (1934-5). When the Japanese attack came in 1937, Yenan proved too remote an area for them to penetrate. (3).
17. Essay answer.

WORK UNIT 11

1. The League of three emperors, those of Austria, Russia and Germany.
2. The rule of thumb applied by Britain whereby her navy had to be larger than the combined fleets of the two next largest navies.
3. Morocco.
4. King Edward VII.

5. To warn Germany of the possibility of war if British naval and oceanic concerns were ignored. It arose when the Kaiser's government sent warships to Agadir to protect German interests' during a revolt against French rule in Morocco. (2).
6. To modernise Turkey.
7. Serbia's main export, pigs, had to be sent to Austria because there was no processing plant in Serbia. At various times Austria put pressure on Serbia by closing the frontier to pig exports on the grounds that there was a danger of swine fever coming into Austrian territories. Between 1906 and 1909 the frontier was closed altogether and this closure period is known as the 'pig war'. (3).
8. Because she was exhausted from the Balkan wars. It is unlikely that she ever contemplated war with Austria without allies. (2).
9. To protect 'German interests' following a revolt against French rule in Morocco.
10. A new type of battleship, far more powerful than any other afloat. Britain's first was named 'Dreadnought' and this gave the name to the type, although individual battleships had different names. The development of dreadnoughts marked a significant build-up in the naval arms' race between Britain and Germany. (3).
11. B.
12. a) The Austro-Hungarian or Habsburg empire.
    b) He meant that, in his opinion, the Balkan League was inspired and sponsored by Russia to further her own ambitions in the Balkans. (2).
    c) Yes. Clearly, Czernin thought that the Monarchy was not doing enough to combat the menace as his remark that 'we stand by with folded arms' illustrates. (2).
    d) Not really. Austria's annexation of Bosnia in 1908 was certainly evidence of very active interest in any threat of encirclement. Between 1908 and 1914 there were signs that the 'war party' in Austria was gaining the upper hand in persuading the emperor to launch a war of destruction against Serbia. Czernin's letter represents a move in this direction by the war party (3).
13. a) C and I.
    b) F, B and C.
    c) D, A and E.
    d) G.
    e) F.
    f) H.
14. a) The boy is meant to be Belgium and the man, Germany. Their relative size is meant to represent the difference in military power between Germany and Belgium (2).
    b) That Belgium had refused to let the German armies through her territory. She had been asked to do so but had refused (2).
    c) The man is shown as big and menacing with a heavy stick symbolising the German army. The boy is shown as courageous as he prepares for the obviously unequal contest. It is a picture of a big bully attacking a little boy and could not have been drawn by an artist who supported the German invasion. (2).
    d) To protect the Channel ports and prevent them falling into enemy hands. This was because of their nearness to Britain and some of her vital seaways. The treaty which guaranteed Belgium neutrality, and, in fact, set up the country in 1839, had been devised by Britain for just this purpose (3).

e) The artist hoped to stimulate patriotic fervour as well as putting the most emotive case for Britain's entry into the war. This was important in a country which at that time had no military conscription and so relied on volunteers to man its armed services (3).

15-18. Essay answers.

WORK UNIT 12

1. Austria, Turkey and her coastline from which an attack could be launched to strike into the heart of Europe. Also to link up with Russia (2).
2. Douglas Haig.
3. Named after Alfred von Schlieffen, the German Chief of Staff, who devised it.
4. A French plan to invade Germany across the Rhine.
5. British Expeditionary Force.
6. Marshal Petain at Verdun.
7. The Allies.
8. General Allenby.
9. The gathering of merchant ships into groups, or convoys, so that they could sail protected by British or Allied warships against 'U' Boat attack.
10. The Zimmerman telegram suggested that Germany might support Mexico's claim for the return of territories taken from her by the USA after the Mexican War in 1848. This enraged American public opinion and made the US's entry into the war on the Allied side almost certain. (2).
11. 1C 2J 3A 4F 5I 6D 7E 8B 9G 10H.
12. B.   13. A.
14. a) Source B. which speaks of an 'immense sixty-five ton rudder' and also a fantail soaring 'a hundred feet into the air'.
    b) Both sources suggest that the sinking seemed like a dream or nightmare; both use the latter word when describing their experiences.
    c) She was torpedoed by a German 'U' Boat.
    d) The USA, because over 100 American citizens were drowned. The US government's reaction was to threaten war unless Germany stopped attacking unarmed merchant vessels including American merchant ships (The 'Lusitania' was British). In consequence, the Germans restricted their submarine campaign until 1917 when they began an all-out campaign against all shipping. This caused the US to enter the war on the Allied side. (3).
    e) It led to the inevitable defeat of Germany because American manpower tipped the balance in favour of the Allies on the Western Front where a war of attrition made the arrival of new 'blood' a decisive factor. (3).

15-18 Essay answers.

WORK UNIT 13

1. A priest who led a protest march to the Winter Palace in St. Petersburg (now Leningrad) in January, 1905. He intended to present a petition to the Tsar pleading for various democratic and social reforms but the Tsar was not in the palace and the marchers were dispersed by rifle fire which caused many casualties. (3).
2. A naval mutiny, sparked off by the unrest following Russia's defeat by Japan in 1904-5.

3. As a prison region. Convicts lived in camps. The area was so remote that escape was virtually impossible. (2).
4. The main industries - coal, steel, railways and banks.
5. He helped Quaker relief agencies trying to deal with the famine in Russia.
6. Traders allowed to set up private businesses under the New Economic Policy.
7. Because they were atheists and opposed to all Church influences.
8. Dora Kaplan.
9. Czech soldiers who had fought in the Tsarist forces against Austria because they were opposed to Austrian rule over what is now Czechoslovakia. After the revolution, they were given permission to travel to Vladivostok so that they could sail west and continue fighting with the Allies against Germany. The Bolshevik forces tried to disarm them so the Czech Legion joined other White armies fighting the communists. (2).
10. Because its leaders had mastered the theory of Marxism and knew how to put in it into practice.
11. 1E 2G 3F 4B 5C 7I 8A 9H.
12. a) The New Economic Policy.
    b) Because of the widespread unrest caused by the communist policy of total nationalisation. This involved the forcibly requisitioning of food and other supplies and led to violent resistance by workers and peasants. The most serious crisis occurred when sailors mutinied at Kronstadt, taking as their slogan, 'Soviets without communism'. The NEP was designed to modify communist policies by allowing a limited amount of private enterprise (3).
    c) Because it was fighting the civil war against 'white' or anti-Bolshevik forces.
    d) Because it allowed some private enterprise.
    e) War Communism,
13. a) German Foreign Minister
    b) They had either been exiled from Russia, or had fled, because of their anti-Tsarist activities.
    c) Because the German government, an imperial monarchy, did not wish to publicise the fact that it was helping 'dangerous' revolutionaries.
    d) The Germans knew that Lenin and his colleagues were opposed to war and would probably take Russia out of the war if they gained power. The first Revolutionary government, led by Kerensky, had continued the war (3).
    e) The Bolshevik takeover of Russia which took place in November (October by Julien calendar was still used in Russia) 1917.
14. a) Source A was written by Leon Trotsky. It condemns the Provisional Government led by Kerensky which it accuses, in essence, of continuing the old regime without the Tsar. In typical communist fashion, it implies that Trotsky and other communists understood the 'creative consciousness' of the working classes whilst their opponents foresaw nothing. With its talk of 'ruling classes', of the demands of 'evolution' and the completion of 'the revolutionary insurrection' it foreshadows most of the Soviet phraseology since the revolution (3).
    Source B was written by Alexander Kerensky. He claims that the Bolsheviks, being opposed to all freedom of choice or opinion, seized power violently even though they knew that the majority of Russian people were against them. He implies that they did it before a Constituent Assembly was summoned because

they knew that such an Assembly would establish a democratic government. (3).

b) Source A, although the language is not very clear.

c) Lenin and his fellow Bolsheviks.

d) They disagreed totally about the mood and wishes of the Russian people in 1917. Source A. claims that the peoples' 'critical understanding' made them support the Bolsheviks, whilst Source B. claims that Russian public opinion favoured the establishment of a democratic system. (2).

e) Both represent the views of men deeply involved in the events of 1917 and on opposite sides. Kerensky spent the rest of his life explaining his overthrow in the terms expressed in Source B. Trotsky put the official party view of why it gained power in Russia. In view of this, neither can be considered unbiased. (2). Source B represents the general western view of how the Bolsheviks gained power (3).

15. 1C 2E 3D 4H 5I 6G 7A 8B 9F

16. A.

17. 1-2-5-4-3-6-7.

18. Essay answers.

WORK UNIT 14

1. In Czechoslovakia.

2. Georges Clemenceau.

3. Treaty of St. Germain.

4. Language spoken by its people.

5. Clause 231, which blamed Germany for starting the war.

6. To give her access to a port.

7. J.M. Keynes.

8. Britain.

9. Yugoslavia *or* Czechoslovakia *or* Hungary *or* Poland.

10. An ex-German or ex-Turkish territory taken over by the League of Nations.

11. a) Germany, where a small group of military men and aristocrats (often the same people) had a disproportionate influence on foreign policy. (2).

b) Austria's declaration of war was an example.

c) Austro-Hungarian empire.

d) By founding the League of Nations to prevent war, and by the application of the principles of 'self-determination' to hitherto subject nationalities. (2).

12. Hungary (B) Italy (A) Bulgaria (B) Rumania (A) Turkey (B)

Germany (B) Poland (A) Austria (B) Greece (A) Yugoslavia (A)

13. B.

14. a) He indicates that the USA is a democracy where the adult population elect their officials at all levels; this make them 'the boss'.

b) Because the 'office' i.e. the Senate, had rejected the Versailles Treaty and also refused to let the USA join the League of Nations. (2).

c) Although Wilson made a desperate appeal to the American people, touring the country making speeches, he suffered a stroke which incapacitated him. The League and Treaty were rejected for a second time by the Senate in March, 1920. (2).

d) The refusal of the USA to join the League seriously weakened it because without the US's power to uphold the treaty arrangements, there was little chance of stopping them being overturned in later years. This was done in the 1930's by Hitler. (2).

15-17. Essay answers.

WORK UNIT 15

1. Woodrow Wilson.
2. The countries carved out of the old empires after the First World War.
3. It was the civil service of the League, in charge of administration.
4. After the Napoleonic War in 1815.
5. Sir Eric Drummond.
6. Geneva, Switzerland.
7. Lithuania and Poland.
8. Silesia, to decide whether Poland or Germany should rule it.
9. To spread communist ideas and promote worldwide revolution against the ruling classes.
10. The Lithuanians.
11. 1G 2D 3A 4C 5F 5E 7H 8B
12. a) Noel Baker is claiming that war became inevitable after the League failed to stop Japanese aggression in Manchuria in 1931. (2).
    b) Because she had invaded Abyssinia (Ethiopia).
    c) No modern war can be fought without oil and Italy had little or no oil supplies of her own.
    d) He is implying that sanctions were ineffective because they were not applied rigourously by some nations, and not applied at all by others. (2).
13. D.
14. C.
15. Essay answer.
16. a) Because the cartoonist considered she had been guilty of military aggressions and because he regarded her as a militaristic nation.
    b) By ignoring the League's resolution which demanded that Japan cease aggression and retire from Manchuria.
    c) China.
    d) If those countries opposed to Japan's action had signed pacts. or alliances, with China, something which was implied in the League concept of 'collective security'.
17. A and D.
18. Essay answers.

WORK UNIT 16

1. A teacher.
2. Fascist gangs in Italy.
3. Because it would have involved fighting Britain, a factor not considered likely by the founders of the alliance.
4. Trentino and Trieste.

5. The bundle of rods and the axe carried by Roman magistrates as a symbol of their power to inflict punishment.
6. Italian troops occupied the Greek island of Corfu for a time until the Greek government paid compensation for the murder of an Italian general at Janina in northern Greece. (2).
7. Named after Sir Samuel Hoare and Pierre Laval, the Foreign Ministers of Britain and France respectively, who negotiated it.
8. Mussolini said that the friendship between Italy and Germany would provide a Rome-Berlin axis around which peace-loving states could revolve.
9. Communist partisans (guerilla fighters against the Germans).
10. When Allied troops invaded the Italian mainland, Mussolini was overthrown and the new Italian government negotiated surrender terms with the Allies.
11. E.
12. D.
13. a) The fascist March on Rome in 1922.
    b) Source B, because it is written by a person not involved in the events and in many cases, although possibly not in this case, not alive at the time they took place. (2).
    c) Columns of fascists were proposing to converge on Rome from different directions to try to influence a change of government in their favour. The King, who was sympathetic to the fascists, invited Mussolini, who was in Milan, to come to Rome and form a government (Source A.) Mussolini went by train and the columns stopped 40 miles short of the capital. (2).
    d) Source B. is objective, having been written by an historian with access to many facts not known at the time. Mussolini's remarks are mere opinion and, in view of what really happened, must be regarded as boastful and designed to impress his audience. (2)
14. 1C 2F 3H 4G 5A 6B 7D 8E
15. a) Because he wanted to create a new 'Roman' empire in Africa.
    b) It is meant to be Hitler.
    c) France.
    d) Italy declared war on France when it became clear that the French were about to surrender. This is 'the stab in the back' referred to in the 'Order of the Day'.
16-18. Essay answers.

WORK UNIT 17

1. George Orwell.
2. Spanish Fascist Party.
3. A right-wing politician whose murder in July, 1936 sparked off the army rebellion against the Popular Front government.
4. To set up naval patrols to prevent supplies reaching either side during the civil war.
5. There were two Generals - Mola and Sunjurjo.
6. Valencia.
7. German planes fighting on the Nationalist (Francoist) side.
8. Spanish 'volunteers' sent to fight with the Germans against Russia in the Second World War.
9. The Nationalists.

10. Francisco Franco.
11. C.
12. B.
13. 8-7-1-4-5-3-6-9-2.
14. a) Anarchism.
    b) Barcelona.
    c) Latifundia
    d) He would not have given the workers such powers and he would not have allowed self-government to separate parts of Spain.
15. a) Franco and his Nationalists who had rebelled against the elected Republican government.
    b) Anarchism.
    c) He uses 'tribe' in a derogatory sense because he is against the trade unions and their methods. He condemns them for their quarrelsome, divisive ways which he regrets because. being a liberal, he is also against Franco and the Spanish right-wing (3).
    d) 1936. It refers to the situation in Spain just before the civil war. It was the chaos and violence of this time which gave Franco and his fellow generals their excuse to rebel in order to restore order but their enemies claimed that right-wingers were as much to blame for the violence as left-wingers (3).
    e) The disunity of Spain as reflected in its politics. This disunity affected the Republican, more than the Nationalist side (2).
    f) The Anarchist who did want a central government. All the others favoured a strong government controlled by them (2).
    g) The International Brigades had good leadership and discipline but were hampered by the political disunity of their Republican masters (2).
16. a) The communists, in particular Soviet Russia.
    b) Nationalised.
    c) The Anarchists who were usually atheists and against Church influence and power.
    d) It is clear from this source that two opposed groups, the Anarchists and Communists, were running Barcelona at the time Orwell describes. The city could be run in either way not by both. A clash was inevitable between the two - and it came later in the war (3).
    e) Essay answer.

WORK UNIT 18

1. Theodore Roosevelt.
2. Assistant Secretary to the Navy.
3. Infantile paralysis.
4. Bing Crosby.
5. Japan.
6. Electricity.
7. The forbidding of the manufacture, sale or consumption of alcoholic liquour.
8. An organisation of American businessmen opposed to Roosevelt's New Deal policies and pledged to 'defend' the Constitution and 'restore respect for private property' - two things they thought were under threat. (2).

9. Herbert Hoover.
10. Four - 1932, 1936, 1940 and 1944.
11. C.
12. Essay answer.
13. (See glossary).
14. 1C 2E 3A 4F 5B 6D.
15. a) Roosevelt's relations with the US Supreme Court who often opposed his New Deal policies.
    b) Roosevelt.
    c) Judges of the Supreme Court.
    d) By showing at least six judges as 'lookalikes' of Roosevelt the cartoonist is referring satirically to Roosevelt's nominees being 'yesmen', or puppets, of the President who would obey him rather than exercise their independent judgement (3).
    e) Roosevelt failed in his attempts to 'pack' the Court with his nominees because such a scheme was opposed by both his Republican opponents and his own Democratic party. (2)
16. Correct order - 1-3-4-2-6-5.
17. a) Source A.
    b) Source D.
    c) Source B.
    d) The American Declaration of Independence.
    e) Communism - because it involves subjection of the private individual and private business to the state.
    f) Italy and Germany.
    g) Hoover thought that only minimum state intervention was permissible if individual liberty was to be assured. Roosevelt thought that true liberty could only be ensured if the government gave support and help to distressed parts of the nation (3).
    h) The writer meant communism or socialism.
    i) Essay answer.

WORK UNIT 19

1. One of the first nazi organisations, the SA, led by Ernst Roehm.
2. From Weimar the town were its administration and government were based.
3. Right-wing ex-soldiers groups.
4. Alfred Hugenberg.
5. German Parliament, and the building in which it met.
6. An alliance between France, Czechoslovakia, Rumania and Yugoslavia.
7. It replaced the old deflated mark and halted runaway inflation.
8. Robert Ley.
9. Brown House.
10. Schutz Staffel (Protection Squad)
11. Essay answers.
12. D.
13. B.
14. 1F 2D 3G 4B 5A 6C 7H 8E

15. a) Germany.
    b) That Germany could rely on Hitler. (2).
    c) That he would uphold the integrity of Germany, restore her pride and take as his watchword, 'Loyalty, honour and order'.
    d) Like most political cartoons it deals in simplified themes, in this case the reliability and strength of Hitler and the confidence Germany can have in his leadership. (2).
    e) He despised them, and based his political propaganda on the premise that they were stupid. The people were to be manipulated by slogans and simplistic appeals to their 'positive' and 'negative' attitudes i.e. the things they liked and the things they did not like. Hitler always emphasised the negative and turned the Germans' attention to groups they did not like, i.e. the Jews, and things they disapproved of, like the Versailles Settlement (3).
    f) Hitler wanted the German people to forget that they had been militarily defeated in 1918 and to remember their grievances about the Peace Settlement. He wanted them to forget the Treaty of Brest Litovsk, a far worse 'diktat' which the Germans imposed on the Russians just before their own defeat (3).
16-17 Essay answers.

WORK UNIT 20

1. 1931.
2. Engelburt Dolfuss.
3. Czechoslovakia or Rumania or Yugoslavia - and, of course France.
4. Luftewaffe.
5. An alliance between Germany and Italy.
6. The Siegfried Line, a series of German defences on the French frontier.
7. The word is German and means 'living space'.
8. Czechoslovakia.
9. Hitler.
10. Hitler's plan for the military occupation of Czechoslovakia.
11. 1C 2E 3A 4G 5B 6D 7F.
12. A.
13. E.
14. a) E
    b) A and D.
    c) D.
    d) F.
    e) C.
    f) B.
15. a) None, because Austria had been occupied by German troops in March of that year. However, the nazis staged this plebiscite as a propaganda exercise; predictably, it showed a majority in favour of the takeover (2).
    b) Because Hitler and the nazis were anti-semites.
    c) To prevent Jews escaping nazi persecution by giving up their faith at the time of the nazi takeover or in the months preceding it.
    d) 1. The regulations regarding Jews in Source A.

2. His broken promises to Chamberlain about not wishing to annex the non Germans.

3. The forcible occupation of Austria and the Sudetenland, later the remainder of Czechoslovakia. (2)

e) The talk of 'stolen provinces' and of native Germans being 'led back' to Germany were untrue. Neither Austria nor the Sudetenland had ever been part of the German empire but were, in fact, ruled by Austro-Hungary until 1918. (2).

f) Essay answer.

16. a) The man on the artist's left is Hitler; the man on his right, Stalin.

b) They indicated the attitudes both men had taken to each other in the years preceding the pact.

c) Poland.

d) Stalin was promised valuable lands previously ruled by Tsarist Russia. These would act as a buffer against possible attack. Hitler was given a free hand to fight Britain and France in the west should his invasion of Poland provoke them to war (2).

e) A. represents the views of a cartoonist, operating in a free country, and expressing the surprise most peoples (including many communists) felt at two such inveterate enemies signing a friendship pact. B. is the official view of a totalitarian state anxious to explain this celebrated 'U' turn in its policy. From the point of view of power politics and the war there is some truth in B. But it ignores the high ideals of communism as spread by the Soviet propaganda machine at the time (3).

f) Because the Nazi and Communists were politically opposed philosophies and both Hitler and Stalin had always proclaimed that they were the champions against each other (3).

g) (You must give your own opinion).

h) Essay answer.

17-18. Essay Answer.

WORK UNIT 21

1. Military chief and for many years the actual ruler of Japan.
2. The Japanese warrior, aristocrat, class.
3. The Japanese way of describing their invasion of China.
4. The code of chivalry and honour practised by samurai.
5. Members of a Japanese patriotic society which aimed to spread Japanese influence and power by armed force if necessary.
6. Manchuria.
7. They favoured Japanese expansion into Manchuria, if necessary at the expense of Russian interests.
8. Hirohito.
9. General Tojo.
10. The Japanese puppet state of Manchuria.
11. 1E 2G 3A 4F 5C 6D 7C 8B
12. D.
13. E.

14. France, Britain and the USA.
15. a) Germany, Italy and Japan.
    b) German and Japanese aggression in Europe and the Far East respectively.
    c) The Japanese against the US fleet at Pearl Harbour, Hawaii.
    d) Isolationist. Most Americans changed their views because of the Japanese attack.
    e) To defeat both Germany and Japan.
16. Essay answers.

WORK UNIT 22

1. US system of aid for Britain and Russia.
2. An artificial harbour towed across to the Normandy beaches during the 'D' Day landings in 1944. It was designed to be used until a large port could be captured (2).
3. The German invasion of Russia. The word means 'redbeard'.
4. The policy of destroying everything in the path of an invader so as to increase his supply problems. It was used extensively in Russia after the German invasion. (2).
5. Pipe Line Under the Ocean.
6. To cut off Japanese supply lines in the Pacific and move nearer the Japanese mainland.
7. It was a series of sea-defences erected by the Germans to stop Allied landings.
8. The Allied airborne landings at Arnhem in 1944.
9. Code-name for landings at Arnhem in 1944.
10. A German flying bomb, first launched against London in June, 1944.
11. a) In Russia; the Russians won.
    b) In the Pacific; the Americans won.
    c) In the Mediterranean; the British won.
    d) In Holland; the Germans won.
    e) In North Africa; the British won.
    f) In Italy; the Allies won.
    g) In North Africa; the British won.
    h) In the Mediterranean; the Germans won.
12. C.
13. E.
14. 1F 2H 3A 4B 5G 6C 7E 8D
15. a) Germany. Operation Barbarossa (See answer 3).
    b) Because France was not defeated until June, 1940 and that autumn was spent in planning an invasion of Britain. When this scheme was abandoned, Hitler turned his troops eastwards.
    c) A. The Germans were stopped and turned back *before* Moscow.
    d) To defeat Russia, her only serious European rival after the fall of France, and to gain 'living space' for German settlers in the east.
    e) The defeat of Germany and the setting up of satellite Soviet states in eastern Europe. Another was the consolidation, instead of the destruction, of communist Russia and Stalin's regime (3).

16. a) The Moehne dam in the Ruhr region of Germany - undamaged.
    b) The dam had been breached by the bouncing bomb raids led by Wing-Commander Guy Gibson of the RAF.
    c) Essay answer.
17. 1D 2A 3C 4F 5E 6B.
18. Essay answer.

WORK UNIT 23

1. Russian workers who tried to copy the feat of Aleksei Stakhanov, a miner, who cut as much coal as 14 men during a 24 hour period in 1935.
2. Winston Churchill, in a speech at Fulton, Missouri, in March, 1946.
3. North Atlantic Treaty Organisation.
4. The so-called nazi Final Solution or the killing of 6,000,000 Jews.
5. One of the two official Soviet newspapers. The word means 'truth'.
6. It means 'Man of steel' and was a name chosen by Stalin himself.
7. Lavrenti Beria.
8. Imre Nagy.
9. Leon Trotsky.
10. New Economic Policy.
11. A.
12. E.
13. 1E 2G 3H 4B 5C 6A 7F 8D.
14. a) The Russian harassment and, finally, blocking of all land routes between Berlin and the West German border.
    b) If no supplies had got through to the French, British and American sectors in Berlin they would have been forced to withdraw - which seems to have been Stalin's aim.
    c) The Allies's unilateral issue of a new currency in their zones.
    d) Russia was exhausted by her efforts and losses in the Second World War, had no atomic weapons and no means of delivering them on to the American mainland even if she had. (2).
    e) The air-lift of supplies into Berlin between June, 1948 and May, 1949. The long-term result was the creation of two German states, the German Democratic Republic (communist) and the German Federal Republic (capitalist) (3).
15. a) A. and B. because both present collectivisation as both desirable and desired by the peasants.
    b) The peasants killed off their cattle and other livestock in protest against collectivisation. The decline was also caused by the mass-deportation of Kulaks described in C.
    c) C. was written and published outside Russia where the author was free to express his own opinions. B. was written in Stalin's Russia and would only have been published with his government's approval, especially on such a sensitive issue. There is little doubt that the author of C. would have been imprisoned or shot had he been known to have written anything critical of the Soviet regime. (3).
    d) The destruction of the Kulaks who, in Stalin's opinion represented a threat to his plans for wholesale collectivisation because they were the richer and

therefore more influential class. (2)

e) It would make the Source more reliable in the sense that the writer had actually experienced life in a Soviet prison camp but possibly unreliable because it deals with an event of which the writer had no direct experience. However, the author was using reliable sources and other accounts seem to confirm this source as being true (3).

f) Essay answer.

16. a) Essay answer.

b) Because they regarded the existence of a large communist country as a threat to their capitalist system in that it might encourage workers' revolts inside their own borders.

c) The German invasion of Russia in 1941.

d) Essay answer.

WORK UNIT 24

1. Secretary General.
2. The administration or civil service.
3. Up to 5 delegates for each country.
4. San Francisco, USA.
5. It is the date that the UN was formed in 1945.
6. France, Britain, Russia, the USA and, first Nationalist, now Communist China.
7. International Monetary Fund.
8. The Hague, Holland.
9. Paris, France.
10. The Baruch Plan.
11. D., neither of the Great Powers (the USA or Soviet Russia) was prepared to allow the UN to 'interfere' in a matter which affected its vital interests.
12. a) Stalin. He wanted to get Red China a seat on the UN Security Council as well as membership of the UN.

b) The USA who regarded Red China as an enemy and a threat to world peace. America had given large amounts of aid to Chiang Kai Shek's Koumintang forces, only to see it lost when the Nationalists were defeated. Chinese participation in the Korean War, where Chinese forces inflicted defeats on US troops, plus the anti-communist 'witch-hunt' inside the USA, increased the American administration's determination to keep China out (3).

c) Essay answer.

13. a) It is referring to the ineffectiveness of the League when faced by Japanese aggression in 1931 and Italian aggression in 1935.

b) President Harry Truman (1945-52) who was determined to support the UN's stand, if necessary by force.

c) To Korea, where North Korean forces had invaded the south in June, 1950.

d) In this case history did not repeat itself. The Korean War ended in a stalemate. The North Korean forces were back where they began the war in 1950. So the cartoonist's optimism was justified, although, in fact, it had been the USA rather than the UN which had controlled the war-effort (3).

14-17. Essay answers.

WORK UNIT 25

1. A system of compensation paid by the EEC to African states plagued by disease, drought, other natural disasters or a drop in world prices affecting their exports (2).
2. The Congo (Zaire).
3. Nigeria.
4. To make the colonial peoples under its rule French in regard to language, culture and customs, and also to integrate them politically with the mother country (2).
5. Abd el Krim.
6. India.
7. A white (European) colonist in Algeria.
8. Ghana under Nkrumah's leadership.
9. Belgium.
10. Namibia, formerly German South West Africa.
11. Kenya African People's Union; Convention People's Party; Kenya Africa National Union; Tanganyika African National Union.
12. D.
13. D.
14. Amin (5) Nyerere (6) Tshombe (2) Lumumba (2) Lugard (3) Nkrumah (4) Mobutu (2) Gowon (3).
15-16. Essay answers.

WORK UNIT 26

1. Mixed marriages in South Africa.
2. People of mixed race in South Africa.
3. Transkei.
4. A society of leading Afrikaaners pledged to uphold white supremacy in economic as well as political matters, and to fight against 'English' influences.
5. Tanzania.
6. That the CAF was successful economically but would have to be broken up because it was unacceptable to the black majority.
7. Portugal.
8. Sir Geoffrey Huggins.
9. Originally a circle of wagons formed by the Voortrekkers to fight off Zulu attacks.
10. The South African police fired on a crowd protesting against the pass laws, killing 60 people.
11. 1B 2E 3G 4A 5F 6D 7C.
12. Central African Federation; Unilateral Declaration of Independence; African National Congress; South West Africa People's Organisation; Patriotic Front.
13. Essay answer.
14. A=Nigeria. C=Zaire. B=Egypt. G=South Africa. E=Kenya. D=Uganda. F=Tanzania.
15. a) Source A. is biassed in favour of the African point of view, B is against. Each list details which reflect badly on what it opposes; for example, A's reference to the tarring of the road to the European hospital, and B's reference to the fate of the 30 original African heads of state.Each contains generalisations which

might be hard to prove i.e. 'Africa is also falling into economic despair' (B) and 'The idea of 'partnership' was forgotten' (A). (3).
   b) Although the opinions in both A. and B. might be disputed, the facts are almost certainly correct. However, in both cases, they have been used the exclusion of any other facts which might throw doubt on their case. One is left wondering if there was any good in the CAF or OAU (3).
   c) Essay answer.
   d) Essay answer.
16. Essay answer.
17. a) Because the Nationalist party represent the Afrikaaners who insist on giving their language equal status with English.
   b) Apartheid. Because it is racist and unfair to the majority population.
   c) Essay answer.

WORK UNIT 27

1. The President proposes to Congress who have the final veto.
2. Obtaining equal rights for negroes under the law.
3. Martin Luther King.
4. A figure of 57 communists who, Senator McCarthy claimed, were working for the US government.
5. Lyndon Johnson.
6. German mark and Japanese yen.
7. A rock festival.
8. A US citizen of Latin American descent.
9. National Security Council.
10. Reduce interest rates.
11. B.
12. F.D. Roosevelt (D) Harry Truman (D) Dwight Eisenhower (R) John Kennedy (D) Lyndon Johnson (D) Richard Nixon (R) Gerald Ford (R) Jimmy Carter (D) Ronald Reagan (R) George Bush (R).
13. C and then D.
14. a) The Civil Rights campaign.
   b) Little Rock, Arkansas, 1957.
   c) Escorting nine black children into hitherto all-white school.
   d) Because the Arkansas state authorities refused to implement the Supreme Court ruling on the matter.
   e) President Eisenhower in his capacity as Commander-in-Chief of the US armed forces, and also as Chief Executive of the USA.
15. 2-4-3-7-1-6-5-8-9
16-17. Essay answers.

WORK UNIT 28

1. The regions of the Far East the USA was prepared to defend against aggression in the late 1940's.
2. The future independence of Korea.3. A truce was signed between the UN forces and the North Korean army which stopped the fighting in 1953.
4. Indonesia.

5. Its Chinese population did not want to be ruled by a Malay-dominated government.
6. Communist guerillas operating behind the South Vietnamese lines on behalf of the North Vietnamese government.
7. South Vietnamese families who fled by sea to escape communist persecution after the North's victory.
8. The French were defeated by the Vietnamese led by Ho Chi Minh and Giap.
9. It escalated US involvement in Vietnam.
10. A route through Laos and Cambodia used to get Russian supplies to North Vietnam.
11. B and then D.
12. India and Canada.
13. 1B 2D 3G 4A 5C 6E 7F.
14. a) Irregular troops who avoid pitched battles with the enemy and engage in sabotage, raiding and ambush.
    b) No, intimidation was used if thought necessary.
    c) Dien Bien Phu.
    d) Geneva.
15. a) After the Second World War and the Japanese surrender.
    b) [See Answer 14 b)].
    c) South Vietnam.
    d) Because of the domino theory regarding the spread of communism in South East Asia. The particular event was the communist victory in China 1949.
    e) Korea.
    f) Essay answer giving your own opinion.
16. a) A=Thailand. D=North Vietnam. C=South Vietnam. B=Cambodia. G=Burma. H=Malayan Federation. I=Indonesia. J=Phillipines. F=China.
    b) Sukarno.
    c) I.
    d) D and C.
    e) H.
    f) J.
    g) A.
    h) D and C.
    i) D and C.
    j) F.
    k) Saigon (South Vietnam) Seoul (South Korea) Rangoon (Burma) Jakarta (Indonesia) Manila (Phillipines) Hanoi (North Vietnam).

WORK UNIT 29

1. The Common Market.
2. A nuclear missile launched underwater from a submarine.
3. It co-ordinates research into nuclear power within the EEC.
4. Norway.
5. Member of the European Parliament.
6. Surplus stores of food and wine resulting from the CAP.
7. West German Parliament
8. Marshal Tito.

9. The East German workers.
10. There was an attempt to liberalise and democratise the Czechoslovak communist system.
11. D.
12. A.
13. Common Agricultural Policy; European Economic Community; Christian Democratic Union; European Free Trade Association; European Coal and Steel Community.
14. a) Source C.
    b) Source C.
    c) Source C.
    d) 1C 2A 3A 4B.
    e) Essay answer with own opinion.
    f) Essay answer
    g) Essay answer.
15. C=Poland. D=Czechoslovakia. I=Hungary. J=Rumania. L=Bulgaria. M=Greece. N=Turkey. F=Italy. H=France. G=Switzerland. O=Russia. E=Austria. A=East Germany. B=West Germany. K=Yugoslavia.
16. Essay answer.

WORK UNIT 31

1. The Great Leap Forward.
2. Lin Piao.
3. The People's Republic of China.
4. Capitalists OR landlords OR rich peasants OR foreigners OR 'bad elements' OR 'Rightists'.
5. Formosa (Taiwan).
6. The USA.
7. Khrushchev and the Soviet system in general.
8. Keeping India neutral (not taking sides in the Cold War).
9. A region between Tibet and Sinkiang province on the Indo-Chinese border. India and China.
10. 1997.
11. A.
12. a) Mao Tse Tung.
    b) The foundation of the People's Republic of China.
    c) October, 1949.
    d) Essay answer
13. a) Because he was a landlord. His likely fate was shooting or imprisonment.
    b) A and B. These sources are concerned with farming. There is also a strong emphasis by both writers on group and communal work (2).
    c) Source C., which suggests that the writer arrived as a stranger in the village but was also going to take charge. His tactics seemed to have been carefully planned before his arrival. Clearly, he was acting under orders (3).
    d) Source C where the writer sets out to gain the villagers' confidence and respect. Such an attitude was in sharp contrast to the landlord/peasant relationship of old China and indicates why, initially at least, the communists

had the support of the peasantry (3).

e) Sources A and B. Evidence now available shows that Mao's government was determined to carry out its policies at all costs and critics and opponents of collectivisation could expect imprisonment and 're-education' at the least. (3).

f) Hardly any of these Sources can be considered reliable. Mao's China was a closed society, insulated by its government from the outside world. It is inconceivable that anything detrimental to the regime would have been publicised outside China. Furthermore, the Chinese communist emphasis on 'brain-washing' and 're-education' meant that a person's only hope of his/her punishment ending would be to 'confess' to all sorts of faults and proclaim the error of their ways. This, plus a fanatical belief in the system by some communists, makes all this documentary evidence suspect, although the technical and practical details may well have been correct (3).

14-16. Essay answers.

WORK UNIT 32

1. Viceroy.
2. A dual system of ruling India whereby Indians ran health, education, industry and finance and British officials the police, law and finance.
3. General Bernard Dyer.
4. The day Nehru proclaimed India 'independent' in 1930.
5. A suggested economic system whereby Britain would give preferential treatment to empire goods and vice versa.
6. Eire. It was no longer part of the Commonwealth.
7. Canada.
8. Land of the pure, plus the initials of various Indian Muslim states.
9. Mackenzie-King.
10. Radcliffe Commission.
11. C and then D.
12. C.
13. A for Afghanistan. K for Kashmir. S for Sind. P for Punjab. The disputed territory is Kashmir.
14. Essay answer.
15 a) A.
    b) B and C.
    c) D.
    d) Essay answer.
16. a) Source B suggests that English language and culture had been prevalent in India for some time. Nehru was educated in England early this century; his father and grandfather were English-speaking. To be instinctively drawn to English habits of thought whilst being so opposed to their continued rule of India indicates how persuasive and deep the English influence was, and suggests that Britain had ruled India for a long time - which, of course, she had. The way they ruled India is indicated by their policy of educating Indian aristocrats to take part in the government (3).
    b) Source D where Gandhi comments that dominion status had pleased even the most anti-British of Empire premiers, South Africa's General Hertzog.

c) High caste Hindus.
d) Eire (Irish Free State).
e) It was too vague and gave no time-scale. i.e. how long would it be before India did attain dominion status? Its date is also significant because by 1929 the dominion status of the white ex-colonies was certain after decisions taken at the 1926 Imperial Conference. This served only to increase Indian dissatisfaction and impatience. (3).
f) Essay answer.
g) The clash between Hindus and Muslims. It was so delicate a matter that it was rarely referred to in official pronouncements. Hindus, in particular, feared that to stress this problem might give the British an excuse to delay independence. (3).

17. Essay answer.

WORK UNIT 33

1. Jawarharlal Nehru.
2. Kerala province.
3. Neutrality.
4. Zulfikar Bhutto.
5. In Amritsar. It is the holiest Sikh shrine.
6. Mororj Desai.
7. Because she had sent troops to storm the Golden Temple.
8. Kashmir.
9. To gain East Pakistani independence from West Pakistan.
10. Russia.
11. (To be found in text).
12. 1E 2F 3A 5C 6G 7H 8D.
13. E.
14. D.
15. a) Source B, which justifies the Chinese action and, in the last sentence, implies that Nehru provoked the hostilities.
    b) Source A favours the Indian point of view more than B. It credits India with taking the initiative in trying to keep peace with China along the border (2).
    c) That neither side knew where the frontier should be. This appears to be incorrect. The Indians knew where they thought it should be - along the line drawn by the British in 1914. The Chinese were very clear as to where they thought the frontier should be, going so far as to occupy NEFA and build a military road through the Aksai Chin. (3).
    d) Both agree that India had tried to live peacefully with China; in fact, Source B gives that as the reason for Chinese surprise when fighting broke out. (2).

16-17. Essay answers.

WORK UNIT 35

1. The supposed difference between Russia and the USA's nuclear capabilities in favour of the former.
2. Openness.
3. Yuri Gagarin.

4. U2 spy-plane pilot, shot down over Russia.
5. A personal telephone link between the Soviet and US leaders.
6. It was a letter send by other Warsaw Pact countries, calling on the Czech's to crush 'anti-socialist forces'. It preceded the 1968 invasion.
7. Armenia
8. Afghanistan.
9. Celebrating its millennium i.e. its 1000th anniversary.
10. A man-made satellite, the first to orbit the earth in 1957.
11. 1C 2A 3E 4G 5B 6D 7F.
12. Intercontinental Ballistic Missile; Strategic Arms Limitation Talks; Organisation of American States.
13. B.
14. D.
15. a) Over Cuba.
    b) Russian Missile launching sites.
    c) Because the island of Cuba is only 100 miles from the US mainland.
    d) Essay answer.
16-17. Essay answers.

Glossary

ABDICATE To give up some office or power. Used particularly with regard to monarchs, i.e. Tsar Nicholas of Russia.

ABSOLUTE MONARCHY A system of government where the ruler is not checked by any form of parliament. **Absolutism:** as practised by the Tsars of Russia and kings of France and Spain.

AFRIKAANER A white South African of Dutch or German descent. A Boer.

AMNESTY The granting of a pardon to convicted offenders, usually political prisoners.

ANARCHY Lack of effective control or government in a country leading to social and political disorder. **Anarchist:** a believer in no central government or authority.

A.N.C. African National Congress (in South Africa).

ANSCHLUSS Proposed union of Germany and Austria. Carried out forcibly by Hitler in 1938.

ANTI-CLERICALISM A policy opposed to Church influence in political, social and educational affairs.

ANTI-SEMITISM Racial prejudice against Jews.

ANZAC Australian and New Zealand Army Corps which landed at Gallipoli on 25th April 1915, a date celebrated as **ANZAC Day**.

APARTHEID Policy of separate development and racial segregation in South Africa.

APPEASEMENT Name of policy pursued by Neville Chamberlain, British prime minister, to try to get a final settlement of German grievances (1937-9).

ARBITRATION The settlement of a dispute through the judgement of a third, neutral party.

ARMISTICE Temporary end to fighting so that a peace can be negotiated. **Armistice Day**, 1918, when fighting stopped on the Western Front.

ASSIMILATION Policy of absorbing Africans into European culture and political life. Pursued by the French in their colonies.

AUTHORITARIAN A regime or person who rules repressively, suppressing individual freedom. A dictatorship or totalitarian state.

AUTONOMY Self-government, usually in a province within a state.

AYATOLLAH A leader of the Shia Moslems in Iran.

BA'ATH An Arab political movement with socialist leanings, strong in Syria and Iraq.

BANTU South African government's name for black people, hence **Bantustans** - black homelands.

BARREL A measure of oil production equal to 42 US gallons or 35 imperial gallons.

BLACK THURSDAY The 24th October 1929 when millions of shares changed hands on the Wall Street, New York Stock Exchange.

BOERS See Afrikaaners.

BOLSHEVIKS Majority group in Russian Social Democratic party. Known as communists after their seizure of power in Russia in 1917.

BONAPARTISM Support for descendants of the Emperor Napoleon Bonaparte.

BOSS Bureau of State Security in South Africa.

BOURGEOSIE The middle classes.

BOYCOTT To refuse to deal with some person, organisation or government. Named after Captain Boycott, the victim of such a policy in 19th century Ireland.

CASTE Hereditary division of Hindu society, consisting of an elite of priests, rulers and warriors, then traders and farmers, and finally of artisans. Those excluded from these divisions are known as **'Untouchables'** and are an under-privileged class.

CALIPH Spiritual ruler of Islam. A position held by the Sultans of Turkey.

CAUDILLO Spanish name for leader. Used by Franco.

CENTRE Political parties which are neither extreme left or right.

CHEKA Russian secret police founded by Lenin.

CHRISTIAN DEMOCRAT Name of centre-right parties in West Germany, Italy, Holland and Norway post-1945.

C.I.A. The US Central Intelligence Agency.

CLERICALS Any French political party in the 19th century which favoured increasing the power of the Church in social and political life.

CO-EXISTENCE A move in the Cold War initiated by Nikita Kruschev, ruler of Russia in the 1950's and 60's. It proposed peaceful rather than violent competition between the two power-blocs whilst accepting that they were hostile to each other.

COLD WAR State of internal tension between Russia and her allies and the USA and her allies which began after the Second World War and continued until at least 1962. It involved the formation of opposing alliances, intensive propaganda campaigns, subversion, infiltration and the support of opposite sides in regional conflicts, i.e. Korea and the Middle East.

COLONY A territory annexed and owned by a foreign power.

COLOUREDS Persons of mixed white and African origin in South Africa.

COMECON Council for Mutual Economic Co-operation. An economic grouping set up be Stalin after the Second World War and including Russia's satellites. It was the economic equivalent of the Warsaw Pact, a military alliance of the same countries.

COMINFORM Communist Information Bureaux.

COMMUNIST The belief, first propounded by Karl Marx and Freidrich Engels, that the private ownership of land, factories banks etc. should be replaced by public ownership, i.e. nationalised. Marx divided people up into classes and conceived the theory of class conflict from which the proletariat (working classes) would eventually triumph. Marx also suggested that once the proletariat had won, all state machinery of government could be abolished but this has not happened so far in communist countries.

CONGRESS An Assembly of delegates or representatives; in the USA the legislative chambers of the government. Used by Indian nationalists as the name of their political party and meant to suggest that they were already the government.

CONSTITUTION The aims and principles of government of a state.

CONSTITUTIONAL AMENDMENT An amendment, change, or addition, to the US Constitution.

CONTAINMENT A policy of the USA during the Cold War which involved the setting up of alliances, and the granting of aid, to countries threatened by a communist takeover.

CONSCRIPTION The liability of fit young men to service in the armed forces of their country. Started by France and now used by most European countries.

CONVOY A group of merchant ships sailing under the protection of warships. Used extensively in the First and Second World Wars to try and prevent successful 'U' Boat attacks.

CORTES Name of the Spanish and Portuguese parliaments.

COUP D'ETAT Violent and illegal seizure of power by a small group.

COVENANT An agreement setting out policies and principles. The most famous in modern times was the Covenant of the League of Nations.

CZECH LEGION A Czech armed force which, whilst being evacuated from Russia after the Bolshevik revolution, became involved in the fighting during the Russian Civil War.

DAIL Lower House of Irish (Eire) Parliament.

DEBTOR NATION A country owed money by other countries.

DEMOCRACY Literally 'rule by the people'. In modern times a system whereby all adults vote for a new government.

D.M.Z. De-militarised zone i.e. a zone without any troops or military installations. Two examples were the Rhineland after 1919 and Korea after 1953.

DEPRESSION A drastic reduction in industrial and trading activity. The US depression, starting in 1929, eventually affected most European countries.

DESPOTISM Rule by one person i.e. a *despot*.

DESEGREGATION The ending of segregation between races or groups of people.

DETENTE Easing of tension between the two power-blocs after an agreement signed at Helsinki in 1975. It followed on from the policy of co-existence.

DIASPORA The dispersal of the Jews after their defeat by the Romans in AD70.

DIET An Assembly or Parliament.

DICTATORSHIP Rule by one person who has usually seized power illegally.

DIKTAT Severe terms dictated to a defeated people after a war i.e. the terms of the Treaty of Versailles concerning Germany in 1919.

DISSIDENT A person who opposes by word or deed a system of government. Used of persecuted critics of the Soviet regime.

DOMINION An independent country within the British Commonwealth. All were ex-colonies, starting with Canada in 1867.

DUMA Russian name for a town council but used to describe the parliament which met in Tsarist days.

E.E.C. European Economic Community or Common Market.

E.F.T.A. European Free Trade Association.

ELITE Top people in a particular sphere of activity, either by virtue of birth, wealth or talent.

EMANCIPATION The setting free of people from unnatural restrictions like slavery. Examples are the emancipation of negroes in the USA and serfs in Russia in the 19th century.

ENCLAVE A piece of territory separated from the rest of the state by a country under different rule. e.g. East and West Pakistan until 1971.

ENTENTE A friendly understanding between previously hostile countries. Example was the Entente Cordiale between Britain and France in 1904.

ENOSIS The proposed political union of Greece and Cyprus.

E.O.K.A Greek terrorist group in Cyprus in the 1950's which aimed to expel the British and establish enosis.

EXECUTIVE COUNCIL The authority in a (British) dependency during colonial days.

EXECUTIVE PRESIDENT A President who is both head of state and head of the government. Example: the President of the USA.

F.A.O. UN Food and Agricutural Organisation.

FASCISM A politcal movement taking its name from the 'fasces', a bundle of rods carried by a Roman magistrate to indicate his right to inflict punishment. A totalitarian system of government, led by a dictator and distinguished by extreme nationalism and the suppression of all opposition. The first fascist regime was established by Benito Mussolini in Italy.

FEDAYUN Palestinian guerilla fighter operating from Egypt against Israeli settlements. The word is Arabic and means 'self-sacrificers'.

FEDERAL A system of government in which several states form a union but retain a large measure of internal self-government. Examples are the USA, Australia and Nigeria.

F.B.I. Federal Bureaux of Investigation, a US law-enforcement agency.

F.L.N. National Liberation Front of Algerian nationalists against French colonial rule.

FRANCHISE The right to vote.

FRELIMO Front for the Liberation of Mozambique from Portugese rule.

FUHRER German word meaning leader. Title adopted by Hitler in 1934.

FREE TRADE Economic policy based on the absence of tariffs or customs duties.

G.A.T.T. General Agreement on Tariffs and Trade.

G.D.R. German Democratic Republic, the official name of East Germany.

G.F.R. German Federal Republic, the official name of West Germany.

G.N.P. Gross National Product.

G.P.U. The initials of the Russian secret police. It became the OGPU (see later).

HABSBURG EMPIRE Another name for the Austro-Hungarian empire, so called because the ruling dynasty were the Habsburgs.

HOLY ROMAN EMPIRE A loose grouping of German states, which,by the 18th century, elected the Habsburg emperor as 'Holy Roman Emperor' as well. The rulers of nine German states elected this monarch and were therefore known as 'Electors'. The most powerful elector (later king) was that of Prussia. From 1714 until 1837 the Electors of Hanover were also Kings of Great Britain and Ireland. The HRE ceased to exist officially in 1806 but it remained a potent idea in the minds of German nationalists working for the unity of their country.

HUMANITARIAN One who works for humane causes.

I.C.B.M. Intercontinental Ballistic Missile.

IMMIGRANTS People who come to live permanently in a foreign country.

IMPERIALISM The extension of power by one country over others to form an empire.

INDEMNITY A fine paid to the victor by the loser in a war. Also known as reparations (or compensation).

INDIGENOUS Belonging to, or created in, a particular country or tribe.

INFALLIBILITY The inability to be wrong. The most famous example is the Doctrine of Papal Infallibility, announced in 1870, which stated that the Pope cannot be wrong when pronouncing 'ex-cathedra' (with authority) because of divine guidance.

INFIDEL One not of the Moslem faith, one of the 'unfaithful'.

INFLATION An increase in prices and a fall in the purchasing power of money.

INTEGRATION The merging of different peoples or races into one country.

INTIFADA Arab uprising against Israeli occupation of their homelands, 1988.

INVESTMENT The buying of stocks and shares with the idea of profiting from interest payments and capital growth.

I.R.A. Irish Republican Army, a terrorist group whose aim is a united Ireland and the end of British rule in Northern Ireland.

IRREDENTIST This means, literally, 'unredeemed' or 'unrecovered' lands. In Italian politics a person who advocates the recovery and re-union of all Italian-speaking districts ruled by another country. It was Italy's irredentist claims to lands ruled by Austro-Hungary which led her to enter the First World War on the side of the Allies in 1915.

ISLAM The name for all those who submit to the Will of Allah as revealed in the Koran. The whole community of Moslems.

ISOLATIONISM The desire of Americans not to be involved in European affairs. Particularly strong in the early 20th century but not US official policy since 1945.

ISVESTIA One of the two official Soviet newspapers. The word means 'News".

JESUITS Members of a Catholic Religious Order, the Society of Jesus, founded by St. Ignatius Loyola in 1534. An extremely dedicated and militant missionary organisation, influential in Catholic countries. In non-Christian and Protestant countries it was notorious for this work, and was often banned or suppressed.

JUNKERS Name for members of the Prussian aristocracy.

K.A.D.U. Kenya African Democratic Union.

K.A.N.U. Kenya African National Union.

K.G.B. Committee of State Security. Soviet secret police.

KIBBUTZ A Jewish agricultural settlement run on cooperative and socialist principles, usually in Israeli.

K.K.K. Klu Klux Klan. A racist and terrorist group opposed to black rights, using intimidation and murder. Founded in the southern states after the Civil War and revived in 1918.

K.M.T. Abbreviation for the Koumintang, the nationalist government of China until 1949.

KORAN Moslem holy book, containing the Will of God as revealed to the Prophet Mohammed.

LAISSEZ-FAIRE Literally 'leave things alone'. The belief that a country functions best without any government interference in trade or industry.

LEBENSRAUM Literally 'living space'. This refers to the German, and in particular, Nazi belief, that Germany would need to obtain territories in eastern Europe if she was to develop properly.

LEFT-WING People of communist or socialist beliefs. The name comes from the positioning of seats in the semi-circular French Chamber of Deputies where conservatives sit on the right, moderates in the centre and socialists on the left.

LEGISLATIVE COUNCIL An advisory council proposing laws for a (British) dependency.

LEGISLATION Law-making.

LIBERAL Spelt with a small 'l' this label denotes people who believe in individual freedom and democratic rule. Liberal parties usually consist of people who share these ideals.

MAGHREB Countries of North-West Africa - Tunisia, Morocco and Algeria.

MAFIA Criminal organisation founded originally in Sicily and established in the USA by Sicilian immigrants.

MANDATES Former German and Turkish colonies placed under League of Nations supervision after the First World War.

MANIFESTO Published policy or programme of a political party or movement.

MEDIATE To negotiate with two rival groups with the aim of bringing them to an agreement.

M.I.R.V. A ballistic missile. The initials stand for Multiple Independently-targeted Re-entry Vehicle.

N.V.D. Name of the Soviet secret police before it became the KGB.

NATIONALISM Patriotic love of one's country or nationality. The desire that a nationality should rule itself and not be governed by others. In extreme forms, like Nazism and fascism, it involves the conquest of other 'inferior' nationalities.

N.A.T.O North Atlantic Treaty Organisation.

NAZI German National Socialist Party run by Hitler. An extreme organisation which believed in dictatorship, the crushing of all opposition by force, the persecution of Jews because of their race and Liberals, Socialists and Communists because of their political beliefs.

NEO-COLONIALISM The way in which ex-colonies are still subject to outside influence by economic and other pressures.

N.E.P. The New Economic Policy introduced by Lenin which involved limited free enterprise.

NIHILISM A Russian belief that everything in the world is bad and must therefore be destroyed. It differs from Anarchism, which claims that governments are the cause of all evil in the world.

N.K.V.D. Name of Russian secret police in Stalin's time.

N.L.F. National Liberation Front, formed to free colonial territories. Two examples are the NLF formed in Yemen and in Vietnam.

O.E.E.C. Organisation for European Economic Cooperation.

O.G.P.U. Central State Political Department, another name for the Soviet secret police. It succeeded the Cheka.

O.P.E.C. Organisation of Petroleum Exporting Countries.

PACIFISM The belief that for an individual to fight in a war is wrong.

PACT Agreement or treaty.

PAN- Literally from the Greek word for 'all'. The belief that all people of one nationality should join together, if possible in a political union. Famous examples are Pan-Slavism, Pan-Germanism and Pan-Africanism.

PARTISAN Anti-German guerrilla fighting in Yugoslavia, Italy or France during the Second World War.

PANZERS German armoured troops.

PIONEER SPIRIT The spirit of the people who had colonised the western regions of the USA, pushing back the 'frontier' year after year during the 18th and 19th centuries. They were pitted against nature, often hostile, the Indians, and the problems created by themselves, i.e. the battle between cattle and arable farmers.

PLEBISCITE A vote by all the people on one issue. A referendum.

P.L.O. Palestine Liberation Organisation, a terrorist group aimed at the liberation of Arab territory from Israel and the establishment of a Palestinian homeland.

POGRAM An organised massacre of jews in Russia.

POLITBURO The chief ruling committee of a communist government.

PRAVDA Name of official Soviet newspaper. The word means 'truth'.

PROLETARIAT In communist terminology the wage earners, or workers, who sell their labour to earn a living.

PROPAGANDA The spreading of a belief or doctrine without regard to any other point of view.

PROHIBITION The forbidding of the manufacture, sale or consumption of alcoholic liquor. Used in particular with reference to the Prohibition period in the USA between 1920 and 1933.

PROTECTION A system of tariffs placed on imports to protect home industries.

PROTECTORATE A country controlled, and protected, by a more powerful country.

PUPPET STATE Name given to a country which is nominally independent but is really controlled by another, more powerful state.

PUTSCH German word meaning armed rising.

RADICAL A person who works for major political reform and change.

REACTIONARY A person opposed to political change.

REFERENDUM A vote on a single issue. A plebiscite.

REICHSTAT Upper House of German Parliament.

REICHSTAG Lower House of German Parliament.

RELIGIOUS ORDER Christian societies of men or women who, having taken vows of poverty, chastity and obedience, live together in communities largely cut off from the world.

REPARATIONS Compensation for damages imposed on the losers by the winners of a war.

Examples, reparations imposed on Germany after the First World War and by Japan on Russia after the Russo-Japanese War.

REPUBLIC A state without a monarch, usually with a President as Head of State.

REVISIONISM The demand to revise, or change, something. Used in connection with the terms of the Versailles Treaty, and by the Chinese in their quarrel with the Soviet leaders about communist theories.

RIGHT-WING A conservative in politics.

RUGGED INDIVIDUALISM The American belief that people and businesses should 'stand on their own feet' and not accept help, or interference, from the federal government.

S.A.L.T. Strategic Arms Limitation Talks.

S.A.M. Surface to air missile.

SANCTIONS Penalties, usually in connection with trade, imposed on a state by other states to force it to change its policies. The League of Nations had the power to impose sanctions.

SATELLITE (See 'Puppet state').

S.E.A.T.O. South East Asia Treaty Organisation.

SECESSION The break away of one part of a country to form a separate state. Ex: Southern States of USA and 'Biafra' from Nigeria..

SEGREGATION Enforced separation of peoples or races.

SENATE The Upper House of several parliaments e.g. the USA and Australia.

SCHUTZATAFFEL (S.S.) Nazi blackshirts.

SOCIAL DEMOCRATS The name of several European socialist parties. Before 1919 such parties often included communists.

SOCIALISM The belief that the state (representing the people), not private individuals, should own the means of production (land and factories), distribution (railways etc.) and exchange (banks). Particularly associated with the writings of Karl Marx but known before his time.

SOVEREIGNTY Supreme power.

STURMABTEILING (S.A.) Nazi brownshirts.

SUFFRAGE The right to vote.

S.W.A.P.O. South West African People's Organisation opposed to South African rule of Namibia.

SYNDICALISM The belief that the power and wealth of a country should be controlled by the workers through their trade union. From the French for trade union, *'syndicat'*.

TARIFFS Taxes on imports as part of a Protectionist policy.

THIRD WORLD A term used to describe countries not allied to the capitalist west or the communist east. Most of these are ex-colonies in Asia and Africa, although Latin American states must be included; they are, in fact, all ex-colonies. These countries are usually poor and relatively undeveloped. The Work Units which deal with their history and problems are 5,6,9,24,25,26,28,33 and 34.

TOTALITARIANISM The dictatorship by one party in a state i.e. the assuming of 'total' control.

TRIBALISM Loyalty to a tribe rather than the country or nation.

T.U.C. Trade Union Congress (in Britain).

T.V.A. Tennessee Valley Authority (in USA).

U2 US spy plane.

U.D.I. Unilateral Declaration of Independence by colonial states without permission of imperial power i.e. Southern Rhodesia in 1965.

ULTIMATUM A final proposal or statement, usually before a war.

U.N.E.S.C.O. United Nations Educational, Scientific and Cultural Organisation.

U.N.I.C.E.F. United Nations International Children's Emergency Fund.

U.N.O. United Nations Organisation.

U.N.R.R.A. United Nations Relief and Rehabilitation Administration.

UNTOUCHABLES Those Hindus outside the caste system. See *Caste*.

U.S.S.R. Union of Soviet Socialist Republics. Soviet Russia.

V1, V2 German weapons in Second World War. The V1 was a flying bomb and the V2 a supersonic rocket bomb.

V.S.O. Voluntary Service Overseas.

VATICAN The Pope's official residence in Rome. *Vatican City* is an independent state ruled by the Pope. It was created by the Lateran Treaty signed between the Church and Italy in 1929.

VETO The right to stop or reject a proposal. The members of the UN Security Council have this right, and so does the President of the USA in connection with bills sent to him by Congress.

VIETCONG Vietnamese guerillas who fought, first, the French, and then the Americans.

VICHY Capital of puppet state set up in southern France following the German victory in 1940. Its leader was Marshal Petain.

WATERGATE Hotel in Washington D.C. in the USA, scene of the burglaries of the Democratic Party headquarters during the 1971 Presidential election. These break-ins led to scandals which culminated in the enforced resignation of President Nixon in 1974.

WELFARE STATE A country with a comprehensive system of social security covering health, education, unemployment and old age.

W.E.U. Western European Union.

W.H.O. World Health Organisation.

Z.A.P.U. Zimbabwe African People's Union.

ZOLLVERIEN A 19th century customs' union of German states headed by Prussia. It proved a useful stepping stone to later, political, union.

ZIONISM The movement for the creation and maintenance of Israel.

Addresses

LONDON AND EAST ANGLIAN GROUP

London
University of London Schools Examination Board
Stewart House, 32 Russell Square, London WC1B 5DN

LREB
London Regional Examinations Board
Lyon House, 104 Wandsworth High Street, London SW18 4LF

EAEB
East Anglian Examinations board
The Lindens, Lexden Road, Colchester, Essex CO3 3RL

MIDLANDS EXAMINING GROUP

Cambridge
University of Cambridge Local Examinations Syndicate
Syndicate Buildings, 1 Hills Road, Cambridge CB1 2EU

O and C
Oxford and Cambridge Schools Examinations Board
10 Trumpington Street, Cambridge and Elsfield Way, Oxford

SUJB
Southern Universities' Joint Board for School Examinations
Cotham Road, Bristol BS6 6DD

WMEB
West Midlands Examinations Board
Norfolk House, Smallbrook Queensway, Birmingham B5 4NJ

EMREB
East Midlands Regional Examinations Board
Robins Wood House, Robins Wood Road, Aspley, Nottingham NG8 3NH

NORTHERN EXAMINATION ASSOCIATION

JMB
Joint Matriculation Board
Devas Street, Manchester M15 6EU

ALSEB
Associated Lancashire Schools Examining Board
12 Harter Street, Manchester M1 6HL

NREB
North Regional Examination Board
Wheatfield Road, Westerhope, Newcastle upon Tyne NE5 5JZ

NWREB
North-West Regional Examinations Board
Orbit House, Albert Street, Eccles, Manchester M30 0WL

YHREB
Yorkshire and Humberside Regional Examinations Board
Harrogate Office - 31-33 Springfield Avenue, Harrogate HG1 2HW
Sheffield Office - Scarsdale House, 136 Derbyshire Lane, Sheffield S8 8SE

NORTHERN IRELAND

NISEC
Northern Ireland Schools Examinations Council
Beechill House, 42 Beechill Road, Belfast BT8 4RS

SCOTLAND

SEB
Scottish Examinations Board
Ironmills Road, Dalkeith, Midlothian EH22 1BR

SOUTHERN EXAMINING GROUP

AEB
The Associated Examining Board
Stag House, Guildford, Surrey GU2 5XJ

Oxford
Oxford Delegacy of Local Examinations
Ewert Place, Summertown, Oxford OX2 7BZ

SREB
Southern Regional Examinations Board
Avondale House, 33 Carlton Crescent, Southampton S)9 4YL

SEREB
South-East Regional Examinations Board
Beloe House, 2-10 Mount Ephraim Road, Tunbridge TN1 1EU

SWEB
South-Western Examinations Board
23-29 Marsh Street, Bristol BS1 4BP

WALES

WJEC
Welsh Joint Education Committee
245 Western Avenue, Cardiff CF5 2YX